Guide to the Software Engineering Body of Knowledge

Trial Version

SWEBOK*

A Project of the Software Engineering Coordinating Committee

Guide to the Software Engineering Body of Knowledge

Trial Version

SWEBOK*

A Project of the Software Engineering Coordinating Committee

Executive Editors
Alain Abran, École de technologie supérieure
James W. Moore, The MITRE Corp.

Editors
Pierre Bourque, École de technologie supérieure
Robert Dupuis, Université du Québec à Montréal

Project Champion
Leonard L. Tripp, Chair, Professional Practices Committee, IEEE Computer Society

IEEE
COMPUTER
SOCIETY
http://computer.org

Los Alamitos, California

Washington • Brussels • Tokyo

© *IEEE – Trial Version 1.00 – May 2001*   *SWEBOK is an official service mark of the IEEE

Library of Congress Cataloging-in-Publication Data

Guide to the software engineering body of knowledge : trial version
      (version 1.00) / executive editors, Alain Abran, James W. Moore;
editors, Pierre Bourque, Robert Dupuis, Leonard L. Tripp.
      p. cm.
1. Software engineering.   2. Computer software--Development.   I.
Abran, Alain, 1949-   . II. Moore, James W., 1948-   .
      QA76.758 .G85   2001
      005.1--dc21

                                                                    2001005442

IEEE Computer Society Press Order Number BP01000
Library of Congress Number 2001005442
ISBN 0-7695-1000-0

Additional copies may be ordered from:

IEEE Computer Society
Customer Service Center
10662 Los Vaqueros Circle
P.O. Box 3014
Los Alamitos, CA 90720-1314
Tel: + 1-714-821-8380
Fax: + 1-714-821-4641
E-mail: cs.books@computer.org

IEEE Service Center
445 Hoes Lane
P.O. Box 1331
Piscataway, NJ 08855-1331
Tel: + 1-732-981-0060
Fax: + 1-732-981-9667
http://shop.ieee.org/store/
customer-service@ieee.org

IEEE Computer Society
Asia/Pacific Office
Watanabe Bldg., 1-4-2
Minami-Aoyama
Minato-ku, Tokyo 107-0062
JAPAN
Tel: + 81-3-3408-3118
Fax: + 81-3-3408-3553
tokyo.ofc@computer.org

Publisher: Angela Burgess
Group Managing Editor, CS Press: Deborah Plummer
Advertising/Promotions: Tom Fink
Production Editor: Bob Werner
Printed in the United States of America

TABLE OF CONTENTS

Important Notice

This is the **Trial** *Version 1.00 of the Guide to the Software Engineering Body of Knowledge. This phase of the project is the Stoneman phase, and previous versions were entitled* **Stoneman** *versions.*

Please register as a user of the Guide at www.swebok.org, after January 2002. You will have the opportunity to share your experiences in using the guide. The results of the experimentation you will make of the guide are of importance to us and the next version of the guide will be based on such results.

Foreword

In 1952, John Tukey, the world-renowned statistician, coined the term *software*. The term *software engineering* was used in the title of a NATO conference held in Germany in 1968. The IEEE Computer Society first published its *Transactions on Software Engineering* in 1972. The committee within the IEEE Computer Society for developing software engineering standards was founded in 1976.

On May 21, 1993, the IEEE Computer Society Board of Governors approved a motion to "establish a steering committee for evaluating, planning, and coordinating actions related to establishing software engineering as a profession." Shortly thereafter, in August 1993, the ACM Council endorsed the "establishment of a Commission on Software Engineering to address a number of questions relating to; 1) the terminology used to describe software engineering and those who work in the software area; 2) the identification of generally accepted and desired standards of good software practice; and 3) our ability to identify, educate, and train individuals who are competent with software engineering and design." The two motions were clearly related and had emerged through informal discussions between volunteers in the two societies.

From September through December of 1993, an ad-hoc committee involving volunteers from both societies met to define an initial set of recommendations to accomplish these tasks. Early on they recognized that the amount of effort and time to accomplish the tasks required a more formal process, and this lead to an agreement, in January 1994, between Laurel Kaleda (then president of the Computer Society) and Gwenn Bell (then president of the ACM) to form a joint steering committee. Mario Barbacci and Stuart Zweben served as co-chairs of the committee. The mission statement of the joint committee was "To establish the appropriate sets(s) of criteria and norms for professional practice of software engineering upon which industrial decisions, professional certification, and educational curricula can be based." The steering committee organized task forces in the following areas:

1. Define Required Body of Knowledge and Recommended Practices;
2. Define Ethics and Professional Standards;
3. Define Educational Curricula for undergraduate, graduate, and continuing education.

The code of ethics and professional practice for software engineering was completed in 1998 and shortly thereafter was approved by both the ACM Council and the Computer Society Board of Governors. It has been adopted by numerous corporations and other organizations and is included in several recent textbooks. A model set of accreditation criteria for software engineering was also completed in 1998, and has been utilized by ABET in defining its criteria for software engineering accreditation. The present document supplies the third component: a guide to the body of knowledge of software engineering.

Each profession is based on a body of knowledge and recommended practices, although they are not always defined in a precise manner. In many cases these are formally documented, usually in a form that permits them to be used for such purposes as accreditation of academic programs, development of education and training programs, certification of specialists, or professional licensing. Generally a professional society or related body maintains custody of such a formal definition. In cases where no such formality is used, the body of knowledge and recommended practices are "generally recognized" by practitioners and may be codified in a variety of ways for different uses.

From 1994 through 1996, the task force on the body of knowledge discussed various options on performing their tasks. By 1996 the task force had concluded that there would be significant cost associated with any reasonable method of establishing a body of knowledge baseline. The task force used a web-based survey to produce a prototype document that served as the basis for the *Guide to the Software Engineering Body of Knowledge* published in this work.

It should be noted that this work does not purport to define the body of knowledge, but rather to serve as a compendium and guide to the body of knowledge that has been developing and evolving over the past four decades. Furthermore, this body of knowledge is not static — the *Guide* must, necessarily, develop and evolve as software engineering matures. Nevertheless, the *Guide* is a valuable element of the software engineering infrastructure. Even in draft form, for example, it has been used to guide the development of several education and training programs in software engineering.

Those who have worked in dedication over the past few years to establish this knowledge baseline hope readers will find this work useful in guiding them towards the knowledge and resources they need in their lifelong career development as software engineering professionals.

Dr. Guylaine M. Pollock, 2000 President, IEEE Computer Society

PREFACE

Software engineering is an emerging discipline and there are unmistakable trends indicating an increasing level of maturity:

- Several universities throughout the world offer undergraduate degrees in software engineering. For example, such degrees are offered at the University of New South Wales (Australia), McMaster University (Canada), the Rochester Institute of Technology (US), the University of Sheffield (UK) and other universities.

- In the US, the Computer Science Accreditation Board (CSAB) and the Accreditation Board for Engineering and Technology (ABET) are cooperating closely and CSAB is expected to be lead society for the accreditation of university software engineering programs.

- The Canadian Information Processing Society has published criteria to accredit software engineering undergraduate university programs.

- The Software Engineering Institute's Capability Maturity Model for Software (SW CMM) and ISO 9000 family of standards are used to assess organizational capability for software engineering.

- The Texas Board of Professional Engineers has begun to license professional software engineers.

- The Association of Professional Engineers and Geoscientists of British Columbia (APEGBC) has begun registering software professional engineers and the Professional Engineers of Ontario (PEO) has also announced requirements for licensing.

- The Association for Computing Machinery (ACM) and the Computer Society of the Institute of Electrical and Electronics Engineers (IEEE) have jointly developed and adopted a Code of Ethics for software engineering professionals[1].

- The Institute for Certification of Computing Professionals (ICCP) offers certification in software development as well as software engineering (www.iccp.org).

All of these efforts are based upon the presumption that there is a Body of Knowledge that should be mastered by practicing software engineers. This Body of Knowledge exists in the literature that has accumulated over the past thirty years. This book provides a Guide to that Body of Knowledge.

PURPOSE

The purpose of this Guide is to provide a consensually-validated characterization of the bounds of the software engineering discipline and to provide a topical access to the Body of Knowledge supporting that discipline. The Body of Knowledge is subdivided into ten Knowledge Areas (KA) and the descriptions of the KAs are designed to discriminate among the various important concepts, permitting readers to find their way quickly to subjects of interest. Upon finding a subject, readers are referred to key papers or book chapters selected because they succinctly present the knowledge.

In browsing the Guide, readers will note that the content is markedly different from Computer Science. Just as electrical engineering is based upon the science of physics, software engineering should be based upon computer science. In both cases, though, the emphasis is necessarily different. Scientists extend our knowledge of the laws of nature while engineers apply those laws of nature to build useful artifacts, under a number of constraints. Therefore, the emphasis of the Guide is placed upon the construction of useful software artifacts.

Readers will also notice that many important aspects of information technology, that may constitute important software engineering knowledge, are not covered in the Guide; they include: specific programming languages, relational databases and networks. This is a consequence of an engineering-based approach. In all fields—not only computing—the designers of engineering curricula have realized that specific technologies are replaced much more rapidly than the engineering work force. An engineer must be equipped with the essential knowledge that supports the selection of the appropriate technology at the appropriate time in the appropriate circumstance. For example, software systems might be built in Fortran using functional decomposition or in C++ using object-oriented techniques. The techniques for integrating and configuring instances of those systems would be quite different. But, the principles and objectives of configuration management remain the same. The Guide therefore does not focus on the rapidly changing technologies, although their general principles are described in relevant Knowledge Areas.

---

[1] The ACM/CS Software Engineering Code of Ethics and other information about the effort can be found at:
http://csciwww.etsu.edu/gotterbarn/SECEPP/

These exclusions demonstrate that this Guide is necessarily incomplete. The Guide includes the software engineering knowledge that is necessary, but not sufficient to a software engineer. Practicing software engineers will need to know many things about computer science, project management and systems engineering—to name a few—that fall outside the Body of Knowledge characterized by this Guide. However, stating that this information should be known by software engineers is not the same as stating that this knowledge falls within the bounds of the software engineering discipline. Instead, it should be stated that software engineers need to know some things taken from other disciplines—and that is the approach adopted by this Guide. So, this Guide characterizes the Body of Knowledge falling within the scope of software engineering and provides references to relevant information from other disciplines.

The emphasis on engineering practice leads the Guide toward a strong relationship with the normative literature. Most of the computer science, information technology and software engineering literature provides information useful to software engineers, but a relatively small portion is normative. A normative document prescribes what an engineer should do in a specified situation rather than providing information that might be helpful. The normative literature is validated by consensus formed among practitioners and is concentrated in standards and related documents. From the beginning, the SWEBOK project was conceived as having a strong relationship to the normative literature of software engineering. The two major standards bodies for software engineering (IEEE Software Engineering Standards Committee and ISO/IEC JTC1/SC7) are represented in the project. Ultimately, we hope that software engineering practice standards will contain principles traceable to the SWEBOK Guide.

INTENDED AUDIENCE

The Guide is oriented toward a variety of audiences, all over the world. It aims to serve public and private organizations in need of a consistent view of software engineering for defining education and training requirements, classifying jobs, developing performance evaluation policies or specifying development tasks. It also addresses practicing, or managing, software engineers and the officials responsible for making public policy regarding licensing and professional guidelines. In addition, professional societies and educators defining the certification rules, accreditation policies for university curricula, and guidelines for professional practice will benefit from SWEBOK, as well as the students learning the software engineering profession and

educators and trainers engaged in defining curricula and course content.

EVOLUTION OF THE GUIDE

From 1993 to 2000, the IEEE Computer Society and the ACM cooperated in promoting the professionalization of software engineering through their joint Software Engineering Coordinating Committee (SWECC). The Code of Ethics was completed under stewardship of the SWECC primarily through volunteer efforts. The SWEBOK project was initiated by the SWECC in 1998.

The SWEBOK project's scope, the variety of communities involved, and the need for broad participation suggested a need for full-time rather than volunteer management. For this purpose, the IEEE-Computer Society contracted the Software Engineering Management Research Laboratory at the Université du Québec à Montréal to manage the effort.

The project plan includes three successive phases: Strawman, Stoneman and Ironman. The publication of this Trial Version of the Guide marks the end of the Stoneman phase of the project. An early prototype, Strawman, demonstrated how the project might be organized. Development of the Ironman version will commence after we gain insight through trial application of the Trial Version of the Guide.

The project team developed two important principles for guiding the project: *transparency* and *consensus*. By transparency, we mean that the development process is itself documented, published, and publicized so that important decisions and status are visible to all concerned parties. By consensus, we mean that the only practical method for legitimizing a statement of this kind is through broad participation and agreement by all significant sectors of the relevant community. By the time the Trial version of the Guide is completed, literally hundreds of contributors and reviewers will have touched the product in some manner. By the time the third phase—the Ironman—is completed, the number of participants will number in the thousands and additional efforts will have been made to reach communities less likely to have participated in the current review process.

Like any software project, the SWEBOK project has many stakeholders—some of which are formally represented. An Industrial Advisory Board, composed of representatives from industry (Boeing, Construx Software, the MITRE Corporation, Rational Software, Raytheon Systems, and SAP Labs-Canada), research agencies (National Institute of Standards and Technology, National Research Council of Canada) and of the Canadian Council of Professional Engineers, and the IEEE Computer Society, have provided financial support for the project. The IAB's generous support permits us to make the products of the SWEBOK project publicly available without any charge (visit http://www.swebok.org). IAB membership is supplemented with the chairs of ISO/IEC JTC1/SC7 and of the related Computing Curricula 2001 initiative. The IAB reviews and approves the project plans, oversees consensus building and review processes, promotes the project, and lends credibility to the effort. In general, it ensures the relevance of the effort to real-world needs From the outset, it was understood that an implicit Body of Knowledge already exists in textbooks on software engineering. To ensure that we took full advantage of existing literature, Steve McConnell, Roger Pressman, and Ian Sommerville—the authors of the three best-selling textbooks on software engineering—served on a Panel of Experts to provide advice on the initial formulation of the project and the structure of the Guide. In addition, the extensive review process involves feedback from relevant communities. In all cases, we seek international participation to maintain a broad scope of relevance.

We organized the development of the Trial version into three public review cycles. The first review cycle focused on the soundness of the proposed breakdown of topics within each KA. Thirty-four domain experts completed this review cycle in April 1999. The reviewer comments, as well as the identities of the reviewers, are available on the project's Web site.

In the second review cycle completed in October 1999, a considerably larger group of professionals, organized into review viewpoints, answered a detailed questionnaire for each KA description. The viewpoints (for example, individual practitioners, educators, and makers of public policy) were formulated to ensure relevance to the Guide's various intended audiences. In all, roughly 200 reviewers provided 5000 comments. The identities of the reviewers, their comments, and the disposition of those comments can be found on the project's web site. In the third review cycle, considering the coherency of the Guide as a whole, we received close to 3500 comments from 378 professionals from 41 countries. These comments, as well as demographic data about the reviewers, are also available at www.swebok.org.

Readers are invited to access the project web site to be informed on the future evolution of the Guide.

LIMITATIONS AND NEXT STEPS

Even though the current version of the Guide has gone through an elaborate development and review process, the following limitations of this process must be recognized and stated:

- Close to five hundred software engineering professionals from 41 countries and representing various viewpoints have participated in the project. Even though this is a significant number of competent software engineering professionals, we cannot and do not claim that this sample represents all viewpoints from around the world and across all industry sectors.

- Even though complementary definitions of what constitutes "generally accepted knowledge" have been developed, the identification of which topics meet this definition within each Knowledge Area remains a matter for continued consensus formation

- The amount of literature that has been published on software engineering is considerable and any selection of reference material remains a matter of judgment. In the case of the SWEBOK, references were selected because they are written in English, readily available, easily readable, and—, taken as a group—, provide coverage of the topics within the KA

- Important and highly relevant reference material written in other languages than English have been omitted from the selected reference material.

- Reports of "field-testing" by its intended audience have not reached the editorial team at the time of publication. We are aware of teams using the Guide for evaluation and development of curriculum as well as for various purposes in industry. Monitoring of such field trials will be the next step in the evolution of the Guide.

Additionally, one must consider that

- Software engineering is an emerging discipline. This is especially true if you compare it to certain more established engineering disciplines. This means notably that the boundaries between the Knowledge Areas of software engineering and between software engineering and its Related Disciplines remain a matter for continued consensus formation;

The contents of this Guide must therefore be viewed as an "informed and reasonable" characterization of the software engineering Body of Knowledge and as baseline document for the Ironman phase. Additionally, please note that the Guide is not attempting nor does it claim to replace or amend in any way laws, rules and procedures that have been defined by official public policy makers around the world regarding the practice and definition of engineering and software engineering in particular.

To address these limitations, the next Ironman phase will begin by monitoring and gathering feedback on actual usage of the Trial version of the Guide by the various intended audiences for a period of roughly two years. Based on the gathered feedback, development of the Ironman version would be initiated in the third year and would follow a still to be determined development and review process. Those interested in performing experimental applications of the Guide are invited to contact the project team.

Alain Abran
École de technologie supérieure

Pierre Bourque
École de Technologie Supérieure

Leonard Tripp
Boeing Commercial Airplane
1999 President
IEEE Computer Society

Executive Editors of the
Guide to the Software
Engineering Body of
Knowledge

Editors of the Guide to
the Software Engineering
Body of Knowledge

Chair of the Professional
Practices Committee,
IEEE Computer Society

James W. Moore
The MITRE Corporation

Robert Dupuis
Université du Québec à Montréal

May 2001

The SWEBOK project web site is http://www.swebok.org/

ACKNOWLEDGMENTS

The SWEBOK editorial team gratefully acknowledges the support provided by the members of the Industrial Advisory Board. Funding for this project has been provided by the ACM, Boeing, the Canadian Council of Professional Engineers, Construx Software, the IEEE Computer Society, the MITRE corporation, the National Institute of Standards and Technology, the National Research Council of Canada, Rational Software, Raytheon, and SAP Labs (Canada). The team is thankful for the counsel provided by the Panel of Experts. The team also appreciates the important work performed by the Knowledge Area specialists. We would also like to express our gratitude for initial work on the Knowledge Area Descriptions completed by Imants Freibergs, Stephen Frezza, Andrew Gray, Vinh T. Ho, Michael Lutz, Larry Reeker, Guy Tremblay, Chris Verhoef, and Sybille Wolff. The editorial team must also acknowledge the indispensable contribution of the hundreds of reviewers.

The editorial team also wishes to thank the following people who contributed to the project in various manners: Mark Ardis, Michel Boivin, Julie Bonneau, Simon Bouchard, François Cossette, Vinh Duong, Gilles Gauthier, Michèle Hébert, Paula Hawthorn, Richard W. Heiman, Vinh T. Ho, Julie Hudon, Lucette Lapointe, Claude Laporte, Luis Molinié, Serge Oligny, Keith Paton, Denis St-Pierre, Dave Rayford, Pascale Tardif, Louise Thibaudeau, Dolores Wallace, Évariste Valery Bevo Wandji, Sybille Wolff, and Michal Young.

Finally, there are surely other people who have contributed to this Guide, either directly or indirectly, whose names we have inadvertently omitted. To those people, we offer our tacit appreciation and apologize for having omitted explicit recognition here.

INDUSTRIAL ADVISORY BOARD

At the time of the publication, the following people formed the Industrial Advisory Board:

Mario R. Barbacci, Software Engineering Institute, representing the IEEE Computer Society

Carl Chang, University of Illinois at Chicago, representing Computing Curricula 2001

François Coallier, Bell Canada, speaking as ISO/IEC JTC 1 / SC7 Chairman

Charles Howell, The MITRE Corporation

Anatol Kark, National Research Council of Canada

Philippe Kruchten, Rational Software

Laure Le Bars, SAP Labs (Canada)

Steve McConnell, Construx Software

Dan Nash, Raytheon Company

Fred Otto, Canadian Council of Professional Engineers (CCPE)

Bryan Pflug, The Boeing Company

Larry Reeker, National Institute of Standards and Technology, Department of Commerce, USA

PANEL OF EXPERTS

At the time of the publication, the following people formed the Panel of Experts:

Steve McConnell, Construx Software

Roger Pressman, R.S. Pressman and Associates

Ian Sommerville, Lancaster University, UK

REVIEW TEAM

The following people participated in the review process of this Guide.

Abbas, Rasha, Australia
Abran, Alain, Canada
Accioly, Carlos, Brazil
Ackerman, Frank, USA
Akiyama, Yoshihiro, Japan
Al-Abdullah, Mohammad, USA
Alarcon, Miren Idoia, Spain
Alawy, Ahmed, USA
Alleman, Glen, USA
Allen, Bob, Canada
Allen, David, USA
Amorosa, Francesco, Italy
Amyot, Daniel, Canada
Andrade, Daniel, Brazil
Arroyo-Figueror, Javier, USA
Ashford, Sonny, USA
Atsushi, Sawada, Japan
Backitis Jr., Frank, USA
Bagert, Donald, USA
Baker, Theodore, USA
Baker, Jr., David, USA
Baldwin, Mark, USA
Bales, David, UK
Bamberger, Judy, USA
Banerjee, Bakul, USA
Barker, Harry, UK
Barnes, Julie, USA
Barney, David, Australia
Barros, Rafael, Colombia
Bastarache, Louis, Canada
Bayer, Steven, USA
Beaulac, Adeline, Canada
Beck, William, USA
Beckman, Kathleen, USA
Below, Doreen, USA
Ben-Menachem, Mordechai, Israel
Benediktsson, Oddur, Iceland
Bergeron, Alain, Canada
Berler, Alexander, Greece
Bernet, Martin, USA
Bernstein, Larry, USA
Bertram, Martin, Germany
Bielikova, Maria, Slovakia
Bierwolf, Robert, The Netherlands

Bisbal, Jesus, Ireland
Boivin, Michel, Canada
Bomitali, Evelino, Italy
Bonderer, Reto, Switzerland
Bonk, Francis, USA
Booch, Grady, USA
Booker, Glenn, USA
Börstler, Jürgen, Sweden
Borzovs, Juris, Latvia
Botting, Richard, USA
Bowen, Thomas, USA
Boyer, Ken, USA
Brashear, Phil, USA
Briggs, Steve, USA
Bright, Daniela, USA
Brosseau, Jim, Canada
Brotbeck, George, USA
Brown, Normand, Canada
Bruhn, Anna, USA
Brune, Kevin, USA
Bryant, Jeanne, USA
Buglione, Luigi, Italy
Burns, Robert, USA
Burnstein, Ilene, USA
Byrne, Edward, USA
Calizaya, Percy, Peru
Carreon, Juan, USA
Carruthers, Kate, Australia
Caruso, Richard, USA
Case, Pam, USA
Cavanaugh, John, USA
Celia, John A., USA
Chalupa Sampaio, Alberto Antonio, Portugal
Chan, F.T., Hong Kong
Chan, Keith, Hong Kong
Chandra, A.K., India
Chang, Wen-Kui, Taiwan
Chapin, Ned, USA
Charette, Robert, USA
Chevrier, Marielle, Canada
Chi, Donald, USA
Chilenski, John, USA
Chow, Keith, Italy
Ciciliani, Ricardo, Argentina

Clark, Glenda, USA
Cleavenger, Darrell, USA
Cloos, Romain, Luxembourg
Coblentz, Brenda, USA
Cohen, Phil, Australia
Collignon, Stephane, Australia
Connors, Kathy Jo, USA
Cooper, Daniel, USA
Councill, Bill, USA
Cox, Margery, USA
Cunin, Pierre-Yves, France
DaLuz, Joseph, USA
Dampier, David, USA
Daneva, Maya, Canada
Davis, Ruth, USA
De Cesare, Sergio, UK
Dekleva, Sasa, USA
del Castillo, Federico, Peru
Del Dago, Gustavo, Argentina
DeWeese, Perry, USA
Di Nunno, Donn, USA
Diaz-Herrera, Jorge, USA
Dieste, Oscar, Spain
Dion, Francis, Canada
Dixon, Wes, USA
Dolado, Javier, Spain
Donaldson, John, UK
Dorofee, Audrey, USA
Douglass, Keith, Canada
Du, Weichang, Canada
Duben, Anthony, USA
Dudash, Edward, USA
Duncan, Scott, USA
Duong, Vinh, Canada
Durham, George, USA
Dutil, Daniel, Canada
Edge, Gary, USA
Edwards, Helen Maria, UK
El-Kadi, Amr, Egypt
Endres, David, USA
Engelmann, Franz, Switzerland
Escue, Marilyn, USA
Espinoza, Marco, Peru
Fay, Istvan, Hungary
Fayad, Mohamed, USA
Fendrich, John, USA
Ferguson, Robert, USA
Fernandez, Eduardo, USA
Fernandez-Sanchez, Jose, Spain
Filgueiras, Lucia, Brazil
Finkelstein, Anthony, UK
Flinchbaugh, Scott, USA
Fortenberry, Kirby, USA

Foster, Henrietta, USA
Fowler, John Jr., USA
Fox, Christopher, USA
Frankl, Phyllis, USA
Freibergs, Imants, Latvia
Frezza, Stephen, USA
Fruehauf, Karol, Switzerland
Fuggetta, Alphonso, Italy
Fujii, Roger, USA
Fuschi, David Luigi, Italy
Gabrini, Philippe, Canada
Gagnon, Eric, Canada
Ganor, Eitan, Israel
Garbajosa, Juan, Spain
Garceau, Benoît, Canada
Garcia-Palencia, Omar, Colombia
Garner, Barry, USA
Gelperin, David, USA
Gersting, Judith, Hawaii
Giesler, Gregg, USA
Gil, Indalecio, Spain
Gilchrist, Thomas, USA
Glass, Robert, USA
Glynn, Garth, UK
Goers, Ron, USA
Gogates, Gregory, USA
Goldsmith, Robin, USA
Goodbrand, Alan, Canada
Gorski, Janusz, Poland
Gresse von Wangenheim, Christiane, Brazil
Grigonis, George, USA
Gupta, Arun, USA
Gustafson, David, USA
Gutcher, Frank, USA
Haas, Bob, USA
Hagar, Jon, USA
Hagstrom, Erick, USA
Hailey, Victoria, Canada
Haller, John, USA
Halstead-Nussloch, Richard, USA
Hamm, Linda, USA
Hankewitz, Lutz, Germany
Harker, Rob, USA
Hart, Ronald, USA
Hart, Hal, USA
Hartner, Clinton, USA
Hayeck, Elie, USA
He, Zhonglin, UK
Hedger, Dick, USA
Hefner, Rick, USA
Heinrich, Mark, USA
Herrmann, Debra, USA
Hesse, Wolfgang, Germany

Hilburn, Thomas, USA
Hill, Michael, USA
Ho, Vinh, Canada
Hodgen, Bruce, Australia
Hodges, Brett, Canada
Hoffman, Michael, USA
Hoganson, Tammy, USA
Hollocker, Chuck, USA
Horch, John, USA
Huang, Hui Min, USA
Hung, Peter, USA
Hung, Chih-Cheng, USA
Hunt, Theresa, USA
Hunter, John, USA
Hvannberg, Ebba Thora, Iceland
Hybertson, Duane, USA
Ikiz, Seckin, Turkey
Iyengar, Dwaraka, USA
Jackelen, George, USA
Jaeger, Dawn, USA
Jahnke, Jens, Canada
Jino, Mario, Brazil
Johnson, Vandy, USA
Jones, Larry, Canada
Jones, Alan, UK
Jones, James, USA
Jones, Paul, USA
Juan-Martinez, Manuel-Fernando, Spain
Juhasz, Zoltan, Hungary
Juristo, Nataiia, Spain
Kaiser, Michael, Switzerland
Kambic, George, USA
Kark, Anatol, Canada
Kasser, Joseph, Australia
Kasser, Joe, USA
Katz, Alf, Australia
Kececi, Nihal, Canada
Kell, Penelope, USA
Kelly, Diane, Canada
Kelly, Frank, USA
Kenett, Ron, Israel
Kenney, Mary L., USA
Kerr, John, USA
Kierzyk, Robert, USA
Kinsner, W., Canada
Kirkpatrick, Harry, USA
Kittiel, Linda, USA
Klappholz, David, USA
Klein, Joshua, Israel
Knight, Claire, UK
Knoke, Peter, USA
Ko, Roy, Hong Kong
Kolewe, Ralph, Canada

Komal, Surinder Singh, Canada
Kovalovsky, Stefan, Austria
Krauth, Péter, Hungary
Krishnan, Nirmala, USA
Kruchten, Philippe, Canada
Kwok, Shui Hung, Canada
Lacroix, Dominique, Canada
LaMotte, Stephen, USA
Land, Susan, USA
Lange, Douglas, USA
Laporte, Claude, Canada
Lawlis, Patricia, USA
Le, Thach, USA
Leavitt, Randal, Canada
LeBel, Réjean, Canada
Leciston, David, USA
Lehman, Meir (Manny), UK
Leigh, William, USA
Lenss, John, USA
Leonard, Eugene, USA
Lethbridge, Timothy, Canada
Leung, Hareton, Hong Kong
Lever, Ronald, The Netherlands
Levesque, Ghislain, Canada
Ley, Earl, USA
Little, Joyce Currie, USA
Logan, Jim, USA
Lounis, Hakim, Canada
Low, Graham, Australia
Lutz, Michael, USA
Lynch, Gary, USA
MacKay, Stephen, Canada
MacKenzie, Garth, USA
MacNeil, Paul, USA
Magel, Kenneth, USA
Mains, Harold, USA
Malak, Renee, USA
Maldonado, José Carlos, Brazil
Marcos, Esperanza, Spain
Marinescu, Radu, Romania
Marm, Waldo, Peru
Marusca, Ioan, Canada
Matlen, Duane, USA
Matsumoto, Yoshihiro, Japan
McBride, Tom, Australia
McCarthy, Glenn, USA
McChesney, Ian, UK
McCormick, Thomas, Canada
McCown, Christian, USA
McDonald, Jim, USA
McGrath Carroll, Sue, USA
McHutchison, Diane, USA
McKinnell, Brian, Canada

McMichael, Robert, USA
McMillan, William, USA
McQuaid, Patricia, USA
Mead, Nancy, USA
Meeuse, Jaap, The Netherlands
Meier, Michael, USA
Melhart, Bonnie, USA
Mengel, Susan, USA
Meredith, Denis, USA
Meyerhoff, Dirk, Germany
Mili, Hafedh, Canada
Miller, Chris, The Netherlands
Miller, Mark, USA
Miller, Keith, USA
Miranda, Eduardo, Canada
Mistrik, Ivan, Germany
Mitasiunas, Antanas, Lithuania
Modell, Howard, USA
Modell, Staiger,USA
Modesitt, Kenneth, USA
Moland, Kathryn, USA
Moreno, Ana, Spain
Mosiuoa, Tseliso, Lesotho
Moudry, James, USA
Mularz, Diane, USA
Mullens, David, USA
Müllerburg, Monika, Germany
Murali, Nagarajan, Australia
Murphy, Mike, USA
Narasimhadevara, Sudha, Canada
Narawane, Ranjana, India
Narayanan, Ramanathan, India
Navarro Ramirez, Daniel, Mexico
Navas Plano, Francisco, Spain
Neumann, Dolly, USA
Nguyen-Kim, Hong, Canada
Nikandros, George, Australia
Nishiyama, Tetsuto, Japan
Nunn, David, USA
O'Donoghue, David, Ireland
Oliver, David John, Australia
Olson, Keith, USA
Ostrom, Donald, USA
Oudshoorn, Michael, Australia
Owen, Cherry, USA
Parrish, Lee, USA
Parsons, Samuel, USA
Patel, Dilip, UK
Paulk, Mark, USA
Pavelka, Jan, Czech Republic
Pawlyszyn, Blanche, USA
Pecceu, Didier, France
Perisic, Branko, Yugoslavia

Peters, Dennis, Canada
Petersen, Erik, Australia
Pfeiffer, Martin, Germany
Phillips, Dwayne, USA
Phipps, Robert, USA
Phister, Jr., Paul, USA
Piattini, Mario, Spain
Piersall, Jeff, USA
Pillai, S.K., India
Pinder, Alan, UK
Pinheiro, Francisco A., Brazil
Poon, Peter, USA
Poppendieck, Mary, USA
Powell, Mace, USA
Predenkoski, Mary, USA
Prescott, Allen, USA
Pressman, Roger, USA
Price, Margaretha, USA
Price, Art, USA
Pullum, Laura, USA
Purser, Keith, USA
Purssey, John, Australia
Pustaver, John, USA
Quinn, Anne, USA
Radnell, David, Australia
Rafea, Ahmed, Egypt
Ramsden, Patrick, Australia
Rao, N.Vyaghrewara, India
Reader, Katherine, USA
Redwine, Samuel, USA
Reed, Karl, Australia
Reedy, Ann, USA
Rios, Joaquin, Spain
Risbec, Philippe, France
Roach, Steve, USA
Robillard, Pierre, Canada
Rocha, Zalkind, Brazil
Rodeiro Iglesias, Javier, Spain
Rodriguez-Dapena, Patricia, Spain
Rogoway, Paul, Israel
Rontondi, Guido, Italy
Rosca, Daniela, USA
Rosenberg, Linda, USA
Rourke, Michael, Australia
Rout, Terry, Australia
Ruocco, Anthony, USA
Rutherfoord, Rebecca, USA
Ryan, Michael, Ireland
Salustri, Filippo, Canada
Salwin, Arthur, USA
Sanden, Bo, USA
Sandmayr, Helmut, Switzerland
Santana Filho, Ozeas Vieira, Brazil

Sato, Tomonobu, Japan
Satyadas, Antony, USA
Schaaf, Robert, USA
Scheper, Charlotte, USA
Schiffel, Jeffrey, USA
Schlicht, Bill, USA
Schrott, William, USA
Schwarm, Stephen, USA
Sebern, Mark, USA
Seffah, Ahmed, Canada
Selby, Nancy, USA
Selph, William, USA
Sen, Dhruba, USA
Senechal, Raymond, USA
Setlur, Atul, USA
Sharp, David, USA
Shepard, Terry, Canada
Shepherd, Alan, Germany
Silva, Andres, Spain
Singer, Carl, USA
Sinnett, Paul, UK
Sintzoff, André, France
Sky, Richard, USA
Smilie, Kevin, USA
Smith, David, USA
Sophatsathit, Peraphon, Thailand
Sorensen, Reed, USA
Soundarajan, Neelam, USA
Sousa Santos, Frederico, Portugal
Spillers, Mark, USA
Spinellis, Diomidis, Greece
Springer, Donald, USA
St-Pierre, Denis, Canada
Staiger, John, USA
Steurs, Stefan, Belgium
Stroulia, Eleni, Canada
Subramanian, K.S., India
Sundaram, Sai, UK
Swanek, James, USA
Swearingen, Sandra, USA
Tamai, Tetsuo, Japan
Tasker, Dan, New Zealand
Taylor, Stanford, USA
Terski, Matt, USA

Thayer, Richard, USA
Thomas, Michael, USA
Thompson, A. Allan, Australia
Thompson, John Barrie, UK
Titus, Jason, USA
Tockey, Steve, USA
Tovar, Edmundo, Spain
Towhidnejad, Massood, USA
Trellue, Patricia, USA
Trèves, Nicolas, France
Troy, Elliot, USA
Tsuneo, Furuyama, Japan
Tuohy, Marsha P., USA
Tuohy, Kenney, USA
Turczyn, Stephen, USA
Upchurch, Richard, USA
Van Duine, Dan, USA
Vander Plaats, Jim, USA
Vegas, Sira, Spain
Verner, June, USA
Villas-Boas, André, Brazil
Vollman, Thomas, USA
Walker, Richard, Australia
Walsh, Bucky, USA
Wang, Yingxu, Sweden
Wear, Larry, USA
Weinstock, Charles, USA
Wenyin, Liu, China
Werner, Linda, USA
White, Stephanie, USA
Whitmire, Scott, USA
Wijbrans, Klaas, The Netherlands
Wijbrans-Roodbergen, Margot, The Netherlands
Wilkie, Frederick, UK
Wilson, Charles, USA
Wilson, Russell, USA
Wilson, Leon, USA
Woechan, Kenneth, USA
Yadin, Aharon, Israel
Yih, Swu, Taiwan
Young, Michal, USA
Yrivarren, Jorge, Peru
Zvegintzov, Nicholas, USA
Zweben, Stu, USA

The following motion was unanimously adopted on April 18, 2001.

The Industrial Advisory Board of the Guide to the Software Engineering Body of Knowledge (SWEBOK) project recognizes that due process was followed in the development of the Guide (Trial Version) and endorses the position that the Guide (Trial Version) is ready for field trials for a period of two years.

The following motion was adopted by the Board of Governors of the
IEEE Computer Society in May 2001.

The Board of Governors of the IEEE Computer Society accepts the Guide to the Software Engineering Body of Knowledge (Trial Version) as fulfilling its development requirements and is ready for field trials for a period of two years.

© IEEE – Trial Version 1.00 – May 2001

CHAPTER 1

INTRODUCTION TO THE GUIDE

In spite of the millions of software professionals worldwide and the ubiquitous presence of software in our society, software engineering has not yet reached the status of a legitimate engineering discipline and a recognized profession.

Originally formed in 1993 by the IEEE Computer Society and the Association for Computing Machinery, the Software Engineering Coordinating Committee (SWECC) has been actively promoting software engineering as a profession and an engineering discipline.

Achieving consensus by the profession on a core body of knowledge is a key milestone in all disciplines and has been identified by the SWECC as crucial for the evolution of software engineering toward a professional status. This Guide, written under the auspices of this committee, is the part of a multi-year project designed to reach this consensus.

What is Software Engineering?

The IEEE Computer Society defines software engineering as

"(1) The application of a systematic, disciplined, quantifiable approach to the development, operation, and maintenance of software; that is, the application of engineering to software.

(2) The study of approaches as in (1)."[1]

What is a Recognized Profession?

For software engineering to be known as a legitimate engineering discipline and a recognized profession, consensus on a core body of knowledge is imperative. This fact is well illustrated by Starr when he defines what can be considered a legitimate discipline and a recognized profession. In his Pulitzer-prize-winning book on the history of the medical profession in the USA, he states that:

"the legitimization of professional authority involves three distinctive claims: first, that the knowledge and competence of the professional have been validated by a community of his or her peers; second, that this consensually validated knowledge rests on rational, scientific grounds; and third, that the professional's judgment and advice are oriented toward a set of substantive values, such as health. These

aspects of legitimacy correspond to the kinds of attributes — collegial, cognitive and moral — usually cited in the term "profession."[2]

What are the Characteristics of a Profession ?

But what are the characteristics of a profession? Gary Ford and Norman Gibbs studied several recognized professions including medicine, law, engineering and accounting[3]. They concluded that an engineering profession is characterized by several components:

- An initial *professional education* in a curriculum validated by society through *accreditation;*
- Registration of fitness to practice via voluntary *certification* or mandatory *licensing;*
- Specialized *skill development* and *continuing professional education;*
- Communal support via a *professional society;*
- A commitment to norms of conduct often prescribed in a *code of ethics.*

This Guide contributes to the first three of these components. Articulating a Body of Knowledge is an essential step toward developing a profession because it represents a broad consensus regarding what a software engineering professional should know. Without such a consensus, no licensing examination can be validated, no curriculum can prepare an individual for an examination, and no criteria can be formulated for accrediting a curriculum. The development of the consensus is also prerequisite to the adoption of coherent skill development and continuing professional education programs in organizations.

What are the Objectives of the SWEBOK Project?

The Guide should not be confused with the Body of Knowledge itself. The Body of Knowledge already exists in the published literature. The purpose of the Guide is to describe what portion of the Body of Knowledge is

---

[1] "IEEE Standard Glossary of Software Engineering Terminology," IEEE, Piscataway, NJ std 610.12-1990, 1990.

[2] P. Starr, The Social Transformation of American Medicine: Basic Books, 1982. p. 15.

[3] G. Ford and N. E. Gibbs, "*A Mature Profession of Software Engineering*," Software Engineering Institute, Carnegie Mellon University, Pittsburgh, Pennsylvania, Technical CMU/SEI-96-TR-004, January 1996.

generally accepted, to organize that portion, and to provide a topical access to it.

The Guide to the Software Engineering Body of Knowledge (SWEBOK) was established with the following five objectives:

1. Promote a consistent view of software engineering worldwide.

2. Clarify the place—and set the boundary—of software engineering with respect to other disciplines such as computer science, project management, computer engineering, and mathematics.

3. Characterize the contents of the software engineering discipline.

4. Provide a topical access to the Software Engineering Body of Knowledge.

5. Provide a foundation for curriculum development and individual certification and licensing material.

The first of these objectives, the consistent worldwide view of software engineering was supported by a development process that has engaged approximately 500 reviewers from 42 countries. (More information regarding the development process can be found in the Preface and on the Web site. Professional and learned societies and public agencies involved in software engineering were officially contacted, made aware of this project and invited to participate in the review process. Knowledge Area Specialists or chapter authors were recruited from North America, the Pacific Rim and Europe. Presentations on the project were made to various international venues and more are scheduled for the upcoming year.

The second of the objectives, the desire to set a boundary, motivates the fundamental organization of the Guide. The material that is recognized as being within software engineering is organized into the ten Knowledge Areas listed in Table 1. Each of the ten KAs is treated as a chapter in this Guide. Table 1. The SWEBOK knowledge areas (KA).

Software requirements

Software design

Software construction

Software testing

Software maintenance

Software configuration management

Software engineering management

Software engineering process

Software engineering tools and methods

Software quality

In establishing a boundary, it is also important to identify what disciplines share a boundary and often a common intersection with software engineering. To this end, the guide also recognizes seven related disciplines, listed in

Table 2 (See also Appendix B). Software engineers should of course know material from these fields (and the KA descriptions may make references to the fields). It is not however an objective of the SWEBOK Guide to characterize the knowledge of the related disciplines but rather what is viewed as specific to software engineering.

Table 2 Related disciplines.

Cognitive sciences and human factors

Computer engineering

Computer science

Management and management science

Mathematics

Project management

Systems engineering

Hierarchical Organization

The organization of the Knowledge Area Descriptions or chapters, shown in Figure 1, supports the third of the project's objectives—a characterization of the contents of software engineering. The detailed specifications provided by the project's editorial team to the Knowledge Area Specialists regarding the contents of the Knowledge Area Descriptions can be found in Appendix A.

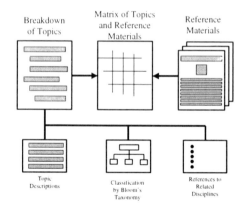

Figure 1 The organization of a KA description

The Guide uses a hierarchical organization to decompose each KA into a set of topics with recognizable labels. A two- or three-level breakdown provides a reasonable way to find topics of interest. The Guide treats the selected topics in a manner compatible with major schools of thought and with breakdowns generally found in industry and in software engineering literature and standards. The breakdowns of topics do not presume particular application domains, business uses, management philosophies, development methods, and so forth. The extent of each topic's description is only that needed to understand the generally accepted nature of the topics and for the reader to successfully find reference material. After all, the Body of Knowledge is found in the reference materials, not in the Guide itself.

Reference Materials and a Matrix

To provide a topical access to the Knowledge—the fourth of the project's objectives—the Guide identifies reference materials for each KA including book chapters, refereed papers, or other well-recognized sources of authoritative information[4]. Each KA description also includes a matrix that relates the reference materials to the listed topics. The total volume of cited literature is intended to be suitable for mastery through the completion of an undergraduate education plus four years of experience.

It should be noted that the Guide does not attempt to be comprehensive in its citations. Much material that is both suitable and excellent is not referenced. Materials were selected, in part, because— taken as a collection—they provide coverage of the described topics.

Depth of Treatment

From the outset, the question arose as to the depth of treatment the Guide should provide. We adopted an approach that supports the fifth of the project's objectives—providing a foundation for curriculum development, certification and licensing. We applied a criterion of *generally accepted* knowledge, which we had to distinguish from advanced and research knowledge (on the grounds of maturity) and from specialized knowledge (on the grounds of generality of application). A second definition of *generally accepted* comes from the Project Management Institute: "The generally accepted knowledge applies to most projects most of the time, and widespread consensus validates its value and effectiveness".[5]

However, generally accepted knowledge does not imply that one should apply the designated knowledge uniformly to all software engineering endeavors—each project's needs determine that—but it does imply that competent, capable software engineers should be equipped with this knowledge for potential application. More precisely, generally accepted knowledge should be included in the study material for a software engineering licensing examination that graduates would take after gaining four years of work experience. Although this criterion is specific to the U.S. style of education and does not necessarily apply to other countries, we deem it useful. However, both

definitions of generally accepted knowledge should be seen as complementary.

Additionally, the KA descriptions are somewhat forward-looking—we're considering not only what is generally accepted today but also what could be generally accepted in three to five years.

Ratings

As an aid notably to curriculum developers and in support of the project's fifth objective, the Guide rates each topic with one of a set of pedagogical categories commonly attributed to Benjamin Bloom[6]. The concept is that educational objectives can be classified into six categories representing increasing depth: knowledge, comprehension, application, analysis, synthesis, and evaluation Results of this exercise for all KAs can be found in Appendix C. This Appendix must however not be viewed as a definitive classification but much more as a starting point for curriculum developers.

KAs from Related Disciplines

A list of disciplines (Related Disciplines) that share a common boundary with software engineering can be found in Appendix B. Appendix B also identifies from an authoritative source a list of KAs of these Related Disciplines.

A proposed Breakdown for an Additional KA

One of the knowledge areas that was not included in this Trial version because there was no consensus on the generally accepted set of reference material is *Component integration*. Since such a consensus may appear in the near future, we include in Appendix D a proposal for a breakdown of topics on that subject. This is intended to serve as a jumpstart for future work on the topic.

We recognize also that Human-Computer Interface is important and we will in future versions indicate a point beyond which the software engineer should seek the help of a specialist. There was also no consensus on a set of reference material on the subject.

THE KNOWLEDGE AREAS

Figure 2 maps out the 10 KAs and the important topics incorporated within them. The first five KAs are presented in traditional waterfall lifecycle sequence. The subsequent Kas are presented in alphabetical order. This is identical to the sequence in which they are presented in the Guide. Brief summaries of the KA descriptions appear next.

---

[4]   Web pages in the Recommended References sections were verified on April 9, 2001.

[5]   Project Management Institute, A Guide to the Project Management Body of Knowledge, Upper Darby, PA, 1996, http://www.pmi.org/publictn/pmboktoc.htm/. "Project" in the quote refers to projects in general.

[6]   See chiron.valdosta.edu/whuitt/col/cogsys/bloom.html for a short description of Bloom's taxonomy. The original source is Bloom, B.S. (Ed.) (1956) Taxonomy of educational objectives: The classification of educational goals: Handbook I, cognitive domain. New York ; Toronto: Longmans, Green.

SOFTWARE REQUIREMENTS (see Figure 2, column a)

A requirement is defined as a property that must be exhibited in order to solve some problem of the real world.

The first knowledge sub-area is the *requirement engineering process*, which introduces the requirements engineering process, orienting the remaining five topics and showing how requirements engineering dovetails with the overall software engineering process. It describes process models, process actors, process support and management and process quality improvement.

The second sub-area is *requirements elicitation*, which is concerned with where requirements come from and how they can be collected by the requirements engineer. It includes requirement sources and techniques for elicitation.

The third sub-area, *requirements analysis*, is concerned with the process of analyzing requirements to:

- detect and resolve conflicts between requirements;

- discover the bounds of the system and how it must interact with its environment;

- elaborate system requirements to software requirements.

Requirements analysis includes requirements classification, conceptual modeling, architectural design and requirements allocation and requirements negotiation.

The fourth sub-area is *software requirements specification*. It describes the structure, quality and verifiability of the requirements document. This may take the form of two documents, or two parts of the same document with different readership and purposes. The first document is the system requirements definition document, and the second is the software requirements specification. The sub-area also describes the document structure and standards and document quality.

The fifth sub-area is *requirements validation* whose aim is to pick up any problems before resources are committed to addressing the requirements. Requirements validation is concerned with the process of examining the requirements document to ensure that it defines the right system (i.e. the system that the user expects). It is subdivided into descriptions of the conduct of requirements reviews, prototyping, model validation and acceptance tests.

The last sub-area is *requirements management*, which is an activity that spans the whole software life-cycle. It is fundamentally about change management and the maintenance of the requirements in a state that accurately mirrors the software to be, or that has been, built. It includes change management, requirements attributes and requirements tracing.

SOFTWARE DESIGN (see Figure 2, column b)

According to the IEEE, software design is an activity that spans the whole software life-cycle. It is fundamentally about change management and the maintenance of the requirements in a state that accurately mirrors the software to be, or that has been, built. The knowledge area is divided into six sub-areas.

The first one presents the *basic concepts* and notions which form an underlying basis to the understanding of the role and scope of software design. These are general concepts, the context of software design, the design process and the enabling techniques for software design.

The second sub-area regroups the *key issues of software design*. They include concurrency, control and handling of events, distribution, error and exception handling, interactive systems and persistence.

The third sub-area is *structure and architecture*, in particular architectural structures and viewpoints, architectural styles, design patterns, and finally families of programs and frameworks.

The fourth sub-area describes *software design quality analysis and evaluation*. While a whole knowledge area is devoted to software quality, this sub-area presents the topics more specifically related to software design. These aspects are quality attributes, quality analysis and evaluation tools and measures.

The fifth one is software *design notations*, which are divided into structural and behavioral descriptions.

The last sub-area covers *software design strategies and methods*. First, general strategies are described, followed by function-oriented methods, then object-oriented methods, data-structure centered design and a group of other methods, like formal and transformational methods.

SOFTWARE CONSTRUCTION (see Figure 2, column c)

Software Construction is a fundamental act of software engineering: the construction of working meaningful software through a combination of coding, validation, and testing (unit testing).

The first and most important method of breaking the subject of software construction into smaller units is to recognize the four principles that most strongly affect the way in which software is constructed. These principles are

the *reduction of complexity*, the *anticipation of diversity*, the *structuring for validation* and the *use of external standards*.

A second and less important method of breaking the subject of software construction into smaller units is to recognize three styles/methods of software construction, namely : *Linguistic, Formal and Visual*.

A synthesis of these two views is presented.

4

SOFTWARE TESTING (see Figure 2, column d)

Software testing consists of the dynamic verification of the behavior of a program on a finite set of test cases, suitably selected from the usually infinite executions domain, against the specified expected behavior. It includes five sub-areas.

It begins with a description of *basic concepts*. First, the testing terminology is presented, then the theoretical foundations of testing are described, with the relationship of testing to other activities.

The second sub-area is the *test levels*. They are divided between the targets and the objectives of the tests.

The third sub-area are the *test techniques* themselves. A first category is grouped on the criterion of the base on which tests are generated, and a second group based on the ignorance of knowledge of implementation. A discussion of how to select and combine the appropriate techniques is presented.

The fourth sub-area covers *test-related measures*. The measures are grouped into those related to the evaluation of the program under test and the evaluation of the tests performed.

The last sub-area describes the *management* specific to the test process. It included management concerns and the test activities.

SOFTWARE MAINTENANCE (see Figure 2, column e)

Once in operation, anomalies are uncovered, operating environments change, and new user requirements surface. The maintenance phase of the lifecycle commences upon delivery but maintenance activities occur much earlier. The Software maintenance knowledge area is dived into six sub-areas.

The first on presents the domain's *basic concepts*, definitions, the main activities and problems of software maintenance.

The second sub-area describes the *maintenance process*, based on the standards IEEE 1219 and ISO/IEC 14764.

The third sub-area regroups *key issues* related to software maintenance. The topics covered are technical, management, cost and estimation and measurement issues.

Techniques for maintenance constitute the fourth sub-area. Those techniques include program comprehension, re-engineering, reverse engineering and impact analysis.

SOFTWARE CONFIGURATION MANAGEMENT (see Figure 2, column f)

Software Configuration Management (SCM) is the discipline of identifying the configuration of a system at distinct points in time for the purpose of systematically controlling changes to the software configuration and maintaining the integrity and traceability of the configuration throughout the system lifecycle. This Knowledge Area includes six sub-areas.

The first sub-area is the *management of the SCM process*. It covers the topics of the organizational context for SCM, constraints and guidance for SCM, planning for SCM, the SCM plan itself and surveillance of SCM.

The second sub-area is *Software configuration identification*, which identifies items to be controlled, establishes identification schemes for the items and their versions, and establishes the tools and techniques to be used in acquiring and managing controlled items. The topics in this sub-area are first the identification of the items to be controlled and the software library.

The third sub-area is the *software configuration control*, which is the management of changes during the software life-cycle. The topics are, first, requesting, evaluating and approving software changes, and, second, implementing software changes, and third deviations and waivers.

The fourth sub-area is *software configuration status accounting*. Its topics are software configuration status information and status reporting.

The fifth sub-area is *software configuration auditing*. Consisting of software functional configuration auditing, software physical configuration auditing and in-process audits of a software baseline.

The last sub-area is *software release management and delivery*, covering software building and software release management.

SOFTWARE ENGINEERING MANAGEMENT (see Figure 2, column g)

Whilst it is true to say that in one sense it should be possible to manage software engineering in the same way as any other (complex) process, there are aspects particular to software products and the software engineering process that complicate effective management. There are three sub-areas for software engineering management.

The first is *organizational management*, comprising policy management, personnel management, communication management, portfolio management and procurement management.

The second sub-area is *process/project management*, including initiation and scope definition, planning, enactment, review and evaluation and closure.

The third and last sub-area is *software engineering measurement*, where general principles about software measurement are covered. The first topics presented are the goals of a measurement program, followed by measurement selection, measuring software and its development, collection of data and, finally, software metric models.

SOFTWARE ENGINEERING PROCESS (see Figure 2, column h)

The Software Engineering Process Knowledge Area is concerned with the definition, implementation, measurement, management, change and improvement of the software engineering process itself. It is divided into six sub-areas.

The first one presents the *basic concepts*: themes and terminology.

The second sub-area is *process infrastructure*, where the Software Engineering Process group concept is described, as well as the Experience Factory.

The third sub-area deals with *measurements specific to software engineering process*. It presents the methodology and measurement paradigms in the field.

The fourth sub-area describes knowledge related to *process definition*: the various types of process definitions, the life-cycle framework models, the software life-cycle models, the notations used to represent these definitions, process definitions methods and automation relative to the various definitions.

The fifth sub-area presents *qualitative process analysis*, especially the process definition review and root cause analysis.

Finally, the sixth sub-area concludes with *process implementation and change*. It describes the paradigms and guidelines for process implementation and change, and the evaluation of the outcome of implementation and change.

SOFTWARE ENGINEERING TOOLS AND METHODS (see Figure 2, column i)

The Software Engineering Tools and Methods knowledge area includes both the software development environments and the development methods knowledge areas identified in the Straw Man version of the guide.

Software development environments are the computer-based tools that are intended to assist the software development process. Development methods impose structure on the software development activity with the goal of making the activity systematic and ultimately more likely to be successful.

The partitioning of the Software Tools section uses the same structure as the Stone Man Version of the Guide to the Software Engineering Body of Knowledge. The first five subsections correspond to the five Knowledge Areas (*Requirements, Design, Construction, Testing, and Maintenance*) and the next four subsections correspond to the remaining Knowledge Areas (*Process, Quality, Configuration Management and Management*). Two additional subsections are provided: one for infrastructure support tools that do not fit in any of the earlier sections, and a Miscellaneous subsection for topics, such as tool integration techniques, that are potentially applicable to all classes of tools.

The *software development methods* section is divided into four subsections: *heuristic methods* dealing with informal approaches, *formal methods* dealing with mathematically based approaches, *prototyping methods* dealing with software development approaches based on various forms of prototyping, and *miscellaneous method issues*.

SOFTWARE QUALITY (see Figure 2, column j)

This chapter deals with software quality considerations that transcend the lifecycle processes. Since software quality is a ubiquitous concern in software engineering, it is considered in many of the other KAs and the reader will notice pointers those KAs through this KA. The Knowledge Area description covers four sub-areas.

The first sub-area describes the *software quality concepts* such as measuring the value of quality, the ISO9126 quality description, dependability and other special types of system and quality needs.

The second sub-area covers the *purpose and planning of software quality assurance (SQA) and V&V (Verification and Validation)*. It includes common planning activities, and both the SQA and V&S plans.

The third sub-area describes the *activities and techniques for SQA and V&V*. It includes static and dynamic techniques as well as other SQA and V&S testing.

The fourth sub-area describes *measurement applied to SQA and V&V*. It includes the fundamentals of measurement, measures, measurement analysis techniques, defect characterization, and additional uses of SQA and V&V data.

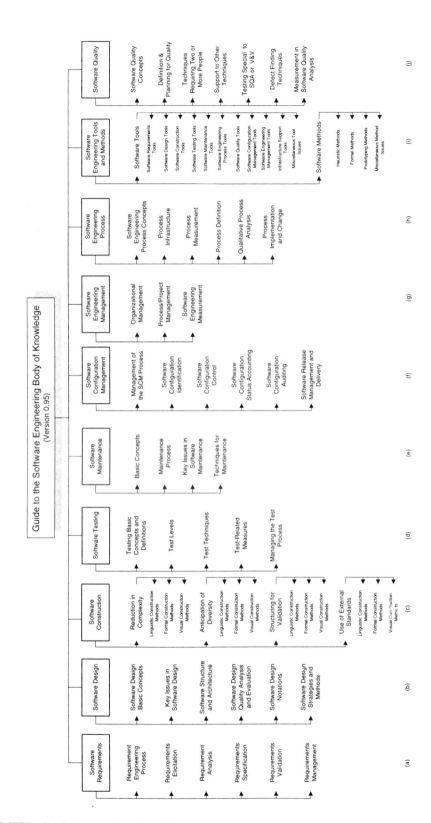

Guide to the Software Engineering Body of Knowledge
(Version 0.95)

(a)	(b)	(c)	(d)	(e)	(f)	(g)	(h)	(i)	(j)
Software Requirements	Software Design	Software Construction	Software Testing	Software Maintenance	Software Configuration Management	Software Engineering Management	Software Engineering Process	Software Engineering Tools and Methods	Software Quality
Requirement Engineering Process	Software Design Basic Concepts	Reduction in Complexity	Testing Basic Concepts and Definitions	Basic Concepts	Management of the SCM Process	Organizational Management	Software Engineering Process Concepts	Software Tools	Software Quality Concepts
Requirements Elicitation	Key Issues in Software Design	Anticipation of Diversity	Test Levels	Maintenance Process	Software Configuration Identification	Process/Project Management	Process Infrastructure	Software Methods	Definition & Planning for Quality
Requirement Analysis	Software Structure and Architecture	Structuring for Validation	Test Techniques	Key Issues in Software Maintenance	Software Configuration Control	Software Engineering Measurement	Process Measurement		Techniques Requiring Two or More People
Requirements Specification	Software Design Quality Analysis and Evaluation	Use of External Standards	Test-Related Measures	Techniques for Maintenance	Software Configuration Status Accounting		Process Definition		Support to Other Techniques
Requirements Validation	Software Design Notations		Managing the Test Process		Software Configuration Auditing		Qualitative Process Analysis		Testing Special to SQA or V&V
Requirements Management	Software Design Strategies and Methods				Software Release Management and Delivery		Process Implementation and Change		Defect Finding Techniques
									Measurement in Software Quality Analysis

Software Construction sub-items (each of Reduction in Complexity, Anticipation of Diversity, Structuring for Validation, Use of External Standards):
- Linguistic Construction Methods
- Formal Construction Methods
- Visual Construction Methods

Software Tools sub-items:
- Software Requirements Tools
- Software Design Tools
- Software Construction Tools
- Software Testing Tools
- Software Maintenance Tools
- Software Engineering Process Tools
- Software Quality Tools
- Software Configuration Management Tools
- Software Engineering Management Tools
- Infrastructure Support Tools
- Miscellaneous Tool Issues

Software Methods sub-items:
- Heuristic Methods
- Formal Methods
- Prototyping Methods
- Miscellaneous Method Issues

CHAPTER 2
SOFTWARE REQUIREMENTS

Pete Sawyer and Gerald Kotonya
Computing Department,
Lancaster University
United Kingdom
{sawyer} {gerald}@comp.lancs.ac.uk

Table of Contents

1   INTRODUCTION

This document proposes a breakdown of the SWEBOK Software Requirements Knowledge Area. The knowledge area is concerned with the acquisition, analysis, specification, validation and management of software requirements. It is widely acknowledged within the software industry that software projects are critically vulnerable when these activities are performed poorly. This has led to the widespread use of the term 'requirements engineering' to denote the systematic handling of requirements. This is the term we use in the rest of this document. Software requirements are one of the products of the requirements engineering process.

Software requirements express the needs and constraints that are placed upon a software product that contribute to the satisfaction of some real world application [Kot00]. The application may be, for example, to solve some business problem or exploit a business opportunity offered by a new market. It is important to understand that, except where the problem is motivated by technology, the problem is an artifact of the problem domain and is generally technology-neutral. The software product alone may satisfy this need (for example, if it is a desktop application), or it may be a component (for example, a speech compression module used in a mobile phone) of a software-intensive system for which satisfaction of the need is an emergent property. In fundamental terms, the way in which the requirements are handled for stand-alone products and components of software-intensive systems is the same.

One of the main objectives of requirements engineering is to discover how to partition the system; to identify which requirements should be allocated to which components. In some systems, all the components will be implemented in software. Others will comprise a mixture of technologies. Almost all will have human users and sometimes it makes sense to consider all components of the system to which requirements should be allocated (for example, to save costs or to exploit human adaptability and resourcefulness). Because of this requirements engineering is fundamentally an activity of systems engineering rather than one that is specific to software engineering. In this respect, the term 'software requirements engineering' is misleading because it implies a narrow scope concerned only with the handling of requirements that have already been acquired and allocated to software components. Since it is increasingly common for practicing software engineers to participate in the elicitation and allocation of requirements, it is essential that the scope of the knowledge area extends to the whole of the requirements engineering process.

One of the fundamental tenets of good software engineering is that there is good communication between system users and system developers. It is the requirements engineer who is the conduit for this communication. They must mediate between the domain of the system user (and other stakeholders) and the technical world of the software engineer. This requires that they possess technical skills, an ability to acquire an understanding of the application domain, and the inter-personal skills to help build consensus between heterogeneous groups of stakeholders [Gog93].

We have tried to avoid domain dependency in the document. The knowledge area document identifies requirements engineering practice and identifies when it is and isn't appropriate. We recognise that desktop software products are different from nuclear reactor control systems and the document should be read in this light. Where we refer to particular tools, methods, notations, SPI models, etc. it does not imply our endorsement of them. They are merely used as examples.

2   DEFINITION OF THE SOFTWARE REQUIREMENTS KNOWLEDGE AREA

This section provides an overview of requirements engineering in which:

♦ the notion of a 'requirement' is defined;

♦ motivations for systems are identified and their relationship to requirements is discussed;

♦ a generic process for analysis of requirements is described, followed by a discussion of why, in practice, organisations often deviate from this process; and

♦ the deliverables of the requirements engineering process and the need to manage requirements are described.

This overview is intended to provide a perspective or 'viewpoint' on the knowledge area that complements the one in Section 3 – Breakdown of topics for the Software Requirements Knowledge Area.

2.1   What is a requirement?

At its most basic, a requirement is a property that must be exhibited in order to solve some problem of the real world [Pfl98, Kot00, Som01, Tha97]. This document refers to requirements on 'systems' rather than 'solutions' because it is concerned with problems that have software-based solutions. Hence, a requirement is a property that must be exhibited by a system developed or adapted to solve a particular problem. The problem may be to automate part of a task of someone who will use the system, to support the business processes of the organisation that has commissioned the system, to correct shortcomings of an existing system, to control a device and many more. The functioning of users, business processes and devices are typically complex. By extension, therefore, the requirements on a system are typically a complex combination of requirements from different people at different levels of an organisation and from the environment in which the system must operate.

Requirements vary in intent and in the kinds of properties they represent. A distinction can be drawn between *product parameters* and *process parameters*. Product parameters are requirements on the system to be developed and can be further classified as [Kot00, Som97]:

♦ Functional requirements on the system such as formatting some text or modulating a signal. Functional requirements are sometimes known as capabilities.

♦ Non-functional requirements that act to constrain the solution. Non-functional requirements are sometimes

known as constraints or quality requirements. They can be further classified according to whether they are (for example) performance requirements, maintainability requirements, safety requirements, reliability requirements, electro-magnetic compatibility requirements and many other types of requirements.

A process parameter is essentially a constraint on the development of the system (e.g. 'the software shall be written in Ada'). These are sometimes known as process requirements.

Requirements must be stated clearly and unambiguously and, where appropriate, quantitatively. It is important to avoid vague and unverifiable requirements that depend for their interpretation on subjective judgement ('the system shall be reliable', 'the system shall be user-friendly'). This is particularly important for non-functional requirements. Two examples of quantified requirements are: that a system must increase a call-center's throughput by 20%; and a requirement that a system shall have a probability of generating a fatal error during any hour of operation of less than $1 * 10^{-8}$. The throughput requirement is at a very high level and will need to be used to derive a number of detailed requirements. The reliability requirement will tightly constrain the system architecture [Dav93, Som01].

Some requirements are emergent properties. That is, requirements that can't be addressed by a single component, but which depend for their satisfaction on how all the system components inter-operate. The throughput requirement for a call-centre given above would, for example, depend upon how the telephone system, information system and the operators all interacted under actual operating conditions. Emergent properties are crucially dependent upon the system architecture.

An essential property of all requirements is that they should be verifiable. It may be difficult or costly to verify certain requirements. For example, verification of the throughput requirement on the call-center may necessitate the development of simulation software. The requirements engineering and V&V personnel must ensure that the requirements can be verified within the available resource constraints.

Some requirements generate implicit process requirements. The choice of verification method is one example. Another might be the use of particularly rigorous analysis techniques (such as formal specification methods) to reduce systemic errors that can lead to inadequate reliability. Process requirements may also be imposed directly by the development organization, their customer, or a third party such as a safety regulator.

Requirements have other attributes in addition to the behavioural property that they express. Common examples include a priority rating to enable trade-offs in the face of finite resources and a status value to enable project progress to me monitored. Every requirement must be uniquely identified so that they can be subjected to configuration control and managed over the entire system life cycle.

2.2 System requirements and process drivers

The literature on requirements engineering sometimes calls system requirements "user requirements". We prefer a restricted definition of the term user requirements in which they denote the requirements of the people who will be the system customers or end-users. System requirements, by contrast, are inclusive of user requirements, requirements of other stakeholders (such as regulatory authorities) and requirements that do not have an identifiable human source. Typical examples of system stakeholders include (but are not restricted to):

♦ Users – the people who will operate the system. Users are often a heterogeneous group comprising people with different roles and requirements.

♦ Customers – the people who have commissioned the system or who represent the system's target market.

♦ Market analysts – a mass-market product will not have a commissioning customer so marketing people are often needed to establish what the market needs and to act as proxy customers.

♦ Regulators – many application domains such as banking and public transport are regulated. Systems in these domains must comply with the requirements of the regulatory authorities.

♦ System developers – these have a legitimate interest in profiting from developing the system by, for example, reusing components in different products. If, in this scenario, a customer of a particular product has specific requirements that compromise the potential for component reuse, the developer must carefully weigh their own stake against those of the customer. For mass-market products, the developer is often the primary stakeholder because they wish to maintain the product in as large a market as possible for as long as possible.

In addition to these human sources of requirements, important system requirements often derive from other devices or systems in the environment, which require some services of the system or act to constrain the system, or even from fundamental characteristics of the application domain [Lou95, Tha97]. For example, a business system may be required to inter-operate with a legacy database and many military systems have to be tolerant of high levels of electro-magnetic radiation. We talk of 'eliciting' requirements but in practice the requirements engineer has to systematically extract and inventory the requirements from a combination of human stakeholders, the system's environment, feasibility studies, market analyses, business plans, analyses of competing products and domain knowledge [Som97].

The elicitation and analysis of system requirements needs to be driven by the need to achieve the overall project aims. To provide this focus, a business case should be made which clearly defines the benefits that the investment must deliver. These should act as a 'reality check' that can be applied to the system requirements to ensure that project focus does not drift. Where there is any doubt about the technical, operational or financial viability of the project, a feasibility analysis should be conducted. This is designed to identify project risks and assess the extent to which they threaten the system's viability. Risks should be documented in the project management plan.

Typical risks include the ability to satisfy non-functional requirements such as performance, or the availability of off-the-shelf components. In some specialised domains, it may be necessary to design simulations to generate data to enable an assessment of the project risks to be made. In domains such as public transport where safety is an issue, a hazard analysis should be conducted from which safety requirements can be identified.

2.3 Overview of requirements analysis

Once the aims of the project have been established, the work of eliciting, analysing and validating the system requirements can commence. This is crucial to gaining a clear understanding of the problem for which the system is to provide a solution and its likely cost [Tha97].

The requirements engineer must strive for completeness by ensuring that all the relevant sources of requirements are identified and consulted. It will usually be infeasible to consult everyone. There may be many of users of a large system, for example. However, representative examples of each class of system stakeholder should be identified and consulted. Although individual stakeholders will be authoritative about aspects of the system that represent their interests or expertise, the requirements engineer has the responsibility to create the 'big picture' to permit for the assurance of completeness with all individual stakeholders.

Elicitation of the stakeholders' requirements is rarely easy and the requirements engineer has to learn a range of techniques for helping people articulate how they do their jobs and what would help them do their jobs better. There are many social and political issues that can affect stakeholders' requirements and their ability or willingness to articulate them and it is necessary to be sensitive to them [Gog93]. In many cases, it is necessary to provide a contextual framework that serves to focus the consultation; to help the stakeholder identify what is possible and help the requirements engineer verify their understanding. Exposing the stakeholders to prototypes may help, and these don't necessarily have to be high fidelity. A series of rough sketches on a flip chart can sometimes serve the same purpose as a software prototype, whilst avoiding the pitfalls of distraction caused by cosmetic features of the software. Walking the stakeholder through a small number of scenarios representing sequences of events in the application domain can also help the stakeholder and requirements engineer to explore the key factors affecting the requirements.

Once identified, the system requirements should be validated by the stakeholders and trade-offs negotiated before further resources are committed to the project. To enable validation, the system requirements are normally kept at a high level and expressed in terms of the application domain rather than in technical terms. Hence the system requirements for an Internet book store will be expressed in terms of books, authors, warehousing and credit card transactions, not in terms of the communication protocols, or key distribution algorithms that may form part of the solution. Too much technical detail at this stage obscures the essential characteristics of the system viewed from the perspective of its customer and users.

Some system requirements may not be satisfiable. Some may be technically infeasible, others may be too costly to implement and some will be mutually incompatible. The requirements engineer must analyse the requirements to understand their implications and how they interact. They must be prioritised and their costs estimated. The goal is to identify the scope of the system and a 'baseline' set of system requirements that is feasible and acceptable. This may necessitate helping stakeholders whose requirements conflict (with each other or with cost or other constraints) to negotiate acceptable trade-offs.

To help the analysis of the system requirements, conceptual models of the system are constructed. These aid understanding of the logical partitioning of the system, its context in the operational environment and the data and control communications between the logical entities. In general, a mix of static (e.g. an object model) and dynamic (e.g. event traces and state diagrams) should be developed to explore different aspects of the system and it's problem domain. However, the choice of which aspects to model is conditioned by the nature of the problem domain.

The system requirements must be analysed in the context of all the applicable constraints. Constraints come from many sources, such as the business environment, the customer's organizational structure and the system's operational environment. They include budget, schedule, technical (non-functional requirements), regulatory and other constraints. Hence, the requirements engineer's job is not restricted to eliciting stakeholders' requirements, but includes making assessments of their feasibility. Requirements that are clearly infeasible should be rejected and the reason for rejection recorded. Requirements that are merely suspected of being infeasible are more difficult. A feasibility study may be justified if, for example, a doubtful requirement is strongly advocated by stakeholders [Kot00, Lou95].

Project resources should be focused on the most important priority requirements. In principle, the requirements should be both *necessary and sufficient* – there should be nothing left out or anything that doesn't need to be included. Achieving this is, of course, difficult. The absence of important requirements information can only be detected by rigorous analysis. Similarly, it may take considerable effort to reach consensus on requirement priorities because one stakeholder's essential requirement may have only cosmetic value to another. In practice, the existence of sufficient resources will allow some non-essential requirements to be satisfied, while insufficient resources may force even strongly advocated requirements to be excluded. Regardless of how the baseline is identified, requirements and V&V personnel must derive acceptance tests that will assure compliance with the requirements before delivery or release of the product.

Eventually, a complete and coherent set of system requirements will emerge as the result of the analysis process. At this point, the principal areas of functionality should be clear. Subsystems or components are defined to handle each principle area of functionality. The system requirements are then allocated or distributed to subsystems/components.

This activity of partitioning and allocation is part of architectural design. Architectural design is a skill that is driven by many factors such as the recognition of reusable architectural 'patterns' or the existence of off-the shelf components. Derivation of the system architecture represents a major milestone in the project and it is crucial to get the architecture right. In particular, the interaction of the system components crucially affects the extent to which the system will exhibit the desired emergent properties. At this point, the system requirements and system architecture are documented, reviewed and 'signed off' as the baseline for subsequent development, project planning and cost estimation.

Except in small-scale systems, it is generally infeasible for software developers to begin detailed design of system components from the system requirements document. The requirements allocated to components that are complex systems in themselves will need to undergo further cycles of analysis in order to add more detail, and to interpret the domain-oriented system requirements for developers who may lack sufficient knowledge of the application domain to interpret them correctly. Hence, a number of detailed technical requirements are typically derived from each high-level system requirement. It is crucial to record and maintain this derivation to enable requirements to be traced. Tracing is crucial to requirements management because it allows, for example, the impact of any subsequent changes to the requirements to be assessed.

Refinement of the requirements and system architecture is where requirements engineering merges with software design. There is no clear-cut boundary but it is rare for requirements analysis to continue beyond 2 or 3 levels of architectural decomposition before responsibility is handed over to the design teams for the individual components.

2.4 Requirements engineering in practice

The overview of requirements analysis given in section 2.3 described the process of eliciting and analysing requirements and deriving the system architecture as if it was a linear sequence of activities. This is an idealised view of the process. This section examines some reasons why a linear process is seldom practicable in the context of real software projects.

There is a general pressure in the software industry for ever-shorter development cycles, and this is particularly pronounced in highly competitive market-driven sectors. Moreover, most projects are constrained in some way by their environment and many are upgrades to or revisions of existing systems where the system architecture is a given. In practice, therefore, it is almost always impractical to implement requirements engineering as a linear, deterministic process where system requirements are elicited from the stakeholders, baselined, allocated and handed over to the software development team. It is certainly a myth that the requirements for large systems are ever perfectly understood or perfectly specified [Som97].

Instead, requirements typically iterate toward a level of quality and detail that is sufficient to permit design and procurement decisions to me made. In some projects, this may result in the requirements being baselined before all their properties are fully understood. This risks expensive rework if problems emerge late in the development process. However, requirements engineers are necessarily constrained by project management plans and must therefore take steps to ensure that the requirements' quality is as high as possible given the available resources. They should, for example, make explicit any assumptions that underpin the requirements, and any known problems.

Even where requirements engineering is well resourced, the level of analysis will seldom be uniformly applied. For example, early in the analysis process experienced engineers are often able to identify where existing or off-the-shelf solutions can be adapted to the implementation of system components. The requirements allocated to these need not be elaborated further, while others, for which a solution is less obvious, may need to be subjected to further analysis. Critical requirements, such as those concerned with public safety, must always be analyzed rigorously.

In almost all cases requirements understanding continues to evolve as design and development proceeds. This often leads to the revision of requirements late in the life cycle. Perhaps the most crucial point of understanding about requirements engineering is that a significant proportion of the requirements *will* change. This is sometimes due to errors in the analysis, but it is frequently an inevitable consequence of change in the 'environment': the customer's operating or business environment; or in the market into which the system must sell, for example. Whatever the cause, it is important to recognise the inevitability of change and adopt measures to mitigate the

effects of change. Change has to be managed by ensuring that proposed changes go through a defined review and approval process, and by applying careful requirements tracing, impact analysis and version management. Hence, the requirements engineering process is not merely a front-end task to software development, but spans the whole development life cycle. In a typical project the activities of the requirements engineer evolve over time from elicitation to change management.

2.5 Products and deliverables

Good requirements engineering requires that the products of the process - the deliverables - are defined. The most fundamental of these in requirements engineering is the requirements document. This often comprises two separate documents (an architecture description may also be developed at this stage - see the knowledge area description for software design):

A document that specifies the system requirements. This is sometimes known as the requirements definition document, user requirements document or, as defined by IEEE std 1362-1998, the concept of operations (ConOps) document. This document serves to define the high-level system requirements from the stakeholders' perspective(s). It also serves as a vehicle for validating the system requirements. Its readership includes representatives of the system stakeholders. It must therefore be couched in terms of the customer's domain. In addition to a list of the system requirements, the requirements definition needs to include background information such as statements of the overall objectives for the system, a description of its target environment and a statement of the constraints and non-functional requirements on the system. It may include conceptual models designed to illustrate the system context, usage scenarios, the principal domain entities, and data, information and work flows [Tha97].

A document that specifies the software requirements. This is sometimes known as the software requirements specification (SRS). The purpose and readership of the SRS is somewhat different than the requirements definition document. In crude terms, the SRS documents the detailed requirements derived from the system requirements, and which have been allocated to software. The non-functional requirements in the requirements definition should have been elaborated and quantified. The principal readership of the SRS can be assumed to have some knowledge of software engineering concepts. This can be reflected in the language and notations used to describe the requirements, and in the detail of models used to illustrate the system. For custom software, the SRS may form the basis of a contract between the developer and customer [Kot00, Tha97].

Requirements documents must be structured so as to minimize the effort needed to read and locate information within them. Failure to achieve this reduces the likelihood that the system will conform to the requirements. It also hinders the ability to make controlled changes to the document as the system and its requirements evolve over time. Standards such as IEEE std 1362-1998 and IEEE std 830-1998 provide templates for requirements documents. Such standards are intended to be generic and need to be tailored to the context in which they are used.

Care must also be taken to describe requirements as precisely as possible. Requirements are usually written in natural language but in the SRS this may be supplemented by formal or semi-formal descriptions. Selection of appropriate notations permits particular requirements and aspects of the system architecture to be described more precisely and concisely than natural language. The general rule is that notations should be used that allow the requirements to be described as precisely as possible. This is particularly crucial for safety-critical and certain other types of dependable systems. However, the choice of notation is often constrained by the training, skills and preferences of the document's authors and readers.

Natural language has many serious shortcomings as a medium for description. Among the most serious are that it is ambiguous and hard to describe complex concepts precisely. Formal notations such as Z or CSP avoid the ambiguity problem because their syntax and semantics are formally defined. However, such notations are not expressive enough to adequately describe every system aspect. Natural language, by contrast, is extraordinarily rich and able to describe, however imperfectly, almost any concept or system property. A natural language is also likely to be the document author and readerships' only *lingua franca*. Because natural language is unavoidable, requirements engineers must be trained to use language simply, concisely and to avoid common causes of mistaken interpretation. These include:

♦ long sentences with complex sub-clauses;

♦ the use of terms with more than one plausible interpretation (ambiguity);

♦ presenting several requirements as a single requirement;

♦ inconsistency in the use of terms such as the use of synonyms.

To counteract these problems, requirements descriptions often adopt a stylized form and use a restricted subset of a natural language. It is good practice, for example, to standardize on a small set of modal verbs to indicate relative priorities. For example, 'shall' is commonly used to indicate that a requirement is mandatory, and 'should' to indicate a requirement that is merely desirable. Hence, the requirement 'The emergency breaks shall be applied to bring the train to a stop if the nose of the train passes a signal at DANGER' is mandatory.

The requirements documents(s) must be subject to validation and verification procedures. The requirements must be validated to ensure that the requirements engineer has understood the requirements. It is also important to verify that a requirements document conforms to company standards, and is understandable, consistent and complete. Formal notations offer the important advantage that they permit the last two properties to be proven (in a restricted sense, at least). The document(s) should be subjected to review by different stakeholders including representatives of the customer and developer. Crucially, requirements documents must be placed under the same configuration management regime as the other deliverables of the development process [Byr94, Ros98].

The requirements document(s) are only the most visible manifestation of the requirements. They exclude information that is not required by the document readership. However this other information is needed in order to manage them. In particular, it is essential that requirements are traced.

One method for tracing requirements is through the construction of a directed acyclic graph (DAG) that records the derivation of requirements and provides audit trails of requirements. As a minimum, requirements need to be traceable backwards to their source (e.g. from a software requirement back to the system requirement(s) from which it was elaborated), and forwards to the design or implementation artifacts that implement them (e.g. from a software requirement to the design document for a component that implements it). Tracing allows the requirements to be managed. In particular, it allows an impact analysis to be performed for a proposed change to one of the requirements.

Modern requirements management tools help maintain tracing information. They typically comprise a database of requirements and a graphical user interface:

♦ to store the requirement descriptions and attributes;

♦ to allow the trace DAGs to be generated automatically;

♦ to allow the propagation of requirements changes to be depicted graphically;

♦ to generate reports on the status of requirements (such as whether they have been analysed, approved, implemented, etc.);

♦ to generate requirements documents that conform to selected standards;

♦ and to apply configuration management to the requirements.

It should be noted that not every organisation has a culture of documenting and managing requirements. It is common for dynamic start-up companies which are driven by a strong 'product vision' and limited resources to view requirements documentation as an unnecessary overhead. Inevitably, however, as these companies expand, as their customer base grows and as their product starts to evolve, they discover that they need to recover the requirements that motivated product features in order to assess the impact of proposed changes. Hence, requirements documentation and management are fundamental to the any requirements engineering process.

3 BREAKDOWN OF TOPICS FOR SOFTWARE REQUIREMENTS

The knowledge area breakdown we have chosen is broadly compatible with the sections of ISO/IEC 12207-1995 that refer to requirements engineering activities. This standard views the software process at 3 different levels as primary, supporting and organizational life cycle processes. In order to keep the breakdown simple, we conflate this structure into a single life cycle process for requirements engineering. The separate topics that we identify include primary life cycle process activities such as requirements elicitation and requirements analysis, along with requirements engineering-specific descriptions of management and, to a lesser degree, organizational processes. Hence, we identify requirements validation and requirements management as separate topics.

We are aware that a risk of this breakdown is that a waterfall-like process may be inferred. To guard against this, the first topic, the requirements engineering process, is designed to provide a high-level overview of requirements engineering by setting out the resources and constraints that requirements engineering operates under and which act to configure the requirements engineering process.

There are, of course, many other ways to structure the breakdown. For example, instead of a process-based structure, we could have used a product-based structure (system requirements, software requirements, prototypes, use-cases, etc.). We have chosen the process-based breakdown to reflect the fact that requirements engineering, if it is to be successful, must be considered as a process with complex, tightly coupled activities (both sequential and concurrent) rather than as a discrete, one-off activity at the outset of a software development project. The breakdown is compatible with that used by many of the works in the recommended reading list (Appendices C and D). See section 4. for an itemised rationale for the breakdown.

The breakdown comprises 6 topics as shown in Table 1 [Kot00, Lou95, Tha97].

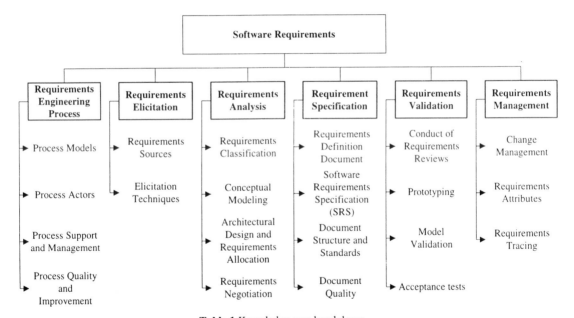

Table 1 Knowledge area breakdown

Figure 1 shows conceptually, how these activities comprise an iterative requirements engineering process. The different activities in requirements engineering are repeated until an acceptable requirements specification document is produced or until external factors such as schedule pressure or lack of resources cause the requirements engineering process to terminate. It is important to note that terminating the requirements engineering process prematurely can have a detrimental effect on the system design. After a final requirements document has been produced, any further changes become part of the requirements management process.

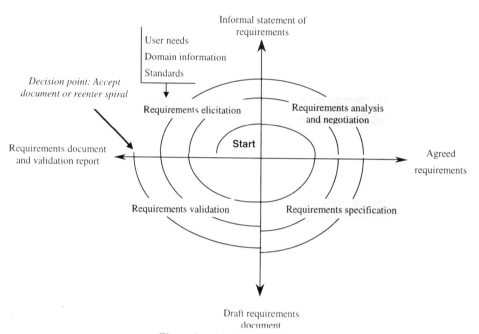

Figure 1 A spiral model of the requirements engineering process

3.1 The requirements engineering process

This section introduces the requirements engineering process, orienting the remaining 5 topics and showing how requirements engineering dovetails with the overall software engineering process.

3.1.1 Process models.

The objective of this subtopic is to provide an understanding that the requirements engineering process:

♦ is not a discrete front-end activity of the software life cycle, but rather, a process that is initiated at the beginning of a project and continues to be refined throughout the life cycle of the software process;

♦ must identify requirements as configuration items, and manage them under the same configuration regime as other products of the development process;

♦ will need to be tailored to the organisation and project context.

In particular, the subtopic is concerned with how the activities of elicitation, analysis, specification, validation and management are configured for different types of project and constraints. The subtopic is also with activities that provide input to the requirements engineering process such as marketing and feasibility studies.

3.1.2 Process actors.

This subtopic introduces the roles of the people who participate in the requirements engineering process. Requirements engineering is fundamentally interdisciplinary and the requirements engineer needs to mediate between the domains of the user and software engineering. There are often many people involved besides the requirements engineer, each of whom have a stake in the system. The stakeholders will vary across different projects but always includes users/operators and customer (who need not be the same) [Gog93]. These need not be homogeneous groups because there may be many users and many customers, each with different concerns. There may also be other stakeholders who are external to the user's/customer's organisation, such as regulatory authorities, whose requirements need to be carefully analysed. The system/software developers are also stakeholders because they have a legitimate interest in profiting from the system. Again, these may be a heterogeneous group in which (for example) the system architect has different concerns from the system tester.

It will not be possible to perfectly satisfy the requirements of every stakeholder and the requirements engineer's job is to negotiate a compromise that is both acceptable to the principal stakeholders and within budgetary, technical, regulatory and other constraints. A prerequisite for this is that all the stakeholders are indentified, the nature of their 'stake' is analysed and their requirements are elicited.

3.1.3   Process support and management.

This subtopic introduces the project management resources required and consumed by the requirements engineering process. This topic merely sets the context for topic 3 (Initiation and scope definition) of the software management KA. Its principal purpose is to make the link from process activities identified in 3.1.1 to issues of cost, human resources, training and tools.

Table 2 shows the links to common themes in other KAs.

3.1.4   Process quality and improvement.

This subtopic is concerned with requirements engineering process quality assessment. Its purpose is to emphasize the key role requirements engineering plays in terms of the cost, timeliness and customer satisfaction of software products [Som97]. It will help to orient the requirements engineering process with quality standards and process improvement models for software and systems. Process quality and improvement is closely related to the software quality KA and the software process KA. Of particular interest are issues of software quality attributes and measurement, and software process definition. This subtopic covers:

*   requirements engineering coverage by process improvement standards and models;

*   requirements engineering measures and benchmarking;

*   improvement planning and implementation

Links to common themes	
Quality	The process quality and improvement subtopic is concerned with quality. It contains links to SPI standards such as the software and systems engineering capability maturity models, the forthcoming ISO/IEC 15504 and ISO 9001-3 guideline. Requirements engineering process is at best peripheral to these and the only work to address requirements engineering processes specifically, is the requirements engineering good practice guide [Som97].
Standards	SPI models/standards as described in the quality theme above. In addition, the life cycle software engineering standard ISO/IEC 12207-1995 describes requirements engineering activities in the context of the primary, supporting and organizational life cycle processes for software.
Measurement	At the process level, requirements measures tend to be relatively coarse-grained and concerned with (e.g.) counting numbers of requirements and numbers and effects of requirements changes. If these indicate room for improvement (as they inevitably will) it is possible to measure the extent and rigour with which requirements 'good practice' is used in a process. These measures can serve to highlight process weaknesses that should be the target improvement efforts.
Tools	General project management tools. Refer to the software management KA.

Table 2 Process quality links to other KAs

3.2   Requirements elicitation

This topic covers what is sometimes termed 'requirements capture', 'requirements discovery' or 'requirements acquisition'. It is concerned with where requirements come from and how they can be collected by the requirements engineer. Requirements elicitation is the first stage in building an understanding of the problem the software is required to solve. It is fundamentally a human activity and is where the stakeholders are identified and relationships established between the development team (usually in the form of the requirements engineer) and the customer.

3.2.1   Requirements sources

In a typical system, there will be many sources of requirements and it is essential that all potential sources are identified and evaluated for their impact on the system. This subtopic is designed to promote awareness of different requirements sources and frameworks for managing them. The main points covered are:

*   Goals. The term 'Goal' (sometimes called 'business concern' or 'critical success factor') refers to the overall, high-level objectives of the system. Goals provide the motivation for a system but are often

vaguely formulated. Requirements engineers need to pay particular attention to assessing the value (relative to priority) and cost of goals. A feasibility study is a relatively low-cost way of doing this [Lou95].

- Domain knowledge. The requirements engineer needs to acquire or to have available knowledge about the application domain. This enables them to infer tacit knowledge that the stakeholders do not articulate, assess the trade-offs that will be necessary between conflicting requirements and sometimes to act as a 'user' champion.

- System stakeholders (see 3.1.2). Many systems have proven unsatisfactory because they have stressed the requirements for one group of stakeholders at the expense of others. Hence, systems are delivered that are hard to use or which subvert the cultural or political structures of the customer organisation. The requirements engineer needs to identify represent and manage the 'viewpoints' of many different types of stakeholder [Kot00].

- The operational environment. Requirements will be derived from the environment in which the software will execute. These may be, for example, timing constraints in a real-time system or interoperability constraints in an office environment. These must be actively sought because they can greatly affect system feasibility, cost, and restrict design choices [Tha97].

- The organizational environment. Many systems are required to support a business process and this may be conditioned by the structure, culture and internal politics of the organisation. The requirements engineer needs to be sensitive to these since, in general, new software systems should not force unplanned change to the business process.

3.2.2 Elicitation techniques

When the requirements sources have been identified the requirements engineer can start eliciting requirements from them. This subtopic concentrates on techniques for getting human stakeholders to articulate their requirements. This is a very difficult area and the requirements engineer needs to be sensitized to the fact that (for example) users may have difficulty describing their tasks, may leave important information unstated, or may be unwilling or unable to cooperate. It is particularly important to understand that elicitation is not a passive activity and that even if cooperative and articulate stakeholders are available, the requirements engineer has to work hard to elicit the right information. A number of techniques will be covered, but the principal ones are [Gog93]:

- Interviews. Interviews are a 'traditional' means of eliciting requirements. It is important to understand the advantages and limitations of interviews and how they should be conducted.

- Scenarios. Scenarios are valuable for providing context to the elicitation of users' requirements. They allow the requirements engineer to provide a framework for questions about users' tasks by permitting 'what if?' and 'how is this done?' questions to be asked. There is a link to 3.3.2. (conceptual modeling) because recent modeling notations have attempted to integrate scenario notations with object-oriented analysis techniques.

- Prototypes. Prototypes are a valuable tool for clarifying unclear requirements. They can act in a similar way to scenarios by providing a context within which users better understand what information they need to provide. There is a wide range of prototyping techniques, which range from paper mock-ups of screen designs to beta-test versions of software products. There is a strong overlap with the use of prototypes for requirements validation (3.5.2).

- Facilitated meetings. The purpose of these is to try to achieve a summative effect whereby a group of people can bring more insight to their requirements than by working individually. They can brainstorm and refine ideas that may be difficult to surface using (e.g.) interviews. Another advantage is that conflicting requirements are surfaced early on in a way that lets the stakeholders recognise where there is conflict. At its best, this technique may result in a richer and more consistent set of requirements than might otherwise be achievable. However, meetings need to be handled carefully (hence the need for a facilitator) to prevent a situation where the critical abilities of the team are eroded by group loyalty, or the requirements reflecting the concerns of a few vociferous (and perhaps senior) people to the detriment of others.

- Observation. The importance of systems' context within the organizational environment has led to the adaptation of observational techniques for requirements elicitation. The requirements engineer learns about users' tasks by immersing themselves in the environment and observing how users interact with their systems and each other. These techniques are relatively new and expensive but are instructive because they illustrate that many user tasks and business processes are too subtle and complex for their actors to describe easily.

Table 3 shows the elicitation techniques links to common themes in other KAs.

Links to common themes	
Quality	The quality of requirements elicitation has a direct effect on product quality. The critical issues are to recognise the relevant sources, to strive to avoid missing important requirements and to accurately report the requirements.
Measurement	Very little work on measurement of requirements elicitation has been carried out.

Table 3 Elicitation techniques links to other KAs

3.3 Requirements analysis

This subtopic is concerned with the process of analysing requirements to:

* detect and resolve conflicts between requirements;

* discover the bounds of the system and how it must interact with its environment;

* elaborate system requirements to software requirements.

The traditional view of requirements analysis was to reduce it to conceptual modeling using one of a number of analysis methods such as SADT or OOA. While conceptual modeling is important, we include the classification of requirements to help inform trade-offs between requirements (requirements classification), and the process of establishing these trade-offs (requirements negotiation) [Dav93].

3.3.1 Requirements classification

There is a strong overlap between requirements classification and requirements attributes (3.6.2). Requirements can be classified on a number of dimensions. Examples include:

* Whether the requirement is functional or non-functional (see 2.1).

* Whether the requirement is derived from one or more high-level requirements, an emergent property (see 2.1), or at a high level and imposed directly on the system by a stakeholder or some other source.

* Whether the requirement is on the product or the process. Requirements on the process constrain, for example, the choice of contractor, the development practices to be adopted, and the standards to be adhered to.

* The requirement priority. In general, the higher the priority, the more essential the requirement is for meeting the overall goals of the system. Often classified on a fixed point scale such as *mandatory, highly desirable, desirable, optional*. Priority often has to be balanced against cost of development and implementation.

* The scope of the requirement. Scope refers to the extent to which a requirement affects the system and system components. Some requirements, particularly certain non-functional ones, have a global scope in that their satisfaction cannot be allocated to a discrete component. Hence a requirement with global scope may strongly affect the system architecture and the design of many components, one with a narrow scope may offer a number of design choices with little impact on the satisfaction of other requirements.

* Volatility/stability. Some requirements will change during the life cycle of the software and even during the development process itself. It is useful if some estimate of the likelihood of a requirement changing can be made. For example, in a banking application, requirements for functions to calculate and credit interest to customers' accounts are likely to be more stable than a requirement to support a particular kind of tax-free account. The former reflect a fundamental feature of the banking domain (that accounts can earn interest), while the latter may be rendered obsolete by a change to government legislation. Flagging requirements that may be volatile can help the software engineer establish a design that is more tolerant of change.

Other classifications may be appropriate, depending upon the development organization's normal practice and the application itself.

3.3.2 Conceptual modeling

The development of models of the problem is fundamental to requirements analysis (see 2.3). The purpose is to aid understanding of the problem rather than to initiate design of the solution. Hence, conceptual models comprise models of entities from the problem domain configured to reflect their real-world relationships and dependencies.

There are several kinds of models that can be developed. These include data and control flows, state models, event traces, user interactions, object models and many others. The factors that influence the choice of model include:

* The nature of the problem. Some types of application demand that certain aspects be analysed particularly rigorously. For example, control flow and state models

19

are likely to be more important for real-time systems than for an information system.

- The expertise of the requirements engineer. It is often more productive to adopt a modeling notation or method that the requirements engineer has experience with. However, it may be appropriate or necessary to adopt a notation that is better supported by tools, imposed as a process requirement (see 3.3.1), or simply 'better'

- The process requirements of the customer. Customers may impose a particular notation or method on 'he requirements engineer. This can conflict with the previous factor.

- The availability of methods and tools. Notations or methods that are poorly supported by training and tools may not reach widespread acceptance even if they are suited to particular types of problem.

Note that in almost all cases, it is useful to start by building a model of the system context. The system context provides an understanding between the intended system and its external environment. This is crucial to understanding the system's context in its operational environment and to identify its interfaces to the environment.

The issue of modeling is tightly coupled with that of methods. For practical purposes, a method is a notation (or set of notations) supported by a process that guides the application of the notations. Methods and notations come and go in fashion. Object-oriented notations are currently in vogue but the issue of what is the 'best' notation is seldom clear. There is little empirical evidence to support claims for the superiority of one notation over another.

Formal modeling using notations based upon discrete mathematics and which are tractable to logical reasoning have made an impact in some specialized domains. These may be imposed by customers or standards or may offer compelling advantages to the analysis of certain critical functions or components.

This topic does not seek to 'teach' a particular modeling style or notation but rather to provide guidance on the purpose and intent of modeling.

3.3.3 Architectural design and requirements allocation

At some point the architecture of the solution must be derived. Architectural design is the point at which requirements engineering overlaps with software or systems design and illustrates how impossible it is to cleanly decouple both tasks [Som01]. This subtopic is closely related to topic 2, in Chapter 3 (software architecture). In many cases, the requirements engineer acts as system architect because the process of analysing and elaborating the requirements demands that the subsystems and components that will be responsible for satisfying the requirements be identified. This is requirements allocation – the assignment of responsibility for satisfying requirements to subsystems.

Allocation is important to permit detailed analysis of requirements. Hence, for example, once a set of requirements have been allocated to a component, they can be further analysed to discover requirements on how the component needs to interact with other components in order to satisfy the allocated requirements. In large projects, allocation stimulates a new round of analysis for each subsystem. As an example, requirements for a particular braking performance for a car (braking distance, safety in poor driving conditions, smoothness of application, pedal pressure required, etc.) may be allocated to the braking hardware (mechanical and hydraulic assemblies) and an anti-lock braking system (ABS). Only when a requirement for an anti-lock system has been identified, and the requirements are allocated to it can the capabilities of the ABS, the braking hardware and emergent properties (such as the car weight) be used to identify the detailed ABS software requirements.

Architectural design is closely identified with conceptual modeling. The mapping from real-world domain entities to computational components not always obvious, so architectural design is identified as a separate sub-topic. The requirements of notations and methods are broadly the same for conceptual modeling and architectural design.

3.3.4 Requirements negotiation

Another name commonly used for this subtopic is 'conflict resolution'. It is concerned with resolving problems with requirements where conflicts occur; between two stakeholders' requiring mutually incompatible features, or between requirements and resources or between capabilities and constraints, for example [Kot00, Som97]. In most cases, it is unwise for the requirements engineer to make a unilateral decision so it is necessary to consult with the stakeholder(s) to reach a consensus on an appropriate trade-off. It is often important for contractual reasons that such decisions are traceable back to the customer. We have classified this as a requirements analysis topic because problems emerge as the result of analysis. However, a strong case can also be made for counting it as part of requirements validation.

Table 4 shows the requirements negotiation links to common themes in other KAs.

Links to common themes	
Quality	The quality of the analysis directly affects product quality. In principle, the more rigorous the analysis, the more confidence can be attached to the software quality.
Measurement	Part of the purpose of analysis is to quantify required properties. This is particularly important for constraints such as reliability or safety requirements where suitable measures need to be identified to allow the requirements to be quantified and verified.

Table 4 Requirements negotiation links to other KAs

3.4 Software requirements specification

This topic is concerned with the structure, quality and verifiability of the requirements document. This may take the form of two documents, or two parts of the same document with different readership and purposes (see 2.5): the requirements definition document and the software requirements specification. The topic stresses that documenting the requirements is the most fundamental precondition for successful requirements handling.

3.4.1 The system requirements definition document

This document (sometimes known as the user requirements document or concept of operations) records the system requirements. It defines the high-level system requirements from the domain perspective. Its readership includes representatives of the system users/customers (marketing may play these roles for market-driven software) so it must be couched in terms of the domain. It must list the system requirements along with background information about the overall objectives for the system, its target environment and a statement of the constraints, assumptions and non-functional requirements. It may include conceptual models designed to illustrate the system context, usage scenarios, the principal domain entities, and data, information and workflows.

3.4.2 The software requirements specification (SRS)

The benefits of the SRS include:

♦ It establishes the basis for agreement between the customers and contractors or suppliers (in market-driven projects, these roles may be played by marketing and development divisions) on what the software product is to do and as well as what it is not expected do. For non-technical readership, the SRS is often accompanied by the requirements definition document.

♦ It forces a rigorous assessment of requirements before design can begin and reduces later redesign.

♦ It provides a realistic basis for estimating product costs, risks and schedules.

♦ Organisations can use a SRS to develop their own validation and verification plans more productively.

♦ Provides an informed basis for transferring a software product to new users or new machines.

♦ Provides a basis for software enhancement

3.4.3 Document structure and standards

Several recommended guides and standards exist to help define the structure of requirements documentation. These include IEEE P1233/D3 guide, IEEE Std. 1233 guide, IEEE std. 830-1998, ISO/IEC 12119-1994. IEEE std 1362-1998 *concept of operations* (ConOps) is a recent standard for a requirements definition document.

3.4.4 Document quality

This is one area where measures can be usefully employed in requirements engineering. There are tangible attributes that can be measured. Moreover, the quality of the requirements document can dramatically affect the quality of the product.

A number of quality indicators have been developed that can be used to relate the quality of an SRS to other project variables such as cost, acceptance, performance, schedule, reproducibility etc. Quality indicators for individual SRS statements include imperatives, directives, weak phrases, options and continuances. Indicators for the entire SRS document include size, readability, specification depth and text structure [Dav93, Ros98, Tha97].

There is a strong overlap with 3.5.1 (the conduct of requirements reviews). Table 5 shows the document quality links to common themes in other KAs.

Links to common themes	
Quality	The quality of the requirements documents dramatically affects the quality of the product.
Measurement	Quality attributes of requirements documents can be identified and measured. See 3.4.4.

Table 5 Document quality links to other KAs

3.5 Requirements validation

It is normal for there to be one or more formally scheduled points in the requirements engineering process where the requirements are validated. The aim is to pick up any problems before resources are committed to addressing the requirements. Requirements validation is concerned with the process of examining the requirements document to ensure that it defines the right system (i.e. the system that the user expects) [Kot00]. There are four important subtopics.

3.5.1 The conduct of requirements reviews.

Perhaps the most common means of validation is by inspection or formal reviews of the requirements document(s). A group of reviewers is constituted with a brief to look for errors, mistaken assumptions, lack of clarity and deviation from standard practice. The composition of the group that conducts the review is important (at least one representative of the customer should be included for a customer-driven project, for example) and it may help to provide guidance on what to look for in the form of checklists.

Reviews may be constituted on completion of the system requirements definition document, the software requirements specification document, the baseline specification for a new release, etc.

3.5.2 Prototyping.

Prototyping is commonly employed for validating the requirements engineer's interpretation of the system requirements, as well as for eliciting new requirements. As with elicitation, there is a range of prototyping techniques and a number of points in the process when prototype validation may be appropriate. The advantage of prototypes is that they can make it easier to interpret the requirements

engineer's assumptions and give useful feedback on why they are wrong. For example, the dynamic behaviour of a user interface can be better understood through an animated prototype than through textual description or graphical models. There are also disadvantages, however. These include the danger of users' attention being distracted from the core underlying functionality by cosmetic issues or quality problems with the prototype. For this reason, several people recommend prototypes that avoid software – such as flip-chart-based mockups. Prototypes may be costly to develop. However, if they avoid the wastage of resources caused by trying to satisfy erroneous requirements, their cost can be more easily justified.

3.5.3 Model validation.

The quality of the models developed during analysis should be validated. For example, in object models, it is useful to perform a static analysis to verify that communication paths exist between objects that, in the stakeholders domain, exchange data. If formal specification notations are used, it is possible to use formal reasoning to prove properties of the specification (e.g. completeness).

3.5.4 Acceptance tests.

An essential property of a system requirement is that it should be possible to validate that the finished product satisfies the requirement. Requirements that can't be validated are really just 'wishes'. An important task is therefore planning how to verify each requirement. In most cases, this is done by designing acceptance tests.

Identifying and designing acceptance test may be difficult for non-functional requirements (see 2.1). To be validated, they must first be analysed to the point where they can be expressed quantitatively.

Table 6 shows the acceptance tests links to common themes in other KAs.

Links to common themes	
Quality	Validation is all about quality - the quality of the requirements.
Measurement	Measurement is important for acceptance tests and definitions of how requirements are to be verified.

Table 6 Acceptance tests links to other KAs

3.6 Requirements management

Requirements management is an activity that spans the whole software life cycle. It is fundamentally about change management and the maintenance of the requirements in a state that accurately mirrors the software to be, or that has been, built [Kot00, Lou95].

There are 3 subtopics concerned with requirements management.

3.6.1 Change management

Change management is central to the management of requirements. This subtopic describes the role of change management, the procedures that need to be in place and the analysis that should be applied to proposed changes. It has strong links to the configuration management knowledge area.

3.6.2 Requirements attributes

Requirements should consist not only of a specification of what is required, but also of ancillary information that helps manage and interpret the requirements. This should include the various classification dimensions of the requirement (see 3.3.1) and the verification method or acceptance test plan. It may also include additional information such as a summary rationale for each requirement, the source of each requirement and a change history. The most fundamental requirements attribute, however, is an identifier that allows the requirements to be uniquely and unambiguously identified. A naming scheme for generating these IDs is an essential feature of a quality system for a requirements engineering process.

3.6.3 Requirements tracing

Requirements tracing is concerned with recovering the source of requirements and predicting the effects of requirements. Tracing is fundamental to performing impact analysis when requirements change. A requirement should be traceable backwards to the requirements and stakeholders that motivated it (from a software requirement back to the system requirement(s) that it helps satisfy, for example). Conversely, a requirement should be traceable forwards into requirements and design entities that satisfy it (for example, from a system requirement into the software requirements that have been elaborated from it and on into the code modules that implement it).

The requirements trace for a typical project will form a complex directed acyclic graph (DAG) of requirements. In the past, development organizations either had to write bespoke tools or manage it manually. This made tracing a short-term overhead on a project and vulnerable to expediency when resources were short. In most cases, this resulted in it either not being done at all or being performed poorly. The availability of modern requirements management tools has improved this situation and the importance of tracing (and requirements management in general) is starting to make an impact in software quality.

Table 7 shows the requirements tracing links to common themes in other KAs.

Links to common themes	
Quality	Requirements management is a level 2 key practice area in the software CMM and this has boosted recognition of its importance for quality.
Measurement	Mature organizations may measure the number of requirements changes and use quantitative measures of impact assessment.

Table 7 Requirements tracing links to other KAs

4 BREAKDOWN RATIONALE

The criterion mentioned below are the criterion described in Appendix A of the Guide: Knowledge Area Description Specifications for the Trial Version of the Guide to the SWEBOK.

Criterion (a): Number of topic breakdowns

One breakdown provided

Criterion (b): Reasonableness

The breakdown is reasonable in that it covers the areas discussed in most requirements engineering texts and standards.

Criterion (c): Generally accepted

The topic breakdowns (shown in Table 1) are generally accepted in that they cover areas typically in texts and standards.

At level A.1 the breakdown is identical to that given in most requirements engineering texts, apart from process improvement. Requirements engineering process improvement is an important emerging area in requirements engineering. We believe this topic adds great value to any the discussion of the requirements engineering as its directly concerned with process quality assessment.

At level A.2 the breakdown is identical to that given in most requirements engineering texts. At level A.3 the breakdown is similar to that discussed in most texts. We have incorporated a reasonably detailed section on requirement characterization to take into account the most commonly discussed ways of characterizing requirements. A.4 the breakdown is similar to that discussed in most texts, apart from document quality assessment. We believe this an important aspect of the requirements specification document and deserves to be treated as a separate sub-section. In A.5 and A.6 the breakdown is similar to that discussed in most texts.

Criterion (d): No specific domains have been assumed

No specific domains have been assumed

Criterion (e): Compatible with various schools of thought

Requirements engineering concept at the process level are general mature and stable.

Criterion (f): Compatible with industry, literature and standards

The breakdown used here has been derived from literature and relevant standards to reflect a consensus of opinion.

Criterion (g): As inclusive as possible

The inclusion of the requirements engineering process A.1 sets the context for all requirements engineering topics. This level is intended to capture the mature and stable concepts in requirements engineering. The subsequent levels all relate to level 1 but are general enough to allow more specific discussion or further breakdown.

Criterion (h): Themes of quality, tools, measurement and standards

The relationship of requirements engineering product quality assurance, tools and standards is provided in the breakdown.

Criterion (i): 2 to 3 levels, 5 to 9 topics at the first level

The proposed breakdown satisfies this criterion.

Criterion (j): Topic names meaningful outside the guide

The topic names satisfy this criterion

Criterion (k): Version 0.1 of the description

Criterion (l): Text on the rationale underlying the proposed breakdowns

This document provides the rationale

5 MATRIX OF TOPICS VS. REFERENCE MATERIAL FOR SOFTWARE REQUIREMENTS

In Table B.1 shows the topic/reference matrix. The table is organized according to requirements engineering topics in section 3. A 'X' indicates that the topic is covered to a reasonable degree in the reference. A 'X' in appearing in main topic but not the sub-topic indicates that the main topic is reasonably covered (in general) but the sub-topic is not covered to any appreciable depth. This situation is quite common in most software engineering texts, where the subject of requirements engineering is viewed in the large context of software engineering.

TOPIC	REFERENCE	[Bry94]	[Dav93]	[Gog93]	[Kot98]	[Lou95]	[Pfl98]	[Ros98]	[Som96]	[Som97]	[Tha97]
Requirements engineering process			X		X				X	X	
Process models					X				X	X	
Process actors			X		X					X	
Process support										X	
Process improvement					X					X	
Requirements elicitation			X	X	X	X	X				
Requirements sources			X	X	X	X	X				
Elicitation techniques			X	X	X	X	X				
Requirements analysis			X		X				X		
Requirements classification			X		X				X		
Conceptual modeling			X		X				X		
Architectural design and requirements allocation			X						X		
Requirements negotiation					X						

TOPIC	REFERENCE									
	[Bry94]	[Dav93]	[Gog93]	[Kot98]	[Lou95]	[Pfl98]	[Ros98]	[Som96]	[Som97]	[Tha97]
Requirement specification	X	X		X		X	X	X		X
The requirements definition document	X	X		X			X	X		X
The software requirements specification (SRS)	X	X		X			X	X		X
Document structure	X	X		X			X			X
Document quality	X	X		X			X			
Requirements validation		X						X		X
The conduct of requirements reviews				X						X
Prototyping		X		X						X
Model validation		X		X						X
Acceptance tests				X						
Requirements management		X		X				X		
Change management				X						
Requirement attributes				X						
Requirements tracing				X						

Table B.1 Topics and their references

Key	Reference
[Byr94]	[Byrne 1994]
[Dav93]	[Davis 1993]
[Gog93]	[Goguen and Linde 1993]
[Kot00]	[Kotonya and Sommerville 2000]
[Lou95]	[Loucopoulos and Karakostas 1995]
[Pfl98]	[Pfleeger 1998]
[Ros98]	[Rosenberg 1998]
[Som01]	[Sommerville 2001]
[Som97]	[Sommervelle and Sawyer 1997]
[Tha97]	[Thayer and Dorfman 1997]

6   RECOMMENDED REFERENCES FOR SOFTWARE REQUIREMENTS

[Byrne 1994]. Byrne, E., "IEEE Standard 830: Recommended Practice for Software Requirements Specification," IEEE International Conference on Requirements Engineering, IEEE Computer Society Press, April 1994, p. 58.

Describes the IEEE Standard 830-1993 for requirements specification.

[Davis 1993]. Davis, A.M., Software Requirements: Objects, Functions and States. Prentice-Hall, 1993.

Provides a way of categorizing software requirements techniques--objects, functions, and states. The author takes an analytical approach by helping the reader analyze which technique is best, rather than imposing one specific technique. Discussion of a wide variety of techniques and their uses is augmented with application illustration using three case studies.

[Goguen and Linde 1993]. Goguen, J., and C. Linde, "Techniques for Requirements Elicitation," International Symposium on Requirements Engineering, San Diego, California: IEEE Computer Society Press, January 1993, pp. 152-164.

This paper is an attempt to address the failings of traditional requirements practice, particularly in eliciting requirements. The paper explores a different paradigm for understanding requirements engineering: the process is seen essentially as a social process, in which requirements emerge and evolve from the discourse between users and developers. The paper describes a number of techniques for requirements elicitation and examines their strengths and weaknesses.

[Kotonya and Sommerville 2000]. Kotonya, G., and I. Sommerville, Requirements Engineering: Processes and Techniques. John Wiley and Sons, 2000.

Introduces requirements engineering to undergraduate and graduate students in computer science, software engineering, and systems engineering. Part I is process-oriented and describes different activities in the requirements engineering process. Part II focuses on requirements engineering techniques, covering the use of structured methods, viewpoint-oriented approaches, and specification of non- functional requirements and of interactive systems. A final chapter presents a case study illustrating a viewpoint-oriented approach. Includes chapter key points and exercises.

[Loucopoulos and Karakostas 1995]. Loucopoulos, P., and V. Karakostas, System Requirements Engineering. McGraw-Hill, 1995.

It provides software professionals with a practical framework for a formal requirements engineering (RE) process. Readers will exchange their RE problem-solving skills in chapters that help them accurately assess the nature of the problems and implement effective solutions.

[Pfleeger 1998]. Pfleeger, S.L., Software Engineering-Theory and Practice. Prentice-Hall, Chap. 4, 1998.

Applies concepts to two common examples: one that represents a typical information system, and one that represents a real-time system. This work features an associated web page containing examples from literature and links to web pages for relevant tool and method vendors.

[Rosenberg 1998]. Rosenberg, L., T.F. Hammer and L.L. Huffman, "Requirements, testing and metrics", 16th Annual Pacific Northwest Software Quality Conference, Oregon, October 1998.

This paper addresses the issue of evaluating the quality of a requirements document. The authors describe a tool developed to parse requirements documents. The Automated Requirements Measurement (ARM) software scans a file containing the text of the requirements specification. The tool searches each line of text for specific words and phrases based on seven quality indicators. ARM has been applied to 56 NASA requirements documents.

[Sommerville 2001]. Sommerville, I. Software Engineering (6th edition), Addison-Wesley, pp. 63-97,

97-147, 2001.

A textbook that presents a general introduction to software engineering, for students in undergraduate and graduate courses and software engineers in commerce and industry. It doesn't describe commercial design methods or CASE systems, but paints a broad picture of software engineering methods and tools.

[Sommerville 1997]. Sommerville, I., and P. Sawyer, Requirements engineering: A Good Practice Guide. John Wiley and Sons, Chap. 1-2, 1997.

Presents guidelines which reflect good practice in requirements engineering, based on the authors' experience in research and in software and systems development. The guidelines range from common sense tips to complex new methods, and can be used in any order, which suits the reader's problems, goals and budget. Guidelines are consistent with ISO 9000 and CMM, are ranked with cost and benefit analysis, include implementation advice, and can be combined and applied to suit an organization's needs.

[Thayer and Dorfman 1997]. Thayer, R.H., and M. Dorfman, Software Requirements Engineering (2nd Ed). IEEE Computer Society Press, pp. 176-205, 389-404, 1997.

A new edition of the comprehensive collection of original and reprinted articles describing the current best practices in requirement engineering focused primarily on software systems but also including hardware and people systems. The 35 papers introduce current issues and basic terminology, and cover the phases of software requirements engineering including elicitation, analysis, specification, verification, and management. Specific discussions feature descriptions of the process developers and users use to review and articulate needs and constraints on development, examine software requirements and documentation, and supply details on management planning and control. Lacks an index.

APPENDIX A – LIST OF FURTHER READINGS

[Ardis 1997]. Ardis, M., "Formal Methods for Telecommunication System Requirements: A survey of Standardized Languages," Annals of Software Engineering, 3, N. Mead, ed., 1997.

[Berzins, et al. 1997]. Berzins, V., et al., "A Requirements Evolution Model for Computer Aided Prototyping," Ninth IEEE International Conference on Software Engineering and Knowledge Engineering, Skokie, Illinois: Knowledge Systems Institute, June 1997, pp. 38-47.

[Beyer and Holtzblatt 1995]. Beyer, H., and Holtzblatt, K., "Apprenticing with the Customer," Communications of the ACM, 38, 5 (May 1995), pp.45-52.

[Bruno and Agarwal 1995]. Bruno, G., and R. Agarwal, "Validating Software Requirements Using Operational Models," Second Sympoium on Software Quality Techniques and Acquisition Criteria, Florence, Italy, May 1995.

[Bucci, et al. 1994]. Bucci, G., et al., "An Object-Oriented Dual Language for Specifying Reactive Systems," IEEE International Conference on Requirements Engineering, IEEE Computer Society Press, April 1994, pp. 6-15.

[Bustard and Lundy 1995]. Bustard, D., and P. Lundy, "Enhancing Soft Systems Analysis with Formal Modeling," Second International Symposium on Requirements Engineering, IEEE Computer Society Press, 1995.

[Chechik and Gannon 1994]. Chechik, M., and J. Gannon, "Automated Verification of Requirements Implementation," ACM Software Engineering Notes, Proceedings of the International Symposium on Software Testing and Analysis, Special Issue (October 1994), pp. 1-15.

[Chung and Nixon 1995]. Chung, L., and B. Nixon, "Dealing with Non-Functional Requirements: Three Experimental Studies of a Process-Oriented Approach," Seventeenth IEEE International Conference on Software Engineering, IEEE Computer Society Press, 1995.

[Ciancarini, et al. 1997]. Ciancarini, P., et al., "Engineering Formal Requirements: An Analysis and Testing Method for Z Documents," Annals of Software Engineering, 3, N. Mead, ed., 1997.

[Crespo 1994]. Crespo, R., "We Need to Identify the Requirements of the Statements of Non-Functional Requirements," International Workshop on Requirements Engineering: Foundations of Software Quality, June 1994.

[Curran, et al. 1994]. Curran, P., et al., "BORIS-R Specification of the Requirements of a Large-Scale Software Intensive System," Conference on Requirements Elicitation for Software-Based Systems, July 1994.

[Darimont and Souquieres 1997]. Darimont, R., and J. Souquieres, "Reusing Operational Requirements: A Process-Oriented Approach," IEEE International Symposium on Requirements Engineering, IEEE Computer Society Press, January 1997.

[Davis and Hsia 1994]. Davis, A., and P. Hsia, "Giving Voice to Requirements Engineering: Guest Editors' Introduction," IEEE Software, 11, 2 (March 1994), pp. 12-16.

[DeFoe 1994]. DeFoe, J., "Requirements Engineering Technology in Industrial Education," IEEE International Conference on Requirements Engineering, IEEE Computer Society Press, April 1994, p. 145.

[Demirors 1997]. Demirors, E., "A Blackboard Framework for Supporting Teams in Software Development," Ninth IEEE International Conference on Software Engineering and Knowledge Engineering, Skokie, Illinois: Knowledge Systems Institute, June 1997, pp. 232-239.

[Diepstraten 1995]. Diepstraten, M., "Command and Control System Requirements Analysis and System Requirements Specification for a Tactical System," First IEEE International Conference on Engineering of Complex Computer Systems, IEEE Computer Society Press, November 1995.

[Dobson and Strens 1994] Dobson, J., and R. Strens, "Organizational Requirements Definition for Information Technology," IEEE International Conference on Requirements Engineering, IEEE Computer Society Press, April 1994, pp. 158-165.

[Duffy, et al. 1995]. Duffy, D., et al., "A Framework for Requirements Analysis Using Automated Reasoning," Seventh International Conference on Advanced Information Systems Engineering (CAiSE '95), Springer-Verlag, 1995.

[Easterbrook and Nuseibeh 1995]. Easterbrook, S., and B. Nuseibeh, "Managing Inconsistencies in an Evolving Specification," Second International Symposium on Requirements Engineering, IEEE Computer Society Press, January 1995.

[Edwards, et al 1995]. Edwards, M., et al., "RECAP: A Requirements Elicitation, Capture, and Analysis Process Prototype Tool for Large Complex Systems," First IEEE International Conference on Engineering of Complex Computer Systems, IEEE Computer Society Press, November 1995.

[El Emam and Madhavji 1995a]. El Emam, K., and N. Madhavji, "Requirements Engineering Practices in Information Systems Development: A Multiple Case Study," Second International Symposium on Requirements Engineering, IEEE Computer Society Press, 1995.

[Fairley and Thayer 1997]. Fairley, R., and R. Thayer, "The Concept of Operations: The Bridge From Operational Requirements to Technical Specifications," Annals of Software Engineering, 3, N. Mead, ed., 1997.

[Fickas and Feather 1995]. Fickas, S., and M. Feather, "Requirements Monitoring in Dynamic Environments," Second International Symposium on Requirements Engineering, IEEE Computer Society Press, 1995.

[Fields, et al. 1995]. Fields, R., et al., "A Task-Centered Approach to Analyzing Human Error Tolerance Requirements," Second International Symposium on Requirements Engineering, IEEE Computer Society Press, 1995.

[Ghajar-Dowlatshahi and Varnekar 1994]. Ghajar-Dowlatshahi, J., and A. Varnekar, "Rapid Prototyping in Requirements Specification Phase of Software Systems," Fourth International Symposium on Systems Engineering, Sunnyvale, California: National Council on Systems Engineering, August 1994, pp. 135-140.

[Gibson 1995]. Gibson, M., "Domain Knowledge Reuse During Requirements Engineering," Seventh International Conference on Advanced Information Systems Engineering (CAiSE '95), Springer-Verlag, 1995.

[Goldin and Berry 1994]. Goldin, L., and D. Berry, "AbstFinder: A Prototype Abstraction Finder for Natural Language Text for Use in Requirements Elicitation: Design, Methodology and Evaluation," IEEE International Conference on Requirements Engineering, IEEE Computer Society Press, April 1994, pp. 84-93.

[Gotel and Finkelstein 1997]. Gotel, O., and A. Finkelstein, "Extending Requirements Traceability: Lessons Learned from an Industrial Case Study," IEEE International Symposium on Requirements Engineering, IEEE Computer Society Press, January 1997.

[Heimdahl 1996]. Heimdahl, M., "Errors Introduced during the TACS II Requirements Specification Effort: A Retrospective Case Study," Eighteenth IEEE International Conference on Software Engineering, IEEE Computer Society Press, 1996.

[Heitmeyer, et al. 1996]. Heitmeyer, C., et al., "Automated Consistency Checking Requirements Specifications," ACM Transactions on Software Engineering and Methodology, 5, 3 (July 1996), pp. 231-261.

[Holtzblatt and Beyer 1995]. Holtzblatt, K., and H. Beyer, "Requirements Gathering: The Human Factor," Communications of the ACM, 38, 5 (May 1995), pp. 31-32.

[Hudlicka 1996]. Hudlicka, E., "Requirements Elicitation with Indirect Knowledge Elicitation Techniques: Comparison of Three Methods," Second IEEE International Conference on Requirements Engineering, IEEE Computer Society Press, April 1996.

[Hughes, et al. 1994]. Hughes, K., et al., "A Taxonomy for Requirements Analysis Techniques," IEEE International Conference on Requirements Engineering, IEEE Computer Society Press, April 1994, pp. 176-179.

[Hughes, et al. 1995]. Hughes, J., et al., "Presenting Ethnography in the Requirements Process," Second IEEE International Symposium on Requirements Engineering, IEEE Computer Society Press, April 1995.

[Hutt 1994]. Hutt, A., Object-Oriented Analysis and Design, New York, New York: Wiley, 1994.

[Jackson 1995]. Jackson, M., Software Requirements and Specifications, Reading, Massachusetts: Addison Wesley, 1995.

[Jackson 1997]. Jackson, M., "The Meaning of Requirements," Annals of Software Engineering, 3, N. Mead, ed., 1997.

[Jones and Britton 1996]. Jones, S., and C. Britton, "Early Elicitation and Definition of Requirements for an Interactive Multimedia Information System," Second IEEE International Conference on Requirements Engineering, IEEE Computer Society Press, April 1996.

[Kirner and Davis 1995]. Kirner, T., and A. Davis, "Nonfunctional Requirements for Real-Time Systems," Advances in Computers, 1996.

[Klein 1997]. Klein, M., "Handling Exceptions in Collaborative Requirements Acquisition," IEEE International Symposium on Requirements Engineering, IEEE Computer Society Press, January 1997.

[Kosman 1997]. Kosman, R., "A Two-Step Methodology to Reduce Requirements Defects," Annals of Software Engineering, 3, N. Mead, ed., 1997.

[Krogstie, et al. 1995]. Krogstie, J., et al., "Towards a Deeper Understanding of Quality in Requirements Engineering," Seventh International Conference on Advanced Information Systems Engineering (CAiSE '95), Springer-Verlag, 1995.

[Lalioti and Theodoulidis 1995]. Lalioti, V., and B. Theodoulidis, "Visual Scenarios for Validation of Requirements Specification," Seventh International Conference on Software Engineering and Knowledge Engineering, Skokie, Illinois: Knowledge Systems Institute, June 1995, pp. 114-116.

[Leite, et al. 1997]. Leite, J., et al., "Enhancing a Requirements Baseline with Scenarios," IEEE International Symposium on Requirements Engineering, IEEE Computer Society Press, January 1997.

[Lerch, et al. 1997]. Lerch, F., et al., "Using Simulation-Based Experiments for Software Requirements Engineering," Annals of Software Engineering, 3, N. Mead, ed., 1997.

[Leveson, et al. 1994]. Leveson, N., et al., "Requirements Specification for Process-Control Systems," IEEE Transactions on Software Engineering, 20,, 9 (September 1994), pp. 684-707.

[Lutz and Woodhouse 1996]. Lutz, R., and R. Woodhouse, "Contributions of SFMEA to Requirements Analysis," Second IEEE International Conference on Requirements Engineering, Computer Society Press, April 1996.

[Lutz and Woodhouse 1997]. Lutz,R., and R. Woodhouse, "Requirements Analysis Using Forward and Backward Search," Annals of Software Engineering, 3, N. Mead, ed., 1997.

[Macaulay 1996]. Macaulay, L., Requirements Engineering, London, UK: Springer, 1996.

[Macfarlane and Reilly 1995]. Macfarlane, I., and I. Reilly, "Requirements Traceability in an Integrated Development Environment," Second IEEE International Symposium on Requirements Engineering, IEEE Computer Society Press, March 1995.

[Maiden and Rugg 1995]. Maiden, N., et al., "Computational Mechanisms for Distributed Requirements Engineering," Seventh International Conference on Software Engineering and Knowledge Engineering, Skokie, Illinois: Knowledge Systems Institute, June 1995, pp. 8-15.

[Mar 1994]. Mar, B., "Requirements for Development of Software Requirements," Fourth International Symposium on Systems Engineering, Sunnyvale, California: National Council on Systems Engineering, August 1994, pp. 39-44.

[Massonet and van Lamsweerde 1997]. Massonet, P., and A. van Lamsweerde, "Analogical Reuse of Requirements Frameworks," IEEE International Symposium on Requirements Engineering, IEEE Computer Society Press, January 1997.

[McFarland and Reilly 1995]. McFarland, I., and I. Reilly, "Requirements Traceability in an Integrated Development Environment," Second International Symposium on Requirements Engineering, IEEE Computer Society Press, 1995.

[Mead 1994]. Mead, N., "The Role of Software Architecture in Requirements Engineering," IEEE International Conference on Requirements Engineering, IEEE Computer Society Press, April 1994, p. 242.

[Mostert and von Solms 1995]. Mostert, D., and S. von Solms, "A Technique to Include Computer Security, Safety, and Resilience Requirements as Part of the Requirements Specification," Journal of Systems and Software, 31, 1 (October 1995), pp. 45-53.

[Mylopoulos, et al. 1995]. Mylopoulos, J., et al., "Multiple Viewpoints Analysis of Software Specification Process," submitted to IEEE Transactions on Software Engineering.

[Nishimura and Honiden 1992]. Nishimura, K., and S. Honiden, "Representing and Using Non-Functional Requirements: A Process-Oriented Approach," submitted to IEEE Transactions on Software Engineering, December 1992.

[Nissen, et al. 1997]. Nissen, H., et al., "View-Directed Requirements Engineering: A Framework and Metamodel," Ninth IEEE International Conference on Software Engineering and Knowledge Engineering, Skokie, Illinois: Knowledge Systems Institute, June 1997, pp. 366-373.

[O'Brien 1996]. O'Brien, L., "From Use Case to Database: Implementing a Requirements Tracking System," Software Development, 4, 2 (February 1996), pp. 43-47.

[Opdahl 1994]. Opdahl, A., "Requirements Engineering for Software Performance," International Workshop on Requirements Engineering: Foundations of Software Quality, June 1994.

[Pinheiro and Goguen 1996]. Pinheiro,F., and J. Goguen, "An Object-Oriented Tool for Tracing Requirements," IEEE Software, 13, 2 (March 1996), pp. 52-64.

[Playle and Schroeder 1996]. Playle, G., and C. Schroeder, "Software Requirements Elicitation: Problems, Tools, and Techniques," Crosstalk: The Journal of Defense Software Engineering, 9, 12 (December 1996), pp. 19-24.

[Pohl, et al. 1994]. Pohl, K., et al., "Applying AI Techniques to Requirements Engineering: The NATURE Prototype," IEEE Workshop on Research Issues in the Intersection Between Software Engineering and Artificial Intelligence, IEEE Computer Society Press, May 1994.

[Porter, et al. 1995]. Porter, A., et al., "Comparing Detection Methods for Software Requirements Inspections: A Replicated Experiment," IEEE Transactions on Software Engineering, 21, 6 (June 1995), pp. 563-575.

[Potts and Hsi 1997]. Potts, C., and I. Hsi, "Abstraction and Context in Requirements Engineering: Toward a Synthesis," Annals of Software Engineering, 3, N. Mead, ed., 1997.

[Potts and Newstetter 1997]. Potts, C., and W. Newstetter., "Naturalistic Inquiry and Requirements Engineering: Reconciling Their Theoretical Foundations," IEEE International Symposium on Requirements Engineering, IEEE Computer Society Press, January 1997.

[Potts, et al. 1995] Potts, C., et al., "An Evaluation of Inquiry-Based Requirements Analysis for an Internet Server," Second International Symposium on Requirements Engineering, IEEE Computer Society Press, 1995.

[Ramesh, et al. 1995]. Ramesh, B., et al., "Implementing Requirements Traceability: A Case Study," Second International Symposium on Requirements Engineering, IEEE Computer Society Press, 1995.

[Regnell, et al. 1995]. Regnell, B., et al., "Improving the Use Case Driven Approach to Requirements Engineering," Second IEEE International Symposium on Requirements Engineering, IEEE Computer Society Press, April 1995.

[Reubenstein 1994]. Reubenstein, H., "The Role of Software Architecture in Software Requirements Engineering," IEEE International Conference on Requirements Engineering, Computer Society Press, April 1994, p. 244.

[Robertson and Robertson 1994]. Robertson, J., and S. Robertson, Complete Systems Analysis, Vols. 1 and 2, Englewood Cliffs, New Jersey: Prentice Hall, 1994.

[Robinson and Fickas 1994]. Robinson, W., and S. Fickas, "Supporting Multi-Perspective Requirements Engineering," IEEE International Conference on Requirements Engineering, IEEE Computer Society Press, April 1994, pp. 206-215.

[Rolland 1994]. Rolland, C., "Modeling and Evolution of Artifacts," IEEE International Conference on Requirements Engineering, IEEE Computer Society Press, April 1994, pp. 216-219.

[Schoening 1994]. Schoening, W., "The Next Big Step in Systems Engineering Tools: Integrating Automated Requirements Tools with Computer Simulated Synthesis and Test," Fourth International Symposium on Systems Engineering, Sunnyvale, California: National Council on Systems Engineering, August 1994, pp. 409-415.

[Shekaran 1994]. Shekaran, M., "The Role of Software Architecture in Requirements Engineering," IEEE International Conference on Requirements Engineering, IEEE Computer Society Press, April 1994, p. 245.

[Siddiqi, et al. 1997]. Siddiqi, J., et al., "Towards Quality Requirements Via Animated Formal Specifications," Annals of Software Engineering, 3, N. Mead, ed., 1997.

[Spanoudakis and Finkelstein 1997]. Spanoudakis, G., and A. Finkelstein, "Reconciling Requirements: A Method for Managing Interference, Inconsistency, and Conflict," Annals of Software Engineering, 3, N. Mead, ed., 1997.

[Stevens 1994]. Stevens, R., "Structured Requirements," Fourth International Symposium on Systems Engineering, Sunnyvale, California: National Council on Systems Engineering, August 1994, pp. 99-104.

[van Lamsweerde, et al. 1995] van Lamsweerde, A., et al., "Goal-Directed Elaboration of Requirements for a Meeting Scheduler: Problems and Lessons Learnt," Second International Symposium on Requirements Engineering, IEEE Computer Society Press, 1995.

[White and Edwards 1995]. White, S., and M. Edwards, "A Requirements Taxonomy for Specifying Complex Systems," First IEEE International Conference on Engineering of Complex Computer Systems, IEEE Computer Society Press, November 1995.

[Wiley 1999]. Wiley, B., Essential System Requirements: A Practical Guide to Event-Driven Methods, Addison-Wesley, 1999.

[Wyder 1996]. Wyder, T., "Capturing Requirements With Use Cases," Software Development, 4, 2 (February 1996), pp. 36-40.

[Yen and Tiao 1997]. Yen, J., and W. Tiao, "A Systematic Tradeoff Analysis for Conflicting Imprecise Requirements," IEEE International Symposium on Requirements Engineering, Computer Society Press, March 1997.

[Yu 1997]. Yu, E., "Towards Modeling and Reasoning Support for Early-Phase Requirements Engineering," IEEE International Symposium on Requirements Engineering, IEEE Computer Society Press, March 1997.

[Zave and Jackson 1996]. Zave, P., and M. Jackson, "Where Do Operations Come From? A Multiparadigm Specification Technique," IEEE Transactions on Software Engineering, 22, 7 (July 1996), pp. 508-528.

APPENDIX B – REFERENCES USED TO WRITE AND JUSTIFY THE DESCRIPTION

[Acosta 1994]. Acosta, R., et al., "A Case Study of Applying Rapid Prototyping Techniques in the Requirements Engineering Environment," IEEE International Conference on Requirements Engineering, IEEE Computer Society Press, April 1994, pp. 66-73.

[Alford 1994]. Alford, M., "Attacking Requirements Complexity Using a Separation of Concerns," IEEE International Conference on Requirements Engineering, IEEE Computer Society Press, April 1994, pp. 2-5.

[Alford 1994]. Alford, M., "Panel Session Issues in Requirements Engineering Technology Transfer: From Researcher to Entrepreneur," IEEE International Conference on Requirements Engineering, IEEE Computer Society Press, April 1994, p. 144.

[Anderson 1985]. Anderson, T., Software Requirements: Specification and Testing, Oxford, UK: Blackwell Publishing, 1985.

[Anderson and Durney 1993]. Anderson, J., and B. Durney, "Using Scenarios in Deficiency-Driven Requirements Engineering," International Symposium on Requirements Engineering, IEEE Computer Society Press, January 1993, pp. 134-141.

[Andriole 1992]. Andriole, S., "Storyboard Prototyping For Requirements Verification," Large Scale Systems, 12 (1987), pp. 231-247. 14.[Andriole 1992]

[Andriole 1995]. Andriole, S., "Interactive Collaborative Requirements Management," Software Development, (September 1995).

[Andriole 1996]. Andriole, S.J., Managing Systems Requirements: Methods, Tools and Cases. McGraw-Hill, 1996.

[Anton and Potts 1998]. Anton, A., and C. Potts, "The Use of Goals to Surface Requirements for Evolving Systems," Twentieth International Conference on Software Engineering, IEEE Computer Society, 1998.

[Ardis, et al. 1995]. Ardis, M., et al., "A Framework for Evaluating Specification Methods for Reactive Systems," Seventeenth IEEE International Conference on Software Engineering, IEEE Computer Society Press, 1995.

[Bickerton and Siddiqi 1993]. Bickerton, M., and J. Siddiqi, "The Classification of Requirements Engineering Methods," IEEE International Symposium on Requirements Engineering, IEEE Computer Society Press, January 1993, pp. 182-186.

[Blanchard and Fabrycky 1998]. Blanchard, B. and Fabrycky, W.J., Systems Engineering Analysis, Prentice Hall, 1998.

[Blum 1983]. Blum, B., "Still More About Prototyping," ACM Software Engineering Notes, 8, 3 (May 1983), pp. 9-11.

[Blum 1993]. Blum, B., "Representing Open Requirements with a Fragment-Based Specification," IEEE Transaction on Systems, Man and Cybernetics, 23, 3 (May-June 1993), pp. 724-736.

[Blyth, et al. 1993a]. Blyth, A., et al., "A Framework for Modelling Evolving Requirements," IEEE International Conference on Computer Software and Applications, IEEE Computer Society Press, 1993.

[Boehm 1994]. Boehm, B., P. Bose, et al., "Software Requirements as Negotiated Win Conditions," Proc. 1st International Conference on Requirements Engineering (ICRE), Colorado Springs, Co, USA, (1994), pp.74-83.

[Boehm, et al. 1995]. Boehm, B., et al., "Software Requirements Negotiation and Renegotiation Aids: A Theory-W Based Spiral Approach," Seventeenth IEEE International Conference on Software Engineering, IEEE Computer Society Press, 1995.

[Brown and Cady 1993]. Brown, P., and K. Cady, "Functional Analysis vs. Object-Oriented Analysis: A View From the Trenches," Third International Symposium on Systems Engineering, Sunnyvale, California: National Council on Systems Engineering, July 1993.

[Byrne 1994]. Byrne, E., "IEEE Standard 830: Recommended Practice for Software Requirements Specification," IEEE International Conference on Requirements Engineering, IEEE Computer Society Press, April 1994, p. 58.

[Burns and McDermid 1994]. Burns, A., and J. McDermid, "Real-Time Safety-Critical Systems: Analysis and Synthesis," IEE Software Engineering Journal, 9, 6 (November 1994), pp. 267-281.

[Checkland and Scholes 1990]. Checkland, P., and J. Scholes, Soft Sysems Methodology in Action. John Wiley and Sons, 1990.

[Chung 1991a]. Chung, L., "Representation and Utilization of Nonfunctional Requirements for Information System Design," Third International Conference on Advanced Information Systems Engineering (CAiSE '90), Springer-Verlag, 1991, pp. 5-30.

[Chung 1999]. Chung, L., Nixon, B.A., Yu. E., Mylopoulos, J., Non-functional Requirements in Software Engineering, Kluwer Academic Publishers, 1999.

[Chung, et al. 1995]. Chung, L., et al., "Using Non-Functional Requirements to Systematically Support Change," Second International Symposium on Requirements Engineering, IEEE Computer Society Press, 1995.

[Connell and Shafer 1989]. Connell, J., and L. Shafer, Structured Rapid Prototyping, Englewood Cliffs, New Jersey, 1989.

[Coombes and McDermid 1994]. Coombes, A., and J. McDermid, "Using Quantitative Physics in Requirements Specification of Safety Critical Systems" Workshop on

Research Issues in the Intersection Between Software Engineering and Artificial Intelligence, Sorrento, Italy, May 1994.

[Costello and Liu 1995]. Costello, R., and D. Liu, "Metrics for Requirements Engineering," Journal of Systems and Software, 29, 1 (April 1995), pp. 39-63.

[Curtis 1994]. Curtis, A., "How to Do and Use Requirements Traceability Effectively," Fourth International Symposium on Systems Engineering, Sunnyvale, California: National Council on Systems Engineering, August 1994, pp. 57-64.

[Davis 1993]. Davis, A.M., Software Requirements: Objects, Functions and States. Prentice-Hall, 1993.

[Davis 1995a]. Davis, A., 201 Principles of Software Development, New York, New York: McGraw Hill, 1995.

[Davis 1995b]. Davis, A., "Software Prototyping," in Advances in Computing, 40, M. Zelkowitz, ed., New York, New York: Academic Press, 1995.

[Davis, et al. 1997]. Davis, A., et al., "Elements Underlying Requirements Specification," Annals of Software Engineering, 3, N. Mead, ed., 1997.

[De Lemos, et al. 1992]. De Lemos, R., et al., "Analysis of Timeliness Requirements in Safety-Critical Systems," Symposium on Formal Techniques in Real-Time and Fault Tolerant Systems, Nijmegen, The Netherlands: Springer Verlag, January 1992, pp. 171-192.

[Dobson 1991]. Dobson, J., "A methodology for analysing human computer-related issues in secure systems," International Conference on Computer Security and Integrity in our Changing World, Espoo, Finland, (1991), pp. 151-170.

[Dobson, et al. 1992]. Dobson, J., et al., "The ORDIT Approach to Requirements Identification," IEEE International Conference on Computer Software and Applications, IEEE Computer Society Press, 1992, pp. 356-361.

[Dorfman and Thayer 1997]. Dorfman, M., and R.H. Thayer, Software Engineering. IEEE Computer Society Press, 1997.

[Easterbrook and Nuseibeh 1996]. Easterbrook, S., and B. Nuseibeh, "Using viewpoints for inconsistency management," Software Engineering Journal, 11, 1, 1996, pp.31-43.

[Ebert 1997]. Ebert, C., "Dealing with Non-Functional Requirements in Large Software Systems," Annals of Software Engineering, 3, N. Mead, ed., 1997.

[El Emam 1997]. EL Amam K., J. Drouin, et al., SPICE: The theory and Practice of Software Process Improvement and Capability Determination. IEEE Computer Society Press, 1997.

[El Emam and Madhavji 1995]. El Emam, K., and N. Madhavji, "Measuring the Success of Requirements Engineering," Second International Symposium on Requirements Engineering, IEEE Computer Society Press, 1995.

[Fagan 1986]. Fagan, M.E., "Advances in Software Inspection," IEEE Transactions on Software Engineering 12, 7, 1986, pp. 744-51.

[Feather 1991]. Feather, M., "Requirements Engineering: Getting Right from Wrong," Third European Software Engineering Conference, Springer Verlag, 1991.

[Fenton 1991]. Fenton, N. E., Software metrics: A rigorous approach. Chapman and Hall, 1991.

[Fiksel 1991]. Fiksel, J., "The Requirements Manager: A Tool for Coordination of Multiple Engineering Disciplines," CALS and CE '91, Washington, D.C., June 1991.

[Finkelstein 1992]. Finkelstein, A., Kramer, J., B. Nuseibeh and M. Goedicke, "Viewpoints: A framework for integrating multiple perspectives in systems development," International Journal of Software Engineering and Knowledge Engineering, 2, 10, (1992), pp.31-58.

[Garlan 1994]. Garlan, D., "The Role of Software Architecture in Requirements Engineering," IEEE International Conference on Requirements Engineering, IEEE Computer Society Press, April 1994, p. 240.

[Gause and Weinberg 1989]. Gause, D.C., and G. M. Weinberg, Exploring Requirements : Quality Before Design, Dorset House, 1989.

[Gilb and Graham 1993]. Gilb, T., and D. Graham, Software Inspection. Wokingham: Addison-Wesley, 1993.

[Goguen and Linde 1993]. Goguen, J., and C. Linde, "Techniques for Requirements Elicitation," International Symposium on Requirements Engineering, IEEE Computer Society Press, January 1993, pp. 152-164.

[Gomaa 1995]. Gomaa, H., "Reusable Software Requirements and Architectures for Families of Systems," Journal of Systems and Software, 28, 3 (March 1995), pp. 189-202.

[Grady 1993a]. Grady, J., Systems Requirements Analysis, New York, New York: McGraw Hill, 1993.

[Graham 1998]. Graham, I., Requirements Engineering and Rapid Development: An Object-Oriented Approach, Addison Wesley, 1998.

[Hadden 1997]. Hadden, R., "Does Managing Requirements Pay Off?," American Programmer, 10, 4 (April 1997), pp. 10-12.

[Hall 1996]. Hall, A., "Using Formal Methods to Develop an ATC Information System," IEEE Software 13, 2, 1996, pp.66-76.

[Hansen, et al. 1991]. Hansen, K., et al., "Specifying and Verifying Requirements of Real-Time Systems," ACM SIGSOFT Conference on Software for Critical Systems, December 1991, pp. 44-54.

[Harel 1988]. Harel, D., "On Visual Formalisms," Communications of the ACM, 31, 5 (May 1988), pp. 8-20.

[Harel 1992]. Harel, D., "Biting the Silver Bullet: Towards a Brighter Future for System Development," IEEE Computer, 25, 1 (January 1992), pp. 8-20.

[Harel and Kahana 1992]. Harel, D., and C. Kahana, "On Statecharts with Overlapping," ACM Transactions on Software Engineering and Methodology, 1, 4 (October 1992), pp. 399-421.

[Harwell 1993]. Harwell, R., et al, "What is a Requirement," Proc 3rd Ann. Int'l Symp. Nat'l Council Systems Eng., (1993), pp.17-24.

[Heimdahl and Leveson 1995]. Heimdahl, M., and N. Leveson, "Completeness and Consistency Analysis of State-Based Requirements," Seventeenth IEEE International Conference on Software Engineering, IEEE Computer Society Press, 1995.

[Hofmann 1993]. Hofmann, H., Requirements Engineering: A Survey of Methods and Tools, Technical Report #TR-93.05, Institute for Informatics, Zurich, Switzerland: University of Zurich, 1993.

[Honour 1994]. Honour, E., "Requirements Management Cost/Benefit Selection Criteria," Fourth International Symposium on Systems Engineering, Sunnyvale, California: National Council on Systems Engineering, August 1994, pp. 149-156.

[Hooks and Stone 1992] Hooks, I., and D. Stone, "Requirements Management: A Case Study — NASA's Assured Crew Return Vehicle," Second Annual International Symposium on Requirements Engineering, Seattle, Washington: National Council on Systems Engineering, July 1992.

[Hsia, et al. 1997]. Hsia, P. et al., "Software Requirements and Acceptance Testing," Annals of Software Engineering, 3, N. Mead, ed., 1997.

[Humphery 1988]. Humphery, W.S., "Characterizing the Software Process," IEEE Software 5, 2 (1988), pp. 73-79.

[Humphery 1989]. Humphery, W., Managing the Software Process, Reading, Massachusetts: Addison Wesley, 1989.

[Hutchings 1995]. Hutchings, A., and S. Knox, "Creating products customers demand," Communications of the ACM, 38, 5, (May 1995), pp. 72-80.

[IEEE 1998a]. IEEE Std 830-1998. IEEE Recommended Practice for Software Requirements Specifications.

[IEEE 1998b]. IEEE Std 1362-1998. IEEE Guide for Information Technology – System Definition – Concept of Operations (ConOps) Document.

[Ince 1994]. Ince, D., ISO 9001 and Software Quality Assurance. London: McGraw-Hill, 1994.

[Jackson and Zave 1995]. Jackson, M., and P. Zave, "Deriving Specifications from Requirements: An Example," Seventeenth IEEE International Conference on Software Engineering, IEEE Computer Society Press, 1995.

[Jarke and Pohl 1994]. Jarke, M., and K. Pohl, "Requirements Engineering in 2001: Virtually Managing a Changing Reality," IEE Software Engineering Journal, 9, 6 (November 1994), pp. 257-266.

[Jarke, et al. 1993]. Jarke, M., et al., "Theories Underlying Requirements Engineering: An Overview of NATURE at Genesis," IEEE International Symposium on Requirements Engineering, IEEE Computer Society Press, January 1993, pp. 19-31.

[Jenkins 1994]. Jenkins, M., "Requirements Capture," Conference on Requirements Elicitation for Software-Based Systems, July 1994.

[Jirotka 1991]. Jirotka, M., Ethnomethodology and Requirements Engineering, Centre for Requirements and Foundations Technical Report, Oxford, UK: Oxford University Computing Laboratory, 1991.

[Kotonya 1999]. Kotonya, G., "Practical Experience with Viewpoint-oriented Requirements Specification," Requirements Engineering, 4, 3, 1999, pp.115-133.

[Kotonya and Sommerville 1996]. Kotonya, G., and I. Sommerville, "Requirements Engineering with viewpoints," Software Engineering, 1, 11, 1996, pp.5-18.

[Kotonya and Sommerville 1998]. Kotonya, G., and I. Sommerville, Requirements Engineering: Processes and Techniques. John Wiley and Sons, 1998.

[Lam, et al. 1997a]. Lam, W., et al., "Ten Steps Towards Systematic Requirements Reuse," IEEE International Symposium on Requirements Engineering, IEEE Computer Society Press, January 1997.

[Leveson 1986]. Leveson, N.G., "Software safety - why, what, and how," Computing surveys, 18, 2, (1986), pp. 125-163.

[Leveson 1995]. Leveson, N.G., Safeware: System Safety and Computers. Reading, Massachusetts: Addison-Wesley, 1995.

[Loucopulos and Karakostas 1995]. Loucopulos, P., and V. Karakostas, Systems Requirements Engineering. McGraw-Hill, 1995.

[Lutz 1993]. Lutz, R., "Analyzing Software Requirements Errors in Safety-Critical, Embedded Systems," IEEE International Symposium on Requirements Engineering, IEEE Computer Society Press, January 1993, pp. 126-133.

[Lutz 1996]. Lutz, R., "Targeting Safety-Related Errors During Software Requirements Analysis," The Journal of Systems and Software, 34, 3 (September 1996), pp. 223-230.

[Maiden and Sutcliffe 1993]. Maiden, N., and A. Sutcliffe, "Requirements Engineering By Example: An Empirical Study," International Symposium on Requirements Engineering, IEEE Computer Society Press, January 1993, pp. 104-111.

[Maiden, et al., 1995] Maiden, N., et al., "How People Categorise Requirements for Reuse: A Natural Approach," Second International Symposium on Requirements Engineering, IEEE Computer Society Press, 1995.

[Mazza 1996]. Mazza, C., J. Fairclough, B. Melton, D. DePablo, A. Scheffer, and R. Stevens, Software Engineering Standards, Prentice-Hall, 1996.

[Mazza 1996]. Mazza, C., J. Fairclough, B. Melton, D. DePablo, A. Scheffer, R. Stevens, M. Jones, G. Alvisi, Software Engineering Guides, Prentice-Hall, 1996.

[Modugno, et al. 1997]. Modugno, F., et al., "Integrating Safety Analysis of Requirements Specification," IEEE International Symposium on Requirements Engineering, IEEE Computer Society Press, January 1997.

[Morris, et al. 1994]. Morris, P., et al., "Requirements and Traceability," International Workshop on Requirements Engineering: Foundations of Software Quality, June 1994.

[Paulk 1996]. Paulk, M.C., C.V. Weber, et al., Capability Maturity Model: Guidelines for Improving the Software Process. Addison-Wesley, 1995.

[Pfleeger 1998]. Pfleeger, S.L., Software Engineering-Theory and Practice. Prentice-Hall, 1998.

[Pohl 1994]. Pohl, K., "The Three Dimensions of Requirements Engineering: A Framework and Its Applications," Information Systems 19, 3 (1994), pp. 243-258.

[Pohl 1999]. Pohl, K., Process-centered Requirements Engineering, Research Studies Press, 1999.

[Potts 1993]. Potts, C., "Choices and Assumptions in Requirements Definition," International Symposium on Requirements Engineering, IEEE Computer Society Press, January 1993, p. 285.

[Potts 1994]. Potts, C., K. Takahashi, et. al., "Inquiry-based Requirements Analysis," IEEE Software, 11, 2, 1994, pp. 21-32.

[Pressman 1997]. Pressman, R.S. Software Engineering: A Practitioner's Approach (4 edition). McGraw-Hill, 1997.

[Ramesh et al. 1997]. Ramesh, B., et al., "Requirements Traceability: Theory and Practice," Annals of Software Engineering, 3, N. Mead, ed., 1997.

[Roberston and Robertson 1999]. Robertson, S., and J. Robertson, Mastering the Requirements Process, Addison Wesley, 1999.

[Rosenberg 1998]. Rosenberg, L., T.F. Hammer and L.L. Huffman, "Requirements, testing and metrics, " 15th Annual Pacific Northwest Software Quality Conference, Utah, October 1998.

[Rudd and Isense 1994]. Rudd, J., and S. Isense, "Twenty-two Tips for a Happier, Healthier Prototype," ACM Interactions, 1, 1, 1994.

[Rzepka 1992]. Rzepka, W., "A Requirements Engineering Testbed: Concept and Status," 2nd IEEE International Conference on Systems Integration, IEEE Computer Society Press, June 1992, pp. 118-126.

[SEI 1995]. A Systems Engineering Capability Model, Version 1.1, CMU/SEI95-MM-003, Software Engineering Institute, 1995.

[Siddiqi and Shekaran 1996]. Siddiqi, J., and M.C. Shekaran, "Requirements Engineering: The Emerging Wisdom," IEEE Software, pp.15-19, 1996.

[Sommerville 1996].Sommerville, I. Software Engineering (5th edition), Addison-Wesley, pp. 63-97, 117-136, 1996.

[Sommerville and Sawyer 1997]. Sommerville, I., and P. Sawyer, "Viewpoints: Principles, Problems, and a Practical Approach to Requirements Engineering," Annals of Software Engineering, 3, N. Mead, ed., 1997.

[Sommerville, et al. 1993]. Sommerville, I., et al., "Integrating Ethnography into the Requirements Engineering Process," International Symposium on Requirements Engineering, IEEE Computer Society Press, January 1993, pp. 165-173.

[Sommerville 1997].Sommerville, I., and P. Sawyer, Requirements engineering: A Good Practice Guide. John Wiley and Sons, 1997

[Stevens 1998]. Stevens, R., P. Brook, K. Jackson and S. Arnold, Systems Engineering, Prentice Hall, 1998.

[Thayer and Dorfman 1990]. Thayer, R., and M. Dorfman, Standards, Guidelines and Examples on System and Software Requirements Engineering. IEEE Computer Society, 1990.

[Thayer and Dorfman 1997]. Thayer, R.H., and M. Dorfman, Software Requirements Engineering (2nd Ed). IEEE Computer Society Press, 1997.

[White 1993]. White, S., "Requirements Engineering in Systems Engineering Practice," IEEE International Symposium on Requirements Engineering, IEEE Computer Society Press, January 1993, pp. 192-193.

[White 1994]. White, S., "Comparative Analysis of Embedded Computer System Requirements Methods," IEEE International Conference on Requirements Engineering, IEEE Computer Society Press, April 1994, pp. 126-134.

CHAPTER 3

SOFTWARE DESIGN

Guy Tremblay
Département d'informatique
Université du Québec à Montréal
C.P. 8888, Succ. Centre-Ville
Montréal, Québec, Canada, H3C 3P8
tremblay.guy@uqam.ca

Table of Contents

1. INTRODUCTION

This chapter presents a description of the Software Design knowledge area for the Guide to the SWEBOK (Stone Man version). First, a general definition of the knowledge area is given. A breakdown of topics is then presented for the knowledge area along with brief descriptions of the various topics. These topic descriptions are also accompanied by references to material that provide more detailed presentation and coverage of these topics. The recommended references are then briefly described, followed by a number of suggestions for further readings.

It is important to stress that various constraints had to be satisfied by the resulting Knowledge Area (KA) description to satisfy the requirements set forth for these descriptions (see Appendix A of the whole Guide to the SWEBOK). Among the major constraints were that the KA description had to describe "generally accepted" knowledge not specific to any application domains or development methods and had to be compatible with typical breakdowns found in the literature. For those interested, Section 4 presents a more detailed Breakdown Rationale explaining how the various requirements for the KA description were met. A final note concerning the requirements was that the KA description had to suggest a list of "Recommended references" with a reasonably *limited* number of entries. Satisfying this requirement meant, sadly, that not all interesting references could be included in the recommended references list, thus the list of further readings.

2. DEFINITION OF SOFTWARE DESIGN

According to the IEEE definition [IEE90], design is both "the process of defining the architecture, components, interfaces, and other characteristics of a system or component" and "the result of [that] process". Viewed as a process, software design is the activity, within the software development life cycle, where software requirements are analyzed in order to produce a description of the internal structure and organization of the system that will serve as the basis for its construction. More precisely, a software design (the result) must describe the architecture of the system, that is, how the system is decomposed and organized into components and must describe the interfaces between these components. It must also describe these components into a level of detail suitable for allowing their construction.

In a classical software development life cycle such as ISO/IEC 12207 Software life cycle processes [ISO95b], software design consist of two activities that fit between software requirements analysis and software coding and testing: i) software architectural design – sometimes called top-level design, where the top-level structure and organization of the system is described and the various components are identified; ii) software detailed design – where each component is sufficiently described to allow for its coding.

Software design plays an important role in the development of a software system in that it allows the developer to produce various models that form a kind of blueprint of the solution to be implemented. These models can be analyzed and evaluated to determine if they will allow the various requirements to be fulfilled. Various alternative solutions and trade-offs can also be examined and evaluated. Finally, the resulting models can be used to plan the subsequent development activities, in addition to being used as input and starting point of the coding and testing activities.

Concerning the scope of the Software Design KA, it is important to note that not all topics containing the word "design" in their names will be discussed in the present KA description. In the terminology of DeMarco [DeM99], the present KA is concerned mainly with D-design (Decomposition design), as discussed in the above paragraphs (mapping a system into component pieces). However, because of its importance within the growing field of Software Architecture, FP-design (Family Pattern design, whose goal is to establish exploitable commonalities over a family of systems) will also be addressed. On the other hand, I-design (Invention design, usually done by system analysts with the objective of conceptualizing and specifying a system to satisfy discovered needs and requirements) will not be addressed, since this latter topic should be considered part of the requirements analysis and specification activity. Finally, also note that because of the requirements that the KA description had to include knowledge not specific to any application domains and the fact that some topics are better addressed in knowledge areas of related disciplines (see Appendix D of the whole Guide), certain specialized areas – for example, User Interface Design or Real-time Design – are not explicitly discussed in the present Software Design KA description. See Section 4 of the present chapter for further details concerning these and other specialized "design" topics. Of course, many of the topics included in the present Software Design KA description may still apply to these specialized areas.

3. BREAKDOWN OF TOPICS FOR SOFTWARE DESIGN

This section presents the breakdown of the Software Design Knowledge Area together with brief descriptions of each of the major topics. Appropriate references are also given for each of the topic. Figure 1 gives a graphical presentation of the top-level decomposition of the breakdown for the Software Design Knowledge Area. The detailed breakdown is presented in the following pages.

Note: The numbers in the reference keys, e.g., [Bud94:8, Pre97:23], indicate specific chapter(s) of the reference. In the case of Mar94, e.g., [Mar94:D], the letters indicates specific entries of the encyclopedia: "D" = Design; "DR" = Design Representation; "DD" = Design of Distributed systems". Note also that, contrary to the matrix presented in Section 5, only the appropriate chapter (or part) number, not the specific sections or pages, have been indicated.

I. Software Design Basic Concepts

This first section introduces a number of concepts and notions which form an underlying basis to the understanding of the role and scope of Software Design.

- General design concepts: Software is not the only field where design is involved. In the general sense, design

can be seen as a form of problem-solving [Bud94:1]. For example, the notion of *wicked* problem – a problem that has no definitive solution – is interesting for understanding the limits of design [Bud94:1]. A number of notions and concepts are also interesting to understand design in its general sense: goals, constraints, alternatives, representations, and solutions [SB93].

- The context of software design: To understand the role and place of software design, it is important to understand the context in which software design fits, i.e., the software development life cycle. Thus, the major characteristics of software requirements analysis vs. software design vs. software construction vs. testing must be understood [ISO95b, LG01:11, Mar94:D, Pfl98:2, Pre97:2].

- The software design process: Software design is generally considered a two steps process: architectural design describes how the system is decomposed and organized into components (the software architecture), whereas detailed design describes the specific behavior of these components [DT97:7, FW83:I, ISO95b, LG01:13, Mar94:D]. The output of this process is a set of models and artifacts that record the major decisions that have been taken [Bud94:2, IEE98, LG01:13, Pre97:13].

- Enabling techniques for software design: According to the Oxford dictionary, a principle is "a basic truth or a general law […] that is used as a basis of reasoning or a guide to action". Such principles for software design, called *enabling techniques* in [BMR+96], are key notions considered fundamental to many different software design approaches, concepts and notions that form a kind of foundation for many of those approaches. Some of the key notions are the following [BCK98:6, BMR+96:6, IEE98, Jal97:5,6, LG01:1,3, Pfl98: 5, Pre97:13,23]:

  - Abstraction: "the process of forgetting information so that things that are different can be treated as if they are the same" [LG01]. In the context of software design, two key abstraction mechanisms are abstraction by parameterization and by specification, which in turn lead to three major kinds of abstraction: procedural abstraction, data abstraction and control (iteration) abstraction [BCK98:6, LG01:1,3,5,6 Jal97:5, Pre97:13].

  - Coupling and cohesion: whereas coupling measures the strength of the relationships that exist *between* modules, cohesion measures how the elements making up a module are related [BCK98:6, Jal97:5, Pfl98:5, Pre97:13].

  - Decomposition and modularization: the operation of decomposing a large system into a number of smaller independent ones, usually with the goal of placing different functionalities or responsibilities in different components [BCK98:6, BMR+96:6, Jal97:5, Pfl98:5, Pre97:13].

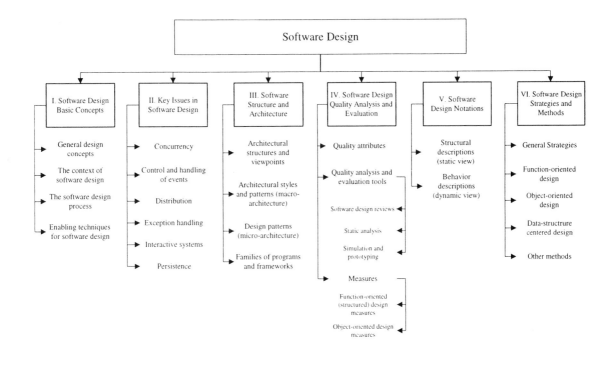

Figure 1 Breakdown of the Software Design KA

- Encapsulation/information hiding: deals with grouping and packaging the elements and internal details of an abstraction and making those details inaccessible [BCK98:6, BMR+96:6, Jal97:6, Pfl98:5, Pre97:13, 23].

- Separation of interface and implementation: involves defining a component by specifying a public interface, known to the clients, separate from the details of how the component is realized [BCK98:6, Bos00:10, LG01:1,9].

- Sufficiency, completeness and primitiveness: deals with ensuring that a software component captures all the important characteristics of an abstraction, and nothing more [BMR+96:6, LG01:5].

II. Key Issues in Software Design

A number of key issues must be dealt with when designing software systems. Some of these are really quality concerns that must be addressed by all systems, for example, performance. Another important issue is how to decompose, organize and package the software components. This is so fundamental that it must be addressed, in one way or another, by all approaches to design; this is discussed in the Enabling techniques and in the Software Design Strategies

topics. On the other hand, there are also other issues that "deal with some aspect of the system's behaviour that is not in the application domain, but which addresses some of the supporting domains" [Bos00]. Such issues, which often cross-cut the system's functionality, have been referred to as *aspects*: "[aspects] tend not to be units of the system's functional decomposition, but rather to be properties that affect the performance or semantics of the components in systemic ways" [KLM+97]. A number of these major, cross-cutting issues are the following (presented in alphabetical order):

- Concurrency: how to decompose the systems into processes, tasks and threads and deal with related efficiency, atomicity, synchronization and scheduling issues [Bos00:5, Mar94:DD, Mey97:30, Pre97:21].

- Control and handling of events: how to organize the flow of data and the flow of control, how to handle reactive and temporal events through various mechanisms, e.g., implicit invocation and call-backs [BCK98:5, Mey97:32, Pfl98:5].

- Distribution: how the software is distributed on the hardware, how the components communicate, how middleware can be used to deal with heterogeneous systems [BCK98:8, BMR+96:2, Bos00:5, Mar94:DD, Mey97:30, Pre97:28].

- Error and exception handling and fault tolerance: how to prevent and tolerate faults and deal with exceptional conditions [LG01:4, Mey97:12, Pfl98:5].

- Interactive systems: which approach to use to interact with users [BCK98:6, BMR+96:2.4, Bos00:5, LG01:13, Mey97:32].
  (Note: this topic is *not* about the specifications of the details of the user interface, which would be considered the task of the UI design, a topic beyond the scope of the current KA.)

- Persistence: how long-lived data is to be handled [Bos00:5, Mey97:31].

III. Software Structure and Architecture

In its strict sense, "*a* software architecture is a description of the subsystems and components of a software system and the relationships between them" [BMR+96:6]. An architecture thus attempts to define the internal *structure* – "the way in which something is constructed or organized" (Oxford dictionary) – of the resulting software. During the mid-90s, however, Software Architecture started to emerge as a broader discipline involved with studying software structures and architectures in a more generic way [SG96]. This gave rise to a number of interesting notions involved with the design of software at different levels of abstraction. Some of these notions can be useful during the architectural design (e.g., architectural style) as well as during the detailed design (e.g., lower-level design patterns) of a *specific* software system. But they can also be useful for designing *generic* systems, leading to the design of families of systems (aka. product lines). Interestingly, most of these notions can be seen as attempts to describe, and thus reuse, generic design knowledge.

- Architectural structures and viewpoints: Different high-level facets of a software design can and should be described and documented. These facets are often called *views*: "a view represents a partial aspect of a software architecture that shows specific properties of a software system" [BMR+96]. These different views pertain to different issues associated with the design of software, for example, the logical view (satisfying the functional requirements) vs. the process view (concurrency issues) vs. the physical view (distribution issues) vs. the development view (how the design is broken down into implementation units). Other authors use different terminologies, e.g., behavioral vs. functional vs. structural vs. data modeling views. The key idea is that a software design is a multi-faceted artifact produced by the design process and generally composed of relatively independent and orthogonal views [BCK98:2, BMR+96:6, BRJ99:31, Bud94:5, IEE98].

- Architectural styles (macro-architectural patterns): An architectural style is "a set of constraints on an architecture [that] define a set or family of architectures that satisfy them" [BCK98:2]. An architectural style can thus be seen as a meta-model that can provide the high-level organization (the *macro*-architecture) of a software system. A number of major styles have been identified by various authors. These styles can (tentatively) be organized as follows [BCK98:5, BMR+96:1.6, Bos00:6, BRJ99:28, Pfl98:5]:

  - General structure (e.g., layers, pipes and filters, blackboard);

  - Distributed systems (e.g., client-server, three-tiers, broker);

  - Interactive systems (e.g., Model-View-Controller, Presentation-Abstraction-Control);

  - Adaptable systems (e.g., micro-kernel, reflection);

  - Other styles (e.g., batch, interpreters, process control, rule-based).

- Design patterns (micro-architectural patterns): Described succinctly, a pattern is "a common solution to a common problem in a given context" [JBR99:p. 447]. Whereas architectural styles can be seen as patterns describing the high-level organization of software systems, thus their *macro*-architecture, other design patterns can be used to describe details at a lower, more local level, thus describing their *micro*-architecture. A wide range of patterns have been discussed in the literature. Such design patterns can (tentatively) be categorized as follows [BCK98:13, BMR+96:1, BRJ99:28]:

  - Creational patterns: e.g., builder, factory, prototype, singleton.

  - Structural patterns: e.g., adapter, bridge, composite, decorator, façade, flyweight, proxy.

  - Behavioral patterns: e.g., command, interpreter, iterator, mediator, memento, observer, state, strategy, template, visitor.

- Families of programs and frameworks: One possible approach to allow the reuse of software designs and components is to design *families* of systems – also known as *software product lines* – which can be done by identifying the commonalities among members of such families and by using reusable and customizable components to account for the variability among the various members of the family [BCK98:15, Bos00:7,10, Pre97:26].
  In the field of OO programming, a key related notion is that of framework [BMR+96:6, Bos00:11, BRJ99:28]: a framework is a partially complete software subsystem which can be extended by appropriately instantiating some specific plug-ins (also known as hot spots).

IV. Software Design Quality Analysis and Evaluation

A whole knowledge area is dedicated to Software Quality (see chapter 11). Here, we simply mention a number of topics more specifically related with software design.

- Quality attributes: Various attributes are generally considered important for obtaining a design of good quality, e.g., various "ilities" (e.g., maintainability, portability, testability, traceability), various "nesses" (e.g., correctness, robustness), including "fitness of purpose" [BMR+96:6, Bos00:5, Bud97:4, Mar94:D, Mey97:3, Pfl98:5]. An interesting distinction is the one between quality attributes discernable at run-time (e.g., performance, security, availability, functionality, usability), those not discernable at run-time (e.g., modifiability, portability, reusability, integrability and testability) and those related with the intrinsic qualities of the architecture (e.g., conceptual integrity, correctness and completeness, buildability) [BCK98:4].

- Quality analysis and evaluation tools: There exists a variety of tools and techniques that can help ensure the quality of a design. These can be decomposed into a number of categories:

  - Software design reviews: informal or semi-formal, often group-based, techniques to verify and ensure the quality of design artifacts, e.g., architecture reviews [BCK98:10], design reviews and inspections [Bud94:4, FW83:VIII, Jal97:5,7, LG01:14, Pfl98:5], scenario-based techniques [BCK98:9, Bos00:5], requirements tracing [DT97:6, Pfl98:10].

  - Static analysis: formal or semi-formal static (non-executable) analysis that can be used to evaluate a design, e.g., fault-tree analysis or automated cross-checking [Jal97:5, Pfl98:5].

  - Simulation and prototyping: dynamic techniques to evaluate a design, e.g., performance simulation or feasibility prototype [BCK98:10, Bos00:5, Bud94:4, Pfl98:5].

- Measures: Formal measures (a.k.a. metrics) can be used to estimate, in a quantitative way, various aspects of the size, structure or quality of a design. Most measures that have been proposed generally depend on the approach used for producing the design. These measures can thus be classified in two broad categories:

  - Function-oriented (structured) design measures: these measures are used for designs developed using the structured design approach, where the emphasis is mostly on functional decomposition. The structure of the design is generally represented as a structure chart (sometimes called a hierarchical diagram), on which various measures can be computed [Jal97:5,7, Pre97:18].

  - Object-oriented design measures: these measures are used for designs based on object-oriented decomposition. The overall structure of the design is often represented as a class diagram, on which various measures can be defined [Jal97:6,7, Pre97:23]. Measures can also be defined on properties of the internal content of each class.

V. Software Design Notations

A large number of notations and languages exist to represent software design artifacts. Some are used mainly to describe the structural organization of a design, whereas others are used to represent the behavior of such software systems. Note that certain notations are used mostly during architectural design whereas others are useful mainly during detailed design, although some can be used in both steps. In addition, some notations are used mostly in the context of certain specific methods (see section VI). Here, we categorize them into notations for describing the structural (static) view vs. the behavioral (dynamic) view.

- Structural descriptions (static view): These notations, mostly (but not always) graphical, can be used to describe and represent the structural aspects of a software design, that is, to describe what the major components are and how they are interconnected (static view).

  - Architecture Description Languages (ADL): textual, often formal, languages used to describe an architecture in terms of components and connectors [BCK98:12];

  - Class and object diagrams: diagrams used to show a set of classes (and objects) and their relationships [BRJ99:8,14, Jal97:5-6];

  - Component diagrams: used to show a set of components ("physical and replaceable part of a system that conforms to and provides the realization of a set of interfaces" [BRJ99]) and their relationships [BRJ99:12,31]

  - CRC Cards: used to denote the name of components (class), their responsibilities and the names of their collaborating components [BRJ99:4, BMR+96];

  - Deployment diagrams: used to show a set of (physical) nodes and their relationships and, thus, to model the physical aspects of a system [BRJ99:30];

  - Entity-Relationship Diagrams (ERD): used to define conceptual models of data stored in information systems [Bud94:6, DT97:4, Mar94:DR];

  - Interface Description Languages (IDL): programming-like languages used to define the interface (name and types of exported operations) of software components [BCK98:8, BJR99:11];

  - Jackson structure diagrams: used to describe the structure of data in terms of sequence, selection and iteration [Bud94.6, Mar94:DR];

  - Structure charts: used to describe the calling structure of programs (which procedure/module calls/is called by which other) [Bud94:6, Jal97:5, Mar94:DR, Pre97:14];

- Behavioral descriptions (dynamic view): These notations and languages are used to describe the dynamic behavior of systems and components. Such notations include various graphical notations (e.g., activity diagrams, DFD, sequence diagrams, state transition diagrams) as well as some textual notations (e.g., formal specification languages, pseudo-code and PDL). Many of these notations are useful mostly, but not exclusively, during detailed design.

- Activity diagrams: used to show the flow of control from activity ("ongoing non-atomic execution within a state machine") to activity [BRJ99:19];

- Collaboration diagrams: used to show the interactions that occur among a group of objects, where the emphasis is on the objects, their links and the messages they exchange on these links [BRJ99:18];

- Data flow diagrams: used to show the flow of data among a set of processes [Bud94:6, Mar94:DR, Pre97:14];

- Decision tables and diagrams: used to represent complex combination of conditions and actions [Pre97:14];

- Flowcharts and structured flowcharts: used to represent the flow of control and the associated actions to be performed [FW83:VII, Mar94:DR, Pre97:14];

- Formal specification languages: textual languages that use basic notions from mathematics (e.g., logic, set, sequence) to rigorously and abstractly define the interface and behavior of software components, often in terms of pre/post-conditions: [Bud94:14, DT97:5, Mey97:11];

- Pseudo-code and Program Design Languages (PDL): structured, programming-like languages used to describe, generally at the detailed design stage, the behavior of a procedure or method [Bud94:6, FW83:VII, Jal97:7, Pre97:12,14];

- Sequence diagrams: used to show the interactions among a group of objects, with the emphasis on the time-ordering of messages [BRJ99:18];

- State transition and statechart diagrams: used to show the flow of control from state to state in a state machine [BRJ99:24, Bud94:6, Mar94:DR, Jal97:7].

VI. Software Design Strategies and Methods

Various general *strategies* can be used to help guide the design process [Bud94:8, Mar94:D]. By contrast with general strategies, *methods* are more specific in that they generally suggest and provide i) a set of notations to be used with the method; ii) a description of the process to be used when following the method; iii) a set of heuristics that provide guidance in using the method [Bud97:7]. Such methods are useful as a means of transferring knowledge and as a common framework for teams of developers [Bud97:7]. In the following paragraphs, a number of general strategies are first briefly mentioned, followed by a number of methods.

- General strategies: Some often cited examples of general strategies useful in the design process are divide-and-conquer and stepwise refinement [FW83:V], top-down vs. bottom-up strategies [Jal97:5, LG01:13], data abstraction and information hiding [FW83:V], use of heuristics [Bud94:7], use of patterns and pattern languages [BMR+96:5], use of an iterative and incremental approach [Pfl98:2].

- Function-oriented (structured) design [DT97:5, FW83:V, Jal97:5, Pre97:13-14]: This is one of the classical approach to software design, where the decomposition is centered around the identification of the major systems functions and their elaboration and refinement in a top-down manner. Structured design is generally used after structured analysis has been performed, thus producing, among other things, dataflow diagrams and associated processes descriptions. Various strategies (e.g., transformation analysis, transaction analysis) and heuristics (e.g., fan-in/fan-out, scope of effect vs. scope of control) have been proposed to transform a DFD into a software architecture generally represented as a structure chart.

- Object-oriented design [DT97:5, FW83:VI, Jal97:6, Mar94:D, Pre97:19,21]: Numerous software design methods based on objects have been proposed. The field evolved from the early object-based design of the mid-1980's (noun = object; verb = method; adjective = attribute) through object-oriented design, where inheritance and polymorphism play a key role, and to the field of component-based design, where meta-information can be defined and accessed (e.g., through reflection). Although object-oriented design's deep roots stem from the concept of data abstraction, the notion of responsibility-driven design has also been proposed as an alternative approach to object-oriented design.

- Data-structure centered design [FW83:III,VII, Mar94:D]: Although less popular in North America than in Europe, there has been some interesting work (e.g., Jackson, Warnier-Orr) on designing a program starting from the data structures it manipulates rather than from the function it performs. The structures of the input and output data are first described (e.g., using Jackson structure diagrams) and then the control structure of the program is developed based on these data structure diagrams. Various heuristics have been proposed to deal with special cases, for example, when there is mismatch between the input and output structures.

- Other methods: Although software design based on functional decomposition or on object-oriented approaches are probably the most well-known methods to software design, other interesting approaches, although probably less "mainstream", do exist, e.g., formal and rigorous methods [Bud94:14, DT97:5,

Mey97:11, Pre97:25], transformational methods [Pfl98:2].

4. BREAKDOWN RATIONALE

This section explains the rationale behind the breakdown of topics for the Software Design KA. This is done informally by going through a number of the requirements described in the "Knowledge Area Description Specifications for the Stone Man Version of the Guide to the SWEBOK" (see Appendix A of the whole Guide) and by trying to explain how these requirements influenced the organization and content of the Software Design KA description.

First and foremost, the breakdown of topics must describe "generally accepted" knowledge, that is, knowledge for which there is a "widespread consensus". Furthermore, and this is clearly where this becomes difficult, such knowledge must be "generally accepted" today and expected to be so in a 3 to 5 years timeframe. This latter requirement first explains why elements related with software architecture (see below), including notions related with architectural styles have been included, even though these are relatively recent topics that might not yet be generally accepted.

The need for the breakdown to be independent of specific application domains, life cycle models, technologies, development methods, etc., and to be compatible with the various schools within software engineering, is particularly apparent within the "Software Design Strategies and Methods" section. In that section, numerous approaches and methods have been included and references given. This is also the case in the "Software Design Notations", which incorporates pointers to many of the existing notations and description techniques for software design artifacts. Although many of the design methods use specific design notations and description techniques, many of these notations are generally useful independently of the particular method that uses them. Note that this is also the approach used in many software engineering books, including the recent UML series of books by Booch, Jacobson and Rumbaugh, which describe "The Unified Modeling Language" apart from "The Unified Software Development Process".

One point worth mentioning about UML is that although "UML" (Unified Modeling Language) is not explicitly mentioned in the Design Notations section, many of its elements are indeed present, for example: class and object diagrams, collaboration diagrams, deployment diagrams, sequence diagrams, statecharts.

The specifications document also specifically asked that the breakdown be as inclusive as possible and that it includes topics related with quality and measurements. Thus, a certain number of topics have been included in the list of topics even though they may not yet be fully considered as generally accepted. For example, although there are a number of books on measures and metrics, design measures *per se* are rarely discussed in detail and few "mainstream"

software engineering books formally discuss this topic. But they are indeed discussed in some books and may become more mainstream in the coming years. Note that although those measures can sometimes be categorized into high-level (architectural) design vs. component-level (detailed) design, the way such measures are defined and used generally depend on the approach used for producing the design, for example, structured vs. object-oriented design. Thus, the measures sub-topics have been divided into function- (structured-) vs. object-oriented design. As the software engineering field matures and classes of software designs evolve, the measures appropriate to each class will become more apparent.

Similarly, there may not yet be a generally accepted list of basic principles and concepts (what was called here the "enabling techniques": see next paragraph for the choice of these terms) on which all authors and software engineers would agree. Only those that seemed the most commonly cited in the literature were included.

As required by the KA Description Specifications, the breakdown is at most three levels deep and use topic names which, based on our survey of the existing literature and on the various reviewers' comments, should be meaningful when cited outside Guide to the SWEBOK. One possible exception might be the use of the terms "enabling techniques", taken from [BMR+96]. In the current context, the term "concept" seemed too general, not specific enough, whereas the term "principle", sometimes used in the literature for some of these notions, sounded too strong (see the definition provided in Section 3).

The rationale for the section "Key Issues in Software Design" is that a number of reviewers of an earlier version suggested that certain topics, not explicitly mentioned in that previous version, be added, e.g., concurrency and multi-threading, exception handling. Although some of these aspects are addressed by some of the existing design methods, it seemed appropriate that these key issues be explicitly identified and that more specific references be given for them, thus the addition of this new section. However, like for the enabling techniques, there does not seem to yet be a complete consensus on what these issues should be, what aspects they should really be addressing, especially since some of those that have been indicated may also be addressed by other topics (e.g., quality). Thus, this section should be seen as a tentative and prototype description that could yet be improved: the author of the Software Design KA Description would gladly welcome any suggestions that could improve and/or refine the content of this section.

In the KA breakdown, as mentioned earlier, an explicit "Software Architecture" section has been included. Here, the notion of "architecture" is to be understood in the large sense of defining the structure, organization and interfaces of the components of a software system, by opposition to producing the "detailed design" of the specific components. This is what really is at the heart of Software Design. Thus, the "Software Architecture" section includes topics which pertain to the macro-architecture of a system – what is now becoming known as "Architecture" *per se*, including notions such as "architectural styles" and "family of programs" – as well as topics related with the micro-architecture of the smaller subsystems – for example, lower-level design patterns which can be used at the detailed design state. Although some of these topics are *relatively* new, they should become much more generally accepted within the 3-5 years timeframe expected from the Guide to the SWEBOK specifications. By contrast, note that no explicit "Detailed Design" section has been included: topics relevant to detailed design can implicitly be found in many places: the "Software Design Notations" and "Software Design Strategies and Methods" sections, "Software Architecture" (design patterns), as well as in "The software design process" subsection.

The "Software Design Strategies and Methods" section has been divided, as is done in many books discussing software design, in a first section that presents general strategies, followed by subsequent sections that present the various classes of approaches (data-, function-, object-oriented or other approaches). For each of these approaches, numerous methods have been proposed and can be found in the software engineering literature. Because of the limit on the number of references, mostly general references have been given, pointers that can then be used as starting point for more specific references.

Another issue, alluded to in the introduction but worth explaining in more detail, is the exclusion of a number of topics which contain the word "design" in their name and which, indeed, pertain to the development of software systems. Among these are the followings: User Interface Design, Real-time Design, Database Design, Participatory Design, Collaborative Design. The first two topics were specifically excluded, in the Straw Man document [BDA+98], from the Software Design KA: User Interface Design was considered to be a related discipline (see the Relevant knowledge areas of related disciplines, where both Computer Science and Cognitive Sciences can be pertinent for UI Design) whereas Real-time Design was considered a specialized sub-field of software design, thus did not have to be addressed in this KA description. The third one, Database Design, can also be considered a relevant (specialized) knowledge area of a related discipline (Computer Science). Note that issues related with user-interfaces and databases still have to be dealt with during the software design process, which is why they are mentioned in the "Key Issues in Software Design" section. However, the specific tasks of designing the details of the user interface or database structure are not considered part of Software Design *per se*. Note also that UI Design is not really part of design for an additional reason: UI Design

deals with specifying the external view of the system, not its internal structure and organization, thus should really be considered part of requirements specification.

As for the last two topics – Participatory and Collaborative Design –, they are more appropriately related with the Requirements Engineering KA, rather than Software Design. In the terminology of DeMarco (DeM99), these latter two topics belong more appropriately to I-Design (invention design, done by system analysts) rather than D-design (decomposition design, done by designers and coders) or FP-design (family pattern design, done by architecture groups). It is mainly D-design and FP-design, with a major emphasis on D-design, that can be considered as generally accepted knowledge related with Software Design.

Finally, concerning standards, there seems to be few standards that *directly* pertain to the design task or work product *per se*. However, standards having some indirect relationships with various issues of Software Design do exist, e.g., OMG standards for UML or CORBA. Since the need for the explicit inclusion of standards in the KA breakdown has been put aside ("Proposed changes to the [...] specifications [...]", Dec. 1999), a few standards having a direct connection with the Software Design KA were included in the Recommended references section. A number of standards related with design in a slightly more indirect fashion were also added to the list of further readings. Finally, additional standards having only an indirect yet not empty connection with design were simply mentioned in the general References section. As for topics related with tools, they are now part of the Software Development Methods and Tools KA.

5. MATRIX OF TOPICS VS. REFERENCE MATERIAL

The figure below presents a matrix showing the coverage of the topics of the Software Design KA by the various recommended references described in more detail in the following section. A number in an entry indicates a specific section or chapter number. A "*" indicates a reference to the whole document, generally either a journal paper or a standard. An interval of the form "n1-n2" indicates a specific range of pages, whereas an interval of the form "n1:n2" indicates a range of sections. For Mar94, the letters refer to one of the encyclopedia's entry: "D" = Design; "DR" = Design Representation; "DD" = Design of Distributed systems".

Note: Only the top two levels of the breakdown have been indicated in the matrix. Otherwise, especially in the "Software Design Notations" subsections, this would have lead to very sparse lines (in an already quite sparse matrix).

	BCK98	BMR+96	Bos00	BRJ99	Bud94	DT97	FW83	IEE98	ISO95b	Ja197	LG01	Mar94	Mey97	Pf198	Pre97	SB93
I. Software Design Basic Concepts																
General design concepts					1											*
The context of software design								*			11.1	D		2.2	2.2 : 2.7	
The software design process	2.1, 2.4				2	266-276	2-22	*	*		13.1 13.2	D			13.8	
Enabling techniques	6.1	6.3	10.3					*		5.1, 5.2, 6.2	1.1, 1.2, 3.1:3.3, 77-85, 5.8, 125-128,9.1:9.3			5.2, 5.5	13.4, 13.5, 23.2	
II. Key issues in software design																
Concurrency			5.4.1									DD	30		21.3	
Control and events	5.2												32.4, 32.5	5.3		
Distribution	8.3, 8.4	2.3	5.4.1									DD	30		28.1	
Exception handling										4.3:4.5			12	5.5		
Interactive systems	6.2	2.4	5.4.1								13.3		32.2			
Persistence			5.4.1										31			
III. Software structure and architecture																
Architectural structures and viewpoints	2.5	6.1		31	5.2				*							
Architectural styles and patterns (macro-arch.)	5.1, 5.2, 5.4	1.1: 1.3, 6.2	6.3.1	28										5.3		
Design patterns (micro-arch.)	13.3	1.1: 1.3		28												
Families of programs and frameworks	15.1, 15.3	6.2	7.1, 7.2, 10.2: 10.4, 11.2, 11.4	28											26.4	
IV. Software design quality analysis and evaluation																
Quality attributes	4.1	6.4	5.2.3		4.1: 4.3							D	3	5.5		
Quality analysis and evaluation	9.1, 9.2, 10.2, 10.3		5.2.1 5.2.2 5.3, 5.4		4.4	266-276	542-576			5.5, 7.3	14.1			5.6, 5.7, 10.5		
Measures										5.6, 6.5, 7.4					18.4, 23.4, 23.5	

	BCK98	BMR+96	Bos00	BRJ99	Bud94	DT97	FW83	IEE98	ISO95b	Jal97	LG01	Mar94	Mey97	Pfl98	Pre97	SB93
V. Software design notations																
Structural descriptions (static)	8.4, 12.1, 12.2	p. 429		4, 8, 11, 12, 14, 30, 31	6.3, 6.4, 6.6					5.3, 6.3		DR			12.3, 12.4	
Behavioral descriptions (dynamic)				18, 19, 24	6.2, 6.7; 6.9, 14.2.2 14.3.2	191-192	485-490, 506-513			5.3, 7.2		DR	11		14.11 12.5	
VI. Software design strategies and methods																
General strategies		5.1: 5.4			7.1, 7.2, 8		304-320, 533-539			5.1.4	13.13	D		2.2		
Function-oriented design						170-180	328-352			5.4					13.5, 13.6, 14.3: 14.5	
OO design						148-159, 160-169	420-436			6.4		D			19.2, 19.3, 21.1: 21.3	
Data-centered design							201-210,5 14-532					D				
Other methods					14	181-192	395-407						11	2.2	25.1: 25.3	

6. RECOMMENDED REFERENCES FOR SOFTWARE DESIGN

In this section, we give a brief presentation of each of the recommended references. Note that few references to existing standards have been included in this list, for the reasons explained in Section 4; instead, references to interesting standards have been included in the list of further readings. Also note that, because of the constraints on the size of the recommended references list, few specific and detailed references have been given for the various design methods; instead, general software engineering textbook references have been given. See the list of further readings in section 7 for more precise and detailed references on such methods, especially for references to various OO design methods.

Finally, also note that, both in this section and the following, only the author(s) and title of the recommended reference are given, together with an appropriate key that then refers to an entry in the general and detailed References section at the end of the chapter.

[BCK98] L. Bass, P. Clements, and R. Kazman. *Software Architecture in Practice,* Addison-Wesley.

A recent and major work on software architecture. It covers all the major topics associated with software architecture: what software architecture is, quality attributes, architectural styles, enabling concepts and techniques (called unit operations), architecture description languages, development of product lines, etc. Furthermore, it presents a number of case studies illustrating major architectural concepts, including a chapter on CORBA and one on the WWW. Some sections also address the issue of product lines design.

[BMR+96] F. Buschmann, R. Meunier, H. Rohnert, P. Sommerlad, and M. Stal. *Pattern-oriented Software Architecture – A System of Patterns,* J. Wiley and Sons.

Probably one of the best and clearest introduction to the notions of software architecture and patterns (both architectural and lower-level ones). Distinct chapters are dedicated to architectural patterns, design patterns and lower-level idioms. Another chapter discusses the relationships between patterns, software architecture, methods, frameworks, etc. This chapter also includes an brief presentation of "enabling techniques for software architecture", e.g., abstraction, encapsulation, information hiding, coupling and cohesion, etc.

[Bos00] J. Bosch. *Design & Use of Software Architectures – Adopting and Evolving a Product-line Approach*, ACM Press.

The first part of this book is about the design of software architectures and proposes a functionality-based approach coupled with subsequent phases of evaluation and transformation of the resulting architecture. These transformations are expressed in terms of different levels of patterns (architectural styles, architectural patterns and design patterns) and the impact they have on a number of key quality factors (performance, maintainability, reliability and security). The second part of the book is more specifically about the design of software product lines, including a whole chapter on OO frameworks.

[BRJ99] G. Booch, J. Rumbaugh, and I. Jacobson. *The Unified Modeling Language User Guide,* Addison-Wesley.

A comprehensive and thorough presentation of the various elements of UML, which incorporates many of the notations mentioned in the "Software Design Notations" section.

[Bud94] D. Budgen. *Software Design,* Addison-Wesley.

One of the few books discussing software design known to the author of the SD KA description – maybe the only one – which is neither a general software engineering textbook nor a book describing a specific software design method. This is probably the book that comes closest to the spirit of the present Software Design KA description, as it discusses topics such as the followings: the nature of design; the software design process; design qualities; design viewpoints; design representations; design strategies and methods (including brief presentations of a number of such methods, e.g., JSP, SSASD, JSD, OOD, etc.). Worth reading to find, in a single book, many notions, views and approaches to/about software design.

[DT97] M. Dorfman and R.H. Thayer (eds.). *Software Engineering,* IEEE Computer Society.

This book contains a collection of papers on software engineering in general. Two chapters deal more specifically with software design. One of them contains a general introduction to software design, briefly presenting the software design process and the notions of software design methods and design viewpoints. The other chapter contains an introduction to object-oriented design and a comparison of some existing OO methods. The following articles are particularly interesting for Software Design:

- D. Budgen, Software Design: An Introduction, pp. 104-115.
- L.M. Northrop, Object-Oriented Development, pp. 148-159.
- A.G. Sutcliffe, Object-Oriented Systems Development: A Survey of Structured Methods, pp.160-169.

- C. Ashworth, Structured Systems Analysis and Design Method (SSADM), pp. 170-180.
- R. Vienneau, A Review of Formal Methods, pp. 181-192.
- J.D. Palmer, Traceability, pp. 266-276.

[FW83] P. Freeman and A.I. Wasserman. *Tutorial on Software Design Techniques*, 4th edition, IEEE Computer Society Press.

Although this is an old book, it is an interesting one because it allows to better understand the evolution of the software design field. This book is a collection of papers where each paper presents a software design technique. The techniques range from basic strategies like stepwise refinement to, at the time, more refined methods such as structured design à la Yourdon and Constantine. An historically important reference. The following articles are particularly interesting:

- P. Freeman, Fundamentals of Design, pp. 2-22.
- D.L. Parnas, On the Criteria to be Used in Decomposing Systems into Modules, pp. 304-309.
- D.L. Parnas, Designing Software for Ease of Extension and Contraction, pp. 310-320.
- W.P. Stevens, G.J. Myers and L.L. Constantine, Structured Design, pp. 328-352.
- G. Booch, Object-Oriented Design, pp. 420-436.
- S.H. Caine and E.K. Gordon, PDL – A Tool for Software Design, pp. 485-490.
- C.M. Yoder and M.L. Schrag, Nassi-Schneiderman Charts: An Alternative to Flowcharts for Design, pp. 506-513.
- M.A. Jackson, Constructive Methods of Program Design, pp. 514-532.
- N. Wirth, Program Development by Stepwise Refinement, pp. 533-539.
- P. Freeman, Toward Improved Review of Software Design, pp. 542-547.
- M.E. Fagan, Design and Code Inspections to Reduce Errors in Program Development, pp. 548-576.

[IEE98] IEEE Std 1016-1998. IEEE Recommended Practice for Software Design Descriptions.

This document describes the information content and recommended organization that should be used for software design descriptions. The attributes describing design entities are briefly described: identification, type, purpose, function, subordinates, dependencies, interfaces, resources, processing and data. How these different elements should be organized is then presented.

[ISO95b] ISO/IEC Std 12207. Information technology – Software life cycle processes.

A detailed description of the ISO/IEC-12207 life cycle model. Clearly shows where Software Design fits in the whole software development life cycle.

[Jal97] P. Jalote. *An integrated approach to software engineering, 2nd ed.,* Springer-Verlag.

A general software engineering textbook with a good coverage of software design, as three chapters discuss this topic: one on function-oriented design, one on object-oriented design, and the other on detailed design. Another interesting point is that all these chapters have a section on measures and metrics.

[LG01] B. Liskov and J. Guttag. *Program Development in Java – Abstraction, Specification, and Object-Oriented Design,* Addison-Wesley, 2000.

A Java version of a classic book on the use of abstraction and specification in software development [LG86]. This new book still discusses, in a clear and insightful way, the notions of procedural vs. data vs. control (iteration) abstractions. It also stresses the importance of appropriate specifications of these abstractions, although this is now done rather informally (with stylized pre/post-conditions in the style of Clu [LG86]). The book also contains a chapter on design patterns. A very good introduction to some of the basic notions of design.

[Mar94] J.J. Marciniak. *Encyclopedia of Software Engineering,* J. Wiley and Sons.

A general software engineering encyclopedia that contains (at least) three interesting articles discussing software design. The first one, "Design" (K. Shumate), is a general overview of design discussing alternative development processes (e.g., waterfall, spiral, prototyping), design methods (structured, data-centered, modular, object-oriented). Some issues related with concurrency are also mentioned. The second one discusses the "Design of distributed systems" (R.M. Adler): communication models, client-server and services models. The third one, "Design representation" (J. Ebert), presents a number of approaches to the representation of design. It is clearly not a detailed presentation of any method; however, it is interesting in that it tries to explicitly identify, for each such method, the kinds of components and connectors used within the representation.

[Mey97] B. Meyer. *Object-Oriented Software Construction (Second Edition),* Prentice-Hall, 2000.

A detailed presentation of the Eiffel OO language and its associated Design-By-Contract approach, which is based on the use of formal assertions (pre/post-conditions, invariants, etc). It introduces the basic concepts of OO design, along with a discussion of many of the key issues associated with software design, e.g., user interface, exceptions, concurrency, persistence.

[Pfl98] S.L. Pfleeger. *Software Engineering – Theory and Practice,* Prentice-Hall.

A general software engineering book with one chapter devoted to design. Briefly presents and discusses some of the major architectural styles and strategies and some of the concepts associated with the issue of concurrency. Another section presents the notions of coupling and cohesion and also deals with the issue of exception handling. Techniques to improve and to evaluate a design are also presented: design by contract, prototyping, reviews. Although this chapter does not delve into any topic, it can be an interesting starting point for a number of issues not discussed in some of the other general software engineering textbooks.

[Pre97] R.S. Pressman. *Software Engineering – A Practitioner's Approach (Fourth Edition),* McGraw-Hill.

A classic general software engineering textbook (4th edition!). It contains over 10 chapters that deal with notions associated with software design in one way or another. The basic concepts and the design methods are presented in two distinct chapters. Furthermore, the topics pertaining to the function-based (structured) approach are separated (part III) from those pertaining to the object-oriented approach (part IV). Independent chapters are also devoted to measures applicable to each of those approaches, a specific section addressing the measures specific to design. A chapter discusses formal methods and another presents the Cleanroom approach. Finally, another chapter discusses client-server systems and distribution issues.

[SB93] G. Smith and G. Browne. Conceptual foundations of design problem-solving, *IEEE Transactions on Systems, Man and Cybernetics,* vol. 23, no. 5 Sep-Oct. 1993, pp. 1209-1219.

A paper that discusses what is design in general. More specifically, it presents the five basic concepts of design: goals, constraints, alternatives, representations, and solutions. The bibliography is a good starting point for obtaining additional references on design in general.

The following section suggests a list of additional reading material related with Software Design. A number of standards are mentioned; additional standards that may be pertinent or applicable to Software Design, although in a somewhat less direct way, are also mentioned, although not further described, in the general References section at the end of the document.

[Boo94] G. Booch. *Object Oriented Analysis and Design with Applications, 2nd ed.*

A classic in the field of OOD. The book introduces a number of notations that were to become part of UML (although sometimes with some slight modifications): class vs. objects diagrams, interaction diagrams, statecharts-like diagrams, module and deployment, process structure diagrams, etc. It also introduces a process to be used for OOA and OOD, both a higher-level (life cycle) process and a lower-level (micro-) process. (Note that a third edition of this book is expected.)

[Cro84] N. Cross (ed.). *Developments in Design Methodology.*

This book consists in a series of papers related to design in general, that is, design in other contexts than software. Still, many notions and principles discussed in some of these papers do apply to Software Design, e.g., the idea of design as wicked-problem solving.

[CY91] P. Coad and E. Yourdon. *Object-Oriented Design.*

This is yet another classic in the field of OOD – note that the second author is one of the father of classical Structured Design. An OOD model developed with their approach consists of the following four components that attempt to separate how some of the key issues should be handled: problem domain, human interaction, task management and data management.

[DW99] D.F. D'Souza and A.C. Wills. *Objects, Components, and Frameworks with UML – The Catalysis Approach.*

A thorough presentation of a specific OO approach with an emphasis on component design. The development of static, dynamic and interaction models is discussed. The notions of components and connectors are presented and illustrated with various approaches (Java Beans, COM, Corba); how to use such components in the development of frameworks is also discussed. Another chapter discusses various aspects of software architecture. The last chapter introduces a pattern system for dealing with both high-level and detailed design, the latter level touching on many key issues of design such as concurrency, distribution, middleware, dialogue independence, etc.

[Fow99] M. Fowler. *Refactoring – Improving the Design of Existing Code.*

A book about how to improve the design of some existing (object-oriented) code. The first chapter is a simple and illustrative example of the approach. Subsequent chapter present various categories of strategies, e.g., composing methods, moving features between objects, organizing data, simplifying conditional expressions, making methods calls simpler.

[FP97] N.E. Fenton and S.L. Pfleeger. *Software Metrics – A Rigorous & Practical Approach (Second Edition).*

This book contains a detailed presentation of numerous software measures and metrics. Although the measures are not necessarily presented based on the software development life cycle, many of those measures, especially those in chapters 7 and 8, are applicable to software design.

[GHJV95] E. Gamma et al. *Design Patterns – Elements of Reusable Object-Oriented Software.*

The seminal work on design patterns. A detailed catalogue of patterns related mostly with the micro-architecture level.

[Hut94] A.T.F. Hutt. *Object Analysis and Design – Description of Methods. Object Analysis and Design – Comparison of Methods.*

These two books describe (first book) and compare (second book), in an outlined manner, a large number of OO analysis and design methods. Useful as a starting point for obtaining additional pointers and references to OOD methods, not so much as a detailed presentation of those methods.

[IEE90] IEEE Std 610.12-1990. IEEE Standard Glossary of Software Engineering Terminology.

This standard is not specifically targeted to Software Design, which is why it has not been included in the recommended references. It describes and briefly explains many of the common terms used in the Software Engineering field, including many terms from Software Design.

[ISO91] ISO/IEC Std 9126. Information technology – Software product evaluation – Quality characteristics and guidelines for their use.

This standard describes six high-level characteristics that describe software quality: functionality, reliability, usability, efficiency, maintainability, portability.

[JBP+91] J. Rumbaugh et al. *Object-Oriented Modeling and Design.*

This book is another classic in the field of OOA and OOD. It was one of the first to introduce the distinctions between object, dynamic and functional modeling. However, contrary to [Boo94] whose emphasis is mostly on design, the emphasis here is slightly more on analysis, although a number of elements do apply to design too.

[JBR99] I. Jacobson, G. Booch, and J. Rumbaugh. *The Unified Software Development Process.*

A detailed and thorough presentation of the Unified Software Development Process proposed by the Rational

Software Corporation. The notion of architecture plays a central role in this development process, the process being said to be architecture-centric. However, the associated notion of architecture seems to be slightly different from the traditional purely design-based one: an architecture description is supposed to contain views not only from the design model but also from the use-case, deployment and implementation models. A whole chapter is devoted to the presentation of the iterative and incremental approach to software development. Another chapter is devoted to design *per se*, whose goal is to produce both the design model, which includes the logical (e.g., class diagrams, collaborations, etc.) and process (active objects) views, and the deployment model (physical view).

[Kru95] P.B. Kruchten. The 4+1 view model of architecture.

A paper that explains in a clear and insightful way the importance of having multiple views to describe an architecture. Here, architecture is understood in the sense mentioned earlier in reference [JBR99], not in its strictly design-related way. The first four views discussed in the paper are the logical, process, development and physical views, whereas the fifth one (the "+1") is the use case view, which binds together the previous views. The views more intimately related with Software Design are the logical and process ones.

[Lar98] C. Larman. *Applying UML and Patterns – An introduction to Object-Oriented Analysis and Design.*

An introductory book that covers object-oriented analysis and design, doing so through a case study used throughout the book. Part IV and VII are dedicated to the design phase. They introduce a number of patterns to guide the assignment of responsibilities to classes and objects. Various issues regarding design are also addressed, e.g., multi-tiers architecture, model-view separation. The patterns of [GHJV95] are also examined in the context of the case study.

[McC93] S. McConnell. *Code Complete.*

Although this book is probably more closely related with Software Construction, it does contain a section on Software Design with a number of interesting chapters, e.g., "Characteristics of a High-Quality Routines", "Three out of Four Programmers Surveyed Prefer Modules", "High-Level Design in Construction". One of these chapters ("Characteristic; [...]") contains an interesting discussion on the use of assertions in the spirit of Meyer's Design-by-Contract; another chapter ("Three [...]") discusses cohesion and coupling as well as information hiding; the other chapter ("High-Level [...]") gives a brief introduction to some design methodologies (structured design, OOD).

[otSESC98] Draft recommended practice for information technology – System design – Architectural description. Technical Report IEEE P1471/D4.1.

"This recommended practice establishes a conceptual framework for architectural description. This framework covers the activities involved in the creation, analysis, and sustainment of architectures of software-intensive systems, and the recording of such architectures in terms of *architectural descriptions*." (from the Abstract)

[Pet92] H. Petroski. *To Engineer is Human – The role of failure in successful design.*

This book is not about software design *per se*. The author, a civil engineer, discusses how a designer, an engineer can and should learn from previous failures and how a design should be seen as a kind of hypothesis to be tested. Interestingly, considering that Software Design is only one out of the 10 knowledge areas for software engineering, the author "take[s] design and engineering to be virtually synonymous".

[PJ00] M. Page-Jones. *Fundamentals of Object-Oriented Design in UML.*

Part III of this book ("Principles of object-oriented design") addresses a number of the enabling techniques in the specific context of OO design. This part of the book contains chapters such as the followings: Encapsulation and connascence; Domains, encumbrance, and cohesion; Type conformance and closed behavior; The perils of inheritance and polymorphism. The book also contains a chapter on the design of software components.

[Pre95] W. Pree. *Design Patterns for Object-Oriented Software Development.*

This book is particularly interesting for its discussion of framework design using what is called the "hot-spot driven" approach to the design of frameworks. The more specific topic of design patterns is better addressed in [BMR+96].

[Rie96] A.J. Riel. *Object-Oriented Design Heuristics.*

This book, targeted mainly towards OO design, presents a large number of heuristics that can be used in software design. Those heuristics address a wide range of issues, both at the architectural level and at the detailed design level.

[SG96] M. Shaw, D. Garlan. *Software architecture: Perspectives on an emerging discipline.*

One of the early book on software architecture that addresses many facets of the topic: architectural styles (including a chapter with a number of small case studies), shared information systems, user-interface architectures, formal specifications, linguistic issues, tools and education.

[Som95] I. Sommerville. *Software Engineering (fifth edition).* Addison-Wesley, 1995.

Part Three is dedicated to software design, giving an overview of a number of topics through the following chapters: the design process, architectural design, OO design, functional design. (Note: a sixth edition may already be available.)

[WBWW90] R. Wirfs-Brock, B. Wilkerson, and L. Wiener. *Designing Object-Oriented Software.*

A book that introduced the notion of responsibility-driven design to OOD. Until then, OOD was often considered synonymous with data abstraction-based design. Although it is true that an object does encapsulate data and associated behavior, focusing strictly on this aspect may not lead, according to the responsibility-driven design approach, to the best design.

[Wie98] R. Wieringa. A Survey of Structured and Object-Oriented Software Specification Methods and Techniques.

An interesting survey article that presents a wide range of notations and methods for specifying software systems and components. It also introduces an interesting framework for comparison based on the kinds of system properties to be specified: functions, behavior, communication or decomposition.

APPENDIX B – REFERENCES USED TO WRITE AND JUSTIFY THE KNOWLEDGE AREA DESCRIPTION

[BCK98] L. Bass, P. Clements, and R. Kazman. *Software Architecture in Practice*. SEI Series in Software Engineering. Addison-Wesley, 1998.

[BDA+98] P. Bourque, R. Dupuis, A. Abran, J.W. Moore, L. Tripp, J. Shyne, B. Pflug, M. Maya, and G. Tremblay. Guide to the software engineering body of knowledge – a straw man version. Technical report, Dépt. d'Informatique, UQAM, Sept. 1998.

[BMR+96] F. Buschmann, R. Meunier, H. Rohnert, P. Sommerlad, and M. Stal. *Pattern-oriented Software Architecture – A System of Patterns*. John Wiley & Sons, 1996.

[Boo94] G. Booch. *Object Oriented Analysis and Design with Applications, 2nd ed.* The Benjamin/Cummings Publishing Company, Inc., 1994.

[Bos00] J. Bosch. *Design & Use of Software Architecture – Adopting and Evolving a Product-line Approach.* ACM Press, 2000.

[BRJ99] G. Booch, J. Rumbauch, and I. Jacobson. *The Unified Modeling Language User Guide*. Addison-Wesley, 1999.

[Bud94] D. Budgen. *Software Design*. Addison-Wesley, 1994.

[Cro84] N. Cross (ed.). *Developments in Design Methodology*. John Wiley & Sons, 1984.

[CY91] P. Coad and E. Yourdon. *Object-Oriented Design*. Yourdon Press, 1991.

[DeM99] T. DeMarco. *The Paradox of Software Architecture and Design*. Stevens Prize Lecture, August 1999.

[DT97] M. Dorfman and R.H. Thayer. *Software Engineering*. IEEE Computer Society Press, 1997.

[DW99] D.F. D'Souza and A.C. Wills. *Objects, Components, and Frameworks with UML – The Catalysis Approach*. Addison-Wesley, 1999.

[Fow99] M. Fowler. *Refactoring – Improving the Design of Existing Code*. Addison-Wesley, 1999.

[FP97] N.E. Fenton and S.L. Pfleeger. *Software Metrics – A Rigorous & Practical Approach (Second Edition)*. International Thomson Computer Press, 1997.

[FW83] P. Freeman and A.I. Wasserman. *Tutorial on Software Design Techniques*, fourth edition. IEEE Computer Society Press, 1983.

[GHJV95] E. Gamma, R. Helm, R. Johnson, and J. Vlissides. *Design Patterns – Elements of Reusable Object-Oriented Software*. Professional Computing Series. Addison-Wesley, 1995.

[Hut94] A.T.F. Hutt. *Object Analysis and Design – Comparison of Methods. Object Analysis and Design – Description of Methods*. John Wiley & Sons, 1994.

[IEE88] IEEE. IEEE Standard Dictionary of Measures to Produce Reliable Software. IEEE Std 982.1-1988, IEEE, 1988.

[IEE88b] IEEE. IEEE Guide for the Use of Standard Dictionary of Measures to Produce Reliable Software. IEEE Std 982.2-1988, IEEE, 1988.

[IEE90] IEEE. IEEE Standard Glossary of Software Engineering Terminology. IEEE Std 610.12-1990, IEEE, 1990.

[IEE98] IEEE. IEEE Recommended Practice for Software Design Descriptions. IEEE Std 1016-1998, IEEE, 1998.

[ISO91] ISO/IEC. Information technology – Software product evaluation – Quality characteristics and guidelines for their use. ISO/IEC Std 9126: 1991, ISO/IEC, 1991.

[ISO95] ISO/IEC. Open distributed processing – Reference model. ISO/IEC Std 10746: 1995, ISO/IEC, 1995.

[ISO95b] ISO/IEC. Information technology – Software life cycle processes. ISO/IEC Std 12207: 1995, ISO/IEC, 1995.

[Jal97] P. Jalote. *An Integrated Approach to Software Engineering, 2nd ed.* Springer, 1997.

[JBP+91] J. Rumbaugh, M. Blaha, W. Premerlani, F. Eddy, and W. Lorensen. *Object-Oriented Modeling and Design*. Prentice-Hall, 1991.

[JBR99] I. Jacobson, G. Booch, and J. Rumbaugh. *The Unified Software Development Process*. Addison-Wesley, 1999.

[JCJO92] I. Jacobson, M. Christerson, P. Jonsson, and G. Overgaard. *Object-Oriented Software Engineering – A Use Case Driven Approach*. Addison-Wesley, 1992.

[KLM+97] G. Kiczales, J. Lamping, A. Mendhekar, C. Maeda, C. Lopes, J.-M. Loingtier, and J. Irwin. Aspect-oriented programming. In *ECOOP '97 – Object-Oriented Programming*, pages 220-242. LNCS-1241, Springer-Verlag, 1997.

[Kru95] P.B. Kruchten. The 4+1 view model of architecture. *IEEE Software*, 12(6):42–50, 1995.

[Lar98] C. Larman. *Applying UML and Patterns – An introduction to Object-Oriented Analysis and Design*. Prentice-Hall, 1998.

[LG86] B. Liskov and J. Guttag. *Abstraction and Specification in Program Development*. The MIT Press, 1986.

[LG01] B. Liskov and J. Guttag. *Program Development in Java – Abstraction, Specification, and Object-Oriented Design*. Addison-Wesley, 2001.

[Mar94] J.J. Marciniak. *Encyclopedia of Software Engineering*. John Wiley & Sons, Inc., 1994.

[McCr93] S. McConnell. *Code Complete*. Microsoft Press, 1993.

[Mey97] B. Meyer. *Object-Oriented Software Construction (Second Edition).* Prentice-Hall, 1997.

[OMG98] OMG. The common object request broker: Architecture and specification. Technical Report Revision 2.2, Object Management Group, February 1998.

[OMG99] UML Revision Task Force. OMG Unified Modeling Language specification, v. 1.3. document ad/99-06-08, Object Management Group, June 1999.

[otSESC98] Architecture Working Group of the Software Engineering Standards Committee. Draft recommended practice for information technology – System design – Architectural description. Technical Report IEEE P1471/D4.1, IEEE, December 1998.

[Pet92] H. Petroski. *To Engineer is Human – The role of failure in successful design.* Vintage Books, 1992.

[Pfl98] S.L. Pfleeger. *Software Engineering – Theory and Practice.* Prentice-Hall, Inc., 1998.

[PJ00] M. Page-Jones. *Fundamentals of Object-Oriented Design in UML.* Addison-Wesley, 2000.

[Pre95] W. Pree. *Design Patterns for Object-Oriented Software Development.* Addison-Wesley and ACM Press, 1995.

[Pre97] R.S. Pressman. *Software Engineering – A Practitioner's Approach (Fourth Edition).* McGraw-Hill, Inc., 1997.

[Rie96] A.J. Riel. *Object-Oriented Design Heuristics.* Addison-Wesley, 1996.

[SB93] G. Smith and G. Browne. Conceptual foundations of design problem-solving. *IEEE Trans. on Systems, Man, and Cybernetics,* 23(5):1209–1219, 1993.

[SG96] M. Shaw, D. Garlan. *Software architecture: Perspectives on an emerging discipline.* Prentice-Hall, 1996.

[Som95] I. Sommerville. *Software Engineering (fifth edition).* Addison-Wesley, 1995.

[WBWW90] R. Wirfs-Brock, B. Wilkerson, and L. Wiener. *Designing Object-Oriented Software.* Prentice-Hall, 1990.

[Wie98] R. Wieringa. A Survey of Structured and Object-Oriented Software Specification Methods and Techniques. *ACM Computing Surveys,* 30(4): 459–527, 1998.

CHAPTER 4

SOFTWARE CONSTRUCTION

Terry Bollinger
The MITRE Corporation
1820 Dolley Madison Blvd.,
W534 McLean, VA, 22102, USA
terry@mitre.org

Philippe Gabrini, Louis Martin
Department of Computer Science
Université du Québec à Montréal
C.P. 8888, Succ. Centre-Ville
Montréal, Québec, H3C 3P8, Canada
{gabrini.philippe, martin.louis}@uqam.ca

Table of Contents

1. INTRODUCTION

Techniques of software construction are largely craft-based. As we come to understand the techniques better, we can explain them in terms of principles that can be explained as part of engineering knowledge. This description will therefore describe the underlying engineering principles in some detail and treat the specific craft-based techniques more briefly, usually just by naming them.

1.1. Annotated table of contents

This chapter is laid out as follows:

1. Introduction - This provides the road map to explain the overall structure of the chapter.

2. Definition - This defines Software Construction and provides links to other Knowledge Areas.

3. Principles of Organization - This explains the **first and most important method** chosen to break the subject matter into smaller sections, using four principles of software construction. The subject matter proper appears in section 5.

4. Styles of Construction - This explains a **second and less important method** chosen to break down the subject matter in each of section 5 into even smaller subsections, using three styles/methods of software construction.

5. Synthesis – This section contains 4 sub-sections, one for each of the four principles (the major dissection); each section contains 3 sub-sub-sections, one for each of the three styles of construction (the minor dissection).

6. Selected References

7. Additional References

8. Standards

9. References to Justify this Knowledge Area

10. Matrix of Reference Material versus Topics

2. DEFINITION OF THE SOFTWARE CONSTRUCTION KNOWLEDGE AREA

The Guide to the Swebok places the chapter on Construction after the one on Design and before the one on Testing. This does not imply **either** that the design stage must be complete before construction starts **or** that the construction stage must be complete before testing starts. In some development styles – such as the classic waterfall - design, construction, and testing are meant to proceed in that order. In others – such as the spiral method - development proceeds in successive steps, where each step consists of a predefined quantity of design, construction, and testing.

An important part of software engineering is to make a rational choice of development style for a given software project.

Software construction is linked to all other KAs, perhaps most strongly to Design, and Testing. This is because the construction process consumes the output of the Design process (KA3) and itself provides one of the inputs to the Testing process (KA5).

Software construction is a fundamental act of software engineering: the construction of working, meaningful software through a combination of coding, validation, and testing (unit testing) by a programmer. Far from being a simple mechanistic "translation" of good design into working software, software construction burrows deeply into difficult issues of software engineering. It requires the establishment of a meaningful dialog[1] between a person and a computer – a "communication of intent" that must reach from the slow and fallible human to a fast and unforgivingly literal computer. Such a dialog requires that the computer perform activities for which it is poorly suited, such as understanding implicit meanings and recognizing the presence of nonsensical or incomplete statements. On the human side, software construction requires that developers be logical, precise, and thorough so that their intentions can be accurately captured and understood by the computer. The relationship works only because each side possesses certain capabilities that the other lacks. In the symbiosis that is software construction, the computer provides astonishing reliability, retention, and (once the need has been explained) speed of performance. Meanwhile, the human being provides creativity and insight into how to solve new, difficult problems, plus the ability to express those solutions with sufficient precision to be meaningful to the computer.

2.1. Software Construction and Software Design

Software construction is closely related to software design (see *Knowledge Area Description for Software Design*). *Software design* analyzes software requirements in order to produce a description of the internal structure and organization of a system that will serve as a basis for its construction. Software design methods are used to express a global solution as a set of smaller solutions and can be applied repeatedly until the resulting parts of the solution are small enough to be handled with confidence by a single developer. It is at this point – that is, when the design process has broken the larger problem up into easier-to-handle chunks – that *software construction* is generally understood to begin. This definition also recognizes the distinction that while software construction necessarily produces executable software, software design does not necessarily produce any executable products at all.

In practice, however, the boundary between design and construction is seldom so clearly defined. Firstly, software construction is influenced by the scale or size of the software product being constructed. Very small projects in which the design problems are already "construction size" may neither require nor need an explicit design phase, and very large projects may require a much more interactive relationship between design and construction as different prototyping alternatives are proposed, tested, and discarded or used. Secondly, many of the techniques of software design also apply to software construction, since dividing problems into smaller parts is just as much a part of construction as it is design. Thirdly, effective design techniques always contain some degree of guessing or approximation in how they define their sub-problems. A few of the resulting approximations will turn out to be wrong, and will require corrective actions during software construction. (While another seemingly obvious solution would be to remove guessing and approximation altogether from design methods, that would contradict the premise that the original problem was too large and complex to be solved in one step. Effective design techniques instead acknowledge risk, work to reduce it, and help make sure that effective alternatives will be available when some choices eventually prove wrong.)

Design and construction both require sophisticated problem solving skills, although the two activities have somewhat different emphases. In design the emphasis is on how to partition a complex problem effectively, while in construction the emphasis is on finding a complete and executable solution to a problem. When software construction techniques do become so well-defined that they can be applied mechanistically, the proper route for the software engineer is to automate those techniques and move on to new problems, ones whose answers are not so well defined. This trend toward automation of well-defined tasks began with the first assemblers and compilers, and it has continued unabated as new generations of tools and computers have made increasingly powerful levels of construction automation possible. Projects that do contain highly repetitive, mechanistic software construction steps should examine their designs, processes, and tools sets more closely for ways to automate such needlessly repetitive steps out of existence.

2.2. The Role of Tools in Construction

In software engineering, a tool is a hardware or software device that is used to support performing a process. An effective tool is one that provides significant improvements in productivity and/or quality. This is a very inclusive definition, however, since it encompasses general-purpose hardware devices such as computers and peripherals that are part of an overall software-engineering environment. *Software construction tools* are a more specific category of tools that are both software-based and used primarily within the construction process. Common examples of software construction tools include compilers, version control systems, debuggers, code generators, specialized

---

[1]   Some reviewers have commented that it is improper even to suggest that computers "understand programs" or "speak languages". However we prefer to retain the language of metaphor to illuminate the material; the reader will understand that such language is metaphorical as opposed to literal.

editors, tools for path and coverage analysis, test scaffolding and documentation tools.

The best software construction tools bridge the gap between methodical computer efficiency and forgetful human creativity. Such tools allow creative minds to express their thoughts easily, but also enforce an appropriate level of rigor. Good tools also improve software quality by allowing people to avoid repetitive or precise work for which a computer is better suited.

2.3. The Role of Integrated Evaluation in Construction

Another important theme of software engineering is the *evaluation* of software products. This includes such diverse activities as peer review of code and test plan, testing, software quality assurance, and measures[2] (see *Knowledge Area Description for Testing* and *Knowledge Area Description for Software Quality Analysis*). Integrated evaluation means that a process (in this case a development process) includes explicit continuous or periodic internal checks to ensure that it is still working correctly. These checks usually consist of evaluations of intermediate work products such as documents, designs, source code, or compiled modules, but they may also look at characteristics of the development process itself. Examples of product evaluations include design reviews, module compilations, and unit tests. An example of process-level evaluation would be periodic re-assessment of a code library to ensure its accuracy, completeness, and self-consistency.

Integrated evaluation in software engineering has yet to reach the stage achieved in hardware engineering where the evaluation is built into the components themselves, e.g. integrated self-test logic and built-in error recovery in complex integrated circuits. Such features were first added to integrated circuits when it was realized the circuits had become so complex that the assumption of perfect start-to-finish reliability was no longer tenable. As with integrated circuits, the purpose of integrated checking in software processes is to ensure that they can operate for long periods without generating nonsensical or hazardously misleading answers.

Historically, software construction has tended to be one of the software engineering steps in which developers were particularly prone to omitting checks on the process. While nearly all developers practice some degree of informal evaluation when constructing software, it is all too common for them to skip needed evaluation steps because they are too confident about the reliability and quality of their own software constructions. Nonetheless, a wide range of automated, semi-automated, and manual evaluation methods have been developed for use in the software construction phase.

---

[2] The word metrics is commonly used by software developers to denote the activity that practitioners in other branches of engineering refer to as measurement.

The simplest and best-known form of software construction evaluation is the use of unit testing after completion of each well-defined software unit. Automated techniques such as compile-time checks and run-time checks help verify the basic integrity of software units, and manual techniques such as code reviews can be used to search for more abstract classes of errors. Tools for extracting measurements of code quality and structure can also be used during construction, although such measurement tools are more commonly applied during integration of large suites of software units. When collecting measurements, it is important that the measurements collected be relevant to the goals of the development process.

2.4. The Role of Standards in Construction

All forms of successful communication require a common language. *Standards* are in many ways best understood as agreements by which both concepts and technologies can become part of the shared "language" of a broader community of users. In many cases, standards are selected by a customer or by an organization. Project managers should consider the use of additional standards selected to be suitable to the specific characteristics of the project.

Software construction is particularly sensitive to the selection of standards, which directly affects such construction-critical issues as programming languages, databases, communication methods, platforms, and tools. Although such choices are often made before construction begins, it is important that the overall software development process take the needs of construction into account when standards are selected.

2.5. Manual and Automated Construction/The Spectrum of Construction Techniques

Manual Construction

Manual construction means solving complex problems in a language that a computer can execute. Practitioners of manual construction need a rich mix of skills that includes the ability to break complex problems down into smaller parts, a disciplined formal-proof-like approach to problem analysis, and the ability to "forecast" how constructions will change over time. Expert manual constructors sometimes use the skills of advanced logicians; they always need to apply the skills they have within a complex, changing environment such as a computer or network.

It would be easy to directly equate manual construction to coding in a programming language, but it would also be an incomplete definition. An effective manual construction process should result in code that fully and correctly processes data for its entire problem space, anticipates and handles all plausible (and some implausible) classes of errors, runs efficiently, and is structured to be resilient and easy-to-change over time. An inadequate manual construction process will in contrast result in code like an amateurish painting, with critical details missing and the entire construction stitched together poorly.

Automated Construction

While no form of software construction can be fully automated, much or all of the overall coordination of the software construction process can be moved from people to the computer – that is, overall control of the construction process can be largely automated. *Automated construction* thus refers to software construction in which an automated tool or environment is primarily responsible for overall coordination of the software construction process. This removal of overall process control can have a large impact on the complexity of the software construction process, since it allows human contributions to be divided up into much smaller, less complex "chunks" that require different problem solving skills to solve. Automated construction is also reuse-intensive construction, since by limiting human options it allows the controlling software to make more effective use of its existing store of effective software problem solutions. Of course, automated construction is not necessarily low cost; sometimes the cost of setting up the machinery is higher than the cost saved in its use.

In its most extreme form, automated construction consists of two related but distinct activities: (1) configuring a baseline system, which means configuring a predefined set of options that provide a workable solution in a typical business context and (2) implementing exceptions in the context of the product's usage. This may include resetting parameters, constructing additional software chunks, building interfaces, and moving data from existing legacy systems and other data sources to the new system. For example, an accounting application for small businesses might lead users through a series of questions that will result in a customized installation of the application. When compared to using manual construction for the same type of problem, this form of automated construction "swallows" huge chunks of the overall software engineering process and replaces them with automated selections that are controlled by the computer. Toolkits provide a less extreme example in which developers still have a great deal of control over the construction process, but that process has been greatly constrained and simplified by the use of predefined components with well-defined relationships to each other.

Automated construction is necessarily tool-intensive construction, since the objective is to move as much of the overall software development process as possible away from the human developer and into automated processes. Automated construction tools tend to take the form of program generators and fully integrated environments that can more easily provide automated control of the construction process. To be effective in coordinating activities, automated construction tools also need to have easy, intuitive interfaces.

Moving Towards Automation

An important goal of software engineering is to move construction continually towards higher levels of automation. That is, when selection from a simple set of options is all that is really required to make software work for a business or system, then the goal of software engineers should continually be to make their systems come as close to that level of simplicity as possible. This not only makes software more accessible, but also makes it safer and more reliable by removing opportunities for error.

The concept of moving towards higher levels of construction automation permeates nearly every aspect of software construction. When simple selections from a list of options will not suffice, software engineers often can still develop application specific tool kits (that is, sets of reusable parts designed to work with each other easily) to provide a somewhat lesser level of control. Even fully manual construction reflects the theme of automation, since many coding techniques and good programming practices are intended to make code modification easier and more automated. For example, even a concept as simple as defining a constant at the beginning of a software module reflects the automation theme, since such constants "automate" the appropriate insertion of new values for the constant in the event that changes to the program are necessary. Similarly, the concept of class inheritance in object-oriented programming helps automate and enforce the conveyance of appropriate sets of methods into new, closely related or derived classes of objects.

2.6. Construction Languages

Construction languages include all forms of communication by which a human can specify an executable problem solution to a computer. The simplest type of construction language is a *configuration language*, in which developers choose from a limited set of predefined options to create new or custom installations of software. The text-based configuration files used in both Windows and Unix operating systems are examples, and the menu-style selection lists of some program generators are another. *Toolkit languages* are used to build applications out of toolkits (integrated sets of application-specific reusable parts), and are more complex than configuration languages. Toolkit languages may be explicitly defined as application programming languages (e.g., scripts), or may simply be implied by the collected set of interfaces of a toolkit. As described below, *programming languages* are the most flexible type of construction languages, but they also contain the least information about both application areas and development processes, and so require the most training and skill to use effectively.

2.7. Programming Languages

Since the fundamental task of software construction is to communicate intent unambiguously between two very different types of entities (people and computers), the interface between the two is most commonly expressed as languages. Programming languages are more literal than natural languages, since no computer yet built has sufficient context and understanding of the natural world to recognize invalid language statements and constructions that would be caught immediately in a natural language. As will be discussed below, programming languages can also borrow from other non-linguistic human skills such as spatial visualization. The particular requirements of an application domain can give rise to the development or use of a specialized, *domain-specific language* such as lex, yacc, PHP, TCL, or TK.

Programming languages are often created in response to the needs of particular application fields, but the quest for more universal or encompassing programming language is ongoing. As in many relatively young disciplines, such quests for universality are as likely to lead to short-lived fads as they are to genuine insights into the fundamentals of software construction. For this very reason, it is important that software construction not be tied too greatly on any programming language or programming methodology. Adherence to suitable programming language standards, and avoiding proprietary feature sets helps avoid language obsolescence.

3. BREAKDOWN OF TOPICS FOR SOFTWARE CONSTRUCTION[3]

3.1. Principles of Organization

The first and most important method of breaking the subject of software construction into smaller units is to recognize the four principles that most strongly affect the way in which software is constructed, namely

- Reduction of Complexity
- Anticipation of Diversity
- Structuring for Validation
- Use of External Standards

These are discussed below.

3.1.1. Reduction of Complexity

This principle of organization reflects the relatively limited ability of people to work with complex systems that have many parts or interactions. A major factor in how people convey intent to computers is the severely limited ability of people to "hold" complex structures and information in their working memory, especially over long periods of time. This need for simplicity in the human-to-computer interface leads to one of the strongest drivers in software construction: *reduction of complexity*. The need to reduce complexity applies to essentially every aspect of the software construction, and is particularly critical to the process of self-verification and testing of software constructions.

There are three main techniques for reducing complexity during software construction:

3.1.1.1 Removal of Complexity

Although trivial in concept, one obvious way to reduce complexity during software construction is to *remove* features or capabilities that are not absolutely required. This may or may not be the right way to handle a given situation, but certainly the general principle of parsimony – that is, of not adding capabilities that clearly will never be needed when constructing software – is valid.

3.1.1.2 Automation of Complexity

A much more powerful technique for removal of complexity is to *automate* the handling of it. That is, a new construction language is created in which features that were previously time-consuming or error-prone for a human to perform are migrated over to the computer in the form of new software capabilities. The history of software is replete with examples of powerful software tools that raised the overall level of development capability of people by allowing them to address a new set of problems. Operating systems are one example of this principle, since they provide a rich construction language by which efficient use of underlying hardware resources can be greatly simplified. Visual construction languages similarly provide automation of the construction of software that otherwise could be very laborious to build.

3.1.1.3 Localization of Complexity

If complexity can neither be removed nor automated, the only remaining option is to *localize* complexity into small "units" or "modules" that are small enough for a person to understand in their entirety, and (perhaps more importantly) sufficiently *isolated* that meaningful assertions can be made about them. This might even lead to components that can be re-used. However, one must be careful, as arbitrarily dividing a very long sequence of code into small "modules" does not help, because the relationships between the modules become extremely complex and difficult to predict. Localization of complexity has a powerful impact on the design of programming languages, as demonstrated by the growth in popularity of object-oriented methods that seek to strictly limit the number of ways to interface to a software module, even though that might end up making components more dependent. Localization is also a key aspect of good design of the broader category of construction languages, since new feature that are too hard to find and use are unlikely to be effective as tools for construction. Classical design admonitions such as the goal of having "cohesion" within modules and to minimize "coupling" are also fundamentally localization of complexity techniques, since they strive to make the

---

[3] An alternate, more traditional, breakdown is presented in Appendix B.

number and interaction of parts within a module easy for a person to understand.

3.1.2. Anticipation of Diversity

This principle has more to do with how people use software than with differences between computers and people. Its motive is simple: *There is no such thing as an unchanging software construction.* Any useful software construction will change in various ways over time, and the *anticipation* of change drives nearly every aspect of software construction. Useful software constructions are unavoidably part of a changing external environment in which they perform useful tasks, and changes in that outside environment trickle in to impact the software constructions in diverse (and often unexpected) ways. In contrast, formal mathematical constructions and formulas can in some sense be stable or unchanging over time, since they represent abstract quantities and relationships that do not require direct "attachment" to a working, physical computational machine. For example, even the software implementations of "universal" mathematical functions must change over time due to external factors such as the need to port them to new machines, and the unavoidable issue of physical limitations on the accuracy of the software on a given machine.

Anticipation of the diversity of ways in which software will change over time is one of the more subtle principles of software construction, yet it is important for the creation of software that can endure over time and add value to future endeavors. Since it includes the ability to anticipate changes due to design errors in software, it also helps to make software robust and error-free. Indeed, one handy definition of "aging" software is that it is software that no longer has the flexibility to accommodate bug fixes without breaking.

There are three main techniques for anticipating change during software construction:

3.1.2.1 Generalization

It is very common for software construction to focus first on highly specific problems with limited, rather specific solutions. This is common because the more general cases often simply are not obvious in the early stages of analysis. Generalization is the process of recognizing how a few specific problem cases fit together as part of some broader framework of problems, and thus can be solved by a single overarching software construction in place of several isolated ones. Generalization of functionality is a distinctly mathematical concept, and not too surprisingly the best generalizations that are developed are often expressed in the language of mathematics. Good design is equally an aspect of generalization, however. For example, software constructions that use stacks to store data are almost always more generalized than similar solutions using arrays behaving as stacks, since fixed sizes immediately place artificial (and usually unnecessary) constraints on the range of problem sizes that the construction can solve.

Generalization anticipates diversity because it creates solutions to entire classes of problems that may not have even been recognized as existing before. Thus just as Newton's general theory of gravity made a small number of formulas applicable to a much broader range of physics problems, a good generalization to a number of discrete software problems often can lead to the easy solution of many other development problems. For example, developing an easily customizable graphics user interface could solve a very broad range of development problems that otherwise would have required individual, labor-intensive development of independent solutions.

Anticipating diversity by using generalization is effective only when the developer finds generalizations that actually correspond to the eventual uses of the software. Developers may have no particular interest (or time) to develop the necessary generalizations under the schedule pressures of typical commercial projects. Even when the time needed is available, it is easy to develop the wrong set of generalizations – that is, to create generalizations that make the software easier to change, but only in ways that prove not to correspond to what is really needed.

For these reasons, generalization is both safer and easier if it can be combined with the next technique of *experimentation*. Change experimentation makes generalization safer by capturing realistic data on which generalizations will be needed, and makes generalization easier by providing schedule-conscious projects with specific data on how generalizations can improve their products.

3.1.2.2 Experimentation

Experimentation means using early (sometimes very early) software constructions in as many different user contexts as possible, and as early in the development process as possible, for the explicit purpose of collecting data on how to generalize the construction. To experiment is to recognize how difficult it is to anticipate all the ways in which software constructions can change.

Obviously, experimentation is a process-level technique rather than a code-level technique, since its goal is to collect data to help guide code-level processes such as generalization. This means that it is constrained by whether the overall development process allows it to be used at the construction level. Construction-level experimentation is most likely to be found in projects that have incorporated experimentation into their overall development process. The Internet-based open source development process that Linus Torvalds used to create the Linux operating system is an example of a process that both allowed and encouraged construction-level use of experimentation. In Torvalds' approach, individual code constructions were very quickly incorporated into an overall product and then redistributed via the Internet, sometimes on the same day. This encouraged further use, experimentation, and updates to the individual constructions. Development environments and languages that support the rapid prototyping style of development also encourage construction-level experimentation.

3.1.2.3 Localization

Localization means keeping anticipated changes as localized in a software construction as possible. It is actually a special case of the earlier principle of *localization of complexity,* since change is a particularly difficult class of complexity. A software construction that can be changed in a common way by making only one change at one location within the construction thus demonstrates good *locality* for that particular class of modifications.

Localization is very common in software construction, and often is used intuitively as the "right way" to construct software. Objects are one example of a localization technique, since good object designs localize implementation changes to within the object. An even simpler example is using compile-time constants to reduce the number of locations in a program that must be changed manually should the constant change. Layered architectures such as those used in communication protocols are yet another example of localization, since good layer designs keep changes from crossing layers.

3.1.3. Structuring for Validation

No matter how carefully a person designs and implements software, the creative nature of non-trivial software construction (that is, of software that is not simply a re-implementation of previously solved problems) means that mistakes and omissions will occur. *Structuring for validation* means building software in such a fashion that such errors and omissions can be ferreted out more easily during unit testing and subsequent testing activities. One important implication of structuring for validation is that software must generally be *modular* in at least one of its major representation spaces, such as in the overall layout of the displayed or printed text of a program. This modularity allows both improved analysis and thorough unit-level testing of such components before they are integrated into higher levels in which their errors may be more difficult to identify. As a principle of construction, structuring for validation generally goes hand-in-hand with anticipation of diversity, since any errors found as a result of validation represent an important type of "diversity" that will require software changes (bug fixes). It is not particularly difficult to write software that cannot really be validated no matter how much it is tested. This is because even moderately large "useful" software components frequently cover such a large range of outputs that exhaustive testing of all possible outputs would take eons with even the fastest computers. *Structuring for validation* thus becomes one important constraint for producing software that can be shown to be acceptably reliable within a reasonable time frame. The concept of *unit testing* parallels structuring for validation, and is used in parallel with the construction process to help ensure that validation occurs before the overall structure gets "out of hand" and can no longer be readily validated.

3.1.4. Use of External Standards

A natural language that is spoken by one person would be of little value in communicating with the rest of the world. Similarly, a construction language that has meaning only within the software for which it was constructed can be a serious roadblock in the long-term use of that software. Such construction languages therefore should either conform to *external standards* such as those used for programming languages, or provide a sufficiently detailed internal "grammar" (e.g., documentation) by which the construction language can later be understood by others. The interplay between reusing external standards and creating new ones is a complex one, as it depends not only on the availability of such standards, but also on realistic assessments of the long-term viability of such external standards. With the advent of the Internet as a major force in software development and interaction, the importance of selecting and using appropriate external standards for how to construct software is more apparent than ever before. Software that must share data and even working modules with other software anywhere in the world obviously must "share" many of the same languages and methods as that other software. The result is that selection and use of external standards – that is, of standards such as language specifications and data formats that were not originated within a software effort – is becoming more important. This is a complex issue, however, because the selection of an external standard may need to take account of such difficult-to-predict issues as the long-term economic viability of a particular software company or organization that promotes that standard. Stability of the standard is especially important. Also, selecting one level of standardization often opens up an entire new set of standardization issues. An example of this is the data description language XML (eXtensible Markup Language). Selecting XML as an external standard answers many questions about how to describe data in an application, but it also raises the issue of whether one of the several customizations of XML to specific problem domains should also be used.

Other examples of external standards include API standards such as mathematics libraries, POSIX and SQL. In addition there are standards such as ISO/IEC 9126 , IEEE Std 1061, and IEEE Std 982, which are used in both Design and Construction.

3.2. Styles of Construction

Section 3.1 explained four principles of organization. A second and less important method of breaking the subject of software construction into smaller units is to recognize three styles/methods of software construction, namely

- Linguistic

- Formal

- Visual

The traditional hierarchical taxonomy places the items in a tree; each item appears in one place only. Such an approach is not suitable for the items used in software construction because some of the items naturally *belong* in more than one place. In the classification that follows, an individual construction method may appear in many different places, rather than in just one. The number of repetitions indicates its breadth of application, and hence its importance in software construction as a whole. Modularity is one example of a construction method that has such broad impacts.

A good construction language moves detailed, repetitive, or memory-intensive construction tasks away from people and into the computer, where such tasks can be performed faster and more reliably. To accomplish this, construction languages must present and receive information in ways that are readily understandable to human senses and capabilities. This need to rely on human capabilities leads to three major styles of software construction interfaces discussed in the subsections below.

Of course, construction languages seldom rely solely on a single style of construction. Linguistic and formal style in particular are both heavily used in most traditional computer languages, and visual styles and models are a major part of how to make software constructions manageable and understandable in programming languages. Relatively new "visual" construction languages such as Visual Basic and Visual Java provide examples that combine all three styles, with complex visual interfaces often constructed entirely through non-textual interactions with the software constructor. Data processing functionality behind the interfaces can then be constructed using more traditional linguistic and formal styles within the same construction language.

3.2.1. Linguistic

Linguistic construction languages make statements of intent in the form of sentences that resemble natural languages such as English or French. In terms of human senses, linguistic constructions are generally conveyed visually as text, although they can (and are) also sometimes conveyed by sound. A major advantage of linguistic construction interfaces is that they are nearly universal among people. A disadvantage is the imprecision of ordinary languages such a English, which makes it hard for people to express needs clearly with sufficient precision when using linguistic interfaces to computers. An example of this problem is the difficulty that most early students of computer science have learning the syntax of even fairly readable languages such as Pascal or Ada.

Linguistic construction methods are distinguished in particular by the use of word-like strings of text to represent complex software constructions, and the combination of such word-like strings into patterns that have a sentence-like syntax. Properly used, each such string should have a strong semantic connotation that provides an immediate intuitive understanding of what will happen when the underlying software construction is executed. For example, the term "search" has an immediate, readily understandable semantic meaning in English, yet the underlying software implementation of such a term in software can be very complex indeed. The most powerful linguistic construction methods allow users to focus almost entirely on the language-like meanings of such term, as opposed (for example) to frittering away mental efforts on examining minor variations of what "search" means in a particular context.

Linguistic construction methods are further characterized by similar use of other "natural" language skills such as using patterns of words to build sentences, paragraphs, or even entire chapters to express software design "thoughts." For example, a pattern such as "search table for out-of-range values" uses word-like text strings to imitate natural language verbs, nouns, prepositions, and adjectives. Just as having an underlying software structure that allows a more natural use of words reduces the number of issues that a user must address to create new software, an underlying software structure that also allows use of familiar higher-level patterns such as sentence further simplifies the expression process.

Finally, it should be noted that as the complexity of a software expression increases, linguistic construction methods begin to overlap unavoidably with visual methods that make it easier to locate and understand large sequences of statements. Thus just as most written versions of natural languages use visual clues such as spaces between words, paragraphs, and section headings to make text easier to "parse" visually, linguistic construction methods rely on methods such as precise indentation to convey structural information visually.

The use of linguistic construction methods is also limited by our inability to program computers to understand the levels of ambiguity typically found in natural languages, where many subtle issues of context and background can drastically influence interpretation. As a result, the linguistic model of construction usually begins to weaken at the more complex levels of construction that correspond to entire paragraphs and chapters of text.

3.2.2. Formal

The precision and rigor of formal and logical reasoning make this style of human thought especially appropriate for conveying human intent accurately into computers, as well as for verifying the completeness and accuracy of a construction. Unfortunately, formal reasoning is not nearly as universal a skill as natural language, since it requires both innate skills that are not as universal as language skills, and also many years of training and practice to use efficiently and accurately. It can also be argued that certain aspects of good formal reasoning, such as the ability to realize all the implications of a new assertion on all parts of a system, cannot be learned by some people no matter how much training they receive. On the other hand, formal reasoning styles are often notorious for focusing on a problem so intently that all "complications" are discarded and only a very small, very pristine subset of the overall problem is actually addressed. This kind of excessively narrow focus at the expense of any complicating issues can be disastrous in software construction, since it can lead to software that is incapable of dealing with the unavoidable complexities of nearly any usable system.

Formal construction methods rely less on intuitive, everyday meanings of words and text strings, and more on definitions that are backed up by precise, unambiguous, and fully formal (or mathematical) definitions. Formal construction methods are at the heart of most forms of system programming, where precision, speed, and verifiability are more important than ease of mapping into ordinary language. Formal constructions also use precisely defined ways of combining symbols that avoid the ambiguity of many natural language constructions. Functions are an obvious example of formal constructions, with their direct parallel to mathematical functions in both form and meaning.

Formal construction techniques also include the wide range of precisely defined methods for representing and implementing "unique" computer problems such as concurrent and multi-threaded programming, which are in effect classes of mathematical problems that have special meaning and utility within computers.

The importance of the formal style of programming cannot be overstated. Just as the precision of mathematics is fundamental to disciplines such as physics and the hard science, the formal style of programming is fundamental to building up a reliable framework of software "results" that will endure over time. While the linguistic and visual styles work well for interfacing with people, these less precise styles can be unsuitable for building the interior of a software system for the same reason that stained glass should not be used to build the supporting arches of a cathedral. Formal construction provides a foundation that can eliminate entire classes of errors or omissions from ever occurring, whereas linguistic and visual construction methods are much more likely to focus on isolated instances of errors or omissions. Indeed, one very real danger in software quality assurance is to focus too much on capturing isolated errors occurring in the linguistic or visual modes of construction, while overlooking the much more grievous (but harder to identify and understand) errors that occur in the formal style of construction.

3.2.3. Visual

Another very powerful and much more universal construction interface style is *visual,* in the sense of the ability to use the same very sophisticated and necessarily natural ability to "navigate" a complex three-dimensional world of images, as perceived primarily through the eye (but also through tactile senses). The visual interface is powerful not only as a way of organizing information for presentation to a human, but also as a way of conceiving and navigating the overall design of a complex software system. Visual methods are particularly important for systems that require many people to work on them – that is, for organizing a software design process – since they allow a natural way for people to "understand" how and where they must communicate with each other. Visual methods are also important for single-person software construction methods, since they provide ways both to present options to people and to make key details of a large body of information "pop out" to the visual system.

Visual construction methods rely much less on the text-oriented constructions of both linguistic and formal construction, and instead rely on direct visual interpretation and placement of visual entities (e.g., "widgets") that represent the underlying software. Visual construction tends to be somewhat limited by the difficulty of making "complex" statements using only movement of visual entities on a display. However, it can also be a very powerful tool in cases where the primary programming task is simply to build and "adjust" a visual interface to a program whose detailed behavior was defined earlier.

Some argue that object-oriented languages belong in this section because the style of reasoning that they encourage is highly visual. For example, experienced object-oriented programmers tend to view their designs literally as objects interacting in spaces of two or more dimensions, and a plethora of object-oriented design tools and techniques (e.g., Unified Modeling Language, or UML) actively encourage this highly visual style of reasoning. Others argue that object-oriented languages are no more inherently visual than procedural ones. They remark that SA/SD is a popular visual notation for procedural systems.

However, object-oriented methods can also suffer from the lack of precision that is part of the more intuitive visual approach. For example, it is common for new – and sometimes not-so-new – programmers in object-oriented languages to define object classes that lack the formal precision that will allow them to work reliably over user-time (that is, long-term system support) and user-space (e.g., relocation to new environments). The visual intuitions that object-oriented languages provide in such cases can be somewhat misleading, because they can make the real problem of how to define a class to be efficient and stable over user-time and user-space seem to be simpler than it really is. A complete object-oriented construction model therefore must explicitly identify the need for formal construction methods throughout the object design process. The alternative can be an object-based system design that, like a complex stained glass window, looks impressive but is too fragile to be used in any but the most carefully designed circumstances.

More explicitly visual programming methods such as those found in Visual C++ and Visual Basic reduce the problem of how to make precise visual statements by "instrumenting" screen objects with complex (and formally precise) objects that lie behind the screen representations. However, this is done at a substantial loss of generality when compared to using C++ with explicit training in both visual and formal construction, since the screen objects are much more tightly constrained in properties.

3.3. Synthesis

The figure that follows combines the four principles of organization with the three styles of construction. Read the diagram by columns to see the principles, by rows to see the styles.

3.3.1. Reduction in Complexity

3.3.1.1 Linguistic Construction Methods

The main technique for reducing complexity in linguistic construction is to make short, semantically "intuitive" text strings and patterns of text stand in for the much more complex underlying software that "implement" the intuitive meanings. Techniques that reduce complexity in linguistic construction include:

- Design patterns
- Software templates

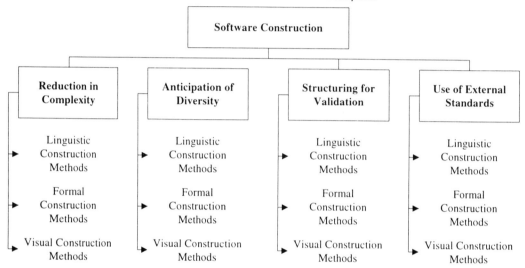

- Functions, procedures, and code blocks
- Objects and data structures
- Encapsulation and abstract data types
- Objects
- Component libraries and frameworks
- Higher-level and domain-specific languages
- Physical organization of source code
- Files and libraries
- Formal inspections

3.3.1.2 Formal Construction Methods

As is the case with linguistic construction methods, formal construction methods reduce complexity by representing complex software constructions as simple text strings. The main difference is that in this case the text strings follow the more precisely defined rules and syntax of formal notations, rather than the "fuzzier" rules of natural language. The reading, writing, and construction of such expressions requires generally more training, but once mastered, the use of formal constructions tends to keep the ambiguity of what is being specified to an absolute minimum. However, as with linguistic construction, the quality of a formal construction is only as good as its underlying implementation. The advantage is that the precision of the formal definitions usually translates into a more precise specification for the software beneath it.

- Traditional functions and procedures
- Functional programming
- Logic programming
- Concurrent and real-time programming techniques
- Spreadsheets
- Program generators
- Mathematical libraries of functions

3.3.1.3 Visual Construction Methods

Especially when compared to the steps needed to build a graphical interface to a program using text-oriented linguistic or formal construction, visual construction can provide drastic reductions in the total effort required. It can also reduce complexity by providing a simple way to select between the elements of a small set of choices.

- Object-oriented programming
- Visual creation and customization of user interfaces
- Visual programming (e.g., visual C++)
- "Style" (visual formatting) aspects of structured programming
- Integrated development environments supporting source browsing

3.3.2. Anticipation of Diversity

3.3.2.1 Linguistic Construction Methods

Linguistic construction anticipates diversity both by permitting extensible definitions of "words," and also by supporting flexible "sentence structures" that allow many different types of intuitively understandable statements to be made with the available vocabulary. An excellent example of using linguistic construction to anticipate diversity is the use of human-readable configuration files to specify software or system settings. Techniques and methods that help anticipate diversity include:

- Information hiding
- Embedded documentation (commenting)
- "Complete and sufficient" method sets
- Object-oriented methods
- Creation of "glue languages" for linking legacy components
- Table-driven software
- Configuration files, internationalization
- Naming and coding styles
- Reuse and repositories
- Self-describing software and hardware (e.g., plug and play)

3.3.2.2 Formal Construction Methods

Diversity in formal construction is handled in terms of precisely defined sets that can vary greatly in size. While mathematical formalizations are capable of very flexible representations of diversity, they require explicit anticipation and preparation for the full range of values that may be needed. A common problem in software construction is to use a formal technique – e.g., a fixed-length vector or array – when what is really needed to accommodate future diversity is a more generic solution that anticipates future growth – e.g., an indefinite variable-length vector. Since more generic solutions are often harder to implement and harder to make efficient, it is important when using formal construction techniques to try to anticipate the full range of future versions.

- Functional parameterization
- Macro parameterization
- Generics
- Objects
- Error handling
- Extensible mathematical frameworks

3.3.2.3 Visual Construction Methods

Provided that the total sets of choices are not overly large, visual construction methods can provide a good way to configure or select options for software or a system. Visual construction methods are analogous to linguistic configuration files in this usage, since both provide easy ways to specify and interpret configuration information.

- Object classes
- Visual configuration specification
- Separation of GUI design and functionality implementation (part of design)

3.3.3. Structuring for Validation

3.3.3.1 Linguistic Construction Methods

Because natural language in general is too ambiguous to allow safe interpretation of completely free-form statements, structuring for validation shows up primarily as rules that at least partially constrain the free use of natural expressions in software. The objective is to make such constructions as "natural" sounding as possible, while not losing the structure and precision needed to ensure consistent interpretations of the source code by both human users and computers.

- Modular design
- Structured programming
- Style guides
- Stepwise refinement

3.3.3.2 Formal Construction Methods

Since mathematics in general is oriented towards proof of hypothesis from a set of axioms, formal construction techniques provide a broad range of techniques to help validate the acceptability of a software unit. Such methods can also be used to "instrument" programs to look for failures based on sets of preconditions.

- Assertion-based programming (static and dynamic)
- State machine logic
- Redundant systems, self-diagnosis, and fail-safe methods
- Hot-spot analysis and performance tuning

- Numerical analysis

3.3.3.3 Visual Construction Methods

Visual construction can provide immediate, active validation of requests and attempted configurations when the visual constructs are "instrumented" to look for invalid feature combinations and warn users immediately of what the problem is.

- "Complete and sufficient" design of object-oriented class methods
- Dynamic validation of visual requests in visual languages

3.3.4. External Standards

3.3.4.1 Linguistic Construction Methods

Traditionally, standardization of programming languages was one of the first areas in which external standards appeared. The goal was (and is) to provide standard meanings and ways of using "words" in each standardized programming language, which makes it possible both for users to understand each other's software, and for the software to be interpreted consistently in diverse environments.

- Standardized programming languages (e.g., Ada 95, C++, etc.)
- Standardized data description languages (e.g., XML, SQL)
- Standardized alphabet representations (e.g., Unicode)

- Standardized documentation (e.g., JavaDoc)
- Inter-process communication standards (e.g., COM, CORBA)
- Component-based software
- Foundation classes (e.g., MFC, JFC)

3.3.4.2 Formal Construction Methods

For formal construction techniques, external standards generally address ways to define precise interfaces and communication methods between software systems and the machines they reside on.

- POSIX standards
- Data communication standards
- Hardware interface standards
- Standardized mathematical representation languages (e.g., MathML)
- Mathematical libraries of functions

3.3.4.3 Visual Construction Methods

Standards for visual interfaces greatly ease the total burden on users by providing familiar, easily understood "look and feel" interfaces for those users.

- Object-oriented language standards
- Standardized screen widgets
- Visual Markup Languages

4. MATRIX OF TOPICS VS. REFERENCE MATERIAL

Topics	Proposed reference material
Software Construction and Software Design	[GLA95] Part III, IV [MAZ96] Part IV [McCO93] Chap. 1, 2, 3
The Role of Tools in Construction	[HUN00] Chap. 3 [MAG93] Chap. 4 [MAZ96] Part IV [McCO93] Chap. 20
The Role of Integrated Evaluation in Construction	[HUM97] [MAG93] Chap. 8 [McCO93] Chap. 31, 32, 33
The Role of Standards in Construction	[IEEE]
Manual and Automated Construction / The Spectrum of Construction Techniques	[HUN00] Chap. 3
Construction Languages	[HUN00] Chap. 3 [SET96]
Programming Languages	[SET96]
A. Reduction in Complexity	
1. Reduction in Complexity (Linguistic)	[BEN00] Chap. 2, 3 [KER99] Chap. 2, 3 [McCO93] Chap. 4 to 19

Topics	Proposed reference material
2. Reduction in Complexity (Formal)	[BOO94] Part II and V [MAG93] Chap. 6 [MEY97] Chap. 6, 10
3. Reduction in Complexity (Visual)	[HOR99] Part II [WAR99] Chap. 1, 2, 3, 4, 5, 10
B. Anticipation of Diversity	
1. Anticipation of Diversity (Linguistic)	[BOO94] Part VI [McCO93] Chap. 30
2. Anticipation of Diversity (Formal)	[BEN00] Chap. 11, 13, 14 [KER99] Chap. 2, 9
3. Anticipation of Diversity (Visual)	[WAR99] Chap. 1, 2, 3, 4, 5, 10
C. Structuring for Validation	
1. Structuring for Validation (Linguistic)	[BEN00] Chap. 4 [KER99] Chap. 1, 5, 6 [MAG93] Chap. 2, 5, 7 [McCO93] Chap. 23, 24, 25, 26
2. Structuring for Validation (Formal)	[MAG93] Chap. 3 [MEY97] Chap. 6, 11
3. Structuring for Validation (Visual)	[HOR99] Part IV [MEY97] Chap. 11
D. Use of External Standards	
1. Use of External Standards (Linguistic)	http://www.xml.org/ http://www.omg.org/corba/beginners.html
2. Use of External Standards (Formal)	Object Constraint Language: http://www.omg.org/uml/
3. Use of External Standards (Visual)	http://www.omg.org/uml/

5. RECOMMENDED REFERENCES FOR SOFTWARE CONSTRUCTION

[BEN00] Bentley, Jon, Programming Pearls (Second Edition). Addison-Wesley, 2000. (Chapters 2, 3, 4, 11, 13 14)[BEN00] Bentley, Jon, Programming Pearls (Second Edition). Addison-Wesley, 2000. (Chapters 2, 3, 4, 11, 13 14)

[BOO94] Booch, Grady, and Bryan, Doug, Software Engineering with Ada (Third edition). Benjamin/Cummings, 1994. (Parts II, IV, V)[HOR99]

[KER99] Kernighan, Brian W., and Pike, Rob, The Practice of Programming. Addison-Wesley, 1999. (Chapters 1, 2, 3, 5, 6, 9)

[MAG93] Maguire, Steve, Writing Solid Code – Microsoft's Techniques for Developing Bug-Free C Software. Microsoft Press, 1993.

[McCO93] McConnell, Steve, Code Complete: A Practical Handbook of Software Construction. Microsoft Press, 1993.

[MEY97] Meyer, Bertrand, Object-Oriented Software Construction (Second Edition). Prentice-Hall, 1997. (Chapters 6, 10, 11)

[SET96] Sethi, Ravi, Programming Languages – Concepts & Constructs (Second Edition). Addison-Wesley, 1996. (Parts II, III, IV, V)

[WAR99] Warren, Nigel, and Bishop, Philip, Java in Practice – Design Styles and Idioms for Effective Java. Addison-Wesley, 1999. (Chapters 1, 2, 3, 4, 5, 10)

APPENDIX A – LIST OF FURTHER READINGS

[BAR98] Barker, Thomas T., *Writing Software Documentation – A Task-Oriented Approach.* Allyn & Bacon, 1998.

[FOW99] Fowler, Martin, *Refactoring – Improving the Design of Existing Code.* Addison-Wesley, 1999.

[GLA95] Glass, Robert L., *Software Creativity.* Prentice-Hall, 1995.

[HEN97] Henricson, Mats, and Nyquist, Erik, *Industrial Strength C++.* Prentice-Hall, 1997.

[HOR99] Horrocks, Ian, *Constructing the User Interface with Statecharts.* Addison-Wesley, 1999.

[HUM97] Humphrey, Watts S., *Introduction to the Personal Software Process.* Addison-Wesley, 1997.

[HUN00] Hunt, Andrew, and Thomas, David, *The Pragmatic Programmer.* Addison-Wesley, 2000.

[MAZ96] Mazza, C., et al., *Software Engineering Guides.* Prentice-Hall, 1996. (Part IV)

Standards

IEEE Std 829-1983 (Reaff 1991), IEEE Standard for Software Test Documentation (ANSI)

IEEE Std 1008-1987 (Reaff 1993), IEEE Standard for Software Unit Testing (ANSI)

IEEE Std 1028-1988 (Reaff 1993), IEEE Standard for Software Reviews and Audits (ANSI)

IEEE Std 1063-1987 (Reaff 1993), IEEE Standard for Software User Documentation (ANSI)

ISO/IEC 12207: 1995 Information technology – Software Life Cycle Processes and IEEE/EIA 12207.0, 12207.1 and 12207.2 ISO/IEC 14674:1999 Information Technology – Software Maintenance

ISO/IEC 14674:1999 Information Technology – Software Maintenance

APPENDIX B – A PROPOSED ALTERNATE BREAKDOWN FOR A SOFTWARE CONSTRUCTION KNOWLEDGE AREA

1. Construction Planning
2. Code Design
3. Data Design and Management
4. Error Processing
5. Source Code Organization
6. Code Documentation
7. Construction Quality Assurance
8. System Integration and Deployment
9. Code Tuning
10. Construction Tools

Source: Adapted from Mc Connell, Steve, "Code Complete: A Practical Handbook of Software Construction," Microsoft Press, 1993.

CHAPTER 5

SOFTWARE TESTING

Antonia Bertolino
Istituto di Elaborazione della Informazione
Consiglio Nazionale delle Ricerche
Research Area of S. Cataldo
56100 PISA (Italy)
bertolino@iei.pi.cnr.it

Table of Contents

1 INTRODUCTION

Testing is an important, mandatory part of software development; it is a technique for evaluating product quality and also for indirectly improving it, by identifying defects and problems.

As more extensively discussed in the *Software Quality* chapter of the Guide to the SWEBOK, the right attitude towards quality is one of prevention: it is obviously much better to avoid problems, rather than repairing them. Testing must be seen as a means primarily for checking whether the prevention has been effective, but also for identifying anomalies in those cases in which, for some reason, it has been not. It is perhaps obvious, but worth recognizing, that even after successfully completing an extensive testing campaign, the software could still contain faults; nor is defect free code a synonymous for quality product. The remedy to system failures that are experienced after delivery is provided by (corrective) maintenance actions. Maintenance topics are covered into the *Software Maintenance* chapter of the Guide to the SWEBOK.

In the years, the view of Software Testing has evolved towards a more constructive attitude. Testing is no longer seen as an activity that starts only after the coding phase is complete, with the limited purpose of detecting failures. Software testing is nowadays seen as an activity that should encompass the whole development process, and is an important part itself of the actual product construction. Indeed, planning for testing should start since the early stages of requirement analysis, and test plans and

procedures must be systematically and continuously refined as the development proceeds. These activities of planning and designing tests constitute themselves a useful input to designers for highlighting potential weaknesses (like, e.g., design oversights or contradictions, and omissions or ambiguities in the documentation).

In the already referred *Software Quality* (SQ) chapter of the Guide to the SWEBOK, activities and techniques for quality analysis are categorized into: *static techniques* (no code execution), and *dynamic techniques* (code execution). Both categories are useful. Although this chapter focuses on testing, that is dynamic (see Sect. 2), static techniques are as important for the purposes of evaluating product quality and finding defects. Static techniques are covered into the SQ Knowledge Area description.

2 DEFINITION OF THE SOFTWARE TESTING KNOWLEDGE AREA

Software testing consists of the **dynamic** verification of the behavior of a program on a **finite** set of test cases, suitably **selected** from the usually infinite executions domain, against the specified **expected** behavior.

In the above definition, and in the following as well, underlined words correspond to key issues in identifying the Knowledge Area of Software Testing. In particular:

*   **dynamic:** this term means *testing always implies executing the program on (valued) inputs*. To be precise, the input value alone is not always sufficient to determine a test, as a complex, non deterministic system might react with different behaviors to a same input, depending on the system state. In the following, though, the term "input" will be maintained, with the implied convention that it also includes a specified input state, in those cases in which it is needed. Different from testing, and complementary with it, are static analysis techniques, such as peer review and inspection (that sometimes are improperly referred to as "static testing"); these are not considered as part of this Knowledge Area (nor is program execution on symbolic inputs, or symbolic evaluation);

*   **finite:** for even simple programs, so many test cases are theoretically possible that exhaustive testing could

require even years to execute. This is why in practice the whole test set can generally be considered infinite. But, the number of executions which can realistically be observed in testing must obviously be finite. Clearly, "enough" testing should be performed to provide reasonable assurance. Indeed, testing always implies a *trade-off* between limited resources and schedules, and inherently unlimited test requirements: this conflict points to well known problems of testing, both technical in nature (criteria for deciding test adequacy) and managerial in nature (estimating the effort to put in testing);

- **selected:** the many proposed *test techniques* essentially differ in how they select the (finite) test set, and testers must be aware that different selection criteria may yield largely different effectiveness. How to identify the most suitable selection criterion under given conditions is a very complex problem; in practice risk analysis techniques and test engineering expertise are applied;

- **expected:** it must be possible (although not always easy) to decide whether the observed outcomes of program execution are acceptable or not, otherwise the testing effort would be useless. The observed behavior may be checked against user's expectations (commonly referred to as testing for validation) or against a specification (testing for verification). The test pass/fail decision is commonly referred in the testing literature to as the *oracle problem*, which can be addressed with different approaches, for instance by human inspection of results or by comparison with an existing reference system. In some situations, the expected behavior may only be partially specified, i.e., only some parts of the actual behavior need to be checked against some stated assertion.

2.1 Conceptual Structure of the Breakdown

Software testing is usually performed at **different levels** along the development process. That is to say, the **target of the test** can vary: a whole system, parts of it (related by purpose, use, behavior, or structure), a single module.

The testing is conducted in view of a specific purpose (**test objective**), which is stated more or less explicitly, and with varying degrees of precision. Stating the objective in precise, quantitative terms allows for establishing control over the test process.

One of testing aims is to expose failures (as many as possible), and many popular **test techniques** have been developed for this objective. These techniques variously attempt to "break" the program, by running one [or more] test[s] drawn from identified classes of (deemed equivalent) executions. The leading principle underlying such techniques is being as much systematic as possible in identifying a representative set of program behaviors (generally in the form of subclasses of the input domain). However, a comprehensive view of the Knowledge Area of Software Testing as a means for quality must include other

as important objectives for testing, e.g., reliability measurement, usability evaluation, contractor's acceptance, for which different approaches would be taken. Note that the test objective varies with the test target, i.e., in general *different purposes are addressed at the different levels of testing.*

The test target and test objective together determine how the test set is identified; both with regard to its consistency -*how much testing is enough for achieving the stated objective?*- and its composition -*which test cases should be selected for achieving the stated objective?*- (although usually the "*for achieving the stated objective*" part is left implicit and only the first part of the two italicized questions above is posed). Criteria for addressing the first question are referred to as *test adequacy criteria*, while for the second as *test selection criteria*.

Sometimes, it can happen that confusion is made between test objectives and techniques. Test techniques are to be viewed as aids that help to ensure the achievement of test objectives. For instance, branch coverage is a popular test technique. Achieving a specified branch coverage measure should not be considered *per se* as the objective of testing: it is a means to improve the chances of finding failures (by systematically exercising every program branch out of a decision point). To avoid such misunderstandings, a clear distinction should be made between **test measures** which evaluate the thoroughness of the test set, like measures of coverage, and those which instead provide an evaluation of the program under test, based on the observed test outputs, like reliability.

Testing concepts, strategies, techniques and measures need to be integrated into a defined and controlled process, which is run by people. The **test process** supports testing activities and provide guidance to testing teams, from test planning to test outputs evaluation, in such a way as to provide justified assurance that the test objectives are met cost-effectively.

Software testing is a very expensive and labor-intensive part of development. For this reason, **tools** are instrumental for automated test execution, test results logging and evaluation, and in general to support test activities. Moreover, in order to enhance cost-effectiveness ratio, a key issue has always been pushing test automation as much as possible.

2.2 Overview

Following the above-presented conceptual scheme, the Software Testing Knowledge Area description is organized as follows.

Part A deals with *Testing Basic Concepts and Definitions*. It covers the basic definitions within the Software Testing field, as well as an introduction to the terminology. In the same part, the scope of the Knowledge Area is laid down, also in relation with other activities.

Part B deals with *Test Levels*. It consists of two (orthogonal) subsections: B.1 lists the levels in which the testing of large software systems is traditionally subdivided. In B.2 testing for specific conditions or properties is instead considered, and is referred to as "Objectives of testing". Clearly not all types of testing apply to every system, nor has every possible type been listed, but those most generally applied.

As said, several *Test Techniques* have been developed in the last two decades according to various criteria, and new ones are still proposed. "Generally accepted" techniques are covered in Part C.

Test-related Measures are dealt in Part D.

Finally, issues relative to *Managing the Test Process* are covered in Part E.

Existing tools and concepts related to supporting and automating the activities into the test process are not addressed here. They are covered within the Knowledge Area description of *Software Engineering Tools and Methods* in this Guide.

3 BREAKDOWN OF TOPICS FOR THE SOFTWARE TESTING KNOWLEDGE AREA

This section gives the list of topics identified for the Software Testing Knowledge Area, with succinct descriptions and references. Two levels of references are provided with topics: the recommended references within brackets, and additional references within parentheses. In particular, the recommended references for Software Testing have been identified into selected book chapters (for instance, Chapter 1 of reference Be is denoted as Be:c1), or, in some cases, sections (for instance, Section 1.4 of Chapter 1 of Be is denoted as Be:c1s1.4). The Further Readings list includes several refereed journal and conference papers and some relevant standards, for a deeper study of the pointed arguments.

A chart in Figure 1 gives a graphical presentation of the top-level decomposition of the breakdown for the Software Testing Knowledge Area. The finer decomposition of the five level 1 topics into the lowest level entries is then summarised by the following five tables (note that two alternative decompositions are proposed for the level 1 topic of Testing Techniques)

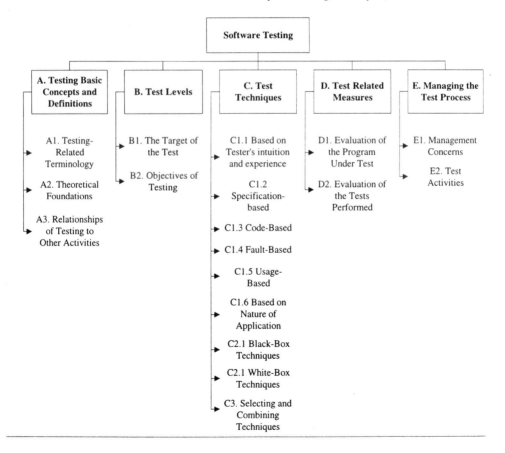

Table 1-A: Decomposition for Testing Basic Concepts and Definitions		
A. Testing Basic Concepts and Definitions	*A1. Testing-related terminology*	Definitions of testing and related terminology
		Faults vs. Failures
	A2. Theoretical foundations	Test selection criteria/Test adequacy criteria (or stopping rules)
		Testing effectiveness/Objectives for testing
		Testing for defect removal
		The oracle problem
		Theoretical and practical limitations of testing
		The problem of infeasible paths
		Testability
	A3. Relationships of testing to other activities	Testing vs. Static Analysis Techniques
		Testing vs. Correctness Proofs and Formal Verification
		Testing vs. Debugging
		Testing vs. Programming
		Testing within SQA
		Testing within Cleanroom
		Testing and Certification

Table 1-B: Decomposition for Test Levels		
B. Test Levels	*B1. The target of the test*	Unit testing
		Integration testing
		System testing
	B2. Objectives of testing	Acceptance/qualification testing
		Installation testing
		Alpha and Beta testing
		Conformance testing/ Functional testing/ Correctness testing
		Reliability achievement and evaluation by testing
		Regression testing
		Performance testing
		Stress testing
		Back-to-back testing
		Recovery testing
		Configuration testing
		Usability testing

Table 1-C: Decomposition for Test Techniques			
C. Test Techniques	C1: (criterion "base on which tests are generated")	*C1.1 Based on tester's intuition and experience*	Ad hoc
		C1.2 Specification-based	Equivalence partitioning
			Boundary-value analysis
			Decision table
			Finite-state machine-based
			Testing from formal specifications
			Random testing
		C1.3 Code-based	Reference models for code-based testing (flow graph, call graph)
			Control flow-based criteria
			Data flow-based criteria
		C1.4 Fault-based	Error guessing
			Mutation testing
		C1.5 Usage-based	Operational profile
			SRET
		C1.6 Based on nature of application	Object-oriented testing
			Component-based testing
			Web-based testing
			GUI testing
			Testing of concurrent programs
			Protocol conformance testing
			Testing of distributed systems
			Testing of real-time systems
			Testing of scientific software
	C2: (criterion "ignorance or knowledge of implementation")	*C2.1 Black-box techniques*	Equivalence partitioning
			Boundary-value analysis
			Decision table
			Finite-state machine-based
			Testing from formal specifications
			Error guessing
			Random testing
			Operational profile
			SRET
		C2.2 White-box techniques	Reference models for code-based testing (flow graph, call graph)
			Control flow-based criteria
			Data flow-based criteria
			Mutation testing
	C3 Selecting and combining techniques		Functional and structural
			Coverage and operational/Saturation effect

Table 1-D: Decomposition for Test Related Measures		
D. Test Related Measures	*D.1 Evaluation of the program under test*	Program measurements to aid in planning and designing testing
		Types, classification and statistics of faults
		Remaining number of defects/Fault density
		Life test, reliability evaluation
		Reliability growth models
	D.2 Evaluation of the tests performed	Coverage/thoroughness measures
		Fault seeding
		Mutation score
		Comparison and relative effectiveness of different techniques

Table 1-E: Decomposition for Managing the Test Process		
E. Managing the Test Process	*E.1 Management concerns*	Attitudes/Egoless programming
		Test process
		Test documentation and workproducts
		Internal vs. independent test team
		Cost/effort estimation and other process measures
		Termination
		Test reuse and test patterns
	E.2 Test activities	Planning
		Test case generation
		Test environment development
		Execution
		Test results evaluation
		Problem reporting/Test log
		Defect tracking

A. Testing Basic Concepts and Definitions

A1. Testing-related terminology

- Definitions of testing and related terminology [Be:c1; Jo:c1,2,3,4; Ly:c2s2.2] (610)

A comprehensive introduction to the Knowledge Area of Software Testing is provided by the core references. Moreover, the IEEE Standard Glossary of Software Engineering Terminology (610) defines terms for the whole field of software engineering, including testing-related terms.

- Faults vs. Failures [Ly:c2s2.2; Jo:c1; Pe:c1; Pf:c7] (FH+; Mo; ZH+:s3.5; 610; 982.2:fig3.1.1-1; 982.2:fig6.1-1)

Many terms are used in the software literature to speak of malfunctioning, notably *fault, failure, error,* and several others. Often these terms are used interchangeably. However, in some cases they are given a more precise meaning (unfortunately, not in consistent ways between different sources), in order to identify the subsequent steps of the cause-effect chain that originates somewhere, e.g., in the head of a designer, and eventually leads to the system's user observing an undesired effect. This terminology is precisely defined in the IEEE Standard 610.12-1990, Standard Glossary of Software Engineering Terminology (610) and is also discussed in more depth in the Software Quality Knowledge Area (Chapter 11, Sect. 7). What is essential to discuss Software Testing, as a minimum, is to clearly distinguish between the *cause* for a malfunctioning, for which either of the terms *fault* or *defect* will be used here, and an undesired effect observed in the system delivered service, that will be called a *failure*. It is important to clarify that testing can reveal failures, but then it is the faults that can and must be removed.

However, it should also be recognized that not always the cause of a failure can be unequivocally identified, i.e., no theoretical criteria exists to uniquely say what the fault was that caused a failure. One may choose to say the fault was what had to be modified to remove the problem, but other modifications could have worked just as well. To avoid ambiguities, some authors instead of faults prefer to speak in terms of *failure-causing inputs* (FH+), i.e., those sets of inputs that when executed cause a failure.

A2. *Theoretical foundations*

- Test selection criteria/Test adequacy criteria (or stopping rules) [Pf:c7s7.3; ZH+:s1.1] (We-b; WW+; ZH+)

A test criterion is a means of deciding which a suitable set of test cases should be. A criterion can be used for selecting the test cases, or for checking if a selected test suite is adequate, i.e., to decide if the testing can be stopped. In mathematical terminology it would be a decision predicate defined on triples (P, S, T), where P is a program, S is the specification (intended here to mean in general sense any relevant source of information for testing) and T is a test set. Some generally used criteria are mentioned in Part C.

- Testing effectiveness/Objectives for testing [Be:c1s1.4; Pe:c21] (FH+)

Testing amounts at observing a sample of program executions. The selection of the sample can be guided by different objectives: it is only in light of the objective pursued that the effectiveness of the test set can be evaluated. This important issue is discussed at some length in the references provided.

- Testing for defect identification [Be:c1; KF+:c1]

In testing for defect identification a successful test is one that causes the system to fail. This is quite different from testing to demonstrate that the software meets its specification, or other desired properties, whereby testing is successful if no (important) failures are observed.

- The oracle problem [Be:c1] (We-a; BS)

An oracle is any (human or mechanical) agent that decides whether a program behaved correctly on a given test, and produces accordingly a verdict of "pass" or "fail". There exist many different kinds of oracles; oracle automation can be very difficult and expensive.

- Theoretical and practical limitations of testing [KF+:c2] (Ho)

Testing theory warns against putting a not justified level of confidence on series of passed tests. Unfortunately, most established results of testing theory are negative ones, i.e., they state what testing can never achieve (as opposed to what it actually achieved). The most famous quotation in this regard is Dijkstra aphorism that "program testing can be used to show the *presence* of bugs, but never to show their absence". The obvious reason is that complete testing is not feasible in real systems. Because of this, testing must be driven based on risk, i.e., testing can also be seen as a risk management strategy.

- The problem of infeasible paths [Be:c3]

Infeasible paths, i.e., control flow paths which cannot be exercised by any input data, are a significant problem in path-oriented testing, and particularly in the automated derivation of test inputs for code-based testing techniques.

- Testability [Be:c3,c13] (BM; BS; VM)

The term of software testability has been recently introduced in the literature with two related, but different meanings: on the one hand as the degree to which it is easy for a system to fulfill a given test coverage criterion, as in (BM); on the other hand, as the likelihood (possibly measured statistically) that the system exposes a failure under testing, *if* it is faulty, as in (VM, BS). Both meanings are important.

A3. *Relationships of testing to other activities*

Here the relation between the Software Testing and other related activities of software engineering is considered. Software Testing is related to, but different from, static analysis techniques, proofs of correctness, debugging and programming. On the other side, it is informative to consider testing from the point of view of software quality analysts, users of CMM and Cleanroom processes, and of certifiers.

- Testing vs. Static Analysis Techniques [Be:c1; Pe:c17p359-360] (1008:p19)
- Testing vs. Correctness Proofs and Formal Verification [Be:c1s5; Pf:c7]
- Testing vs. Debugging [Be:c1s2.1] (1008:p19)
- Testing vs. Programming [Be:c1s2.3]
- Testing within SQA (see the SQ Chapter in this Guide)
- Testing within CMM (Po:p117-123)
- Testing within Cleanroom [Pf:c8s8.9]
- Testing and Certification (WK+)

B. Test Levels

B1. *The target of the test*

Testing of large software systems usually involves more steps [Be:c1; Jo:c12; Pf:c7].

Three big test stages can be conceptually distinguished, namely Unit, Integration and System. No process model is implied in this Guide, nor any of those three stages is assumed to have a higher importance than the other two. Depending on the development model followed, these three stages will be adopted and combined in different paradigms, and quite often more than one iteration between them is necessary.

- Unit testing [Be:c1; Pe:c17; Pf:c7s7.3] (1008)

Unit testing verifies the functioning in isolation of software pieces that are separately testable. Depending on the context, these could be the individual subprograms or a larger component made of tightly related units. A test unit is defined more precisely in the IEEE Standard for Software Unit Testing [1008], that also describes an integrated approach to systematic and documented unit testing. Typically, unit testing occurs with access to the code being tested and with the support of debugging tools, and might involve the same programmers. Clearly, unit testing starts after coding is quite mature, for instance after a clean compile.

- Integration testing [Jo:c12,13; Pf:c7s7.4]

Integration testing is the process of verifying the interaction between system components (possibly, and hopefully, already tested in isolation). Classical integration testing strategies, such as top-down or bottom-up, are used with traditional, hierarchically structured systems. Modern systematic integration strategies are rather architecture driven, which implies integrating the software components or subsystems based on identified functional threads: integration testing is a continuous activity, at each stage of which testers must abstract away lower level perspectives and concentrate on the perspectives of the level they are integrating. Except for small, simple systems, systematic, incremental integration testing strategies are to be preferred to putting all components together at once, that is pictorially said "big-bang" testing.

- System testing [Jo:c14; Pf:c8]

System testing is concerned with the behavior of a whole system. The majority of functional failures should have been already identified during unit and integration testing. System testing should compare the system to the non-functional system requirements, such as security, speed, accuracy, and reliability. External interfaces to other applications, utilities, hardware devices, or the operating environment are also evaluated at this level.

B2. Objectives of Testing [Pe:c8; Pf:c8s8.3]

Testing of a software system (or subsystem) can be aimed at verifying different properties. Test cases can be designed to check that the functional specifications are correctly implemented, which is variously referred to in the literature as conformance testing, "correctness" testing, functional testing. However several other non-functional properties need to be tested as well, including conformance, reliability and usability among many others.

References cited above give essentially a collection of the potential different purposes. The topics separately listed below (with the same or additional references) are those most often cited in the literature. Note that some kinds of testing are more appropriate for custom made packages (e.g., installation testing), while others for generic products (e.g., beta testing).

- Acceptance/qualification testing [Pe:c10; Pf:c8s8.5] (12207:s5.3.9)

Acceptance testing checks the system behavior against the customer's requirements (the "contract"); the customers undertake (or specify) typical tasks to check their requirements. This testing activity may or may not involve the developers of the system.

- Installation testing [Pe:c9; Pf:c8s8.6]

After completion of system and acceptance testing, the system is verified upon installation in the target environment, i.e., system testing is conducted according to the hardware configuration requirements. Installation procedures are also verified.

- Alpha and Beta testing [KF+:c13]

Before releasing the system, sometimes it is given in use to a small representative set of potential users, in-house (alpha testing) or external (beta testing), who report potential experienced problems with use of the product. Alpha and beta use is often uncontrolled, i.e., the testing does not refer to a test plan.

- Conformance testing/Functional testing/Correctness testing [KF+:c7; Pe:c8] (WK+)

Conformance testing is aimed at verifying whether the observed behavior of the tested system conforms to its specification.

- Reliability achievement and evaluation by testing [Pf:c8s.8.4; Ly:c7] (Ha; Musa and Ackermann in Po:p146-154)

By testing failures can be detected, and afterwards, if the faults that are the cause of the identified failures are efficaciously removed, the software will be more reliable. In this sense, testing is a means to improve reliability. On the other hand, by randomly generating test cases accordingly to the operational profile, statistical measures of reliability can be derived. Using reliability growth models, both objectives can be pursued together (see also part D.1).

- Regression testing [KF+:c7; Pe:c11,c12; Pf:c8s8.1] (RH)

According to (610), regression testing is the "selective retesting of a system or component to verify that modifications have not caused unintended effects [...]". In practice, the idea is to show that previously passed tests, still do. [Be] defines it as any repetition of tests intended to show that the software's behavior is unchanged except insofar as required. Obviously a tradeoff must be found between the assurance given by regression testing every time a change is made and the resources required to do that.

Regression testing can be conducted at each of the test levels in B.1, and may apply to functional and non-functional testing.

- Performance testing [Pe:c17; Pf:c8s8.3] (WK+)

This is specifically aimed at verifying that the system meets the specified performance requirements, e.g., capacity and response time. A specific kind of performance testing is volume testing (Pe:p185, p487; Pf:p349), in which internal program or system limitations are tried.

- Stress testing [Pe:c17; Pf:c8s8.3]

Stress testing exercises a system at the maximum design load as well as beyond it.

- Back-to-back testing

A same test set is presented to two implemented versions of a system, and the results are compared with each other.

- Recovery testing [Pe:c17; Pf:c8s8.3]

It is aimed at verifying system restart capabilities after a "disaster".

- Configuration testing [KF+:c8; Pf:c8s8.3]

In those cases in which a system is built to serve different users, configuration testing analyzes the system under the various specified configurations.

- Usability testing [Pe:c8; Pf:c8s8.3]

It evaluates the ease of using and learning the system (and system user documentation) by the end users, as well as the effectiveness of system functioning in supporting user tasks, and finally the ability of recovering from user's errors.

C. Test Techniques

In this section, two alternative classifications of test techniques are proposed. It is arduous to find a homogeneous criterion for classifying all techniques, as there exist many and very disparate.

The first classification, from C1.1 to C1.6, is based on how tests are generated, i.e., respectively from: tester's intuition and expertise, the specifications, the code structure, the (real or artificial) faults to be discovered, the field usage or finally the nature of application, which in some case can require knowledge of specific test problems and of specific test techniques.

The second classification is the classical distinction of test techniques between *black-box* and *white-box* (pictorial terms derived from the world of integrated circuit testing). Test techniques are here classified according to whether the tests rely on information about how the software has been designed and coded (white-box, somewhere also said glass-box), or instead only rely on the input/output behavior, without no assumption about what happens in between the "pins" (precisely, the entry/exit points) of the system (black box). Clearly this second classification is more coarse than the first one, and it does not allow us to categorize the techniques specialized on the nature of application (section C1.6) nor ad hoc approaches, because these can be either black-box or white-box. Also note that as new technologies such as Object Oriented or Component-based become more and more widespread, this split becomes more of a theoretical than a practical scope, as information about code and design is hidden or simply not available.

A final section, *C3*, deals with combined use of more techniques.

C1: CLASSIFICATION "based on how tests are generated"

C1.1 Based on tester's intuition and experience [KF+:c1]

Perhaps the most widely practiced technique remains *ad hoc testing*: tests are derived relying on the tester skill and

intuition ("exploratory" testing), and on his/her experience with similar programs. While a more systematic approach is advised, ad hoc testing might be useful (but only if the tester is really expert!) to identify special tests, not easily "captured" by formalized techniques. Moreover it must be reminded that this technique may yield largely varying degrees of effectiveness.

C1.2 Specification-based

- Equivalence partitioning [Jo:c6; KF+:c7]

The input domain is subdivided into a collection of subsets, or "equivalent classes", which are deemed equivalent according to a specified relation, and a representative set of tests (sometimes even one) is taken from within each class.

- Boundary-value analysis [Jo:c5; KF+:c7]

Test cases are chosen on and near the boundaries of the input domain of variables, with the underlying rationale that many defects tend to concentrate near the extreme values of inputs. A simple, and often worth, extension of this technique is *Robustness Testing*, whereby test cases are also chosen outside the domain, in fact to test program robustness to unexpected, erroneous inputs.

- Decision table [Be:c10s3] (Jo:c7)

Decision tables represent logical relationships between conditions (roughly, inputs) and actions (roughly, outputs). Test cases are systematically derived by considering every possible combination of conditions and actions. A related techniques is *Cause-effect graphing* [Pf:c8].

- Finite-state machine-based [Be:c11; Jo:c4s4.3.2]

By modeling a program as a finite state machine, tests can be selected in order to cover states and transitions on it, applying different techniques. This technique is suitable for transaction-processing, reactive, embedded and real-time systems.

- Testing from formal specifications [ZH+:s2.2] (BG+; DF; HP)

Giving the specifications in a formal language (i.e., one with precisely defined syntax and semantics) allows for automatic derivation of functional test cases from the specifications, and at the same time provides a reference output, an oracle, for checking test results. Methods for deriving test cases from model-based (DF, HP) or algebraic specifications (BG+) are distinguished.

- Random testing [Be:c13; KF+:c7]

Tests are generated purely random (not to be confused with statistical testing from the operational profile, where the random generation is biased towards reproducing field usage, see C1.5). Actually, therefore, it is difficult to categorize this technique under the scheme of "base on which tests are generated". It is put under the Specification-based entry, as at least the domain must be known, to be able to pick random points within it.

C1.3   Code-based

• Reference models for code-based testing (flowgraph, call graph) [Be:c3; Jo:c4].

In code-based testing techniques, the control structure of a program is graphically represented using a flowgraph, i.e., a directed graph whose nodes and arcs correspond to program elements. For instance, nodes may represent statements or uninterrupted sequences of statements, and arcs the transfer of control between nodes.

• Control flow-based criteria [Be:c3; Jo:c9] (ZH+:s2.1.1)

Control flow-based coverage criteria aim at covering all the statements or the blocks in a program, or specified combinations of them. Several coverage criteria have been proposed (like Decision/Condition Coverage), in the attempt to get good approximations for the exhaustive coverage of all control flow paths, that is unfeasible for all but trivial programs.

• Data flow-based criteria [Be:c5] (Jo:c10; ZH+:s2.1.2)

In data flow-based testing, the control flowgraph is annotated with information about how the program variables are defined and used. Different criteria exercise with varying degrees of precision how a value assigned to a variable is used along different control flow paths. A reference notion is a definition-use pair, which is a triple (d,u,V) such that: V is a variable, d is a node in which V is defined, and u is a node in which V is used; and such that there exists a path between d and u in which the definition of V in d is used in u.

C1.4   Fault-based (Mo)

With different degrees of formalization, fault based testing techniques devise test cases specifically aimed at revealing categories of likely or pre-defined faults.

• Error guessing [KF+:c7]

In error guessing, test cases are specifically designed by testers trying to figure out those, which could be the most plausible faults in the given program. A good source of information is the history of faults discovered in earlier projects, as well as tester's expertise.

• Mutation testing [Pe:c17; ZH+:s3.2-s3.3]

A mutant is a slightly modified version of the program under test, differing from it by a small, syntactic change. Every test case exercises both the original and all generated mutants: If a test case is successful in identifying the difference between the program and a mutant, the latter is said to be killed. Originally conceived as a technique to evaluate a test set (see D.2.2), mutation testing is also a testing criterion in itself: either tests are randomly generated until enough mutants are killed or tests are specifically designed to kill (survived) mutants. In the latter case, mutation testing can also be categorized as a code-based technique. The underlying assumption of mutation testing, the coupling effect, is that by looking for simple

syntactic faults, also more complex, (i.e., real) faults will be found. For the technique to be effective, a high number of mutants must be automatically derived in systematic way.

C1.5   Usage-based

• Operational profile [Jo:c14s14.7.2; Ly:c5; Pf:c8]

In testing for reliability evaluation, the test environment must reproduce as closely as possible the product use in operation. In fact, from the observed test results one wants to infer the future reliability in operation. To do this, inputs are assigned a probability distribution, or profile, according to their occurrence in actual operation.

• (Musa's) SRET [Ly:c6]

Software Reliability Engineered Testing (SRET) is a testing methodology encompassing the whole development process, whereby testing is "designed and guided by reliability objectives and expected relative usage and criticality of different functions in the field".

C1.6   Based on nature of application

The above techniques apply to all types of software, and their classification is based on how test cases are derived. However, for some kinds of applications some additional know-how is required for test derivation. Here below a list of few "specialized" testing fields is provided, based on the nature of the application under test.

• Object-oriented testing [Jo:c15; Pf:c7s7.5] (Bi)

• Component-based testing

• Web-based testing

• GUI testing (OA+)

• Testing of concurrent programs (CT)

• Protocol conformance testing (Sidhu and Leung in Po:p102-115; BP)

• Testing of distributed systems

• Testing of real-time systems (Sc)

• Testing of scientific software

C2: CLASSIFICATION "ignorance or knowledge of implementation"

As explained at the beginning of Section C, here below an alternative classification of the same test techniques cited so far is proposed (just the headings are mentioned), based on whether knowledge of implementation is exploited to derive the test cases (white-box), or not (black-box).

C2.1   Black-box techniques

• Equivalence partitioning [Jo:c6; KF+:c7]

• Boundary-value analysis [Jo:c5; KF+:c7]

• Decision table [Be:c10s3] (Jo:c7)

• Finite-state machine-based [Be:c11; Jo:c4s4.3.2]

• Testing from formal specifications [ZH+:s2.2] (BG+; DF; HP)

- Error guessing [KF+:c7]
- Random testing [Be:c13; KF+:c7]
- Operational profile [Jo:c14s14.7.2; Ly:c5; Pf:c8]
- (Musa's) SRET [Ly:c6]

C2.2   White-box techniques

- Reference models for code-based testing (flowgraph, call graph) [Be:c3; Jo:c4].
- Control flow-based criteria [Be:c3; Jo:c9] (ZH+:s2.1.1)
- Data flow-based criteria [Be:c5] (Jo:c10; ZH+:s2.1.2)
- Mutation testing [Pe:c17; ZH+:s3.2-s3.3]

C3   Selecting and combining techniques

- Functional and structural [Be:c1s.2.2; Jo:c1, c11s11.3; Pe:c17] (Po:p3-4; Po:Appendix 2)

Specification-based and code-based test techniques are often contrasted as functional vs. structural testing. These two approaches to test selection are not to be seen as alternative, but rather as complementary: in fact, they use different sources of information, and have proved to highlight different kinds of problems. They should be used in combination, compatibly with budget availability.

- Coverage and operational/Saturation effect (Ha; Ly:p541-547; Ze)

Test cases can be selected in deterministic way, according to one of the various listed techniques, or randomly drawn from some distribution of inputs, such as it is usually done in reliability testing. There are interesting considerations one should be aware of, about the different implications of each approach.

D. Test related measures

Measurement is instrumental to quality analysis. Indeed, product evaluation is effective only when based on quantitative measures. Measurement is instrumental also to the optimal planning and execution of tests, and several process measures can be used by the test manager to monitor progress. Measures relative to the test process for management purposes are considered in part E.

A wider coverage of the topic of quality measurement, including fundamentals, measures and techniques for measurement, is provided in the Software Quality chapter of the Guide to the SWEBOK. A comprehensive reference is provided by the IEEE Standard. 982.2 "Guide for the Use of IEEE Standard Dictionary of Measures to Produce Reliable Software", which was originally conceived as a guide to using the companion standard 982.1, that is the Dictionary. However, the guide is also a valid and very useful reference by itself, for selection and application of measures in a project.

Test related measures can be divided into two classes: those relative to evaluating the program under test, and those relative to evaluating the test set. The first class, for instance, includes measures that count and predict either faults (e.g., fault density) or failures (e.g., reliability). The second class instead evaluates the test suites against selected test criteria; notably, this is what is usually done by measuring the code coverage achieved by the executed tests.

D1. Evaluation of the program under test (982.2)

- Program measurements to aid in planning and designing testing. [Be:c7s4.2; Jo:c9] (982.2:sA16, BMa)

Measures based on program size (e.g., Source Lines of Code, function points) or on program structure (e.g., complexity) is useful information to guide the testing. Structural measures can also include measurements among program modules, in terms of the frequency with which modules call each other.

- Types, classification and statistics of faults [Be:c2; Jo:c1; Pf:c7] (1044, 1044.1; Be:Appendix; Ly:c9; KF+:c4, Appendix A)

The testing literature is rich of classifications and taxonomies of faults. Testing allows for discovering defects. To make testing more effective it is important to know which types of faults could be found in the application under test, and the relative frequency with which these faults have occurred in the past. This information can be very useful to make quality predictions as well as for process improvement. The topic "Defect Characterization" is also covered more deeply in the SQA Knowledge Area. An IEEE standard on how to classify software "anomalies" (1044) exists, with a relative guide (1044.1) to implement it. An important property for fault classification is orthogonality, i.e., ensuring that each fault can be unequivocally identified as belonging to one class.

- Fault density [Pe:c20] (982.2:sA1; Ly:c9)

In common industrial practice a product under test is assessed by counting and classifying the discovered faults by their types (see also A1). For each fault class, fault density is measured by the ratio between the number of faults found and the size of the program.

- Life test, reliability evaluation [Pf:c8] (Musa and Ackermann in Po:p146-154)

A statistical estimate of software reliability, that can be obtained by operational testing (see in B.2), can be used to evaluate a product and decide if testing can be stopped.

- Reliability growth models [Ly:c7; Pf:c8] (Ly:c3, c4)

Reliability growth models provide a prediction of reliability based on the failures observed under operational testing. They assume in general that the faults that caused the observed failures are fixed (although some models also accept imperfect fixes) and thus, on average, the product reliability exhibits an increasing trend. There exist now tens of published models, laid down on some common assumptions as well as on differing ones. Notably, the models are divided into *failures-count* and *time-between-failures* models.

D2. Evaluation of the tests performed

*   Coverage/thoroughness measures [Jo:c9; Pf:c7] (982.2:sA5-sA6)

Several test adequacy criteria require the test cases to systematically exercise a set of elements identified in the program or in the specification (see Part C). To evaluate the thoroughness of the executed tests, testers can monitor the elements covered, so that they can dynamically measure the ratio (often expressed as a fraction of 100%) between covered elements and the total number. For example, one can measure the percentage of covered branches in the program flowgraph, or of exercised functional requirements among those listed in the specification document. Code-based adequacy criteria require appropriate instrumentation of the program under test.

*   Fault seeding [Pf:c7] (ZH+:s3.1)

Some faults are artificially introduced into the program before test. When the tests are executed, part of these seeded faults will be revealed, as well as possibly genuine faults. Depending on which and how many of the artificial faults are hit, testing effectiveness can be evaluated; also, one could estimate how many of the genuine faults should remain.

*   Mutation score [ZH+:s3.2-s3.3]

Mutation testing has been described before (within C1.4). The proportion between killed mutants and the total number of generated mutants can be a measure of the effectiveness of the executed test set.

*   Comparison and relative effectiveness of different techniques [Jo:c8,c11; Pe:c17; ZH+:s5] (FW; Weyuker in Po p64-72; FH+)

Several studies have been recently conducted to compare the relative effectiveness of different test techniques. It is important to be precise relative to the property against which the techniques are being assessed, i.e., what "effectiveness" is exactly meant for. Possible interpretations are how many tests are needed to find the first failure, or the ratio of the number of faults found by the testing to all the faults found during and after the testing, or of how much reliability is improved. Analytical and empirical comparisons between different techniques have been conducted according to each of the above specified notions of "effectiveness".

E. Managing the Test Process

E1. Management concerns

*   Attitudes/Egoless programming [Be:c13s3.2; Pf:c7]

A very important component of successful testing is a positive and collaborative attitude towards testing activities. Managers should revert a negative vision of testers as the destroyers of developers' work and as heavy budget consumers. On the contrary, they should foster a common culture towards software quality, by which early failure discover is an objective for all involved people, and not only of testers.

*   Test process [Be:c13; Pe:c1,c2,c3,c4; Pf:c8] (Po:p10-11; Po:Appendix 1; 12207:s5.3.9;s5.4.2;s6.4;s6.5)

A process is defined as "a set of interrelated activities, which transform inputs into outputs"[12207]. Test activities conducted at different levels (see B.1) must be organized, together with people, tools, policies, measurements, into a well defined process, which is integral part to the life cycle. This test process needs control and continuous improvement. In the IEEE/EIA Standard 12207.0 testing is not described as a stand alone process, but principles for testing activities are included along with the five primary life cycle processes, as well as along with the supporting process.

*   Test documentation and workproducts [Be:c13s5; KF+:c12; Pe:c19; Pf:c8s8.8] (829)

Documentation is an integral part of the formalization of the test process. The IEEE standard for Software Test Documentation [829] provides a good description of test documents and of their relationship with one another and with the testing process. Test documents includes, among others, Test Plan, Test Design Specification, Test Procedure Specification, Test Case Specification, Test Log and Test Incident or Problem Report. The program under test, with specified version and identified hw/sw requirements before testing can begin, is documented as the Test Item. Test documentation should be produced and continually updated, at the same standards as other types of documentation in development.

*   Internal vs. independent test team [Be:c13s2.2-2.3; KF+:c15; Pe:c4; Pf:c8]

Formalization of the test process requires formalizing the test team organization as well. The test team can be composed of members internal to the project team (but not directly involved in code development), or of external members, in the latter case bringing in an unbiased, independent perspective, or finally of both internal and external members. The decision will be determined by considerations of costs, schedule, maturity levels of the involved organizations, and criticality of the application.

*   Cost/effort estimation and other process measures [Pe:c4, c21] (Pe: Appendix B; Po:p139-145; 982.2:sA8-sA9)

In addition to those discussed in Part D, several measures relative to the resources spent on testing, as well as to the relative effectiveness in fault finding of the different test phases, are used by managers to control and improve the test process. These test measures may cover such aspects as: number of test cases specified, number of test cases executed, number of test cases passed, number of test cases failed, and similar.

Evaluation of test phase reports is often combined with root cause analysis to evaluate test process effectiveness in finding faults as early as possible. Moreover, the resources that are worth spending in testing should be commensurate to the use/criticality of the application: the techniques listed in part C have different costs, and yield different levels of confidence in product reliability.

- Termination [Be:c2s2.4; Pe:c2]

A critical task of the test manager is to decide how much testing is enough and when a test stage can be terminated. Thoroughness measures such as achieved code coverage or functional completeness, as well as estimates of fault density or of operational reliability, provide useful support, but are not sufficient by themselves. The decision involves also considerations about the costs and risks incurred by potentially remaining failures, as opposed to the costs implied by further continuing to test.

- Test reuse and test patterns [Be:c13s5]

To carry out testing or maintenance in an organized and cost/effective way, the means used to test each part of the system should be reused systematically. At all levels of testing, test scripts, test cases, and expected results should be carefully defined and documented so that they may be reused. This repository of test materials must be configuration controlled, so that changes to system requirements or design can be reflected in changes to the scope of the tests conducted.

The test solutions adopted for testing some application type under certain circumstances, with the motivations behind the decisions taken, form a test pattern, that can itself be documented for later reuse in similar projects.

E2. Test Activities

Here below a brief overview of test activities is given; as often implied by the following description, successful management of test activities strongly depends from the Software Configuration Management process (see Chapter 7 in this Guide).

- Planning [KF+:c12; Pe:c19; Pf:c7s7.6] (829:s4; 1008:s1, s2, s3)

Like any other part of project management, testing activities must be planned. Key aspects of test planning include co-ordination of personnel needed, management of available test facilities and equipment (which may include magnetic media, test plans and procedures), and planning for possible undesirable outcomes. If more than one baseline of the system is being maintained, then a major planning consideration is the time and effort needed to ensure the test environment is set to the proper configuration.

- Test case generation [KF+:c7] (Po:c2; 1008:s4, s5)

Generation of test cases is based on the level of testing to be performed, and the particular testing techniques. Test cases should be configuration controlled and include the expected results for each test.

- Test environment development [KF+:c11]

The environment used for testing should be compatible with the software development environment. It should facilitate development and control of test cases, as well as logging and recovery of expected results, scripts, and other testing materials.

- Execution [Be:c13; KF+:c11] (1008:s6, s7;)

Execution of tests is generally performed by testing engineers with oversight by quality assurance personnel and, in some cases, customer representatives. Execution of tests should embody the basic principles of scientific experimentation: everything done during testing should be performed and documented clearly enough that another person could replicate the same results. Hence testing should be performed in accordance with documented procedures using a clearly defined version of the system under test.

- Test results evaluation [Pe:c20,c21] (Po:p18-20; Po:p131-138)

The results of testing must be evaluated to determine if the test was successful, and to derive specific test measures. In most cases, 'successful' means that the system performed as expected, and did not have any major unexpected outcomes. On the other side, not all unexpected outcomes are necessarily faults, but could be judged as just noise. Before a failure can be removed, analysis and debugging effort is needed to isolate, identify and describe it. When test results are particularly important, a formal review board may be convened to evaluate test results.

- Problem reporting/Test log [KF+:c5; Pe:c20] (829:s9-s10)

All testing activities should be entered into a test log to identify when a test was conducted, who performed the test, what system configuration was the basis for testing, and other relevant identification information. Unexpected or incorrect test results should be recorded in a problem reporting system. The problem reporting system's data forms the basis for later debugging and fixing the problems which were observed as failures during testing. Also anomalies not classified as faults could be documented, in case they later turn out to be more serious than judged. Test Reports are also an input to the Change Management system (which is a part of the Configuration Management system).

- Defect tracking [KF+:c6]

Failures observed during testing are often due to faults or defects in the system. Such defects should be analyzed to determine when they were introduced into the system, what kind of error caused them to be created (e.g. poorly defined requirements, incorrect variable declaration, memory leak, programming syntax error, etc.), and when they could have been first observed in the system. Defect tracking information is used to determine what aspects of system development need improvement and how effective have been previous analyses and testing.

4 BREAKDOWN RATIONALE

The conceptual scheme followed in decomposing the Software Testing Knowledge Area is described in Section 2.1. Level 1 topics include five entries, labeled from A to E, that correspond to the fundamental and complementary concerns forming the Software Testing knowledge: Basic Concepts and Definitions, Levels, Techniques, Measures, and Process. There is not a standard way to decompose the Software Testing Knowledge Area, each book on Software Testing would structure its table of contents in different ways. However any thorough book on Software Testing would cover these five topics. A sixth level 1 topic would be Test Tools. These are not covered here, but in the *Software Engineering Tools and Methods* chapter of the Guide to the SWEBOK.

The breakdown is three levels deep. The second level is for making the decomposition more understandable. The selection of level 3 topics, that are the subjects of study, has been quite difficult. Finding a breakdown of topics that is "generally accepted" by all different communities of potential users of the Guide to the SWEBOK is challenging for Software Testing, because there still exists a wide gap between the literature on Software Testing and current industrial test practice. There are topics that have been taking a relevant position in the academic literature for many years now, but are not generally used in industry, for example data-flow based or mutation testing. The position taken in writing this document has been to include any relevant topics in the literature, even those that are likely not considered so relevant by practitioners at the current time. The proposed breakdown of topics for Software Testing is thus considered as an inclusive list, from which each stakeholder can pick according to his/her needs.

However, under the precise definition for "generally accepted" adopted in the Guide to the SWEBOK (i.e., *knowledge to be included in the study material of a software engineering with four years of work experience*), some of the included topics (like the examples above) would be only lightly (if at all) covered in a curriculum of a software engineer with four years of experience. The recommended references have been therefore selected accordingly, i.e., they provide reading material according to this meaning of "generally accepted", while the more advanced topics are covered in the Further Reading list.

5 MATRIX OF TOPICS VS. REFERENCE MATERIAL

A. Testing Basic Concepts and Definitions	[Be]	[Jo]	[Ly]	[KF+]	[Pe]	[Pf]	[ZH+]
Definitions of testing and related terminology	C1	C1,2,3,4	C2S2.2				
Faults vs. Failures		C1	C2S2.2		C1	C7	
Test selection criteria/Test adequacy criteria (or stopping rules)						C7S7.3	S1.1
Testing effectiveness/Objectives for testing	C1S1.4				C21		
Testing for defect identification	C1			C1			
The oracle problem	C1						
Theoretical and practical limitations of testing					C2		
The problem of infeasible paths	C3						
Testability	C3,13						
Testing vs. Static Analysis Techniques	C1				C17		
Testing vs. Correctness Proofs and Formal Verification	C1S5					C7	
Testing vs. Debugging	C1S2.1						
Testing vs. Programming	C1S2.3						
Testing within SQA							
Testing within CMM							
Testing within Cleanroom						C8S8.9	
Testing and Certification							

B. Test Levels	[Be]	[Jo]	[Ly]	[KF+]	[Pe]	[Pf]
Unit testing	C1				C17	C7S7.3
Integration testing		C12,13				C7S7.4
System testing		C14				C8
Acceptance/qualification testing					C10	C8S8.5
Installation testing					C9	C8S8.6
Alpha and Beta testing				C13		
Conformance testing/ Functional testing/ Correctness testing				C7	C8	
Reliability achievement and evaluation by testing			C7			C8S8.4
Regression testing				C7	C11,12	C8S8.1
Performance testing					C17	C8S8.3
Stress testing					C17	C8S8.3
Back-to-back testing						
Recovery testing					C17	C8S8.3
Configuration testing				C8		C8S8.3
Usability testing					C8	C8S8.3

C. Test Techniques	[Be]	[Jo]	[Ly]	[KF+]	[Pe]	[Pf]	[ZH+]
Ad hoc				C1			
Equivalence partitioning		C6		C7			
Boundary-value analysis		C5		C7			
Decision table	C10S3						
Finite-state machine-based	C11	C4S4.3.2					
Testing from formal specifications							S2.2
Random testing	C13			C7			
Reference models for code-based testing (flow graph, call graph)	C3	C4					
Control flow-based criteria	C3	C9				C7	
Data flow-based criteria	C5						
Error guessing						C7	
Mutation testing					C17		S3.2, 3.3
Operational profile		C14S14.7.2	C5			C8	
SRET			C6				
Object-oriented testing		C15				C7S7.5	
Component-based testing							
Web-based testing							
GUI testing							
Testing of concurrent programs							
Protocol conformance testing							
Testing of distributed systems							
Testing of real-time systems							
Testing of scientific software							
Functional and structural	C1S2.2	C1,11S11.3				C17	
Coverage and operational/Saturation effect							

D. Test Related Measures	[Be]	[Jo]	[Ly]	[KF+]	[Pe]	[Pf]	[ZH+]
Program measurements to aid in planning and designing testing.	C7S4.2	C9					
Types, classification and statistics of faults	C2	C1				C7	
Remaining number of defects/Fault density					C20		
Life test, reliability evaluation						C8	
Reliability growth models			C7			C8	
Coverage/thoroughness measures		C9				C7	
Fault seeding						C7	
Mutation score							S3.2, 3.3
Comparison and relative effectiveness of different techniques		C8,11			C17		S5

E. Managing the Test Process	[Be]	[Jo]	[Ly]	[KF+]	[Pe]	[Pf]
Attitudes/Egoless programming	C13S3.2					C7
Test process	C13				C1,2,3,4	C8
Test documentation and workproducts	C13S5			C12	C19	C8S8.8
Internal vs. independent test team	C13S2.2,2.3			C15	C4	C8
Cost/effort estimation and other process measures					C4,21	
Termination	C2S2.4				C2	
Test reuse and test patterns	C13					
Planning				C12	C19	C7S7.6
Test case generation				C7		
Test environment development				C11		
Execution	C13			C11		
Test results evaluation					C20,21	
Problem reporting/Test log				C5	C20	
Defect tracking				C6		

6 RECOMMENDED REFERENCES FOR SOFTWARE TESTING

Be   Beizer, B. *Software Testing Techniques* 2nd Edition. Van Nostrand Reinhold, 1990. [Chapters 1, 2, 3, 5, 7s4, 10s3, 11, 13]

Jo   Jorgensen, P.C., *Software Testing A Craftsman's Approach*, CRC Press. 1995. [Chapters 1, 2, 3, 4, 5, 6, 7, 8, 11, 12, 13, 14, 15]

KF+   Kaner, C., Falk, J., and Nguyen, H. Q., *Testing Computer Software*, 2nd Edition, Wiley, 1999. [Chapters 1, 2, 5, 6, 7, 8, 11, 12, 13, 15]

Ly   Lyu, M.R. (Ed.), *Handbook of Software Reliability Engineering*, Mc-Graw-Hill/IEEE, 1996. [Chapters 2s2.2, 5, 6, 7]

Pe   Perry, W. *Effective Methods for Software Testing*, Wiley, 1995. [Chapters 1, 2, 3, 4, 9, 10, 11, 12, 17, 19, 20, 21]

Pf   Pfleeger, S.L. *Software Engineering Theory and Practice*, Prentice Hall, 1998. [Chapters 7, 8]

ZH+   Zhu, H., Hall, P.A.V., and May, J.H.R. Software Unit Test Coverage and Adequacy. *ACM Computing Surveys*, 29, 4 (Dec. 1997) 366-427. [Sections 1, 2.2, 3.2, 3.3,

APPENDIX A – LIST OF FURTHER READINGS

Books

Be   Beizer, B. *Software Testing Techniques* 2nd Edition. Van Nostrand Reinhold, 1990.

Bi   Binder, R. V., *Testing Object-Oriented Systems Models, Patterns, and Tools*, Addison-Wesley, 2000.

Jo   Jorgensen, P.C., *Software Testing A Craftsman's Approach*, CRC Press, 1995.

KF+   Kaner, C., Falk, J., and Nguyen, H. Q., *Testing Computer Software*, 2nd Edition, Wiley, 1999.

Ly   Lyu, M.R. (Ed.), *Handbook of Software Reliability Engineering*, Mc-Graw-Hill/IEEE, 1996.

Pe   Perry, W. *Effective Methods for Software Testing*, Wiley, 1995.

Po   Poston, R.M. *Automating Specification-based Software Testing*, IEEE, 1996.

Survey Papers

ZH+   Zhu, H., Hall, P.A.V., and May, J.H.R. Software Unit Test Coverage and Adequacy. *ACM Computing Surveys*, 29, 4 (Dec. 1997) 366-427.

Specific Papers

BG+   Bernot, G., Gaudel, M.C., and Marre, B. Software Testing Based On Formal Specifications: a Theory and a Tool. *Software Engineering Journal* (Nov. 1991) 387-405.

BM   Bache, R., and Müllerburg, M. Measures of Testability as a Basis for Quality Assurance. *Software Engineering Journal*, 5 (March 1990) 86-92.

BMa   Bertolino, A., Marrè, M. "How many paths are needed for branch testing?", *The Journal of Systems and Software*, Vol. 35, No. 2, 1996, pp.95-106.

BP   Bochmann, G.V., and Petrenko, A. Protocol Testing: Review of Methods and Relevance for Software Testing. *ACM Proc. Int. Symposium on Sw Testing and Analysis (ISSTA' 94)*, (Seattle, Washington, USA, August 1994) 109-124.

BS   Bertolino, A., and Strigini, L. On the Use of Testability Measures for Dependability Assessment. *IEEE Transactions on Software Engineering*, 22, 2 (Feb. 1996) 97-108.

CT   Carver, R.H., and Tai, K.C., Replay and testing for concurrent programs. *IEEE Software* (March 1991) 66-74

DF   Dick, J., and Faivre, A. Automating The Generation and Sequencing of Test Cases From Model-Based Specifications. *FME'93: Industrial-Strenght Formal Method*, LNCS 670, Springer Verlag, 1993, 268-284.

FH+   Frankl, P., Hamlet, D., Littlewood B., and Strigini, L. Evaluating testing methods by delivered reliability. *IEEE Transactions on Software Engineering*, 24, 8, (August 1998), 586-601.

FW   Frankl, P., and Weyuker, E. A formal analysis of the fault detecting ability of testing methods. *IEEE Transactions on Software Engineering*, 19, 3, (March 1993), 202-

Ha   Hamlet, D. Are we testing for true reliability? *IEEE Software* (July 1992) 21-27.

Ho   Howden, W.E., Reliability of the Path Analysis Testing Strategy. *IEEE Transactions on Software Engineering*, 2, 3, (Sept. 1976) 208-215

HP   Horcher, H., and Peleska, J. Using Formal Specifications to Support Software Testing. *Software Quality Journal*, 4 (1995) 309-327.

Mo   Morell, L.J. A Theory of Fault-Based Testing. *IEEE Transactions on Software Engineering* 16, 8 (August 1990), 844-857.

MZ   Mitchell, B., and Zeil, S.J. A Reliability Model Combining Representative and Directed Testing. *ACM/IEEE Proc. Int. Conf. Sw Engineering ICSE 18* (Berlin, Germany, March 1996) 506-514.

OA+   Ostrand, T., Anodide, A., Foster, H., and Goradia, T. A Visual Test Development Environment for GUI Systems. *ACM Proc. Int. Symposium on Sw Testing and Analysis (ISSTA' 98)*, (Clearwater Beach, Florida, USA, March 1998) 82-92.

OB   Ostrand, T.J., and Balcer, M. J. The Category-Partition Method for Specifying and Generating Functional Tests. *Communications of ACM*, 31, 3 (June 1988), 676-686.

RH   Rothermel, G., and Harrold, M.J., Analyzing Regression Test Selection Techniques. *IEEE Transactions on Software Engineering*, 22, 8 (Aug. 1996) 529-

Sc   Schütz, W. Fundamental Issues in Testing Distributed Real-Time Systems. *Real-Time Systems Journal*. 7, 2, (Sept. 1994) 129-157.

VM   Voas, J.M., and Miller, K.W. Software Testability: The New Verification. *IEEE Software*, (May 1995) 17-28.

We-a Weyuker, E.J. On Testing Non-testable Programs. *The Computer Journal*, 25, 4, (1982) 465-470

We-b Weyuker, E.J. Assessing Test Data Adequacy through Program Inference. *ACM Trans. on Programming Languages and Systems*, 5, 4, (October 1983) 641-655

WK+   Wakid, S.A., Kuhn D.R., and Wallace, D.R. Toward Credible IT Testing and Certification, *IEEE Software*, (August 1999) 39-47.

WW+ Weyuker, E.J., Weiss, S.N, and Hamlet, D.
Comparison of Program Test Strategies in *Proc.*
*Symposium on Testing, Analysis and Verification TAV
4* (Victoria, British Columbia, October 1991), ACM
Press, 1-10.

Standards

610 IEEE Std 610.12-1990, Standard Glossary of Software
Engineering Terminology.

829 IEEE Std 829-1998, Standard for Software Test
Documentation.

982.2 IEEE Std 982.2-1998, Guide for the Use of IEEE
Standard Dictionary of Measures to Produce Reliable
Software.

1008 IEEE Std 1008-1987 (R 1993), Standard for Software
Unit Testing.

1044 IEEE Std 1044-1993, Standard Classification for
Software Anomalies.

1044.1 IEEE Std 1044.1-1995, Guide to Classification for
Software Anomalies.

12207 IEEE/EIA 12207.0-1996, Industry Implementation
of Int. Std. ISO/IEC 12207:1995, Standard for
Information Technology-Software Life cycle
processes.

CHAPTER 6

SOFTWARE MAINTENANCE

Thomas M. Pigoski
Technical Software Services (TECHSOFT), Inc.
31 West Garden Street, Suite 100
Pensacola, Florida 32501 USA
+1 850 469 0086
tmpigoski@techsoft.com

Table of Contents

Acronyms

CASE	Computer Aided Software Engineering
CM	Configuration Management
CMM	Capability Maturity Model
ICSM	International Conference on Software Maintenance
PSM	Practical Software and Systems Measurement
SCM	Software Configuration Management
SW-CMM	Capability Maturity Model for Software
SQA	Software Quality Assurance
V&V	Verification and Validation
WCRE	Working Conference on Reverse Engineering

1. INTRODUCTION

Software engineering is the application of engineering to software. The life cycle paradigm for software includes: requirements, design, construction, testing, and maintenance. This chapter addresses the maintenance portion of software engineering and the software life cycle.

Software maintenance is an integral part of a software life cycle. However, it has not historically received the same degree of attention as the other phases. Historically, development has had a much higher profile than maintenance in most organizations. This is now changing as organizations strive to obtain the most out of their development investment by keeping software operating as long as possible. Concerns about the Year 2000 (Y2K) rollover did bring significant attention to this important phase. Further, the Open Source paradigm has brought attention to the issue of maintaining code developed by others. Maintenance is also expensive. For these reasons, there is an opportunity to pursue further research to enhance productivity of maintenance activities.

This chapter presents an overview of the Knowledge Area of software maintenance. Brief descriptions of the topics are provided so that the reader can select the appropriate reference material according to his/her needs.

2. DEFINITION OF THE SOFTWARE MAINTENANCE KNOWLEDGE AREA

This section provides a definition of the Software Maintenance Knowledge Area.

Software development efforts result in delivery of a software product that satisfies user requirements. Accordingly, the software product must change or evolve. Once in operation, anomalies are uncovered, operating environments change, and new user requirements surface.

The maintenance phase of the life cycle commences upon delivery but maintenance activities occur much earlier.

Software maintenance sustains the software product throughout its life cycle. Modification requests are logged and tracked, the impact of proposed changes is determined, code is modified, testing is conducted, and a new version of the software product is released. Training is provided to users.

3. BREAKDOWN OF TOPICS FOR THE SOFTWARE MAINTENANCE KNOWLEDGE AREA

The breakdown of topics for software maintenance is a decomposition of software engineering topics that are "generally accepted" in the software maintenance community. They are general in nature and are not tied to any particular domain, model, or business needs. The presented topics can be used by small and medium sized organizations, as well as by larger ones. Organizations should use those topics that are appropriate for their unique situations. The topics are consistent with what is found in current software engineering literature and standards. The common themes of quality, measurement, and standards are included in the breakdown of topics.

The breakdown of topics, along with a brief description of each, is provided in this section. Key references are provided.

3.1. Basic Concepts

3.1.1 Definitions and Terminology [IEEE1219:s3.1.12; ISO12207:s3.1,s5.5; ISO14764:s6.1]

Software maintenance is defined in the IEEE Standard for Software Maintenance, IEEE 1219 [IEEE 1219], as the modification of a software product after delivery to correct faults, to improve performance or other attributes, or to adapt the product to a modified environment. The standard also addresses maintenance activities prior to delivery of the software product but only in an information annex of the standard.

The ISO/IEC 12207 Standard for Life Cycle Processes [ISO/IEC 12207], essentially depicts maintenance as one of the primary life cycle processes and describes maintenance as the process of a software product undergoing "modification to code and associated documentation due to a problem or the need for improvement. The objective is to modify existing software product while preserving its integrity." [ISO/IEC 12207] Of note is that ISO/IEC 12207 describes an activity called "Process Implementation." That activity establishes the maintenance plan and procedures that are later used during the maintenance process.

ISO/IEC 14764 [ISO14764], the International Standard for Software Maintenance, defines software maintenance in the same terms as ISO/IEC 12207 and places emphasis on the predelivery aspects of maintenance, e.g., planning.

The SWEBOK definition, generally accepted by software researchers and practitioners, is as follows:

SOFTWARE MAINTENANCE: The totality of activities required to provide cost-effective support to a software system. Activities are performed during the predelivery stage as well as the postdelivery stage. Predelivery activities include planning for postdelivery operations, supportability, and logistics determination. Postdelivery activities include software modification, training, and operating a help desk.

A maintainer is defined by ISO/IEC 12207 as an organization that performs maintenance activities [ISO12207].

ISO/IEC 12207 identifies the primary activities of software maintenance as: process implementation; problem and modification analysis; modification implementation; maintenance review/acceptance; migration; and retirement. These activities are discussed in a later section. They are further defined by the tasks in ISO/IEC 12207.

3.1.2 Majority of Maintenance Costs [AH93:pp63-90; Pre97:c27s27.1.2; Pig97:c3]

A common perception of maintenance is that it is merely fixing bugs. However, studies and surveys over the years have indicated that the majority, over 80%, of the maintenance effort is used for non-corrective actions [AH 93] [Pre97] [Pig97]. This perception is perpetuated by users submitting problem reports that in reality are major enhancements to the system. This inclusion of enhancement requests with problem reports contributes to some of the misconceptions regarding maintenance. Software evolves over its life cycle, as evidenced by the fact that over 80% of the effort after initial delivery goes to implement non-corrective actions. Thus, maintenance is similar to software development, although some unique processes are employed.

The focus of software development is to solve problems or to obtain business advantage through producing code. The generated code implements stated requirements and should operate correctly. Maintainers look back at development products and also the present by working with users and operators. Maintainers also look forward to anticipate problems and to consider functional changes.

3.1.3 The Nature of Maintenance [Pfl98:c10s10.2]

Pfleeger [Pfl98] states that maintenance has a broader scope than development, with more changes to track and control. Thus, configuration management is an important aspect of software evolution and maintenance.

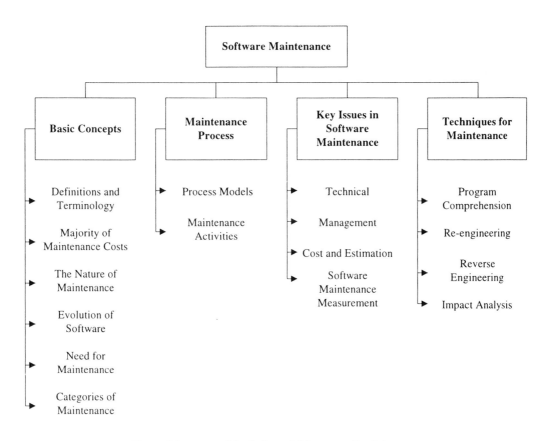

Figure 1 Summary of the Software Maintenance Breakdown

Maintenance, however, can learn from the development effort. Contact with the developers and early involvement by the maintainer helps the maintenance effort. However, it is difficult sometimes when the developers are no longer around. Maintenance must take the products of the development, e.g., code, documentation, and evolve/maintain them over the life cycle. Chapter 10 of the Guide to the SWEBOK discusses how tools can aid maintenance.

3.1.4 Evolution of Software [Leh97:pp108-124; Pfl98: c10s10.1;Art88:c1s1.0,s1.1,s1.2,c11,s1.1,s1.2]

The area of software maintenance and evolution of systems was first addressed by Lehman in 1969. His research led to an investigation of the evolution of OS/360 [LB85] and continues today on the Feedback, Evolution, and Software Technology (FEAST) research at Imperial College, England.

Over a period of twenty years, that research led to the formulation of eight Laws of Evolution [Leh97]. Simply put, Lehman stated that maintenance is really evolutionary developments and that maintenance decisions are aided by understanding what happens to systems (and software) over

time. Others state that maintenance is really continued development, except that there is an extra input (or constraint) – the existing software system.

Key points from Lehman include that large systems are never complete and continue to evolve. As they evolve, they grow more complex unless some action is taken to reduce the complexity. As systems demonstrate regular behavior and trends, these can be measured and predicted. Pfleeger [Pfl98] and Arthur [Art88] have excellent discussions regarding software evolution.

3.1.5 Need for Maintenance [Pfl98:c10.s10.2; Pig97: c2s2.3; TG97:c1]

Maintenance is needed to ensure that the system continues to satisfy user requirements. Maintenance is applicable to systems developed using any software development model (e.g., spiral). The system changes due to corrective and non-corrective software actions. Maintenance must be performed in order to:

Correct errors.

Correct requirements and design flaws.

Improve the design.

Make enhancements.

Interface with other systems.

Convert programs so that different hardware, software, system features, and telecommunications facilities can be used.

Migrate legacy systems.

Retire systems.

The four major aspects that maintenance focuses on are [Pf98]:

Maintaining control over the system's day-to-day functions.

Maintaining control over system modification.

Perfecting existing acceptable functions.

Preventing system performance from degrading to unacceptable levels.

Accordingly, software must evolve and be maintained.

3.1.6 Categories of Maintenance [Art88:c1s1.2; DT97:c8s5; IEEE1219:s3.1.1,s3.1.2,s3.1.7,A.1.7; ISO14764:s4.1,s4.3, s4.10,s4.11,s6.2; Pf98: c10s10.2; Pig97:c2s2.3]

Lehman developed the concept of software evolution. E. B. Swanson of UCLA was one of the first to examine what really happens in evolution and maintenance, using empirical data from industry maintainers. Swanson believed that, by studying the maintenance phase of the life cycle, a better understanding of the maintenance phase would result. Swanson was able to create three different categories of maintenance: corrective, adaptive, and perfective. [Art88] [DT97]. There have been updated and a new category has been defined by the International Organization of Standards (ISO) in the Standard for Software Maintenance standard ISO/IEC 14764, [ISO14764] and by the IEEE Computer Society [IEEE 1219]. The categories of maintenance defined by ISO/IEC are as follows:

Corrective maintenance. Reactive modification of a software product performed after delivery to correct discovered problems.

Adaptive maintenance. Modification of a software product performed after delivery to keep a software product usable in a changed or changing environment.

Perfective maintenance. Modification of a software product after delivery to improve performance or maintainability.

Preventive maintenance. Modification of a software product after delivery to detect and correct latent faults in the software product before they become effective faults.

The ISO Standard on Software Maintenance [ISO14764] classifies Adaptive and Perfective maintenance as

enhancements. It also classifies Corrective and Preventive maintenance as corrections. Preventive maintenance, the newest category, is defined as maintenance performed for the purpose of preventing problems before they occur. Preventive maintenance is most often performed on software products where safety is critical.

3.2. Maintenance Process

The need for software processes is well documented. The Capability Maturity Model for Software (SW-CMM) provides a means to measure levels of maturity. Of importance, is that there is a direct correlation between levels of maturity and cost savings. The higher the level of maturity, the greater the cost savings. The SW-CMM applies equally to maintenance and maintainers should have a documented maintenance process

3.2.1 Maintenance Process Models [IEEE1219:s4; ISO14764:s8; ISO12207:s5.5; Pig97:c5; TG97:c2; Par86:c7s1]

Process models provide needed operations and detailed inputs/outputs to those operations. Maintenance process models are provided in the software maintenance standards, IEEE 1219 [IEEE 1219] and ISO/IEC 14764 [ISO14764].

The maintenance process model described in IEEE 1219 [IEEE 1219], the Standard for Software Maintenance, starts the software maintenance effort during the post-delivery stage and discusses items such as planning for maintenance and measures outside the process model. That process model with the IEEE maintenance phases is depicted in Figure 2.

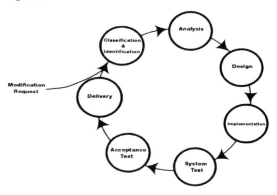

Figure 2 The IEEE Maintenance Process Activities

ISO/IEC 14764 [ISO14764] is an elaboration of the maintenance process of ISO/IEC 12207 [ISO12207]. The activities of the ISO/IEC maintenance process are similar to those of IEEE although they are aggregated a little differently. The maintenance process activities developed by ISO/IEC are shown in Figure 3.

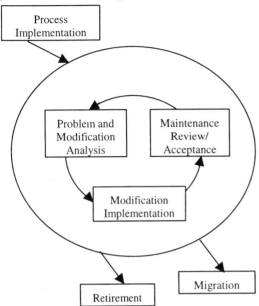

Figure 3 ISO/IEC Maintenance Process Activities

Each of the ISO/IEC 14764 primary software maintenance activities is further broken down into tasks as follows.

Process Implementation tasks are:

Develop maintenance plans and procedures.

Establish procedures for Modification Requests.

Implement the CM process.

Problem and Modification tasks are:

Perform initial analysis.

Verify the problem.

Develop options for implementing the modification.

Document the results.

Obtain approval for modification option.

Modification Implementation tasks are:

Perform detailed analysis.

Develop, code, and test the modification.

Maintenance Review/Acceptance tasks are:

Conduct reviews.

Obtain approval for modification.

Migration tasks are:

Ensure that migration is in accordance with ISO/IEC 12207.

Develop a migration plan.

Notify users of migration plans.

Conduct parallel operations.

Notify user that migration has started.

Conduct a post-operation review.

Ensure that old data is accessible.

Software Retirement tasks are:

Develop a retirement plan.

Notify users of retirement plans.

Conduct parallel operations.

Notify user that retirement has started.

Ensure that old data is accessible.

Takang and Grubb [TG97] provide a history of maintenance process models leading up to the development of the IEEE and ISO/IEC process models. A good overview of a generic maintenance process is given by Parikh [Par86]

3.2.2 Maintenance Activities

Maintenance activities are similar to those of software development. Maintainers perform analysis, design, coding, testing, and documenting. Maintainers must track requirements just as they do in development. Maintainers must update documentation as baselines change. However, for software maintenance, the activities involve processes unique to maintenance. Chapter 10 discusses how tools can be used to help in the maintenance effort.

3.2.2.1 *Unique Activities [Pfl98:c10s10.2; Art88:c3; DT97: c8s9.1; IEEE1219:s4.1,s4.2; ISO14764: s8.2.2.1, s,8.3.2.1]*

Maintainers must possess an intimate knowledge of the code's structure and content [Pfl98]. That knowledge is used by maintainers to perform impact analysis. Impact analysis identifies all systems and system products affected by a change request and develops an estimate of the resources needed to accomplish the change [Art88]. Additionally, the risk of making the change is determined. The change request, sometimes called a modification request and often called a problem report, must first be analyzed and translated into software terms [DT97]. The maintainer then identifies the affected components. Several potential solutions are provided and then a recommendation is made as to the best course of action.

Problem solving skills are very important for maintenance. Maintainers must also be concerned about the "ripple effect" of any proposed changes.

3.2.2.2 *Supporting Activities [IEEE1219:A.7,A.11; Pig97: c10s10.2,c18; ISO12207:c6,c7]*

Maintainers may also perform supporting activities such as configuration management (CM), verification and validation, quality assurance, reviews, audits, and conducting user training. Often these supporting activities are performed by separate entities. The IEEE Standard for

Software Maintenance, IEEE 1219 [IEEE 1219], describes CM as a critical element of the maintenance process. CM procedures should provide for the verification, validation, and certification of each step required to identify, authorize, implement, and release the software product. Training of maintainers, a supporting process, is also a needed activity [Pig97] [ISO12207].

3.2.2.2.1 Configuration management [ISO12207:s6.2; IEEE1219: A.11; Art88:c2,c10; Pfl98:c10s10.5; TG97:c7]

It is not sufficient to simply track modification requests or problem reports. The software product and any changes made to it must be controlled. This control is established by implementing and enforcing an approved software configuration management (SCM) process. SCM provides support and makes the job of the maintainer easier. Chapter 7 of the Guide to the SWEBOK provides details of SCM and discusses the process by which change requests are submitted, evaluated, and approved. SCM for maintenance is different than for development in that a change request initiates the maintenance process. The SCM process is implemented by developing and following a CM Plan and operating procedures. Maintainers participate in Configuration Control Boards to determine when enhancements should stop and perhaps migration is necessary. Problem severity is often used to decide how and when a problem will be fixed.

3.2.2.2.2 Quality [ISO12207:s6.3; IEEE1219:A.7; Art98: c7s4]

It is not sufficient to simply hope that increased quality will result from the maintenance of software. It must be planned and processes implemented to support the maintenance process. The activities and techniques for Software Quality Assurance (SQA) and V&V must be selected in concert with all other processes to achieve the level of quality desired. This is implemented by developing and following SQA and V&V plans and procedures. Details of software quality are covered in chapter 11 of the Guide to the SWEBOK.

3.2.2.2.3 Maintenance Planning Activity [IEEE1219:A.3; ISO14764:s7; Pig97:c7,c8]

An important activity for software maintenance is planning. Whereas developments typically can last for 1-2 years, the operation and maintenance phase typically lasts for many years. Developing accurate estimates of resources is a key element of maintenance planning. Those resources, which include costs, should be included in project planning budgets. Maintenance planning should begin with the decision to develop a new system and should consider quality objectives. A concept and then a maintenance plan should be developed. The concept for maintenance should address:

The scope of software maintenance.

The tailoring of the postdelivery process.

The designation of who will provide maintenance.

An estimate of life cycle costs.

Once the maintenance concept is determined, the next step is to develop the maintenance plan. The maintenance plan should be prepared during software development and should specify how users will request modifications or report problems. Maintenance planning [Pig97] is addressed in IEEE 1219 [IEEE 1219]and ISO/IEC 14764. [ISO14764] ISO/IEC14764 [ISO14764] provides guidelines for a maintenance plan.

3.3. Key Issues in Software Maintenance

It is important to understand that software maintenance provides unique technical and management problems for software engineers. Trying to find a defect in a 500K line of code system that the maintainer did not develop is a challenge for the maintainer. Similarly, competing with software developers for resources is a constant battle. Planning for a future release, while coding the next release, and sending out emergency patches for the current release, is also a challenge. The following discusses some of the technical and management problems relating to software evolution and maintenance.

3.3.1 Technical Problems

3.3.1.1 Limited understanding [Pfl98:c10s10.3; TG97:c3; DT97: c8s11.4]

Practitioners and researchers indicate that some 40% to 60% of the maintenance effort is devoted to understanding the software to be modified. Thus, the topic of program comprehension is one of interest to maintainers. Comprehension is more difficult for text-based representation. It is often difficult to trace the evolution of the software through its versions, changes are not documented, and the developers are usually not around to explain the code. Thus, maintainers have a limited understanding of the software and must learn the software on their own.

3.3.1.2 Testing [Pfl98:c10s10.3; Art88:c9]

The cost of repeating full testing on a major piece of software can be significant in terms of time and money. Regression testing, the selective retesting of a system or component to verify the modifications have not caused unintended effects, is important to maintenance. Research efforts into areas such as "slicing" look at this topic. Finding time to test is often difficult [Plf98]. Chapter 5 of the Guide to the SWEBOK provides details of testing.

3.3.1.3 Impact analysis [DT97:c8s10.1-3; Pfl98: c10s10.5; Art88:c3]

The software and the organization must both undergo impact analysis. Critical skills, documentation, and processes are needed for this area. Impact analysis is necessary for risk abatement. Software designed for maintainability facilitates impact analysis.

3.3.1.4 Maintainability [ISO14764:s6.8s6.8.1;Pfl98: c8s8.4;Pig97:c16]

The IEEE Computer Society [IEEE610.12] defines maintainability as the ease with which software can be maintained, enhanced, adapted, or corrected to satisfy specified requirements. ISO/IEC defines maintainability as one of the quality characteristics. Maintainability features must be incorporated into the software development effort to reduce life cycle costs. If this is done, the quality of evolution and maintenance of the code can improve. Maintainability is often a problem in maintenance because maintainability is not incorporated into the software development process, documentation is lacking, and program comprehension is difficult. Maintainability can be achieved by including it in requirements, design, and construction. Chapters 2, 3, and 4 provide details of these topics. Maintainability can be enhanced by defining coding standards, documentation standards, and standard test tools in the software development phase of the life cycle.

3.3.2 Management

3.3.2.1 Alignment with organizational issues [DT97: c8s6; Pfl98:c10s10.3]

Dorfman and Thayer [DT97] relate that return on investment is not clear with maintenance. Thus, there is a constant struggle to obtain resources.

3.3.2.2 Staffing [Pfl98:c10s10.3; Dek92:pp10-17; Par86: c4s8-s11; DT97:c8s6]

Maintenance personnel often are viewed as second class citizens [Pfl98] and morale suffers [DT97]. Maintenance is not viewed as glamorous work. Deklava provides a list of staffing related problems based on survey data [Dek92].

3.3.2.3 Process issues [DT97:c8s3]

Maintenance requires several activities that are not found in software development, (e.g., help desk support). These present challenges to management [DT97].

3.3.2.4 Organizational Aspects of Maintenance

The team that develops the software is not always used to maintain the system once it is operational. A maintainer must be identified and there are several options as discussed below.

3.3.2.4.1 The Maintainer [Pfl98:c10s10.2; Pig97:c2s2.5; Par86: c4s7; TG97:c8]

Often, a separate team (or maintainer) is employed to ensure that the system runs properly and evolves to satisfy changing needs of the users. There are many pros and cons to having the original developer or a separate team maintain the software [Pfl98] [Pig97] [Par86]. That decision should be made on a case-by-case basis.

3.3.2.4.2 Outsourcing [DT97:c8s7;Pig97: c9s9.1,s9.2]

Outsourcing of maintenance is becoming a major industry. Large corporations are outsourcing entire operations, including software maintenance. More often outsourcing is done for peripheral software, as companies are unwilling to release the software used in its core business. One of the major challenges is for the outsource maintenance company to determine the scope of the effort. Outsourcing companies typically spend a number of months assessing the software before it will accept a contract [DT97]. Another challenge is the transition of the software to the outsourced company [Pig97].

3.3.2.4.3 Organizational Structure [Pig97:c12s12.1-s12.3]

Based on the fact there are almost as many organizational structures as there are software maintenance organizations, an organizational structure for maintenance is best developed on a case-by-case basis. What is important is the delegation or designation of maintenance responsibility to a group [Pig97], regardless of the organizational structure. As with other efforts, maintenance will only be successful with full management support.

3.3.3 Maintenance Cost and Maintenance Cost Estimation

Software engineers must understand the different categories of maintenance, previously discussed, in order to address the cost of maintenance. For planning purposes, estimating costs is an important aspect of software maintenance.

3.3.3.1 Cost [Pfl98:c10s10.3; Art88:c3; Pig97:c3s3.1-3; Pre97: c27s27.2.2]

Maintenance consumes a major share of life cycle costs. Understanding the categories of maintenance helps to understand why maintenance is so costly. Also understanding the factors that influence the maintainability of a system can help to contain costs. Pfleeger [Pfl98] addresses some of the technical and non-technical factors affecting maintenance.

Impact analysis identifies all systems and system products affected by a change request and develops an estimate of the resources needed to accomplish the change [Art88]. It is performed after a change request enters the CM process. It is used in concert with the cost estimation techniques discussed below.

3.3.3.2 Cost estimation [Boe81:c30; Jon98:c27; Pig97:c8; Pfl98:c10s10.3]

Maintenance cost estimates are affected by many technical and non-technical factors. Primary approaches to cost estimating include use of parametric models and experience. Most often a combination of these is used to estimate costs.

3.3.3.3 Parametric models [Boe81:c30; Jon98:c27; Pfl98:c10s10.3]

One of the works in the area of parametric models for estimating was performed by Boehm [Boe81]. COCOMO (derived from COnstructive COst Model), puts the software life cycle and the quantitative life cycle relationships into a hierarchy of software cost-estimation models [Pfl98]. Of significance is that data from past projects is needed in order to use the models. Jones [Jon98] discusses all aspects of estimating costs including function points, and provides a detailed chapter on maintenance estimating. Chapter 8 of the Guide to the SWEBOK provides additional details regarding models.

3.3.3.4 Experience [Pig97:c8; ISO14764:s7,s7.2,s7.2.1, c7s7.2.4]

Experience should be used to augment data from parametric models. Sound judgment, reason, a work breakdown structure, educated guesses, and use of empirical/historical data are several approaches. Clearly the best approach to maintenance estimation is to use empirical data and experience. That data should be provided as a result of a measurement program. In practice, cost estimation relies much more on experience than parametric models. The Software Engineering Institute has conducted research into performing cost estimation based on historical data.

3.3.4 Software Maintenance Measurement [GC87:c2; TG97: c6s6.1-3; AI98:A.2]

Software life cycle costs are growing and a strategy for maintenance is needed. Software measurement need to be a part of that strategy. Grady and Caswell [GC87] discuss establishing a corporate-wide software measures program. The Practical Software and Systems Measurement (PSM) project describes an issue-driven measurement process [http://www.psmsc.com] that is used by many organizations and is quite practical. Software measures are vital for software process improvement but the process must be measurable. Additional discussion of measurement is contained in chapters 8 and 11 of the Guide to the SWEBOK.

3.3.4.1 Specific Measures [CG90:s2-3; SKV94:pp239-249; IEEE1219:Table3; Pig97:c14s14.6; TG97: c6s6.4]

There are software measures that are common to all efforts and the Software Engineering Institute (SEI) identified these as: size; effort; schedule; and quality [Pig97]. Those are a good starting point for a maintainer.

Takang and Grubb [TG97] group software measures into areas of: size; complexity; quality; understandability; maintainability; and cost estimation.

Documentation regarding specific software measures to use in maintenance is not often published. Typically generic software engineering measures are used and the maintainer determines which ones are appropriate for their organization. IEEE 1219 [IEEE 1219] provides suggested measures for software programs. Stark, et al [SKV94] provide a suggested list of software maintenance measures used at NASA's Mission Operations Directorate. That list includes:

> Software size
>
> Software staffing
>
> Maintenance request number/status
>
> Software enhancement numbers/status
>
> Computer resource utilization
>
> Fault density
>
> Software volatility
>
> Discrepancy report open duration
>
> Break/fix ratio
>
> Software reliability
>
> Design complexity
>
> Fault type distribution

3.4. Techniques for Maintenance

Effective software maintenance is performed using techniques specific to maintenance. The following provides some of the best practice techniques used by maintainers.

3.4.1 Program Comprehension [Arn92:c14; DT97: c8s11.4; TG97:c3]

Programmers spend considerable time in reading and comprehending programs in order to implement changes. Code browsers are a key tool in program comprehension. Clear and concise documentation can aid in program comprehension. Based on the importance of this subtopic, an annual IEEE Computer Society workshop is now held to address program comprehension. The website http://www.seg.iit.nrc.ca/projects/easse provides a number of papers on comprehension and tools for assisting comprehension processes. Takang and Grubb [TG97] provide a detailed chapter on comprehension.

3.4.2 Re-engineering [Arn92:c1,c3-6, c8s11.4; IEEE1219: B.2; DT97:c8s11.4]

Re-engineering is defined as the examination and alteration of the subject system to reconstitute it in a new form, and the subsequent implementation of the new form. Dorfman and Thayer [DT97] state that re-engineering is the most radical (and expensive) form of alteration. Others believe that re-engineering can be used for minor changes. Re-engineering is often not undertaken to improve maintainability but is used to replace aging legacy systems.

Arnold [Arn92] provides a comprehensive compendium of topics, e.g., concepts, tools and techniques, case studies, and risks and benefits associated with re-engineering. Refactoring, a program transformation that reorganizes a program without changing its behavior, is now being used in reverse engineering to improve the structure of object-oriented programs.

3.4.3 *Reverse engineering* [Arn92:c12; DT97:c8s11.3; IEEE1219:B.3; TG97:c4]

Reverse engineering is the process of analyzing a subject system to identify the system's components and their inter-relationships and to create representations of the system in another form or at higher levels of abstraction. Reverse engineering is passive, it does not change the system, or result in a new one. A simple reverse engineering effort may merely produce call graphs and control flow graphs from source code. One type of reverse engineering is redocumentation. Another type is design recovery [DT97]. Date Reverse Engineering has gained great importance over the last few years. Reverse engineering topics are discussed at the annual Working Conference on Reverse Engineering (WCRE).

3.4.4 *Impact Analysis* [Plf98:c10s10.5; Art88:c3]

Impact analysis identifies all systems and system products affected by a change request and develops an estimate of the resources needed to accomplish the change [Art88]. It is performed after a change request enters the configuration management process. Arthur [Art88] states that the objectives of impact analysis are:

> Determine the scope of a change in order to plan and implement work.

> Develop accurate estimates of resources needed to perform the work.

> Analyze the cost/benefits of the requested change.

> Communicate to others the complexity of a given change.

Resources

Beside the references listed in this chapter, there are other resources available to learn more about software maintenance. The IEEE Computer Society sponsors the annual *International Conference on Software Maintenance (ICSM)*. That conference, started in 1983, provides a Proceedings, which incorporates numerous research and practical industry papers concerning evolution and maintenance topics. Other venues, which address these topics, include:

4. BREAKDOWN RATIONALE

The breakdown of topics for software maintenance is a decomposition of software engineering topics that are "generally accepted" in the software maintenance community. They are general in nature. There is agreement in the literature and in the standards on the topics.

A detailed discussion of the rationale for the proposed breakdown, keyed to the Guide to the SWEBOK development criteria, is given in Appendix B. The following is a narrative description of the rationale for the breakdown.

The Basic Concepts sub-area was selected as the initial topic in order to introduce Software Maintenance. The subtopics are needed to provide definitions and to emphasize why there is a need for maintenance. Categories are critical to understand the underlying meaning of maintenance.

Maintenance Process is needed to provide the current references and standards needed to implement the maintenance process.

The Maintenance Activities sub-topic is needed to differentiate maintenance from development and to show the relationship to other software engineering activities.

The sub-area on the Key Issues of Software Maintenance was chosen to ensure that the software engineers fully comprehended these problems.

Every organization is concerned with who will perform maintenance. The Management topic provides some options regarding who can perform maintenance. Every software maintenance reference discusses the fact that maintenance consumes a large portion of the life cycle costs. The topic on Cost and Cost Estimation was provided to ensure that the readers select references to help with this difficult task.

The Software Maintenance Measurement topic is one that is not addressed very well in the literature. Most maintenance books barely touch on the topic. Measurement information is most often found in generalized measurement books. This topic was chosen to highlight the need for unique maintenance measures and to provide specific maintenance measurement references.

The Techniques topic was provided to introduce some of the generally accepted techniques used in maintenance operations.

5. MATRIX OF TOPICS VS. REFERENCE MATERIAL

Topics	AH 93	IEEE 610.12	AI 98	Arn 92	Art 88	Boe 81	CG 90	Dek 92	DT 97	GC 87	IEEE 1219	ISO 12207	ISO 14764	Jon 98	Leh 97	Par 86	Pfl 98	Pig 97	Pre 97	SKV 94	TG 97
1. Basic Concepts																					
1.1 Definitions and Terminology											s3.1.12	s3.1. s5.5	s6.1								
1.2 Majority of Maintenance Costs	pp 63-90																	c3	c27. s27.1.2		
1.3 Nature of Maintenance																	c10 s10.2				
1.4 Evolution of Software					c1 s1.0 s1.1 s1.2 c11 s11 s12										pp 108-124		c10 s10.1				
1.5 Need for Maintenance																	c10 s10.2	c2 s2.3			c1
1.6 Categories of Maintenance					c1 s1.2				c8 s5		c3 s3.1. s3.1.1 s3.1.2 s3.1.7 A.1.7		s4.1 s4.3 s4.10 s4.11 s6.2				c10 s10.2	c2 s2.3			
2. Maintenance Process																					
2.1 Maintenance Process Models											s4	s5.5	s8			c7,s1		c5			c2
2.2 Maintenance Activities																					
Unique Activities					c3				c8 s9.1		s4.1. s4.2		s8.2.2.1, s8.3.2.1				c10 s10.2				
Supporting Activities											A.7. A.11	c6,c7					c10 s10.2, c18				
Configuration Management					c2 c10						A.11	s6.2					c10 s10.5				c7
Quality					c7 s4						A.7	s6.3									
Maintenance Planning Activity											A.33		c7					c7.c8			
3. Key Issues in Software Maintenance																					
3.1 Technical																					
Limited Understanding									c8 s11.4								c10 s10.3				c3
Testing					c9												c1 s10.3				
Impact Analysis					c3				c8 s10.1 s10.2 s10.3								c10 s10.5				
Maintainability		s3											s6.8, s6.8.1				c8 s8.4	c16			
3.2 Management																					
Alignment with organizational issues									c8 s6								c10 s10.3				
Staffing								pp 10-17	c8 s6							c4. s8-11	c10 s10.3				c1. s1.8
Process issues									c8. s3												
Organizational																					
The Maintainer																c4 s7	c10 s10.2	c2 s2.5			c8
Outsourcing									c8 s7									c9 s9.1. s9.2			
Organizational Structure																		c12 s12.1 s12.2 s12.3			

Topics	AH 93	IEEE 610.12	AI 98	Arn 92	Art 88	Boe 81	CG 90	Dek 92	DT 97	GC 87	IEEE 1219	ISO 1220 7	ISO 1476 4	Jon 98	Leh 97	Par 86	Pfl 98	Pig 97	Pre 97	SKV 94	TG 97
3.3 Maintenance Cost and Maintenance Cost Estimation																					
Cost				c3													c10 s10. 3	c3 s3.1- 3	c27 s27. 2.2		
Cost estimation					c30									c27			c10 s10. 3	c8			
Parametric models					c30									c27			c10 s10. 3				
Experience													s7 s7.2. s7.2. 1. s7.2. 4					c8			
3.4 Software Maintenance Measurement						s2-3					Table 3							c14 s14. 6	pp 239- 249	c6 s6.4
4. Techniques for Maintenance																					
4.1 Program Comprehension				c14					c8 s11. 4												c3
4.2 Re-engineering				c1.3- 6					c8 s11. 4	B.2											
4.3 Reverse Engineering				c12					c8 s11. 3	B.3											c4
4.4 Impact Analysis				c3													c10 s10. 5				

6. RECOMMENDED REFERENCES FOR SOFTWARE MAINTENANCE

The following set of references provides a strong foundation to acquire knowledge on specific topics identified in the breakdown. They were chosen to provide coverage of all aspects of software maintenance. Priority was given to standards, maintenance specific publications, and then general software engineering publications.

References

[AH93] A. Abran and H. Nguyenkim, "Measurement of the Maintenance Process from a Demand-Based Perspective," *Journal of Software Maintenance: Research and Practice*, Vol 5, no 2, 1993 [pp63-90].

[AI98] ANSI/IEEE STD 1061. *IEEE Standard for a Software Quality Metrics Methodology*. IEEE Computer Society Press, 1998. [s4, A.1, A.2]

[Arn92] R.S. Arnold. *Software Reengineering*. IEEE Computer Society, 1993. [c1,c3-6,c12,c14]

[Art88] L.J. Arthur. *Software Evolution: The Software Maintenance Challenge*. John Wiley & Sons, 1988. [c1s1.0,s1.1,s1.2; c2, c3, c7s4, c9, c10,c11s1.1,s1.2]

[Boe81] B.W. Boehm. *Software Engineering Economics*. Prentice-Hall, 1981. [c30]

[CG90] D.N. Card and R. L. Glass, *Measuring Software Design Quality*, Prentice Hall, 1990. [s1.1,1.3,c2-3]

[Dek92] S. Dekleva. Delphi Study of Software Maintenance Problems. *Proceedings of the International Conference on Software Maintenance*, 1992. [pp10-17]

[DT97] M. Dorfman and R. H. Thayer. *Software Engineering*. IEEE Computer Society Press, 1997. [c8s3, c8s5, c8s6, c8s7, c8s9.1, c8s10.1-3, c8s11.3-4]

[GC87] R.B. Grady and D. L. Caswell. *Software Metrics: Establishing a Company-wide Program*. Prentice-Hall, 1987. [c2, c3]

[IEEE610.12] IEEE STD 610.12: *IEEE Standard Glossary of Software Engineering Terminology*, 1990. [s3]

[IEEE1219] *IEEE STD 1219: Standard for Software Maintenance*, 1998. [s3.1.1,s3.1.2,s3.1.7,s4,s4.1,s4.2, A.1.7,A.3,A.7,A.11, Table3, B.2-3]

[ISO12207] *ISO/IEC 12207: Information Technology-Software Life Cycle Processes*, 1995. [s3.1, s5.5, c6, s6.2,s6.3, c7]

[ISO14764] *ISO/IEC 14764: Software Engineering-Software Maintenance*, 2000. [s4.1,s4.3,s4.10,s4.11,s6.1, s6.2,s6.8,s6.8.1,s7,s7.2,s7.2.1,s7.2.4,s8,s8.2.2.1,s8.3.2.1]

[Jon98] T. C. Jones. *Estimating Software Costs*. McGraw-Hill, 1998. [c27]

[Leh97] M.M Lehman, Laws of Software Evolution Revisited, EWSPT96, October 1996, LNCS 1149, Springer Verlag, 1997. [pp108-124]

[Par86] G. Parikh. *Handbook of Software Maintenance*. John Wiley & Sons, 1986. [c4s7-11, c7s1]

[Pfl98] S.L. Pfleeger. *Software Engineering—Theory and Practice*. Prentice Hall, 1998. [c8s8.4,c10s10.1,s10.2, s10.3,s10.5]

[Pig97] T.M. Pigoski. *Practical Software Maintenance: Best Practices for Managing your Software Investment*.

Wiley, 1997. [c2s2.3,s2.5, c3, c3s3.1-3, c5, c7, c8, c9s9.1-2, c10s10.2, c12s12.1-3, c14s4-5, c14 s14.6, c16, c18]

[Pre97] R.S. Pressman. *Software Engineering: A Practitioner's Approach.* McGraw-Hill, fourth edition, 1997. [c27s27.2.1-2]

[SKV94] G.E. Stark, L. C. Kern, and C. V. Vowell. *A Software Metric Set for Program Maintenance Management.* Journal of Systems and Software, Vol. 24, no. 3, March 1994. [pp239-249]

[TG97] A. Takang and P. Grubb. *Software Maintenance Concepts and Practice.* International Thomson Computer Press, 1996. [c1, c1s1.8, c2, c3, c4, c6s6.1-4, c7, c8]

APPENDIX A – LIST OF FURTHER READINGS

Beside the recommended references listed in this chapter, there are other resources available to learn more about software maintenance. The IEEE Computer Society sponsors the annual *International Conference on Software Maintenance (ICSM)*. That conference, started in 1983, provides a Proceedings, which incorporates numerous research and practical industry papers concerning evolution and maintenance topics. Other venues, which address these topics, include:

> The Workshop on Software Change and Evolution (SCE). [HTTP://www.dur.ac.uk/~dcs0elb/csm/sce99/]
>
> Manny Lehman's work on the FEAST project at the Imperial College in England continues to provide valuable research into software evolution. [HTTP://www-dse.doc.ic.uk/~mml/]
>
> The International Workshop on Empirical Studies of Software Maintenance (WESS). [HTTP://computer.org/conferences/calendar/htm]
>
> The Research Institute for Software Evolution (RISE) at the University of Durham, England, concentrates its research on software maintenance and evolution. [HTTP://www.dur.ac.uk/csm]
>
> The Seventh Working Conference on Reverse Engineering (WCRE-2000). [HTTP://computer.org/conferences/calendar/htm]
>
> The Conference on Software Maintenance and Reengineering (CSMR). [HTTP://www.uni-koblenz.de/ ~ist/SCSMR2000/]

The *Journal of Software Maintenance*, published by John Wiley & Sons, also is an excellent resource for maintenance.

A list of additional readings is also provided to identify additional reference material for the Knowledge Area of Software Maintenance. These references also contain generally accepted knowledge.

References

[AH93] A. Abran and H. Hguyenkim, "Measurement of the Maintenance Process from a Demand-Based Perspective," *Journal of Software Maintenance: Research and Practice*, Vol 5, no 2, 1993.

[AI98] ANSI/IEEE STD 1061. *IEEE Standard for a Software Quality Metrics Methodology*. IEEE Computer Society Press, 1998.

[Arn92] R.S. Arnold. *Software Reengineering*. IEEE Computer Society, 1992.

[Art88] L.J. Arthur. *Software Evolution: The Software Maintenance Challenge*. John Wiley & Sons, 1988.

[Bas85] V.R. Basili, "Quantitative Evaluation of Software Methodology," *Proceedings First Pan-Pacific Computer Conference*, September 1985.

[Boe81] B.W. Boehm. *Software Engineering Economics*. Prentice-Hall, 1981.

[BBHMMY] C. Boldyreff, E. Burd, R. Hather, R. Mortimer, M. Munro, and E. Younger, "The AMES Approach to Application Understanding: A Case Study," *Proceedings of the International Conference on Software Maintenance-1995*, IEEE Computer Society Press, Los Alamitos, CA, 1995.

[CM94] M.A. Capretz and M. Munro, "Software Configuration Management Issues in the Maintenance of Existing Systems," *Journal of Software Maintenance*, Vol. 6, no.2, 1994.

[CG90] D.N. Card and R. L. Glass, *Measuring Software Design Quality*, Prentice Hall, 1990.

[Car92] J. Cardow, "You Can't Teach Software Maintenance!," *Proceedings of the Sixth Annual Meeting and Conference of the Software Management Association*, 1992.

[Dek92] S. M. Dekleva. Delphi Study of Software Maintenance Problems. *Proceedings of the International Conference on Software Maintenance*, 1992.

[DT97] M. Dorfman and R. H. Thayer. *Software Engineering*. IEEE Computer Society Press, 1997.

[GC87] R.B. Grady and D. L. Caswell. *Software Metrics: Establishing a Company-wide Program*. Prentice-Hall, 1987.

[Gra92] R.B. Grady, *Practical Software Metrics for Project Management and Process Improvement*, Prentice-Hall, Inc., Englewood Cliffs, NJ, 1992.

[IEEE610.12] IEEE STD 610.2: *IEEE Standard Glossary of Software Engineering Terminology*, 1990.

[IEEE1219] *IEEE STD 1219: Standard for Software Maintenance*, 1998.

[ISO12207] *ISO/IEC 12207: Information Technology-Software Life Cycle Processes*, 1995.

[ISO14764] *ISO/IEC 14764: Software Engineering-Software Maintenance*, 2000.

[ISO15271] ISO/IEC TR 15271, *Information Technology - Guide for ISO/IEC 12207, (Software Life Cycle Process)*

[Jon98] T.C. Jones. *Estimating Software Costs*. McGraw-Hill, 1998.

[LB85] M.M. Lehman and L.A. Belady, *Program Evolution – Processes of Software Change*, Academic Press Inc. (London) Ltd., 1985.

[Leh97] M.M. Lehman, Laws of Software Evolution Revisited, EWSPT96, October 1996, LNCS 1149, Springer Verlag, 1997.

[KSV95] T.M. Khoshgoftaar, R.M. Szabo, and J.M. Voas, "Detecting Program Module with Low Testability," *Proceedings of the International Conference on Software Maintenance-1995*, IEEE Computer Society Press, Los Alamitos, CA, 1995.

[OHA91] P.W. Oman, J. Hagemeister, and D. Ash, *A Definition and Taxonomy for Software Maintainability*, University of Idaho, Software Engineering Test Lab, Technical Report, 91-08 TR, November 1991.

[OH92] P. Oman and J. Hagemeister, "Metrics for Assessing Software System Maintainability," *Proceedings of the International Conference on Software Maintenance-1992*, IEEE Computer Society Press, Los Alamitos, CA, 1992.

[Par86] G. Parikh. *Handbook of Software Maintenance*. John Wiley & Sons, 1986.

[Pfl98] S. L. Pfleeger. *Software Engineering—Theory and Practice*. Prentice Hall, 1998.

[Pig93] T.M. Pigoski, "Maintainable Software: Why You Want It and How to Get It," *Proceedings of the Third Software Engineering Research Forum-November 1993*, University of West Florida Press, Pensacola, FL, 1993.

[Pig94] T.M. Pigoski. "Software Maintenance," *Encyclopedia of Software Engineering*, John Wiley & Sons, New York, NY, 1994.

[Pig97] T.M. Pigoski. *Practical Software Maintenance: Best Practices for Managing your Software Investment*. Wiley, 1997.

[PM97] L.H. Putman and W. Myers. *Industrial Strength Software – Effective Management Using Measurement*, IEEE Computer Society Press, Los Alamitos, CA, 1997.

[Pre97] R.S. Pressman. *Software Engineering: A Practitioner's Approach*. McGraw-Hill, fourth edition, 1997.

[Scha99] S.R. Schach, *Classical and Object-Oriented Software Engineering With UML and C++*, McGraw-Hill, 1999

[Sch87] N.F. Schneidewind. *The State of Software Maintenance. Proceedings of the IEEE*, 1987.

[Schn97] S.L. Schneberger, *Client/Server Software Maintenance*, McGraw-Hill, 1997.

[Som01] I. Sommerville. *Software Engineering*. Addison-Wesley, sixth edition, 2001.

[SKV94] G.E. Stark, L. C. Kern, and C. V. Vowell. *A Software Metric Set for Program Maintenance Management*. Journal of Systems and Software, 1994.

[TG97] A. Takang and P. Grubb. *Software Maintenance Concepts and Practice*. International Thomson Computer Press, 1997.

[VCBKB] J.D. Vallett, S.E. Condon, L. Briand, Y.M. Kim and V.R. Basili, "Building on Experience Factory for Maintenance," *Proceedings of the Software Engineering Workshop*, Software Engineering Laboratory, 1994.

APPENDIX B – REFERENCES USED TO WRITE AND JUSTIFY THE SOFTWARE MAINTENANCE DESCRIPTION

The following set of references was chosen to provide coverage of all aspects of software evolution and maintenance. Priority was given to standards, maintenance specific publications, and then general software engineering publications.

References

[AH93] A. Abran and H. Hguyenkim, "Measurement of the Maintenance Process from a Demand-Based Perspective," *Journal of Software Maintenance: Research and Practice*, Vol. 5, no 2, 1993.

[AI98] ANSI/IEEE STD 1061. *IEEE Standard for a Software Quality Metrics Methodology*. IEEE Computer Society Press, 1998.

[Arn92] R.S. Arnold. *Software Reengineering*. IEEE Computer Society, 1992.

[Art88] L.J. Arthur. *Software Evolution: The Software Maintenance Challenge*. John Wiley & Sons, 1988.

[Bas85] V. R. Basili, "Quantitative Evaluation of Software Methodology," *Proceedings First Pan-Pacific Computer Conference*, September 1985.

[Boe81] B.W. Boehm. *Software Engineering Economics*. Prentice-Hall, 1981.

[BBHMMY] C. Boldyreff, E. Burd, R. Hather, R. Mortimer, M. Munro, and E. Younger, "The AMES Approach to Application Understanding: A Case Study," *Proceedings of the International Conference on Software Maintenance-1995*, IEEE Computer Society Press, Los Alamitos, CA, 1995.

[CG90] D.N. Card and R.L. Glass, *Measuring Software Design Quality*, Prentice Hall, 1990.

[Dek92] S. M. Dekleva. Delphi Study of Software Maintenance Problems. *Proceedings of the International Conference on Software Maintenance*, 1992.

[DT97] M. Dorfman and R. H. Thayer. *Software Engineering*. IEEE Computer Society Press, 1997.

[GC87] R. B. Grady and D. L. Caswell. *Software Metrics: Establishing a Company-wide Program*. Prentice-Hall, 1987.

[IEEE610.12] IEEE STD 610.2: *IEEE Standard Glossary of Software Engineering Terminology*, 1990.

[IEEE1219] *IEEE STD 1219: Standard for Software Maintenance*, 1998.

[ISO12207] *ISO/IEC 12207: Information Technology-Software Life Cycle Processes*, 1995.

[ISO14764] *ISO/IEC 14764: Software Engineering-Software Maintenance*, 2000.

[Jon98] T.C. Jones. *Estimating Software Costs*. McGraw-Hill, 1998.

[Leh97] M.M. Lehman, Laws of Software Evolution Revisited, EWSPT96, October 1996, LNCS 1149, Springer Verlag, 1997.

[Par86] G. Parikh. *Handbook of Software Maintenance*. John Wiley & Sons, 1986.

[Pfl98] S.L. Pfleeger. *Software Engineering—Theory and Practice*. Prentice Hall, 1998.

[Pig93] T.M. Pigoski, "Maintainable Software: Why You Want It and How to Get It," *Proceedings of the Third Software Engineering Research Forum-November 1993*, University of West Florida Press, Pensacola, FL, 1993.

[Pig97] T.M. Pigoski. *Practical Software Maintenance: Best Practices for Managing your Software Investment*. Wiley, 1997.

[Pre97] R.S. Pressman. *Software Engineering: A Practitioner's Approach*. McGraw-Hill, fourth edition, 1997.

[SKV94] G.E. Stark, L.C. Kern, and C.V. Vowell. *A Software Metric Set for Program Maintenance Management*. Journal of Systems and Software, 1994.

[TG97] A. Takang and P. Grubb. *Software Maintenance Concepts and Practice*. International Thomson Computer Press, 1997.

APPENDIX C – DETAILED BREAKDOWN RATIONALE

Criterion (a): Number of topic breakdowns

One breakdown is provided.

Criterion (b): Reasonableness

The breakdowns are reasonable in that they cover the areas typically discussed in texts and standards, although there is less discussion regarding the pre-maintenance activities, e.g., planning. Other topics such as measures are also often not addressed although they are getting more attention now.

Criterion (c): Generally Accepted

The breakdowns are generally accepted in that they cover the areas typically discussed in texts and standards.

Criterion (d): No specific Application Domains

No specific application domains are assumed.

Criterion (e): Compatibility with Various Schools of Thought

Software maintenance concepts are stable and mature.

Criterion (f): Compatible with Industry, Literature, and Standards

The breakdown was derived from the literature and key standards reflecting consensus opinion. The extent to which industry implements the software maintenance concepts in the literature and in standards varies by company and project.

Criterion (g): As Inclusive as Possible

The primary topics are addressed within the page constraints of the chapter.

Criterion (h): Themes of Quality, Measurement, and Standards

Quality, Measurement and standards are discussed.

Criterion (i): 2 to 3 levels, 5 to 9 topics at the first level

The proposed breakdown satisfies this criterion.

Criterion (j): Topic Names Meaningful Outside the Guide

Wording is meaningful. Version 0.7/0.8 reviews indicated that the wording is meaningful.

Criterion (k) Vincenti Categorization

Topics were applied to the Vincenti Categorization.

Criterion (l): Topics only sufficiently described to allow reader to select appropriate material

A tutorial on maintenance was not provided. Generally accepted concepts were introduced with appropriate references for additional reading were provided.

Criterion (m): Text on the Rationale Underlying the Proposed Breakdowns

The Software Maintenance Theory and Practice was selected as the initial topic in order to introduce the topic. The subtopics are needed to provide definitions and to emphasis why there is a need for maintenance. Categories are critical to understand the underlying meaning of maintenance. All pertinent texts use a similar introduction.

The Maintenance Activities subtopic is needed to differentiate maintenance from development and to show the relationship to other software engineering activities. The subtopic on the Problems of Software Maintenance was chosen to ensure that the software engineers fully comprehended these problems.

Maintenance Process is needed to provide the current references and standards needed to implement the maintenance process.

Every organization is concerned with who will perform maintenance. The Organizational Aspect of Maintenance provides some options. There is always a discussion that maintenance is hard. Every software maintenance reference discusses the fact that maintenance consumes a large portion of the life cycle costs. The topic on Cost and Cost Estimation was provided to ensure that the readers select references to help with this difficult task.

The Software Maintenance Measurements topic is one that is not addressed very well in the literature. Most maintenance books barely touch on the topic. Measurement information is most often found in generalized measurement books. This topic was chosen to highlight the need for unique maintenance measures and to provide specify maintenance measurement references.

The Techniques topic was provided to introduce some of the generally accepted techniques used in maintenance operations.

Finally, there are other resources besides textbooks and periodicals that are useful to software engineers who wish to learn more about software maintenance. This topic is provided to list these additional resources.

CHAPTER 7

SOFTWARE CONFIGURATION MANAGEMENT

John A. Scott and David Nisse
Lawrence Livermore National Laboratory
7000 East Avenue
P.O. Box 808, L-632
Livermore, CA 94550, USA
(925) 423-7655
scott7@llnl.gov

Table of Contents

1   INTRODUCTION

This paper presents an overview of the knowledge area of software configuration management (SCM) for the Guide to the Software Engineering Body of Knowledge (SWEBOK) project. A breakdown of topics is presented for the knowledge area along with a succinct description of each topic. References are given to materials that provide more in-depth coverage of the key areas of software configuration management. Important knowledge areas of related disciplines are also identified.

Keywords

Software configuration management, software configuration identification, software configuration control, software configuration status accounting, software configuration auditing, software release management.

Acronyms

CCB	Configuration Control Board
CM	Configuration Management
DBMS	Database Management System
FCA	Functional Configuration Audit
PCA	Physical Configuration Audit

SCI	Software Configuration Item
SCR	Software Change Request
SCM	Software Configuration Management
SCMP	Software Configuration Management Plan
SCSA	Software Configuration Status Accounting
SDD	Software Design Description
SQA	Software Quality Assurance
SRS	Software Requirements Specification

2   DEFINITION OF THE SCM KNOWLEDGE AREA

A system can be defined as a collection of components organized to accomplish a specific function or set of functions [IEEE 610]. The configuration of a system is the function and/or physical characteristics of hardware, firmware, software or a combination thereof as set forth in technical documentation and achieved in a product [Buckley]. It can also be thought of as a collection of specific versions of hardware, firmware, or software items combined according to specific build procedures to accomplish a particular purpose. Configuration management (CM), then, is the discipline of identifying the configuration of a system at distinct points in time for the purpose of systematically controlling changes to the configuration and maintaining the integrity and traceability of the configuration throughout the system life cycle [Bersoff, (3)]. CM is formally defined [IEEE 610] as:

> "A discipline applying technical and administrative direction and surveillance to: identify and document the functional and physical characteristics of a configuration item, control changes to those characteristics, record and report change processing and implementation status, and verify compliance with specified requirements."

The concepts of configuration management apply to all items to be controlled although there are some differences in implementation between hardware CM and software CM.

This chapter presents a breakdown of the key software configuration management (SCM) concepts along with a succinct description of each concept. The concepts are generally accepted in that they cover the areas typically addressed in texts and standards. The descriptions cover the primary activities of SCM and are only intended to be sufficient for allowing the reader to select appropriate reference material according to the reader's needs. The SCM activities are: the management of the software configuration management process, software configuration identification, software configuration control, software configuration status accounting, software configuration auditing, and software release management and delivery.

Figure 1 shows a stylized representation of these activities

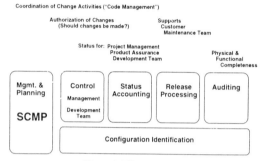

Figure 1. SCM Activities

Following the breakdown of SCM topics, key references for SCM are listed along with a cross-reference of topics that each listed reference covers. Finally, topics in related disciplines that are important to SCM are identified.

3   BREAKDOWN OF TOPICS FOR SCM

Breakdown of Topics

An outline of the breakdown of topics is shown below in Figure 2. Following the chart, a brief description of each breakdown topic is provided. The breakdown covers the concepts and activities of SCM. The variety of SCM tools and tool systems now available, as well as the variety of characteristics of the projects to which they are applied, may make the implementation of these concepts and the nature of the activities appear quite different from project to project. However, the underlying concepts and types of activities still apply.

I. Management of the SCM Process

Software configuration management is a supporting software life cycle process [ISO/IEC 12207] that benefits project and line management, development and maintenance activities, assurance activities, and the customers and users of the end product. From a management perspective, SCM controls the evolution and integrity of a product by identifying its elements, managing and controlling change, and verifying, recording and reporting on configuration information. From the

developer's perspective, SCM facilitates the development and change implementation activities. A successful SCM implementation requires careful planning and management. This, in turn, requires an understanding of the organizational context for, and the constraints placed upon, the design and implementation of the SCM process.

I.A Organizational Context for SCM

To plan an SCM process for a project, it is necessary to understand the organizational structure and the relationships among organizational elements. SCM interacts with several other activities or organizational elements.

SCM, like other processes such as software quality assurance and software verification and validation (V&V), is categorized as a supporting life cycle process. The organizational elements responsible for these processes may be structured in various ways. Although the responsibility for performing certain SCM tasks might be assigned to other organizations, such as the development organization, the overall responsibility for SCM typically rests with a distinct organizational element or designated individual.

Software is frequently developed as part of a larger system containing hardware and firmware elements. In this case, SCM activities take place in parallel with hardware and firmware CM activities and must be consistent with system level CM. Buckley [5] describes SCM within this context. Note that firmware contains hardware and software and, therefore, both hardware and software CM concepts are applicable.

SCM is closely related to the software quality assurance (SQA) activity. The goals of SQA can be characterized [Humphrey] as monitoring the software and its development process, ensuring compliance with standards and procedures, and ensuring that product, process, and standards defects are visible to management. SCM activities help in accomplishing these SQA goals. In some project contexts, e.g. see [IEEE 730], specific SQA requirements prescribe certain SCM activities.

SCM might also interface with an organization's quality assurance activity on issues such as records management and non-conforming items. Regarding the former, some items under SCM control might also be project records subject to provisions of the organization's quality assurance program. Managing non-conforming items is usually the responsibility of the quality assurance activity, however, SCM might assist with tracking and reporting on software items that fall in this category.

Perhaps the closest relationship is with the software development and maintenance organizations. The environment for software engineering includes such things as the:

- software life cycle model and its resulting plans and schedules,

- project strategies such as concurrent or distributed development activities,
- software reuse processes,
- development and target platforms, and
- software development tools.

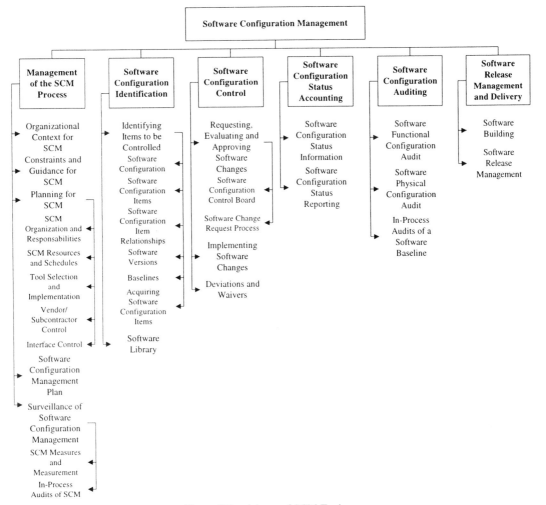

Figure 2 Breakdown of SCM Topics

This environment is also the environment within which many of the software configuration control tasks are conducted. Frequently, the same tools support development, maintenance and SCM purposes.

I.B Constraints and Guidance for SCM

Constraints affecting, and guidance for, the SCM process come from a number of sources. Policies and procedures set forth at corporate or other organizational levels might influence or prescribe the design and implementation of the SCM process for a given project. In addition, the contract between the acquirer and the supplier might contain provisions affecting the SCM process. For example, certain configuration audits might be required or it might be specified that certain items be placed under configuration management. When software products to be developed have the potential to affect the public safety, external regulatory bodies may impose constraints. For example, see [USNRC]. Finally, the particular software life cycle model chosen for a software project and the tools selected to implement the software affect the design and implementation of the SCM process [Bersoff, (4)].

Guidance for designing and implementing an SCM process can also be obtained from 'best practice' as reflected in the standards on software engineering issued by the various standards organizations. Moore [31] provides a roadmap to these organizations and their standards. Best practice is also reflected in process improvement and process assessment models such as the Software Engineering Institute's Capability Maturity Model (SEI/CMM) [Paulk] and the International Organization for Standardization's Software Process Improvement and Capability determination project (ISO SPICE) [El Emam].

I.C Planning for SCM

The planning of an SCM process for a given project should be consistent with the organizational context, applicable constraints, commonly accepted guidance, and the nature of the project (e.g., size and criticality). The major activities covered are Software Configuration Identification, Software Configuration Control, Software Configuration Status Accounting, Software Configuration Auditing, and Software Release Management and Delivery. In addition, issues such as organization and responsibilities, resources and schedules, tool selection and implementation, vendor and subcontractor control, and interface control are typically considered. The results of the planning activity are recorded in a Software Configuration Management Plan (SCMP). The SCMP is typically subject to SQA review and audit.

I.C.1 SCM Organization and Responsibilities

To prevent confusion about who will perform given SCM activities or tasks, organizations to be involved in the SCM process need to be clearly identified. Specific responsibilities for given SCM activities or tasks also need to be assigned to organizational entities, either by title or organizational element. The overall authority and reporting channels for SCM should also be identified, although this might be accomplished in the project management or quality assurance planning.

I.C.2 SCM Resources and Schedules

The planning for SCM identifies the staff and tools involved in carrying out SCM activities and tasks. It addresses schedule questions by establishing necessary sequences of SCM tasks and identifying their relationships to the project schedules and milestones established in the project management planning. Any training requirements necessary for implementing the plans and training new staff members are also specified.

I.C.3 Tool Selection and Implementation

Different types of tool capabilities, and procedures for their use, support the SCM activities. Depending on the situation, these tool capabilities can be made available with some combination of manual tools, automated tools providing a single SCM capability, automated tools integrating a range of SCM (and, perhaps other) capabilities, or integrated tool environments that serve the needs of multiple participants in the software development

process (e.g., SCM, development, V&V). Automated tool support becomes increasingly important, and increasingly difficult to establish, as projects grow in size and as project environments get more complex. These tool capabilities provide support for:

- the SCM Library,
- the software change request (SCR) and approval procedures,
- code (and related work products) and change management tasks,
- reporting software configuration status and collecting SCM measurements,
- software auditing,
- managing and tracking software documentation,
- performing software builds, and
- managing and tracking software releases and their distribution.

The use of tools in these areas increases the potential for obtaining product and process measurements to be used for project management and process improvement purposes. Royce [37] describes seven core measures of value in managing software processes. Information available from the various SCM tools relates to Royce's Work and Progress management indicator and to his quality indicators of Change Traffic and Stability, Breakage and Modularity, Rework and Adaptability, and MTBF (mean time between failures) and Maturity. Reporting on these indicators can be organized in various ways, such as by software configuration item or by type of change requested. Details on specific goals and measures for software processes are described in [Grady].

Figure 3 shows a representative mapping of tool capabilities and procedures to the SCM Activities.

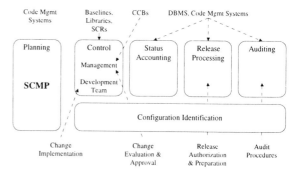

Figure 3 Characterization of SCM Tools and Related Procedures

In this example, code management systems support the operation of software libraries by controlling access to library elements, coordinating the activities of multiple users, and helping to enforce operating procedures. Other tools support the process of building software and release

© IEEE – Trial Version 1.00 – May 2001

documentation from the software elements contained in the libraries. Tools for managing software change requests support the change control procedures applied to controlled software items. Other tools can provide database management and reporting capabilities for management, development, and quality assurance activities. As mentioned above, the capabilities of several tool types might be integrated into SCM systems, which, in turn, are closely coupled to various other software activities.

The planning activity assesses the SCM tool needs for a given project within the context of the software engineering environment to be used and selects the tools to be used for SCM. The planning considers issues that might arise in the implementation of these tools, particularly if some form of culture change is necessary. An overview of SCM systems and selection considerations is given in [Dart, (7)], a recent case study on selecting an SCM system is given in [Midha], and [Hoek] provides a current web-based resource listing web links to various SCM tools.

I.C.4 Vendor/Subcontractor Control

A software project might acquire or make use of purchased software products, such as compilers. The planning for SCM considers if and how these items will be taken under configuration control (e.g., integrated into the project libraries) and how changes or updates will be evaluated and managed.

Similar considerations apply to subcontracted software. In this case, the SCM requirements to be imposed on the subcontractor's SCM process as part of the subcontract and the means for monitoring compliance also need to be established. The latter includes consideration of what SCM information must be available for effective compliance monitoring.

I.C.5 Interface Control

When a software item will interface with another software or hardware item, a change to either item can affect the other. The planning for the SCM process considers how the interfacing items will be identified and how changes to the items will be managed and communicated. The SCM role may be part of a larger system-level process for interface specification and control and may involve interface specifications, interface control plans, and interface control documents. In this case, SCM planning for interface control takes place within the context of the system level process. A discussion of the performance of interface control activities is given in [Berlack].

I.D Software Configuration Management Plan

The results of SCM planning for a given project are recorded in a Software Configuration Management Plan (SCMP). The SCMP is a 'living document' that serves as a reference for the SCM process. It is maintained (i.e., updated and approved) as necessary during the software life cycle. In implementing the plans contained in the SCMP, it is typically necessary to develop a number of more detailed, subordinate procedures that define how specific requirements will be carried out during day-to-day activities.

Guidance for the creation and maintenance of an SCMP, based on the information produced by the planning activity, is available from a number of sources, such as [IEEE 828 and IEEE 1042]. This reference provides requirements for the information to be contained in an SCMP. It also defines and describes six categories of SCM information to be included in an SCMP:

1. Introduction (purpose, scope, terms used)

2. SCM Management (organization, responsibilities, authorities, applicable policies, directives, and procedures)

3. SCM Activities (configuration identification, configuration control, etc.)

4. SCM Schedules (coordination with other project activities)

5. SCM Resources (tools, physical, and human resources)

6. SCMP Maintenance

I.E Surveillance of Software Configuration Management

After the SCM process has been implemented, some degree of surveillance may be conducted to ensure that the provisions of the SCMP are properly carried out (e.g., see [Buckley]). There are likely to be specific SQA requirements for ensuring compliance with specified SCM processes and procedures. This could involve an SCM authority ensuring that the defined SCM tasks are performed correctly by those with the assigned responsibility. The software quality assurance authority, as part of a compliance auditing activity, might also perform this surveillance.

The use of integrated SCM tools that have capabilities for process control can make the surveillance task easier. Some tools facilitate process compliance while providing flexibility for the developer to adapt procedures. Other tools enforce process, leaving the developer less flexibility. Surveillance requirements and the level of developer flexibility to be provided are important considerations in tool selection.

I.E.1 SCM Measures and Measurement

SCM measures can be designed to provide specific information on the evolving product or to provide insight into the functioning of the SCM process. A related goal of monitoring the SCM process is to discover opportunities for process improvement. Quantitative measurements against SCM process measures provide a good means for monitoring the effectiveness of SCM activities on an ongoing basis. These measurements are useful in characterizing the current state of the process as well as in providing a basis for making comparisons over time. Analysis of the measurements may produce insights leading to process changes and corresponding updates to the SCMP.

The software libraries and the various SCM tool capabilities provide sources for extracting information about the characteristics of the SCM process (as well as providing project and management information). For example, information about the processing time required for various types of changes would be useful in an evaluation of the criteria for determining what levels of authority are optimal for authorizing certain types of changes.

Care must be taken to keep the focus of the surveillance on the insights that can be gained from the measurements, not on the measurements themselves.

I.E.2 In-process Audits of SCM

Audits can be carried out during the development process to investigate the current status of specific elements of the configuration or to assess the implementation of the SCM process. In-process auditing of SCM provides a more formal mechanism for monitoring selected aspects of the process and may be coordinated with the SQA auditing function.

II. Software Configuration Identification

The software configuration identification activity identifies items to be controlled, establishes identification schemes for the items and their versions, and establishes the tools and techniques to be used in acquiring and managing controlled items. These activities provide the basis for the other SCM activities.

II.A Identifying Items to be Controlled

A first step in controlling change is to identify the software items to be controlled. This involves understanding the software configuration within the context of the system configuration, selecting software configuration items, developing a strategy for labeling software items and describing their relationships, and identifying the baselines to be used, along with the procedure for a baseline's acquisition of the items.

II.A.1 Software Configuration

A software configuration is the set of functional and physical characteristics of software as set forth in the technical documentation or achieved in a product [IEEE 610]. It can be viewed as a part of an overall system configuration.

II.A.2 Software Configuration Item

A software configuration item (SCI) is an aggregation of software that is designated for configuration management and is treated as a single entity in the SCM process [IEEE 610]. A variety of items, in addition to the code itself, are typically controlled by SCM. Software items with potential to become SCIs include plans, specifications and design documentation, testing materials, software tools, source and executable code, code libraries, data and data dictionaries, and documentation for installation, maintenance, operations and software use.

Selecting SCIs is an important process that must achieve a balance between providing adequate visibility for project control purposes and providing a manageable number of controlled items. A list of criteria for SCI selection is given in [Berlack].

II.A.3 Software Configuration Item Relationships

The structural relationships among the selected SCIs, and their constituent parts, affect other SCM activities or tasks, such as software building or analyzing the impact of proposed changes. Proper tracking of these relationships is also important for supporting traceability verifications. The design of the identification scheme for SCIs should consider the need to map the identified items to the software structure as well as the need to support the evolution of the software items and their relationships.

II.A.4 Software Versions

Software items evolve as a software project proceeds. A *version* of a software item is a particular identified and specified item. It can be thought of as a state of an evolving item [Conradi]. A *revision* is a new version of an item that is intended to replace the old version of the item. A *variant* is a new version of an item that will be added to the configuration without replacing the old version. The management of software versions in various software engineering environments is a current research topic; for example, see [Conradi], [Estublier], and [Sommerville, (39)].

II.A.5 Baseline

A software baseline is a set of software items formally designated and fixed at a specific time during the software life cycle. The term is also used to refer to a particular version of a software item that has been agreed upon. In either case, the baseline can only be changed through formal change control procedures. A baseline, together with all approved changes to the baseline, represents the current approved configuration.

Commonly used baselines are the functional, allocated, developmental, and product baselines; e.g. see [Berlack]. The functional baseline corresponds to the reviewed system requirements. The allocated baseline corresponds to the reviewed software requirements specification and software interface requirements specification. The developmental baseline represents the evolving software configuration at selected times during the software life cycle. Change authority for this baseline typically rests primarily with the development organization, but may be shared by other organizations (e.g., SCM or Test). The product baseline corresponds to the completed software product delivered for system integration. The baselines to be used for a given project, along with their associated levels of authority needed for change approval, are typically identified in the SCMP.

II.A.6 Acquiring Software Configuration Items

Software configuration items are placed under SCM control at different times; i.e. they are incorporated into a particular baseline at a particular point in the software life cycle. The triggering event is the completion of some form of formal acceptance task, such as a formal review. Figure 4 characterizes the growth of baselined items as the life cycle proceeds. This figure is based on a waterfall model for purposes of illustration only; the subscripts used in the figure indicate versions of the evolving items. The software change request (SCR) is described in section III.A.

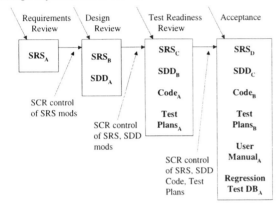

Figure 4 Acquisition of Items

Following the acquisition of an SCI, changes to the item must be formally approved as appropriate for the SCI and the baseline involved, as defined in the SCMP. Following the approval, the item is incorporated into the software baseline according to the appropriate procedure.

II.B Software Library

A software library is a controlled collection of software and related documentation designed to aid in software development, use, and maintenance [IEEE 610]. It is also instrumental in software release and delivery activities. Several types of libraries might be used, each corresponding to a particular level of maturity of the software item. For example a working library could support coding and a project support library could support testing, whereas a master library could be used for finished products. An appropriate level of SCM control (associated baseline and level of authority for change) is associated with each library. Security, in terms of access control and the backup facilities, is a key aspect of library management. A model of a software library is described in [Berlack].

The tool(s) used for each library must support the SCM control needs for that library, both in terms of controlling SCIs and controlling access to the library. At the working library level, this is a code management capability serving

developers, maintainers and SCM. It is focused on managing the versions of software items while supporting the activities of multiple developers. At higher levels of control, access is more restricted and SCM is the primary user.

These libraries are also an important source of information for measurements of work and progress.

III. Software Configuration Control

Software configuration control is concerned with managing changes during the software life cycle. It covers the process for determining what changes to make, the authority for approving certain changes, support for the implementation of those changes, and the concept of formal deviations and waivers from project requirements. Information derived from these activities is useful in measuring change traffic, breakage, and aspects of rework.

III.A. Requesting, Evaluating and Approving Software Changes

The first step in managing changes to controlled items is determining what changes to make. The software change request process (see Figure 5) provides formal procedures for submitting and recording change requests, evaluating the potential cost and impact of a proposed change, and accepting, modifying or rejecting the proposed change. Requests for changes to software configuration items may be originated by anyone at any point in the software life cycle and may include a suggested solution and requested priority. One source of change requests is the initiation of corrective action in response to problem reports. Regardless of the source, the type of change (e.g. defect or enhancement) usually recorded on the SCR.

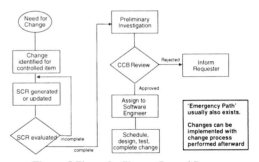

Figure 5 Flow of a Change Control Process

This provides an opportunity for tracking defects and collecting change activity measurements by change type. Once an SCR is received, a technical evaluation (also known as an impact analysis) is performed to determine the extent of modifications that would be necessary should the change request be accepted. A good understanding of the relationships among software (and possibly, hardware) items is important for this task. Finally, an established authority, commensurate with the affected baseline, the SCI involved, and the nature of the change, will evaluate the technical and managerial aspects of the change request and either accept, modify, reject or defer the proposed change.

III.A.1. Software Configuration Control Board

The authority for accepting or rejecting proposed changes rests with an entity typically known as a Configuration Control Board (CCB). In smaller projects, this authority actually may reside with the responsible leader or an assigned individual rather than a multi-person board. There can be multiple levels of change authority depending on a variety of criteria, such as the criticality of the item involved, the nature of the change (e.g., impact on budget and schedule), or the current point in the life cycle. The composition of the CCBs used for a given system varies depending on these criteria (an SCM representative would always be present). All stakeholders, appropriate to the level of the CCB, are represented. When the scope of authority of a CCB is strictly software, it is known as a software configuration control board (SCCB). The activities of the CCB are typically subject to SQA audit or review.

III.A.2 Software Change Request Process

An effective SCR process requires the use of supporting tools and procedures ranging from paper forms and a documented procedure to an electronic tool for originating change requests, enforcing the flow of the change process, capturing CCB decisions, and reporting change process information. A link between this tool capability and the problem reporting system can facilitate the tracking of solutions for reported problems. Change process descriptions and supporting forms (information) are given in a variety of references, e.g. [Berlack] and [IEEE 1042]. Typically, change management tools are tailored to local processes and tool suites and are often locally developed. The current trend is towards integration of these kinds of tools within a suite referred to as a software engineering environment.

III.B. Implementing Software Changes

Approved change requests are implemented using the defined software procedures in accordance with the applicable schedule requirements. Since a number of approved change requests might be implemented simultaneously, it is necessary to provide a means for tracking which change requests are incorporated into particular software versions and baselines. As part of the closure of the change process, completed changes may undergo configuration audits and SQA verification. This includes ensuring that only approved changes were made. The change request process described above will typically document the SCM (and other) approval information for the change.

The actual implementation of a change is supported by the library tool capabilities that provide version management

and code repository support. At a minimum, these tools provide check-in/out and associated version control capabilities. More powerful tools can support parallel development and geographically distributed environments. These tools may be manifested as separate specialized applications under control of an independent SCM group. They may also appear as an integrated part of the software development environment. Finally, they may be as elementary as a rudimentary change control system provided with an operating system.

III.C. Deviations and Waivers

The constraints imposed on a software development effort or the specifications produced during the development activities might contain provisions that cannot be satisfied at the designated point in the life cycle. A deviation is an authorization to depart from a provision prior to the development of the item. A waiver is an authorization to use an item, following its development, that departs from the provision in some way. In these cases, a formal process is used for gaining approval for deviations to, or waivers of, the provisions.

IV. Software Configuration Status Accounting

Software configuration status accounting (SCSA) is the recording and reporting of information needed for effective management of the software configuration. The design of the SCSA capability can be viewed from an information systems perspective, utilizing accepted information systems design techniques.

IV.A. Software Configuration Status Information

The SCSA activity designs and operates a system for the capture and reporting of necessary information as the life cycle proceeds. As in any information system, the configuration status information to be managed for the evolving configurations must be identified, collected, and maintained. Various information and measurements are needed to support the SCM process and to meet the configuration status reporting needs of management, software engineering, and other related activities. The types of information available include the approved configuration identification as well as the identification and current implementation status of changes, deviations and waivers. A partial list of important data elements is given in [Berlack].

Some form of automated tool support is necessary to accomplish the SCSA data collection and reporting tasks. This could be a database capability, such as a relational or object-oriented database management system. This could be a stand-alone tool or a capability of a larger, integrated tool environment.

IV.B. Software Configuration Status Reporting

Reported information can be used by various organizational and project elements, including the development team, the maintenance team, project management, and quality assurance activities. Reporting can take the form of ad hoc queries to answer specific questions or the periodic production of pre-designed reports. Some information produced by the status accounting activity during the course of the life cycle might become quality assurance records.

In addition to reporting the current status of the configuration, the information obtained by SCSA can serve as a basis for various measurements of interest to management, development, and SCM. Examples include the number of change requests per SCI and the average time needed to implement a change request.

V. Software Configuration Auditing

A software audit is an activity performed to independently evaluate the conformance of software products and processes to applicable regulations, standards, guidelines, plans, and procedures [IEEE 1028]. Audits are conducted according to a well-defined process consisting of various auditor roles and responsibilities. Consequently, each audit must be carefully planned. An audit can require a number of individuals to perform a variety of tasks over a fairly short period of time. Tools to support the planning and conduct of an audit can greatly facilitate the process. Guidance for conducting software audits is available in various references, such as [Berlack], [Buckley], and [IEEE 1028].

The software configuration auditing activity determines the extent to which an item satisfies the required functional and physical characteristics. Informal audits of this type can be conducted at key points in the life cycle. Two types of formal audits might be required by the governing contract (e.g., in contracts covering critical software): the Functional Configuration Audit (FCA) and the Physical Configuration Audit (PCA). Successful completion of these audits can be a prerequisite for the establishment of the product baseline. Buckley [5] contrasts the purposes of the FCA and PCA in hardware versus software contexts and recommends careful evaluation of the need for the software FCA and PCA before performing them.

V.A. Software Functional Configuration Audit

The purpose of the software FCA is to ensure that the audited software item is consistent with its governing specifications. The output of the software verification and validation activities is a key input to this audit.

V.B. Software Physical Configuration Audit

The purpose of the software PCA is to ensure that the design and reference documentation is consistent with the as-built software product.

V.C. In-process Audits of a Software Baseline

As mentioned above, audits can be carried out during the development process to investigate the current status of specific elements of the configuration. In this case, an audit could be applied to sampled baseline items to ensure that performance was consistent with specification or to ensure

that evolving documentation was staying consistent with the developing baseline item.

VI. Software Release Management and Delivery

The term "release" is used in this context to refer to the distribution of a software configuration item outside the development activity. This includes internal releases as well as distribution to customers. When different versions of a software item are available for delivery, such as versions for different platforms or versions with varying capabilities, it is frequently necessary to recreate specific versions and package the correct materials for delivery of the version. The software library is a key element in accomplishing release and delivery tasks.

VI.A. Software Building

Software building is the activity of combining the correct versions of software items, using the appropriate configuration data, into an executable program for delivery to a customer or other recipient, such as the testing activity. For systems with hardware or firmware, the executable is delivered to the system building activity. Build instructions ensure that the proper build steps are taken and in the correct sequence. In addition to building software for new releases, it is usually also necessary for SCM to have the capability to reproduce previous releases for recovery, testing, or additional release purposes.

Software is built using particular versions of supporting tools, such as compilers. It might be necessary to rebuild an exact copy of a previously built software item. In this case, the supporting tools and associated build instructions need to be under SCM control to ensure availability of the correct versions of the tools.

A tool capability is useful for selecting the correct versions of software items for a given target environment and for automating the process of building the software from the selected versions and appropriate configuration data. For large projects with parallel development or distributed development environments, this tool capability is necessary. Most software development environments provide this capability. These tools vary in complexity from requiring the engineer to learn a specialized scripting language to graphics-oriented approaches that hide much of the complexity of an "intelligent" build facility.

The build process and products are often subject to SQA verification. Outputs of the build process might be needed for future reference and may become quality assurance records.

VI.B Software Release Management

Software release management encompasses the identification, packaging and delivery of the elements of a product, for example, the executable, documentation, release notes, and configuration data. Given that product changes can be occurring on a continuing basis, one issue for release management is determining when to issue a release. The severity of the problems addressed by the release and measurements of the fault densities of prior releases affect this decision [Sommerville, (38)]. The packaging task must identify which product items are to be delivered and select the correct variants of those items, given the intended application of the product. The set of information documenting the physical contents of a release is known as a version description document and may exist in hardcopy or electronic form. The release notes typically describe new capabilities, known problems, and platform requirements necessary for proper product operation. The package to be released also contains loading or upgrading instructions. The latter can be complicated by the fact that some current users might have versions that are several releases old. Finally, in some cases, the release management activity might be required to track the distribution of the product to various customers or target systems. An example would be a case where the supplier was required to notify a customer of newly reported problems.

A tool capability is needed for supporting these release management functions. It is useful to have a connection with the tool capability supporting the change request process in order to map release contents to the SCRs that have been received. This tool capability might also maintain information on various target platforms and on various customer environments.

4 BREAKDOWN RATIONALE

One of the primary goals of the Guide to the SWEBOK is to arrive at a breakdown that is 'generally accepted'. Consequently, the breakdown of SCM topics was developed largely by attempting to synthesize the topics covered in the literature and in recognized standards, which tend to reflect consensus opinion. The topic on Software Release Management and Delivery is an exception since it has not commonly been broken out separately in the past. The precedent for this was set by the ISO/IEC 12207 standard [23], which identifies a 'Release Management and Delivery' activity.

There is widespread agreement in the literature on the SCM activity areas and their key concepts. However, there continues to be active research on implementation aspects of SCM. Examples are found in ICSE workshops on SCM such as [Estublier] and [Sommerville, (39)].

5 MATRIX OF TOPICS VS. REFERENCE MATERIAL

Table 1. Coverage of the Breakdown Topics by the Recommended References

	Babich	Berlack	Buckley	Conradi	Dart	Hoek	IEEE 828	IEEE/EIA 12207	Midha	Moore	Paulk	Pressman	Royce	Sommerville
I. Management of the SCM Process														
A. Organizational Context for SCM		C4	C2		C2		4.2.1							
B. Constraints and Guidance for SCM		C5					4.1, 4.2.3			X				
C. Planning for SCM					C2			6.2.1						C33
1. SCM Organization and Responsibilities		C7	C3				4.2							
2. SCM Resources and Schedules		C7	C3				4.4, 4.5							
3. Tool Selection and Implementation		C15		C6	C3, App A	X				X		C29		
4. Vendor/Subcontractor Control		C13	C11				4.3.6							
5. Interface Control		C12					4.3.5							
D. SCM Plan		C7	C3				4				L2-81			
E. Surveillance of SCM											L2-87			
1. SCM Measures and Measurement			C3										202,283-	
2. In-Process Audits of SCM			C15											
II. Software Configuration Identification								6.2.2						
A. Identifying Items to be Controlled		C8					4.3.1				L2-83			C33
1. Software Configuration			C4,6									C9		
2. Software Configuration Item			C4,6	C2								C9		
3. Software Configuration Item Relationships				C2								C9		
4. Software Versions	C2			C3,C4,C5								C9		
5. Baseline	C5		C4									C9		
6. Acquiring Software Configuration Items			C4											
B. Software Library	C2,5	C14	C4				4.3.1				L2-82			C33
III. Software Configuration Control								6.2.3			L2-84			
A. Requesting, Evaluating and Approving Software Changes							4.3.2					C9		C33
1. Software Configuration Control Board		C9	C9,11									C9		
2. Software Change Request Process		C9	C9,11									C9		

	Babich	Berlack	Buckley	Conradi	Dart	Hoek	IEEE 828	IEEE/EIA 12207	Midha	Moore	Paulk	Pressman	Royce	Sommerville
B. Implementing Software Changes	C6	C9	C9,11				4.3.2.4					C9		C33
C. Deviations & Waivers		C9	C12											
IV. Software Configuration Status Accounting								6.2.4			L2-85	C9		C33
A. Software Configuration Status Inf.		C10	C13				4.3.3							
B. Software Configuration Status Rptg.		C10	C13											
V. Software Configuration Auditing							4.3.4	6.2.5			L2-86	C9,C17		
A. Software Functional Configuration Audit		C11	C15											
B. Software Physical Configuration Audit		C11	C15											
C. In-Process Audits of a Software Baseline			C15											
VI. Software Release Management and Delivery								6.2.6						
A. Software Building	C6													C33
B. Software Release Management														C33

6 RECOMMENDED REFERENCES FOR SCM

Cross Reference Matrix

Table 1, in Appendix A, provides a cross reference between the recommended references and the topics of the breakdown. Note that, where a recommended reference is also shown in the Further Reading section, the cross reference reflects the full text rather than just the specific passage referenced in the Recommended References.

Recommended References

Specific recommendations are made here to provide additional information on the topics of the SCM breakdown.

W.A. Babich, Software Configuration Management, Coordination for Team Productivity, Addison-Wesley, 1986 [1]

Pages 20-43 address the basics of code management.

H.R. Berlack, Software Configuration Management, Wiley 1992 [2]

See pages 101-175 on configuration identification, configuration control and configuration status accounting, and pages 202-206 on libraries.

F.J. Buckley, Implementing Configuration Management: Hardware, Software, and Firmware 2nd edition, IEEE Computer Society Press, 1996 [5]

See pages 10-19 on organizational context, pages 21-38 on CM planning, and 228-250 on CM auditing.

R. Conradi and B. Westfechtel, "Version Models for Software Configuration Management", ACM Computing Surveys, vol. 30, no. 2, June 1998 [6]

An in-depth article on version models used in software configuration management. It defines fundamental concepts and provides a detailed view of versioning paradigms. The versioning characteristics of various SCM systems are discussed.

S.A. Dart, Spectrum of Functionality in Configuration Management Systems [7]

This report covers features of various CM systems and the scope of issues concerning users of CM systems. As of this writing, the report can be found on the Internet at: http://www.sei.cmu.edu/about/website/search.html

Hoek, "Configuration Management Yellow Pages," [13]

This web page provides a current compilation of SCM resources.
ht:p://www.cmtoday.com/yp/configuration_management.html

IEEE/EIA Std 12207.0-1996, Software Life Cycle Processes, [20] and IEEE/EIA Std 12207.1-1996, Software Life Cycle Processes - Life Cycle Data, [21]

These standards provide the ISO/IEC view of software processes along with specific information on life cycle data keyed to software engineering standards of other standards bodies.

IEEE Std.828-1990, IEEE Standard for Software Configuration Management Plans [17] and IEEE Std.1042-1987, IEEE Guide to Software Configuration Management [19]

These standards focus on SCM activities by specifying requirements and guidance for preparing the SCMP. These standards reflect commonly accepted practice for software configuration management.

A.K. Midha, "Software Configuration Management for the 21st Century", Bell Technical Labs Journal, vol. 2 no. 1, Winter 1997, pp. 154-165 [30]

This article discusses the characteristics of SCM systems, assessment of SCM needs in a particular environment, and the issue of selecting and implementing an SCM system. It is a current case study on this issue.

J.W. Moore, Software Engineering Standards, A User's Road Map, IEEE Computer Society Press, 1998 [31]

Pages 118-119 cover SCM and pages 194-223 cover the perspective of the 12207 standards.

M.C. Paulk, et al., Key Practices of the Capability Maturity Model, Software Engineering Institute, 1993 [32]

Pages 180-191 cover the SCM key process area of the SEI CMM.

R.S. Pressman, Software Engineering: A Practitioner's Approach, 4th edition, McGraw-Hill, 1997 [36]

Pages 209-226 address SCM in the context of a textbook on software engineering.

Walker Royce, Software Project Management, A Unified Framework, Addison-Wesley, 1998 [37]

Pages 188-202 and 283-298 cover measures of interest to software project management that are closely related to SCM.

I. Sommerville, Software Engineering, 5th edition, Addison-Wesley, 1996 [38]

Pages 675-696 cover SCM with an emphasis on software building and release management.

APPENDIX A – LIST OF FURTHER READINGS

The following set of references was chosen to provide coverage of all aspects of SCM, from various perspectives and to varying levels of detail. The author and title are cited; the complete reference is given in the References section. Some items overlap with those in the Recommended References since they cover the full texts rather than specific passages.

W.A. Babich, Software Configuration Management, Coordination for Team Productivity [1]

This text is focused on code management issues from the perspective of the development team.

H.R. Berlack, Software Configuration Management [2]

This textbook provides detailed, comprehensive coverage of the concepts of software configuration management. This is one of the more recent texts with this focus.

F.J. Buckley, Implementing Configuration Management: Hardware, Software, and Firmware [5]

This text presents an integrated view of configuration management for projects in which software, hardware and firmware are involved. It is a recent text that provides a view of software configuration management from a systems perspective.

J. Estublier, Software Configuration Management, ICSE SCM-4 and SCM-5 Workshops Selected Papers [10]

These workshop proceedings are representative of current experience and research on SCM. This reference is included with the intention of directing the reader to the whole class of conference and workshop proceedings.

The suite of IEEE/EIA and ISO/IEC 12207 standards, [20]-[24]

These standards cover software life cycle processes and address SCM in that context. These standards reflect commonly accepted practices for software life cycle processes. Note - the developing ISO/IEC TR 15504 (SPICE99) expands on SCM within the context of the ISO/IEC 12207 standard.

IEEE Std.1042-1987, IEEE Guide to Software Configuration Management [19]

This standard provides guidance, keyed to IEEE 828, for preparing the SCMP.

J.W. Moore, Software Engineering Standards, A User's Road Map [31]

This text provides a comprehensive view of current standards and standards activities in the area of software engineering.

APPENDIX B – REFERENCES USED TO WRITE AND
JUSTIFY THE KNOWLEDGE AREA DESCRIPTION

These references were used in preparing this paper; the
recommended references for SCM are listed in Section 3.1.

1. W.A. Babich, Software Configuration Management:
   Coordination for Team Productivity, Addison-Wesley,
   Reading, Massachusetts, 1986.

2. H.R. Berlack, Software Configuration Management,
   John Wiley & Sons, New York, 1992.

3. E.H. Bersoff, "Elements of Software Configuration
   Management," Software Engineering, M. Dorfman and
   R.H. Thayer ed., IEEE Computer Society Press, Los
   Alamitos, CA, 1997.

4. E.H. Bersoff and A.M. Davis, "Impacts of Life Cycle
   Models on Software Configuration Management,"
   Communications of the ACM, Vol. 34, No. 8, August
   1991, pp104-118.

5. F.J. Buckley, Implementing Configuration
   Management: Hardware, Software, and Firmware,
   Second Edition, IEEE Computer Society Press, Los
   Alamitos, CA, 1996.

6. R. Conradi and B. Westfechtel, "Version Models for
   Software Configuration Management," ACM
   Computing Surveys, Vol. 30, No. 2, June 1998, pp.
   232-282.

7. S.A. Dart, Spectrum of Functionality in Configuration
   Management Systems, Technical Report CMU/SEI-90-
   TR-11, Software Engineering Institute, Carnegie
   Mellon University, 1990.

8. S.A. Dart, "Concepts in Configuration Management
   Systems," Proceedings of the Third International
   Workshop on Software Configuration Management,
   ACM Press, New York, 1991, pp1-18.

9. Khaled El Emam, et al., SPICE, The Theory and
   Practice of Software Process Improvement and
   Capability Determination, IEEE Computer Society,
   Los Alamitos, CA, 1998.

10. J. Estublier, Software Configuration Management,
    ICSE SCM-4 and SCM-5 Workshops Selected Papers,
    Springer-Verlag, Berlin, 1995.

11. P.H. Feiler, Configuration Management Models in
    Commercial Environments, Technical Report
    CMU/SEI-91-TR-7, Software Engineering Institute,
    Carnegie Mellon University, 1991.

12. R.B. Grady, Practical Software Metrics for Project
    Management and Process Improvement, Prentice-Hall,
    Englewook Cliffs, NJ, 1992.

13. Hoek, "Configuration Management Yellow Pages,"
    http://www.cs.colorado.edu/users/andre/configuration_
    management.html

14. W.S. Humphrey, Managing the Software Process,
    Addison-Wesley, Reading, MA, 1989.

15. IEEE Std.610.12-1990, IEEE Standard Glossary of
    Software Engineering Terminology, IEEE, Piscataway,
    NJ, 1990.

16. IEEE Std.730-1998, IEEE Standard for Software
    Quality Assurance Plans, IEEE, Piscataway, NJ, 1998.

17. IEEE Std.828-1998, IEEE Standard for Software
    Configuration Management Plans, IEEE, Piscataway,
    NJ, 1998.

18. IEEE Std.1028-1997, IEEE Standard for Software
    Reviews, IEEE, Piscataway, NJ, 1997.

19. IEEE Std.1042-1987, IEEE Guide to Software
    Configuration Management, IEEE, Piscataway, NJ,
    1987.

20. IEEE/EIA Std 12207.0-1996, Software Life Cycle
    Processes, IEEE, Piscataway, NJ, 1996.

21. IEEE/EIA Std 12207.1-1996, Guide for Software Life
    Cycle Processes – Life Cycle Data, IEEE, Piscataway,
    NJ, 1996.

22. IEEE/EIA Std 12207.2-1996, Guide for Software Life
    Cycle Processes – Implementation Considerations,
    IEEE, Piscataway, NJ, 1996.

23. ISO/IEC 12207:1995(E), Information Technology -
    Software Life Cycle Processes, ISO/IEC, Geneve,
    Switzerland, 1995.

24. ISO/IEC TR 15846:1998, Information Technology -
    Software Life Cycle Processes - Configuration
    Management , ISO/IEC, Geneve, Switzerland, 1998.

25. ISO/DIS 9004-7 (now ISO 10007), Quality
    Management and Quality System Elements, Guidelines
    for Configuration Management, International
    Organization for Standardization, Geneve,
    Switzerland, 1993.

26. P. Jalote, An Integrated Approach to Software
    Engineering, Springer-Verlag, New York, 1997

27. John J. Marciniak and Donald J. Reifer, Software
    Acquisition Management, Managing the Acquisition of
    Custom Software Systems, John Wiley & Sons, 1990.

28. J.J. Marciniak, "Reviews and Audits," Software
    Engineering, M. Dorfman and R.H. Thayer ed., IEEE
    Computer Society Press, Los Alamitos, CA, 1997.

29. K. Meiser, "Software Configuration Management
    Terminology," Crosstalk, 1995,
    http://www.stsc.hill.af.mil/crosstalk/1995/jan/terms.ht
    ml, February 1999.

30. A.K. Midha, "Software Configuration Management for
    the 21st Century," Bell Labs Technical Journal, Winter
    1997.

31. J.W. Moore, Software Engineering Standards, A
    User's Roadmap, IEEE Computer Society, Los
    Alamitos, CA, 1998.

32. M.C. Paulk, et al., Key Practices of the Capability Maturity Model, Version 1.1, Technical Report CMU/SEI-93-TR-025, Software Engineering Institute, Carnegie Mellon University, 1993

33. M.C. Paulk, et al., The Capability Maturity Model, Guidelines for Improving the Software Process, Addison-Wesley, Reading, Massachusetts, 1995.

34. S.L. Pfleeger, Software Engineering: Theory and Practice, Prentice Hall, Upper Saddle River, NJ, 1998

35. R.K. Port, "Software Configuration Management Technology Report, September 1994, " http://www.stsc.hill.af.mil/cm/REPORT.html, February 1999.

36. R.S. Pressman, Software Engineering: A Practitioner's Approach, McGraw-Hill, New York, 1997.

37. Walker Royce, Software Project Management, A United Framework, Addison-Wesley, Reading, Massachusetts, 1998.

38. Sommerville, Software Engineering, Fifth Edition, Addison-Wesley, Reading, Massachusetts, 1995.

39. Sommerville, Software Configuration Management, ICSE SCM-6 Workshop, Selected Papers, Springer-Verlag, Berlin, 1996.

40. USNRC Regulatory Guide 1.169, Configuration Management Plans for Digital Computer Software Used in Safety Systems of Nuclear Power Plants, U.S. Nuclear Regulatory Commission, Washington DC, 1997.

41. J.P. Vincent, et al., Software Quality Assurance, Prentice-Hall, Englewood Cliffs, NJ, 1988.

42. W.G. Vincenti, What Engineers Know and How They Know It, The Johns Hopkins University Press, Baltimore, MD, 1990.

43. D. Whitgift, Methods and Tools for Software Configuration Management, John Wiley & Sons, Chichester, England, 1991.

M.C. Paulk, et al., Key Practices of the Capability Maturity Model [32]

This report describes the key practices that could be evaluated in assessing software process maturity. Therefore, the section on SCM key practices provides a view of SCM from a software process assessment perspective.

R.S. Pressman, Software Engineering: A Practitioner's Approach [36]

This reference and the Sommerville reference address SCM in the context of a textbook on software engineering.

I. Sommerville, Software Engineering [38]

This reference and the Pressman reference address SCM in the context of a textbook on software engineering.

J.P. Vincent, et al., Software Quality Assurance [41]

In this text, SCM is described from the perspective of a complete set of assurance processes for a software development project.

D. Whitgift, Methods and Tools for Software Configuration Management [43]

This text covers the concepts and principles of SCM. It provides detailed information on the practical questions of implementing and using tools. This text is out of print but still available in libraries.

Criterion (a): Number of topic breakdowns

One breakdown is provided.

Criterion (b): Reasonableness

The breakdowns are reasonable in that they cover the areas typically discussed in texts and standards, although there is somewhat less discussion of release management as a separate topic. In response to comments on version 0.5 of the paper, the tool discussion under 'Planning for SCM' has been expanded. The various tool subheadings used throughout the text have been removed (so they do not appear as topics), however, the supporting text has been retained and incorporated into the next higher level topics.

Criterion (c): Generally Accepted

The breakdowns are generally accepted in that they cover the areas typically discussed in texts and standards.

At level 1, the breakdown is identical to that given in IEC 12207 (Section 6.2) except that the term "Management of the Software Configuration Management Process" was used instead of "Process Implementation" and the term "Software Configuration Auditing" was used instead of "Configuration Evaluation." The typical texts discuss Software Configuration Management Planning (our topic A.3); We have expanded this to a "management of the process" concept in order to capture related ideas expressed in many of the references that we have used. These ideas are captured in topics A.1 (organizational context), A.2 (constraints and guidance), and A.4 (surveillance of the SCM process). A similar comparison can also be made to [Buckley] except for the addition of "Software Release Management and Delivery."

We have chosen to include the word "Software" as a prefix to most of the configuration topics to distinguish the topics from hardware CM or system level CM activities. We would reserve "Configuration Management" for system purposes and then use HCM and SCM for hardware and software respectively.

The topic A.1, "Software Configuration Management Organizational Context," covers key topics addressed in multiple texts and articles and it appears within the level 1 headings consistently with the placement used in the references. This new term on organizational context was included as a placeholder for capturing three concepts found in the references. First, [Buckley] discusses SCM in the overall context of a project with hardware, software, and firmware elements. We believe that this is a link to a related discipline of system engineering. (This is similar to what IEEE 828 discusses under the heading of "Interface Control"). Second, SCM is one of the product assurance processes supporting a project, or in IEC 12207 terminology, one of the supporting lifecycle processes. The processes are closely related and, therefore, interfaces to them should be considered in planning for SCM. Finally,

some of the tools for implementing SCM might be the same tools used by the developers. Therefore, in planning SCM, there should be awareness that the implementation of SCM is strongly affected by the environment chosen for the development activities.

The inclusion of the topic "Release Management and Delivery" is somewhat controversial since the majority of texts on software configuration management devote little or no attention to the topic. We believe that most writers assume the library function of configuration identification would support release management and delivery but, perhaps, assume that these activities are the responsibility of project or line management. The IEC 12207 standard, however, has established this as a required area for SCM. Since this has occurred and since this topic should be recognized somewhere in the overall description of software activities, "Release Management and Delivery" has been included.

Criterion (d): No Specific Application Domains

No specific application domains have been assumed.

Criterion (e): Compatible with Various Schools of Thought

SCM concepts are fairly stable and mature.

Criterion (f): Compatible with Industry, Literature, and Standards

The breakdown was derived from the literature and from key standards reflecting consensus opinion. The extent to which industry implements the SCM concepts in the literature and in standards varies by company and project.

Criterion (g): As Inclusive as Possible

The inclusion of the level 1 topic on management of SCM expands the planning concept into a larger area that can cover all management-related topics, such as surveillance of the SCM process. For each level 1 topic, the level 2 topics categorize the main areas in various references' discussions of the level 1 topic. These are intended to be general enough to allow an open-ended set of subordinate level 3 topics on specific issues. The level 3 topics cover specifics found in the literature but are not intended to provide an exhaustive breakdown of the level 2 topic.

Criterion (h): Themes of Quality and Measurement

The relationship of SCM to product assurance and measurement is provided for in the breakdowns. The description also conveys the role of SCM in achieving a consistent, verified, and validated product.

Criterion (i): 2 to 3 levels, 5 to 9 topics at the first level

The proposed breakdown satisfies this criterion.

Criterion (j): Topic Names Meaningful Outside the Guide

For the most part, we believe this is the case. Some terms, such a "Baselines" or "Physical Configuration Audit" require some explanation but they are obviously the terms to use since appear throughout the literature.

Criterion (k): Topics only sufficiently described to allow reader to select appropriate material

We believe this has been accomplished. We have not attempted to provide a tutorial on SCM.

Criterion (l): Text on the Rationale Underlying the Proposed Breakdowns

This document provides the rationale.

CHAPTER 8

SOFTWARE ENGINEERING MANAGEMENT

Stephen G. MacDonell and Andrew R. Gray

University of Otago,
Dunedin, New Zealand
+64 3 479 8135 (phone) +64 3 479 8311 (fax)
stevemac@infoscience.otago.ac.nz

Table of Contents

1 INTRODUCTION

This is the current draft (version 0.9) of the knowledge area description for *Software Engineering Management*. The primary goals of this document are to:

1) define the *Software Engineering Management* knowledge area,

2) present a breakdown of the knowledge area in an hierarchical topic framework,

3) provide a list of references that addresses the topics in the breakdown,

4) provide a topic-reference matrix,

5) provide a list of further readings and supplementary references that also address topics in this knowledge area.

2 DEFINITION OF THE SOFTWARE ENGINEERING MANAGEMENT KNOWLEDGE AREA

Before defining the *Software Engineering Management* knowledge area it is first necessary to set out the scope or context in which it is placed. As an organizational process, it is also important that its relationship to other related standards and to other knowledge areas is clear.

2.1 Scope and definition

The scope of this knowledge area follows the general focus of the Guide; that is, "emphasis... is placed upon the construction of useful software artifacts" (page i, Preface to the Guide to the SWEBOK). As a result we are principally concerned with issues related to software *development* – the *acquisition* of software solutions receives less attention here.

Software engineering is characterized in this Guide according to the IEEE definition: "(1) The application of a systematic, disciplined, quantifiable approach to the development, operation, and maintenance of software; that is, the application of engineering to software." *Management* generally incorporates the following activities: planning, coordinating, measuring, monitoring, controlling and reporting. Combining these two definitions leads us to an understanding of *Software Engineering Management*: the application of management activities – planning, coordinating, measuring, monitoring, controlling and reporting – to ensure that the development of software is systematic, disciplined and measured.

The *Software Engineering Management* knowledge area therefore addresses the management of software development and the measurement and modeling of software development. Whilst measurement is an important aspect of all Guide to the SWEBOK knowledge areas, it is here that the topic is most focused, particularly with regard to issues involved in goal-driven measurement selection, model development and testing for the purposes of software engineering management.

2.2 The management of software engineering

Whilst it is true to say that in one sense it should be possible to manage software engineering in the same way as any other (complex) process, there are aspects particular to software products and the software engineering process that complicate effective management – just a few of them are as follows:

- the perception of clients is such that there is a lack of appreciation for the complexity inherent in software engineering, particularly in relation to the impact of changing requirements

- related to the point just made, it is almost inevitable that the software engineering process itself will generate the need for new or changed client requirements

- as a result, software is often built in an iterative process rather than a concrete sequence of closed tasks

- software engineering necessarily incorporates aspects of creativity and discipline – maintaining an appropriate balance between the two is often difficult

- unlike many other disciplines, we are largely lacking an underlying theory (e.g. engineering is founded on the principles of physics and mathematics)

- software engineers create intangible products that cannot easily be tested in the same sense that a physical product can

- the degree of novelty and complexity of the software we are asked to build is extremely high, in that most (if not all) of the common and simple products have already been built

- we are faced with an extremely rapid rate of change in the underlying technology.

2.3 Relationship to general management and project management

With respect to software engineering, management activities occur at two levels. Aspects of general organizational management are relevant in terms of their impact on software engineering. For instance, planning at the strategic, tactical and operational level, organizational culture and behavior, and functional enterprise management in terms of procurement, supply chain management, marketing, sales, and distribution all have an influence, albeit indirectly, on an organization's software engineering process. Perhaps more pertinent to this knowledge area is the notion of project management, as "the construction of useful software artifacts" is normally managed in the form of (perhaps programs of) individual projects. In this regard we find extensive support in the Guide to the Project Management Body of Knowledge (PMBOK) [PMI, 1996], which itself includes the following project management knowledge areas: integration, scope, time, cost, quality, human resource, communications, risk, and procurement. Clearly all of these topics have direct relevance to this knowledge area. Rather than attempt to duplicate the content of the Guide to the PMBOK here, which would be both impossible and inappropriate, we instead provide a cross-reference table at the end of this document so that the relationship between the two is evident.

2.4 Relationship to other Guide to the SWEBOK knowledge areas and standards

Not unexpectedly this knowledge area is closely related to others in the Guide to the SWEBOK, and reading the following knowledge area documents in conjunction with this one would be particularly useful. Material that is covered in these separate documents is not duplicated here.

Software Configuration Management, as this deals with the administration, monitoring and control of collections of [software] components.

Software Engineering Process, where these process activities must be managed.

Software Quality, as quality is constantly a goal of management and is an aim of many activities that must be managed.

In order to provide a broader context in which these knowledge areas can be considered it is useful to map them to the IEEE/EIA Standard for Information Technology (ISO/IEC 12207) – *Software life cycle processes*. This sees the four management-oriented knowledge areas principally aligned to '6. Supporting Life Cycle Processes' and to '7. Organizational Life Cycle Processes' as follows:

Guide to the SWEBOK	ISO/IEC 12207
Chapter 7 Software Configuration Management	6.2 Configuration Management
Chapter 8 Software Engineering Management	7.1 Management
Chapter 9 Software Engineering Process	7.3 Improvement
Chapter 11 Software Quality	6.3 Quality Assurance 6.6 Joint Review 6.4 Verification 6.7 Audit 6.5 Validation

Chapters 2 through 6 of the Guide to the SWEBOK represent the phases of the software development process (and map to sections 5.3 Development and 5.5 Maintenance of ISO/IEC 12207). Clearly each process must be managed – issues of particular relevance to each process are dealt with in the associated knowledge area. Our focus is on the relevant aspects of enterprise, process and project management as they apply to software engineering rather than to individual development processes.

2.5 Management and measurement

As alluded to above, the *Software Engineering Management* knowledge area consists of both the management process and measurement sub-areas. Whilst these two topics are often regarded as being separate, and indeed they do possess many mutually unique aspects, their close relationship has led to their combined treatment here as part of the Guide to the SWEBOK. Unfortunately the public perception of the software industry is that it delivers products late, over budget, with poor quality and uncertain functionality. Measurement-informed management – an assumed principle of any true engineering discipline – can help to turn this perception around. In essence, management without measurement, qualitative and quantitative, suggests a lack of rigor, and measurement without management suggests a lack of purpose or context. In the same way, however, management and measurement without expert knowledge is equally ineffectual so we must be careful to avoid over-emphasizing the quantitative aspects of *Software Engineering Management*. Effective management requires a combination of both numbers and stories.

The following working definitions are adopted here:

Management process refers to the activities that are undertaken in order to ensure that the software development process is performed in a manner consistent with the organization's policies, goals, and standards.

Measurement (a.k.a. Metrics) refers to the assignment of values and labels to aspects of software development (products, processes, and resources as defined by [Fenton and Pfleeger, 1997]) and the models that are derived from them whether these models are developed using statistical, expert knowledge, or other techniques.

The management process sub-area makes extensive use of the measurement sub-area. This exchange between the two sub-areas occurs continuously throughout the software development processes.

3 BREAKDOWN OF TOPICS FOR SOFTWARE ENGINEERING MANAGEMENT

As the *Software Engineering Management* knowledge area is viewed here as an organizational process that incorporates the notion of process and project management, we have created a breakdown that is both topic-based and life cycle-based. There are three major topic areas: organizational management, which deals with high-level management activities that have a relevant but somewhat indirect impact on software engineering; process/project management, which deals with generally accepted software engineering management activities; and software engineering measurement, which deals with the effective development and implementation of measurement programs in software engineering organizations. Within each main topic area relevant sub-topics are listed, and described where necessary. In particular, further explanation is provided in the process/project management and software engineering measurement topic areas where

distinct issues relating to software engineering management warrant more detailed attention.

A. Organizational management

1. Policy management – organizational policies and standards provide the framework in which software engineering is undertaken. As such, they operationalize overall organizational strategies and have an indirect influence on the software engineering process and its management. It is important that those charged with the management of software engineering both understand and influence the development, dissemination, deployment and enforcement of policies and standards. [Pfle: c2; Reif: c2; Somm: c30; Thay: c2,c4]

   1. Means of policy development
   2. Policy dissemination and enforcement
   3. Development and deployment of standards

2. Personnel management – policies and procedures used at the organizational level to recruit, select, motivate and reward personnel also affect the management of software engineering teams and individuals. It is acknowledged that in order to recruit and retain high-quality personnel in the software engineering industry it is vital that training, motivation, career development and the like are given adequate attention. [F&P: c11; Pfle: c3; Press: c3; Reif: c7,c8; Somm: c28; Thay: c7,c8]

   1. Hiring and retention
   2. Training and motivation
   3. Mentoring for career development

3. Communication management – even if project-based communication is effective, an organization is unlikely to survive long-term without clear policies and procedures that are applicable in the wider context. An awareness of communication channels (formal and informal), conventions in terms of terminology, form and style, mechanisms for feedback and the impact of organizational structures on communication, has an indirect but important influence on communication within the software engineering process. [Press: c3; Somm: c28; Thay: c1,c3]

   1. Communication channels and media
   2. Meeting procedures

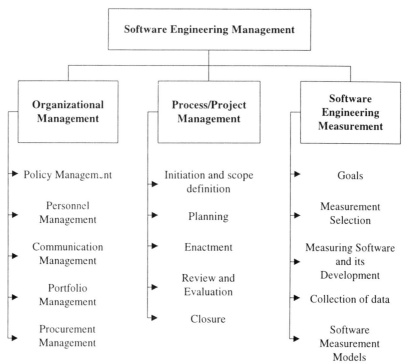

```
                    Software Engineering Management

        Organizational          Process/Project          Software
         Management              Management              Engineering
                                                         Measurement


    ▶ Policy Management      ▶ Initiation and scope      ▶  Goals
                                  definition
        Personnel                                           Measurement
     ▶  Management           ▶  Planning                    Selection

        Communication        ▶  Enactment                   Measuring Software
     ▶  Management                                       ▶   and its
                                Review and                   Development
        Portfolio           ▶  Evaluation
     ▶  Management                                       ▶  Collection of data
                            ▶  Closure
        Procurement                                          Software
     ▶  Management                                           Measurement
                                                            Models
```

3. Written presentations
4. Oral presentations
5. Negotiation

4. Portfolio management – organizations that deal with multiple clients and/or multiple projects are often faced with the need to prioritize their effort in terms of the projects they undertake. It is important that those involved in software engineering management both contribute to and are guided by the organizational management of project portfolios, where portfolios are constructed in light of the advantages and disadvantages of undertaking individual projects using a variety of cost/benefit and similar analysis methods. [Press: c10]

1. Strategy development and coordination

2. General investment management techniques

3. Project selection

4. Portfolio construction (risk minimization and value maximization)

5. Procurement management – in cases where an organization outsources (part of) their operation to an external agency this process must be managed effectively in order to ensure a successful outcome. As it is not uncommon for organizations to purchase some or all of their software engineering activity in such a way, organizational policies and procedures should exist to facilitate effective provider-consumer relationships. [Press: c5; Reif: c15; Somm: c2]

1. Procurement planning and selection

2. Supplier contract management

B. Process/project management (largely following 7.1 ISO/IEC 12207 Management Process)

1. Initiation and scope definition – the focus of this set of activities is on the effective determination of process and/or project requirements via various elicitation methods and the assessment of the process/project's feasibility from a variety of standpoints. Once feasibility has been established, the remaining task within this process is the specification of requirements review and modification procedures (see also Chapter 2 of the Guide to the SWEBOK).

1. Determination and negotiation of requirements – methods of requirements engineering, elicitation (e.g. observation), analysis (e.g. data modelling, use case modelling), specification, and validation (e.g. prototyping) must be selected and applied in cognizance of various stakeholder perspectives. This leads to the determination of process/project scope, objectives and constraints. This is always an important activity, as it sets the visible boundaries for the set of tasks being undertaken, and is particularly so where the novelty of the undertaking is high. [D&T: c4; Pfle: c4; Press: c5,c11,c12; Somm: c4-11]

2. Feasibility analysis (technical, operational, financial, social/political) – the software engineering manager must be assured that adequate capability and resources are available in the form of people, expertise, facilities, infrastructure, and support (either internally or externally) to ensure that the process/project can be successfully completed in a timely and cost-effective manner (using, for example, a requirement-capability matrix). This often requires some 'ball-park' estimation of effort and cost based on appropriate methods (e.g. expert-informed analogy techniques). [Press: c10]

3. Process for the review and revision of requirements – given the inevitability of change, it is vital that agreement among stakeholders is reached at this early point as to the means by which scope and requirements are to be reviewed and revised (e.g. via agreed change management procedures). This clearly implies that scope and requirements will not be 'set in stone' but can and should be revisited at pre-determined points as the process occurs (e.g. at design reviews, acceptance tests). If changes are accepted then some form of traceability analysis and risk analysis (see below) should be used to ascertain the impact of those changes. A managed change approach should also be useful when it comes time to review the outcome of the process/project, as the scope and requirements should form the basis for evaluation of success. [Somm: c4]

2. Planning – the iterative planning process is informed by the scope and requirements and the establishment of feasibility. At this point, software processes are evaluated and the most appropriate (given the nature of the process/project, its degree of novelty, its functional and technical complexity, its quality requirements, and so on) is selected. Where relevant, the project itself is then planned in the form of an hierarchical decomposition of tasks, the associated deliverables of each task are specified and characterized in terms of quality and other attributes in line with stated requirements, and detailed effort, schedule and cost estimation is undertaken. Resources are then allocated to tasks so as to optimize personnel productivity (at individual, team, and organizational levels), equipment and materials utilization and adherence to schedule. Detailed risk management is undertaken and the 'risk profile' of the process/project is discussed among and accepted by all relevant stakeholders. Comprehensive quality management processes are determined as part of the planning process in the form of procedures and responsibilities for quality assurance, verification and validation (see also Chapter 11 of the Guide to the SWEBOK). As an iterative process, it is vital that the processes and responsibilities for ongoing plan management, review and revision are also clearly stated and agreed.

1. Process planning – selection of the appropriate software process (e.g. spiral, cleanroom) and the specification and deployment of appropriate process standards are undertaken in the light of the particular scope and requirements of the process/project. Relevant methods and tools are also selected. [D&T: c5,c11; Pfle: c2; Press: c2; Reif: c1,c2,c4; Somm: c1; Thay: c3]

2. Project planning – appropriate methods and tools are used to decompose the project into tasks, with associated inputs, outputs and completion conditions (e.g. work breakdown structure). [D&T: c10; Pfle: c3; Press: c3,c5; Reif: c3,c4; Somm: c3; Thay: c4,c6]

3. Determine deliverables – the product(s) of each task (e.g. high level architectural design, inspection report) are specified and characterized. [Pfle: c3; Press: c3,c7; Somm: c3; Thay: c4]

4. Effort, schedule and cost estimation – based on the breakdown of tasks, inputs and outputs, the expected effort range required for each is determined using a calibrated estimation model based on historical size-effort data where available and relevant (e.g. analogy-based estimation, function point analysis); task dependencies are established and potential bottlenecks are identified using suitable methods (e.g. critical path analysis); bottlenecks are resolved where possible and the expected schedule of tasks with projected start times, durations and end times is produced (e.g. PERT chart); resource requirements (people, tools) are translated into cost estimates. [D&T: c10; F&P: c12; Pfle: c3; Press: c5,c7; Reif: c4,c5; Somm: c3,c29; Thay: c5]

5. Resource allocation – equipment, facilities and people are associated with the scheduled tasks, including the allocation of responsibilities for completion (using, for example, a Gantt chart). This activity is informed and constrained by the availability of resources and their optimal use under these circumstances, as well as by issues relating to personnel e.g. productivity of individuals/teams, team dynamics, organizational and team structures. [Pfle: c3; Press: c5; Reif: c7,c8; Somm: c3; Thay: c6,c7]

6. Risk management – risk identification and analysis (what can go wrong, how and why, and what are the likely consequences), critical risk assessment (which are the most significant risks in terms of exposure, which can we do

something about in terms of leverage), risk mitigation and contingency planning (formulating a strategy to deal with risks and to manage the risk profile) are all undertaken. Risk assessment methods (e.g. decision trees and process simulations) should be used in order to highlight and evaluate risks. Project abandonment policies should also be determined at this point in discussion with all other stakeholders. [D&T: c10; Pfle: c3; Press: c6; Reif: c11; Thay: c4]

7. Quality management – quality is defined in terms of pertinent attributes of the specific process/project and any associated product(s), perhaps in both quantitative and qualitative terms. (These quality attributes will have been determined in the specification of detailed requirements.) Thresholds for adherence to quality are set for each attribute as appropriate to stakeholder expectations for the software at hand. Procedures relating to ongoing software quality assurance (SQA) throughout the process and for product (deliverable) verification and validation are also specified at this stage (e.g. reviews and inspections) (see also Chapter 11 of the Guide to the SWEBOK). [D&T: c7,c9; Press: c8; Reif: c10; Somm: c30,c31; Thay: c9,c10]

8. Plan management – in an environment where change is an expectation rather than a shock, it is vital that plans are themselves managed. This requires that adherence to plans is systematically directed, monitored, reviewed, reported, and, where appropriate, revised. Plans associated with other management-oriented support processes (e.g. documentation, configuration management and problem resolution) also need to be managed in the same manner. [Somm: c3; Thay: c4]

3. Enactment – the plans are then implemented and the processes embodied in the plans are enacted. Throughout, there is a focus on adherence to the plans, with an over-riding expectation that such adherence will lead to the successful satisfaction of stakeholder requirements and achievement of the process/project objectives. Fundamental to enactment are the ongoing management activities of measuring, monitoring, controlling and reporting.

1. Implementation of plans – the process is initiated and the process/project activities are undertaken according to the schedule. In the process, resources are utilized (e.g. personnel effort, funding) and deliverables are produced (e.g. architectural design documents, test cases). [Pfle: c3; Somm: c3]

2. Implementation of measurement process – the measurement process is enacted alongside the software development process/project, ensuring that relevant and useful data is collected (see also section C of this knowledge area breakdown). [F&P: c13,c14; Press: c4; Reif: c9,c10,c12; Thay: c3,c10]

3. Monitor process – adherence to the various plans is systematically assessed continually and at pre-determined intervals. Outputs and completion conditions for each task are analyzed, deliverables are evaluated in terms of their required characteristics (e.g. via joint reviews, test audits), effort expenditure, schedule adherence and costs to date are investigated, resource usage is examined, the process/project risk profile is revisited, and adherence to quality requirements is evaluated. Measurement data is modeled and analyzed. Variance analysis based on the deviation of actual from expected outcomes and values is undertaken. This may be in the form of cost overruns, schedule slippage and the like. Outlier identification and analysis of quality and other measurement data is performed (e.g. defect density analysis). Risk exposure and leverage are recalculated and decisions trees, simulations and so on are re-run in the light of new data. These activities enable problem detection and exception identification based on exceeded thresholds. Outcomes are reported as needed and certainly where acceptable thresholds are surpassed. [D&T: c7,c9,c10; Press: c7; Reif: c9,c10; Somm: c31; Thay: c3;c9]

4. Control process – the outcomes of the process monitoring activities provide the basis on which action decisions are taken. Where appropriate, and where the impact and associated risks are modeled and managed, changes can be made to the process/project. This may take the form of corrective action (e.g. re-testing certain components), it may involve the incorporation of contingencies so that similar occurrences are avoided (e.g. the decision to use prototyping to assist in requirements validation), and/or it may entail the revision of the various plans and other project documents (e.g. requirements specification) to accommodate the unexpected outcomes and their flow-on implications. In some instances it may lead to abandonment of the process/project. In all cases, change control and configuration management procedures are adhered to (see Chapter 7 of the Guide to the SWEBOK), decisions are documented and communicated to all relevant parties, plans are revisited and revised where necessary, and relevant data is recorded in the central database (see also section C of this knowledge area breakdown). [D&T: c10; Press: c9; Reif: c9,c10; Thay: c3,c9]

5. Reporting – at specified and agreed periods, adherence to the plans is reported, both within the organization (e.g. to the project portfolio steering committee) and to external stakeholders (e.g. clients, users). Reports of this nature should focus on overall adherence as opposed to the detailed reporting required frequently within the process/project team. [Reif: c9,c10; Thay: c3,c10]

4. Review and evaluation – at critical points in the process/project overall progress towards achievement of the stated objectives and satisfaction of stakeholder requirements is evaluated. Similarly, assessments of the effectiveness of the overall process to date, the personnel involved, and the tools and methods employed are also undertaken at particular milestones.

   1. Determining satisfaction of requirements – since attaining stakeholder (user and customer) satisfaction is one of our principal aims, it is important that progress towards this aim is formally and periodically assessed. This occurs at the achievement of major process/project milestones (e.g. confirmation of software design architecture, software integration joint review). Variances from expectations are identified and appropriate action is taken. As in the Control process activity above, in all cases change control and configuration management procedures are adhered to (see Chapter 7 of the Guide to the SWEBOK), decisions are documented and communicated to all relevant parties, plans are revisited and revised where necessary, and relevant data is recorded in the central database (see also section C of this knowledge area breakdown). [Reif: c9,c10; Thay: c3,c10]

   2. Reviewing and evaluating performance – periodic performance reviews for process/project personnel provide insights as to the likelihood of adherence to plans as well as possible areas of difficulty (e.g. team member conflicts). The various methods, tools and techniques employed are evaluated for their effectiveness and appropriateness, and the process itself is systematically and periodically assessed for its relevance, utility and efficacy in the process/project context (see also the other SWEBOK chapters). Where appropriate, changes are made and managed. [D&T: c7; Pfle: c7,c8; Press: c8; Reif: c9,c10; Thay: c3,c10]

5. Closure – the process/project reaches closure when all of the plans and embodied processes have been enacted and completed. At this stage the criteria for process/project success are revisited. Once closure is established, archival, *post mortem* and process improvement activities are performed.

   1. Determining closure – the tasks as specified in the plans are complete and satisfactory achievement of completion criteria is confirmed. All planned products have been delivered with acceptable characteristics. Requirements are checked off and confirmed as satisfied and the objectives of the process/project have been achieved. These processes generally involve all stakeholders and result in the documentation of client acceptance and any remaining known problem reports. [D&T: c7; Reif: c9,c10; Thay: c3,c10]

   2. Closure activities – after closure has been confirmed, archival of process/project materials takes place in line with stakeholder-agreed methods, location and duration. The organization's measurement database is updated with final process/project data and post-project analyses are undertaken. A process/project *post mortem* is undertaken so that issues, problems and opportunities encountered during the process (particularly via Review and Evaluation) are analyzed, lessons are drawn from the process, and are fed into organizational learning and improvement endeavors (see also Chapter 9 of the Guide to the SWEBOK). [Pfle: c11; Somm: c31]

   (Software then moves into operation, maintenance and, perhaps eventually, retirement. Whilst these tasks also need to be managed they are not explicitly addressed here – software maintenance as a set of activities is addressed in Chapter 6 of the Guide to the SWEBOK, and the other topics (software operation and retirement) are outside the scope of the Guide.)

C. **Software engineering measurement**

1. Determining the goals of a measurement program – the *ad hoc* approach to software engineering measurement that characterized early efforts – that is, measuring everything possible – often failed to provide genuine insights in terms of organizational improvement, or worse, it led to spurious outcomes that did not generalize to other cases. Each measurement endeavor should be guided by organizational objectives and driven by an over-riding goal that has organizational improvement at its foundation. In this way, measurement effort expenditure should ultimately result in some sort of cost-effective gain to the organization, based on justified prioritization of efforts. An emerging international standard, ISO/IEC FCD 15939, describes a generic process that defines the activities and tasks necessary to implement a software measurement process and includes as well a measurement information model. [ISO/IEC, 2000]

1. Organizational objectives – organizational strategies inform software engineering management in terms of identifying the broad issues and objectives that hold principal relevance at the organizational level (e.g. being first-to-market with new products). [F&P: c3,c13; Press: c4]

2. Software process improvement goals – organizational objectives are translated into specific software-related goals that, if achieved, can assist the organization in attaining its objectives (e.g. optimizing software development with a view to shortening the product life-cycle whilst maintaining process and product quality). [F&P: c3,c13; Pfle: c12; Press: c4; Reif: c2; Somm: c31]

2. Measurement selection – development of an effective measurement process is informed by the organizational objectives and software process improvement goals as specified. This provides the necessary context for more specific and detailed measurement selection. Some understanding of the validity, accuracy and reliability of the selected measures is also crucial in terms of assessing the value of the measurement program and the confidence that can be placed in the results generated from it.

   1. Goal-driven measurement selection – once software process improvement goals are set, we are then in a position to utilize a decomposition process in order to ask questions of direct relevance and interest, leading finally to the selection of useful and relevant measures (e.g. the Goal/Question/Metric approach incorporates just such a decomposition process). In relation to shortening the product life-cycle we may adopt a measurement goal of maximizing software development productivity. In turn, we might ask questions such as: how much effort is expended on rework? what is the range of developer productivity rates? is developer productivity in line with changes in developer experience? All require quite different measures in order to provide the answers needed to achieve the over-riding goals. [F&P: c1,c3,c13,c14; Reif: c12; Thay: c10]

   2. Measurement validity – an awareness of issues relating to measurement validity and reliability is essential if the measurement program is to provide effective and bounded results. In particular, an appreciation of measurement scales and the implications of each scale type in relation to the subsequent selection of data analysis methods is especially important. [F&P: c2; Pfle: c11]

3. Measuring software and its development – whilst the application of measurement to software engineering can be complex, particularly in terms of modeling and analysis methods (see below), there are several aspects of software engineering measurement that are fundamental and that underlie much of the more advanced measurement and analysis processes. Furthermore, achievement of process and product improvement efforts can only be assessed if a set of baseline measures has been established. Software engineering management therefore includes, as a minimum, the measurement of product size, product structure, resource utilization and product and process quality.

   1. Size measurement – software product size is most often assessed by measures of length (e.g. lines of source code in a module, pages in a requirements specification document) or functionality (e.g. function points in a specification or design, COCOMO evaluation of a system design). The standard for functional size measurement methods is [ISO/IEC 1998] and additional supporting standards are under development. A number of specific methods, suitable for different purposes, are available. [F&P: c7; Press: c4,c18,c23; Reif: c12; Somm: c30].

   2. Structure measurement – a diverse range of measures of software product structure may be applied to both high- and low-level design and code artifacts to reflect control-flow (e.g. the cyclomatic number, code knots), data-flow (e.g. measures of slicing), nesting (e.g. nesting polynomial measure, the BAND measure), control structures (e.g. the vector measure, the NPATH measure), and modular structure and interaction (e.g. information flow, tree-based measures, coupling and cohesion). [F&P: c8; Press: c18,c23]

   3. Resource measurement – whilst some effort can be made to assess the utilization of tools and hardware, the primary resource that needs to be managed in software engineering is personnel. As a result the main measures of interest are those related to productivity of individuals and of teams (e.g. using a measure of function points produced per unit of person-effort) and their associated levels of experience in software engineering in general and perhaps in particular technologies. [F&P: c3,c11; Somm: c29]

   4. Quality measurement – as a multi-dimensional attribute, quality measurement is less straightforward to define than those above. Furthermore, some of the dimensions of quality (e.g. usability, maintainability, and value to the client) are likely to require measurement in qualitative rather than quantitative form. A more detailed discussion of software quality

128

assessment is provided in Chapter 11 of the Guide to the SWEBOK. [F&P: c9,c10; Press: c4; Reif: c12; Somm: c30]

4. Collection of data – when developing a measurement process it is important to ensure that the *optimal* set of measures is chosen. By optimal it is not just meant that the measures are those that necessarily provide the greatest (predictive) power for the desired purpose. It is also important that the cost of data collection is minimized or at least balanced against the benefits to be gained from the outputs of the program. The possibility of reusing measures collected for other purposes is also considered as part of the collection process. The data collected is also useful from the perspective of enabling appropriate models to be developed for analysis, classification and prediction.

   1. Survey techniques and form design – data collection forms and questionnaires are pilot tested before they are used on actual processes/projects. Forms are logically laid out, require minimum completion, and make use of default values where possible. Assistance for form and survey completion is made available. [F&P: c4,c5]

   2. Automated and manual data collection – all data collection has associated costs, both direct (in terms of people employed and software purchased) and indirect (in the costs of interruptions and delays as measurement data are analyzed). For this reason, the measurement process is treated as an *investment* in the development process, with justification for expenditure and quantification of the resulting benefits. Procedures relating to data collection detail the point at which the data is available, the way in which it is collected, the personnel responsible for collection, and the cost associated with collection. Where possible, unobtrusive automated data collection is preferred. This information is important in ensuring that that program is actually feasible. The potential exists for a measurement process to be created, only to find that some of the data cannot physically be collected, or not in sufficient quantities. [F&P: c5; Press: c4; Somm: c30]

5. Software measurement models – as the data is collected and the measurement database is populated we become able to build models using both data and knowledge. These models exist for the purposes of analysis, classification and prediction. Such models need to be evaluated to ensure that their levels of accuracy are sufficient and that their limitations are known and understood. The refinement of models, which takes place both during and after projects are completed, is another important activity. The

implementation of measurement models is more management-oriented since the use of such models has an influential effect on personnel behavior.

1. Model building, calibration and evaluation – the goal-driven approach to measurement informs the model building process to the extent that models are constructed to answer relevant questions and achieve software improvement goals. This process is also influenced by the implied limitations of particular measurement scales in relation to the choice of analysis method. The models are calibrated (by using particularly relevant observations e.g. recent projects, projects using similar technology) and their effectiveness is evaluated (e.g. by testing their performance on holdout samples). [F&P: c4,c6,c13; Pfle: c3,c11,c12; Somm: c29]

2. Implementation, interpretation and refinement of models – the calibrated models are applied to the process/project (see Process/project enactment), their outcomes are interpreted and evaluated in the context of the process/project, and the models are then refined where appropriate. [F&P: c6; Pfle: c3,c11,c12; Press: c4; Somm: c29]

4 BREAKDOWN RATIONALE

The following subsections each describe how the proposed draft of the knowledge area description meets the criteria given in the project guidelines.

One or two breakdowns with identical topics

A single breakdown of topics is shown.

Soundness and reasonableness

The primary references and secondary sources were examined quite thoroughly in order to list all main topics. The division of the management process into life-cycle based topics seems both plausible and useful in terms of educational presentation.

Generally acceptable

In our view the material in this knowledge area description meets the criterion of being generally acceptable in terms of being "applicable to most projects, most of the time" and having "widespread consensus about their value and usefulness" [PMI, 1996]. These topics are those that receive the greatest coverage in both the original texts and additional materials suggested here.

Similarly, the Industrial Advisory Board definition of "study material of a software engineering licensing exam that a graduate would pass after completing four years of work experience" appears to be met. However, in this case the specific responsibilities of the graduate will obviously influence in what areas they have the opportunity to gain experience. Project management is often a more senior position and as such, graduates with four years of practice may not have had significant experience in managing, at least large-scale, projects.

The importance of measurement and its role in better management practices is widely acknowledged and so its importance can only increase in coming years. Effective measurement has become one of the cornerstones of organizational maturity.

Compatible with various schools of thought within software engineering

Excluding debate on measurement theoretic issues there is little intense debate in the measurement field. There is nothing that appears to be controversial in the management process sub-area.

Compatible with breakdown in industry, literatures, and standards

The breakdown is in line with others proposed, and is particularly aligned with the IEEE/EIA Standard for Information Technology (ISO/IEC 12207) – *Software life cycle processes* and the Guide to the Project Management Body of Knowledge.

Depth and node density

The suggested guidelines have been met here.

Meaningful topic names

Key terms on software measures and measurement methods have been defined in [ISO/IEC 2000] on the basis of the

ISO international vocabulary of metrology [ISO93]. Nevertheless, readers will encounter terminology differences in the literature; for example, the term "metrics" is sometimes used in place of "measures". We recognize that this could make less obvious the connection between this work and many papers and books (including [Fenton and Pfleeger, 1997]).

Brevity of topic descriptions

Although they have been expanded significantly between the last draft and this, the descriptions remain adequately brief and to the point.

Specific reference material

Additional reference material for more specialized topics not covered adequately in the primary reference material has been added.

Proposed reference material (publicly available)

All material is publicly available.

Maximum number of core reference materials is 15

We have adhered to this limit.

Preference to IEEE or ACM copyrighted material

This is evident in the selection of reference material, especially the collections of papers.

5 MATRIX OF TOPICS VS. REFERENCE MATERIAL

The level of granularity used in Table 1 is a mixture of second and third level topics, depending on the specificity of the topic in question.

Topic	D&T	F&P	Pfle	Press	Reif	Somm	Thay
A. Organizational Management							
Policy management			Ch. 2		Ch. 2	Ch. 30	Ch. 2,4
Personnel management		Ch. 11	Ch. 3	Ch. 3	Ch. 7,8	Ch. 28	Ch. 7,8
Communication management				Ch. 3		Ch. 28	Ch. 1,3
Portfolio management				Ch. 10			
Procurement management				Ch. 5	Ch. 15	Ch. 2	
B. Process/project Management							
Initiation and scope definition							
Determination and negotiation of requirements	Ch. 4		Ch. 4	Ch. 5,11,12		Ch. 4-11	
Feasibility analysis				Ch. 10			
Review/revision of requirements						Ch. 4	
Planning							
Process planning	Ch. 5,11		Ch. 2	Ch. 2	Ch. 1,2,4	Ch. 1	Ch. 3
Project planning	Ch. 10		Ch. 3	Ch. 3,5	Ch. 3,4	Ch. 3	Ch. 4,6
Determine deliverables			Ch. 3	Ch. 3,7		Ch. 3	Ch. 4
Effort, schedule and cost estimation	Ch. 10	Ch. 12	Ch. 3	Ch. 5,7	Ch. 4,5	Ch. 3,29	Ch. 5
Resource allocation			Ch. 3	Ch. 5	Ch. 7,8	Ch. 3	Ch. 6,7
Risk management	Ch. 10		Ch. 3	Ch. 6	Ch. 11		Ch. 4
Quality management	Ch. 7,9			Ch. 8	Ch. 10	Ch. 30,31	Ch. 9,10
Plan management						Ch. 3	Ch. 4

Topic	D&T	F&P	Pfle	Press	Reif	Somm	Thay
Enactment							
Implementation of plans			Ch. 3			Ch. 3	
Implementation of measurement process		Ch. 13,14		Ch. 4	Ch. 9,10,12		Ch. 3,10
Monitor process	Ch. 7,9,10			Ch. 7	Ch. 9,10	Ch. 31	Ch. 3,9
Control process	Ch. 10			Ch. 9	Ch. 9,10		Ch. 3,9
Reporting					Ch. 9,10		Ch. 3,10
Review and evaluation							
Determining satisfaction of requirements					Ch. 9,10		Ch. 3,10
Reviewing and evaluating performance	Ch. 7		Ch. 7,8	Ch. 8	Ch. 9,10		Ch. 3,10
Closure							
Determining closure	Ch. 7				Ch. 9,10		Ch. 3,10
Closure activities			Ch. 11			Ch. 31	
C. Software Engineering Measurement							
Determining the goals of a measurement program							
Organizational objectives		Ch. 3,13		Ch. 4			
Software process improvement goals		Ch. 3,13	Ch. 12	Ch. 4	Ch. 2	Ch 31	
Measurement selection							
Goal-driven measurement selection		Ch. 1,3,13, 14			Ch. 12		Ch. 10
Measurement validity		Ch. 2	Ch. 11				
Measuring software and its development							
Size measurement		Ch. 7		Ch. 4,18,23	Ch. 12	Ch. 30	
Structure measurement		Ch. 8		Ch. 18,23			
Resource measurement		Ch. 3,11				Ch. 29	
Quality measurement		Ch. 9,10		Ch. 4	Ch. 12	Ch. 30	
Collection of data							
Survey techniques and form design		Ch. 4,5					
Automated and manual data collection		Ch. 5		Ch. 4		Ch. 30	
Software measurement models							
Model building, calibration and evaluation		Ch. 4,6,13	Ch. 3,11,12			Ch. 29	
Implementation, interpretation and refinement of models		Ch. 6	Ch. 3,11,12	Ch. 4		Ch. 29	

Table 1: Topics and their references

6 RECOMMENDED REFERENCES FOR SOFTWARE ENGINEERING MANAGEMENT

The Topic-Reference matrix shown above requires the following references to be included in the Guide to the SWEBOK.

1) [D&T: Dorfman and Thayer, 1997] Merlin Dorfman and Richard H. Thayer (eds.). 1997. *Software engineering*. IEEE Computer Society. [Chapters 4, 5, 7, 9-11]

2) [F&P: Fenton and Pfleeger, 1997] Norman E. Fenton and Shari Lawrence Pfleeger. 1997. *Software metrics: a rigorous and practical approach*. PWS Publishing Company. [Chapters 1-14]

3) [Pfle: Pfleeger, 1998] Shari Lawrence Pfleeger. 1998. *Software engineering: theory and practice*. Prentice Hall. [Chapters 2-4, 7, 8, 11, 12]

4) [Press: Pressman, 1997] Roger S. Pressman. 1997. *Software engineering: a practitioner's approach. (Fourth edition)* McGraw-Hill. [Chapters 2-12, 18, 23]

5) [Reif: Reifer, 1997] Donald J. Reifer (ed.). 1997. *Software management*, 5th edition. IEEE Computer Society. [Chapters 1-5, 7-12, 15]

6) [Somm: Sommerville, 1996] Ian Sommerville. 1996. *Software engineering*. Addison-Wesley. [Chapters 1-11, 28-31]

7) [Thay: Thayer, 1997] Richard H. Thayer (ed.). 1997. *Software engineering project management*. IEEE Computer Society. [Chapters 1-10]

Appendix A – List of Further Readings

The following readings are useful sources of information for this knowledge area.

Process/Project Management:

Adler, T.R., Leonard, J.G. and Nordgren, R.K. Improving risk management: moving from risk elimination to risk avoidance. *Information and Software Technology* 41: 29-34 (1999).

Baines, R. Across disciplines: risk, design, method, process, and tools. *IEEE Soft.* (July/Aug): 61-64 (1998)

Binder, R.V. Can a manufacturing quality model work for software? *IEEE Soft.* (September/October): 101-102,105 (1997).

Boehm, B.W. and DeMarco, T. Software risk management (Guest editors' introduction). *IEEE Soft.* (May/June): 17-19 (1997).

Carr, M.J. Risk management may not be for everyone. *IEEE Soft.* (May/June): 21,24 (1997).

Charette, R.N. Large-scale project management is risk management. *IEEE Soft.* (July): 110-117 (1996).

Charette, R.N., Adams, K.M. and White, M.B. Managing risk in software maintenance. *IEEE Soft.* (May/June): 43-50 (1997).

Collier, B., DeMarco, T. and Fearey, P. A defined process for project postmortem review. *IEEE Soft.* (July): 65-72 (1996).

Conrow, E.H. and Shishido, P.S. Implementing risk management on software intensive projects. *IEEE Soft.* (May/June): 83-89 (1997).

DeMarco, T. and Lister, T. *Peopleware: productive projects and teams.* Dorset House Publishing, 1987.

DeMarco, T. and Miller, A. Managing large software projects. *IEEE Soft.* (July): 24-27 (1996).

Favaro, J. and Pfleeger, S.L. Making software development investment decisions. *ACM SIGSoft Software Engineering Notes* 23(5): 69-74 (1998).

Fayad, M.E and Cline, M. Managing object-oriented software development. *Computer* (Sept): 26-31 (1996)

Fleming, R. A fresh perspective on old problems. *IEEE Soft.* (January/February): 106-113 (1999).

Garvey, P.R., Phair, D.J. and Wilson, J.A. An information architecture for risk assessment and management. *IEEE Soft.* (May/June): 25-34 (1997).

Gemmer, A. Risk management: moving beyond process. *Computer* (May): 33-43 (1997).

Glass, R.L. The ups and downs of programmer stress. *Communications of the ACM* 40(4): 17-19 (1997).

Glass, R.L. Short-term and long-term remedies for runaway projects. *Comm. ACM* 41(7): 13-15 (1998).

Glass, R.L. How not to prepare for a consulting assignment, and other ugly consultancy truths. *Communications of the ACM* 41(12): 11-13 (1998).

Henry, S.M. and Stevens, K.T. Using Belbin's leadership role to improve team effectiveness: an empirical investigation. *Journal of Systems and Software* 44: 241-250 (1999).

Hohmann, L. Coaching the rookie manager. *IEEE Soft.* (January/February): 16-19 (1999).

Hsia, P. Making software development visible. *IEEE Soft.* (March): 23-26 (1996).

Humphrey, W.S. *Managing Technical People: Innovation, Teamwork, and the Software Process.* Addison-Wesley, 1997.

Jackman, M. Homeopathic remedies for team toxicity. *IEEE Soft.* (July/August): 43-45 (1998).

Kansala, K. Integrating risk assessment with cost estimation. *IEEE Soft.* (May/June): 61-67 (1997).

Karlsson, J. and Ryan, K. A cost-value aproach for prioritizing requirements. *IEEE Soft.* (September/October): 87-74 (1997).

Karolak, D.W. *Software engineering risk management.* IEEE Computer Society, 1996.

Keil, M., Cule, P.E., Lyytinen, K. and Schmict, R.C. A framework for identifying software project risks. *Communications of the ACM* 41(11): 76-83 (1998).

Kitchenham, B. and Linkman, S. Estimates, uncertainty, and risk. *IEEE Soft.* (May/June): 69-74 (1997).

Leung, H.K.N. A risk index for software producers. *Software Maintenance: Research and Practice* 8: 281-294 (1996).

Lister, T. Risk management is project management for adults. *IEEE Soft.* (May/June): 20,22 (1997).

Mackey, K. Why bad things happen to good projects. *IEEE Soft.* (May): 27-32 (1996).

Mackey, K. Beyond Dilbert: creating cultures that work. *IEEE Soft.* (January-February): 48-49 (1998).

Madachy, R.J. Heuristic risk assessment using cost factors. *IEEE Soft.* (May/June): 51-59 (1997).

Martin, C. The need for software risk management tools. *Application Development Trends.* p.20,22.

McConell, S.C. *Rapid Development: Taming Wild Software Schedules.* Microsoft Press, 1996.

McConell, S.C. *Software Project Survival Guide.* Microsoft Press, 1997.

Moynihan, T. How experienced project managers assess risk. *IEEE Soft.* (May/June): 35-41 (1997).

Nesi, P. Managing OO projects better. *IEEE Soft.* (July/August): 50-60 (1998).

Nolan, A.J. Learning from success. *IEEE Soft.* (January/February): 97-105 (1999).

Parris, K.V.C. Implementing accountability. *IEEE Soft.* (July): 83-93 (1996).

Putnam, L.H. and Myers, W. *Industrial Strength Software: Effective Management Using Measurement.* Los Alamitos CA, IEEE Computer Society Press (1997) 309p.

Rodrigues, A.G. and Williams, T.M. System dynamics in software project management: towards the development of a formal integrated framework. *European Journal of Information Systems* 6: 51-66 (1997).

Ropponen, J. and Lyytinen, K. Can software risk management improve system development: an exploratory study. *European Journal of Information Systems* 6: 41-50 (1997).

Schmidt, C., Dart, P., Johnston, L., Sterling, L. and Thorne, P. Disincentives for communicating risk: a risk paradox. *Information and Software Technology* 41: 403-411 (1999).

Slaughter, S.A., Harter, D.E. and Krishnan, M.S. Evaluating the cost of software quality. *Communications of the ACM* 41(8): 67-73 (1998).

van Scoy, R.L. Software development risk: opportunity, not problem. CMU/SEI-92-TR-30, Software Engineering Institute, Carnegie Mellon University, 1992.

van Solingen, R., Berghout, E. and van Latum, F. Interrupts: just a minute never is. *IEEE Soft.* (September/October): 97-103 (1998).

Whitten, N. *Managing Software Development Projects: Formulas for Success.* Wiley, 1995.

Williams, R.C., Walker, J.A. and Dorofee, A.J. Putting risk management into practice. *IEEE Soft.* (May/June): 75-82 (1997).

Software Engineering Measurement:

Briand, L.C., Morasca, S. and Basili, V.R. Property-based software engineering measurement. *IEEE Transactions on Software Engineering* 22(1): 68-86 (1996).

Briand, L., El Emam, K. and Morasca, S. On the application of measurement theory in software engineering. *Empirical Software Engineering* 1: 61-88 (1996).

Briand, L.C., Morasca, S. and Basili, V.R. Response to: Comments on "Property-based software engineering measurement: refining the additivy properties". *IEEE Transactions on Software Engineering* 23(3): 196-197 (1997).

Brooks, F.P., Jr. No silver bullet: essence and accidents of software engineering. *Computer* (Apr.): 10-19 (1987).

Davis, A.M. Predictions and farewells. *IEEE Soft.* (July/August): 6-9 (1998).

Fenton, N.E. and Pfleeger, S.L. *Software Metrics: A Rigorous and Practical Approach.* London, International Thomson Computer Press (1997) 638p.

Fuggetta, A., Lavazza, L., Morasca, S., Cinti, S., Oldano, G. and Orazi, E. Applying GQM in an industrial software factory. *ACM Transactions on Software Engineering and Methodology* 7(4): 411-448 (1998).

Glass, R.L. The realities of software technology payoffs. *Communications of the ACM* 42(2): 74-79 (1999).

Grable, R., Jernigan, J., Pogue, C. and Divis, D. Metrics for small projects: experiences at the SED. *IEEE Soft.* (March/April): 21-29 (1999).

Grady, R.B. and Caswell, D.L. *Software Metrics: Establishing A Company-Wide Program.* Englewood Cliffs NJ, USA, Prentice-Hall (1987).

Hall, T. and Fenton, N. Implementing effective software metrics programs. *IEEE Soft.* (Mar/Apr): 55-64 (1997).

Kautz, K. Making sense of measurement for small organizations. *IEEE Soft.* (March/April): 14-20 (1999).

Kernighan, B. and Pike, R. Finding performance improvements. *IEEE Soft.* (March/April): 61-65 (1999).

McConnell, S. Software engineering principles. *IEEE Soft.* (March/April): 6-8 (1999).

Offen, R.J. and Jeffery, R. Establishing software measurement programs. *IEEE Soft.* (Mar/Apr): 45-53 (1997).

Pfleeger, S.L. Assessing measurement (Guest editor's introduction). *IEEE Soft.* (Mar/Apr): 25-26 (1997).

Pfleeger, S.L., Jeffery, R., Curtis, B. and Kitchenham, B. Status report on software measurement. *IEEE Soft.* (March/April): 33-43 (1997).

Robillard, P.N. The role of knowledge in software development. *Comm. of the ACM* 42(1): 87-92 (1999).

van Latum, F., van Solingen, R., Oivo, M., Hoisl, B., Rombach, D. and Ruhe, G. Adopting GQM-based measurement in an industrial environment. *IEEE Soft.* (January-February): 78-86 (1998).

Zelkowitz, M.V. and Wallace, D.R. Experimental models for validating technology. *Computer* (May): 23-31 (1998).

APPENDIX B – REFERENCES USED TO WRITE AND JUSTIFY THE DESCRIPTION

[IEEE/EIA, 1998] IEEE/EIA. 1998. Standard for Information Technology (ISO/IEC 12207) – *Software life cycle processes.* Institute of Electrical and Electronics Engineers/Electronic Industries Association Engineering Department.

[ISO93] ISO 1993. *International Vocabulary of Basic and General Terms in Metrology*, International Organization for Standardization.

[ISO/IEC, 1998] ISO/IEC 1998. 14143-1 *Software engineering - Software measurement - Functional size measurement - Definition of concepts,* International Organization for Standardization/International Electrotechnical Commission.

[ISO/IEC, 1999] ISO/IEC. 1999. Draft Technical Report (DTR) 16326 – *Software engineering – guide for the application of ISO/IEC 12207 to project management.* International Organization for Standardization/International Electrotechnical Commission.

[ISO/IEC, 2000] ISO/IEC Committee Draft (CD) 15939: Information technology - Software Measurement Process, International Organization for Standardization/International Electrotechnical Commission.

[Moore, 1998] James W. Moore. 1998. *Software engineering standards: a user's road map.* IEEE Computer Society.

[PMI, 1996] Project Management Institute Standards Committee. 1996. *A guide to the project management body of knowledge (PMBOK).* Project Management Institute.

APPENDIX C – TABLE OF CORRESPONDENCE WITH PMBOK

PMBOK Knowledge Areas	PMBOK Knowledge Area Processes	7.1 ISO/IEC 12207 Management Process Activities				
		7.1.1 Initiation and Scope Definition	7.1.2 Planning	7.1.3 Enactment	7.1.4 Review and Evaluation	7.1.5 Closure
4. Project Integration Management	4.1 Project Plan Development	X	X			
	4.2 Project Plan Execution			X	X	
	4.3 Overall Change Control			X	X	
5. Project Scope Management	5.1 Initiation	X		X		
	5.2 Scope Planning	X	X			
	5.3 Scope Definition	X	X			
	5.4 Scope Verification	X			X	X
	5.5 Scope Change Control	X	X	X	X	
6. Project Time Management	6.1 Activity Definition	X	X			
	6.2 Activity Sequencing		X			
	6.3 Activity Duration Estimating		X	X	X	
	6.4 Schedule Development		X			
	6.5 Schedule Control			X	X	
7. Project Cost Management	7.1 Resources Planning	X	X			
	7.2 Cost Estimating	X	X	X		
	7.3 Cost Budgeting		X			
	7.4 Cost Control			X	X	
8. Project Quality Management	8.1 Quality Planning	X	X			
	8.2 Quality Assurance			X	X	
	8.3 Quality Control			X	X	
9. Project Human Resource Management	9.1 Organizational Planning	X	X		X	
	9.2 Staff Acquisition	X		X		
	9.3 Team Development	X		X		
10. Project Communications Management	10.1 Communications Planning	X	X			
	10.2 Information Distribution			X		
	10.3 Performance Reporting			X	X	
	10.4 Administrative Closure			X		X
11. Project Risk Management	11.1 Risk Identification	X		X		
	11.2 Risk Quantification	X		X		
	11.3 Risk Response Development		X	X	X	
	11.4 Risk Response Control	X	X	X	X	
12. Project Procurement Management	12.1 Procurement Planning	X	X			
	12.2 Solicitation Planning	X	X			
	12.3 Solicitation	X		X		
	12.4 Source Selection	X		X	X	
	12.5 Contract Administration			X	X	
	12.6 Contract Close-out		X			X

Table 2: Correspondence between PMBOK knowledge areas and ISO/IEC 12207 management process activities (taken from ISO/IEC Draft Technical Report (DTR) 16326)

CHAPTER 9

SOFTWARE ENGINEERING PROCESS

Khaled El Emam
Institute for Information Technology
National Research Council
Building M-50, Montreal Road
Ottawa, Ontario K1A 0R6, Canada
+1 (613) 998 4260
Khaled.el-emam@iit.nrc.ca

Table of Contents

Keywords

software process, software process improvement, software process modeling, software process measurement, organizational change, software process assessment.

Acronyms

CBA IPI	CMM Based Appraisal for Internal Process Improvement
CMM	Capability Maturity Model
EF	Experience Factory
FP	Function Points
G/Q/M	Goal/Question/Metric
HRM	Human Resources Management
IDEAL	Initiating-Diagnosing-Establishing-Acting-Leaning (model)
MIS	Management Information Systems
PDCA	Plan-Do-Check-Act (cycle)
QIP	Quality Improvement Paradigm
ROI	Return on Investment
SCE	Software Capability Evaluation
SEPG	Software Engineering Process Group
SW-CMM	Capability Maturity Model for Software

1   INTRODUCTION

The software engineering process Knowledge Area has witnessed dramatic growth over the last decade. This was partly due to a recognition by major acquirers of systems where software is a major component that process issues can have an important impact on the ability of their suppliers to deliver. Therefore, they encouraged a focus on the software engineering process as a way to remedy this. Furthermore, the academic community has recently pursued an active research agenda in developing new tools and techniques to support software engineering processes, and also empirically studying these processes and their improvement. It should also be recognized that many software engineering process issues are closely related to other disciplines, namely those in the management sciences, albeit they have used a different terminology. The industrial adoption of software engineering process technology has also been increasing, as demonstrated by a number of published success stories. Therefore, there is in fact an extensive body of knowledge on the software engineering process.

2   DEFINITION OF THE SOFTWARE ENGINEERING PROCESS KNOWLEDGE AREA

The software engineering process Knowledge Area (KA) can potentially be examined at two levels. The first level encompasses the technical and managerial activities within the software engineering process that are performed during software acquisition, development, maintenance, and retirement. The second is the meta-level, which is concerned with the definition, implementation, measurement, management, change and improvement of the software engineering process itself. The latter we will term *software process engineering*.

The first level is covered by the other KA's of this Guide to the Software Engineering Body of Knowledge. This Knowledge Area is concerned with the second: **software process engineering**.

2.1 Scope

This Knowledge Area does not explicitly address the following topics:

- Human resources management (for example, as embodied in the People CMM [30][31])
- Systems engineering processes

While important topics in themselves, they are outside the direct scope of software process engineering. However, where relevant, interfaces (or references to interfaces) to HRM and systems engineering will be addressed.

2.2 Currency of Material

The software process engineering discipline is rapidly changing, with new paradigms and new models. The breakdown and references included here are pertinent at the time of writing. An attempt has been made to focus on concepts to shield the knowledge area description from changes in the field, but of course this cannot be 100% successful, and therefore the material here must be evolved over time. A good example is the on-going CMM Integration effort (see http://www.sei.cmu.edu/cmmi/products/models.html for the latest document suite) and the Team Software Process effort [71], both of which are likely to have a considerable influence on the software process community once widely disseminated, and would therefore have to be accommodated in the knowledge area description.

In addition, where Internet addresses are provided for reference material, these addresses were verified at the time of press. However, there are no guarantees that the documents will still be available on-line at the same location in the future.

2.3 Structure of the KA

To structure this KA in a way that is directly related to practice, we have defined a generic process model for software process engineering (see **Figure 1**). This model identifies the activities that are performed in a process engineering context. The topics are mapped to these activities. The advantage of such a structure is that one can see, in practice, where each of the topics is relevant, and provides an overall rationale for the topics. This generic model is based on the PDCA (plan-do-check-act) cycle (also see [79]).

3 BREAKDOWN OF TOPICS FOR SOFTWARE ENGINEERING PROCESS AND BREAKDOWN RATIONALE

The following figure shows the breakdown of topics in this knowledge area. Further explanation is provided in the subsequent sections.

Software Engineering Process Concepts
    Themes
    Terminology
Process Infrastructure
    The Software Engineering Process Group
    The Experience Factory
Process Measurement
    Methodology in Process Measurement
    Process Measurement Paradigms
        Analytic Paradigm
        Benchmarking Paradigm
Process Definition
    Types of Process Definitions
    Life Cycle Framework Models
    Software Life Cycle Process Models
    Notations for Process Definitions
    Process Definition Methods
    Automation
Qualitative Process Analysis
    Process Definition Review
    Root Cause Analysis
Process Implementation and Change
    Paradigms for Process Implementation and Change
    Guidelines for Process Implementation and Change
    Evaluating the Outcome of Process Implementation and Change

3.1 Software Engineering Process Concepts

3.1.1 Themes

Dowson [35] notes that "All process work is ultimately directed at 'software process assessment and improvement'". This means that the objective is to implement new or better processes in actual practices, be they individual, project or organizational practices.

 © *IEEE – Trial Version 1.00 – May 2001*

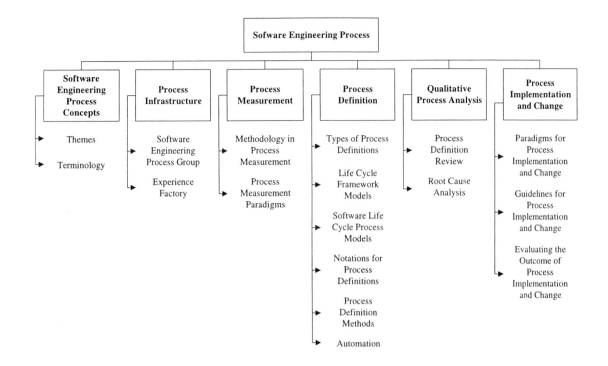

We describe the main topics in the software process engineering (i.e., the meta-level that has been alluded to earlier) area in terms of a cycle of process change, based on the commonly known PDCA cycle. This cycle highlights that individual process engineering topics are part of a larger process to improve practice, and that process evaluation and feedback is an important element of process engineering.

Software process engineering consists of four activities as illustrated in the model in **Figure 1**. The activities are sequenced in an iterative cycle allowing for continuous feedback and improvement of the software process.

The "Establish Process Infrastructure" activity consists of establishing commitment to process implementation and change (including obtaining management buy-in), and putting in place an appropriate infrastructure (resources and responsibilities) to make it happen.

The activities "Planning of Process Implementation and Change" and "Process Implementation and Change" are the core ones in process engineering, in that they are essential for any long-lasting benefit from process engineering to accrue. In the planning activity the objective is to understand the current business objectives and process needs of the organization[1], identify its strengths and weaknesses, and make a plan for process implementation and change. In "Process Implementation and Change", the

objective is to execute the plan, deploy new processes (which may involve, for example, the deployment of tools and training of staff), and/or change existing processes.

The fourth activity, "Process Evaluation" is concerned with finding out how well the implementation and change went; whether the expected benefits materialized. This is then used as input for subsequent cycles.

At the centre of the cycle is the "Process Experience Base". This is intended to capture lessons from past iterations of the cycle (e.g., previous evaluations, process definitions, and plans). Evaluation lessons can be qualitative or quantitative. No assumptions are made about the nature or technology of this "Process Experience Base", only that it be a persistent storage. It is expected that during subsequent iterations of the cycle, previous experiences will be adapted and reused. It is also important to continuously re-assess the utility of information in the experience base to ensure that obsolete information does not accumulate.

With this cycle as a framework, it is possible to map the topics in this knowledge area to the specific activities where they would be most relevant. This mapping is also shown in **Figure 1**. The bulleted boxes contain the Knowledge Area topics.

It should be noted that this cycle is not intended to imply that software process engineering is relevant to only large organizations. To the contrary, process-related activities can, and have been, performed successfully by small organizations, teams, and individuals. The way the activities defined in the cycle are performed would be

---

[1] The term "organization" is meant in a loose sense here. It could be a project, a team, or even an individual.

different depending on the context. Where it is relevant, we will present examples of approaches for small organizations.

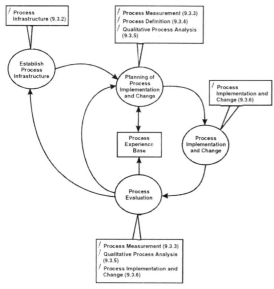

Figure 1 A model of the software process engineering cycle, and the relationship of its activities to the KA topics. The circles are the activities in the process engineering cycle. The square in the middle of the cycle is a data store. The bulleted boxes are the topics in this Knowledge Area that map to each of the activities in the cycle. The numbers refer to the topic sections in this chapter.

The topics in this KA are as follows:

Process Infrastructure: This is concerned with putting in place an infrastructure for software process engineering.

Process Measurement: This is concerned with quantitative techniques to diagnose software processes; to identify strengths and weaknesses. This can be performed to initiate process implementation and change, and afterwards to evaluate the consequences of process implementation and change.

Process Definition: This is concerned with defining processes in the form of models, plus the automated support that is available for the modeling task, and for enacting the models during the software process.

Qualitative Process Analysis: This is concerned with qualitative techniques to analyze software processes, to identify strengths and weaknesses. This can be performed to initiate process implementation and change, and afterwards to evaluate the consequences of process implementation and change.

Process Implementation and Change: This is concerned with deploying processes for the first time and with changing existing process. This topic focuses on organizational change. It describes the paradigms, infrastructure, and critical success factors necessary for successful process implementation and change. Within the scope of this topic, we also present some conceptual issues about the evaluation of process change.

The main, generally accepted, themes in the software engineering process field have been described by Dowson in [35]. His themes are a subset of the topics that we cover in this KA. Below are Dowson's themes:

- Process definition: covered in topic 3.4 of this KA breakdown

- Process assessment: covered in topic 3.3 of this KA breakdown

- Process improvement: covered in topics 3.2 and 3.6 of this KA breakdown

- Process support: covered in topic 3.4 of this KA breakdown

We also add one theme in this KA description, namely the qualitative process analysis (covered in topic 3.5).

3.1.2 Terminology

There is no single universal source of terminology for the software engineering process field, but good sources that define important terms are [51][96], and the vocabulary (Part 9) in the ISO/IEC TR 15504 documents [81].

3.2 Process Infrastructure

At the initiation of process engineering, it is necessary to have an appropriate infrastructure in place. This includes having the resources (competent staff, tools and funding), as well as the assignment of responsibilities. This is an indication of management commitment to and ownership of the process engineering effort. Various committees may have to be established, such as a steering committee to oversee the process engineering effort.

It is widely recognized that a team separate from the developers/maintainers must be set up and tasked with process analysis, implementation and change [16]. The main reason for this is that the priority of the developers/maintainers is to produce systems or releases, and therefore process engineering activities will not receive as much attention as they deserve or need. This, however, should not mean that the project organization is not involved in the process engineering effort at all. To the contrary, their involvement is essential. Especially in a small organization, outside help (e.g., consultants) may be required to assist in making up a process team.

Two types of infrastructure are have been used in practice: the Experience Factory [8][9] and the Software Engineering Process Group [54]. The IDEAL handbook [100] provides

 © IEEE – Trial Version 1.00 – May 2001

a good description of infrastructure for process improvement in general.

3.2.1 The Software Engineering Process Group

The SEPG is intended to be the central focus for process improvement within an organization. The SEPG typically has the following ongoing activities:

- Obtains and maintains the support of all levels of management
- Facilitates software process assessments (see below)
- Works with line managers whose projects are affected by changes in software engineering practice
- Maintains collaborative working relationships with software engineers
- Arranges and supports any training or continuing education related to process implementation and change
- Tracks, monitors, and reports on the status of particular improvement efforts
- Facilitates the creation and maintenance of process definitions
- Maintains a process database
- Provides process consultation to development projects and management
- Participate in integrating software engineering processes with other organizational processes, such as systems engineering

Fowler and Rifkin [54] suggest the establishment of a steering committee consisting of line and supervisory management. This would allow management to guide process implementation and change, align this effort with strategic and business goals of the organization, and also provides them with visibility. Furthermore, technical working groups may be established to focus on specific issues, such as selecting a new design method to setting up a measurement program.

3.2.2 The Experience Factory

The concept of the EF separates the project organization (e.g., the software development organization) from the improvement organization. The project organization focuses on the development and maintenance of applications. The EF is concerned with improvement. Their relationship is depicted in **Figure 2**.

The EF is intended to institutionalize the collective learning of an organization by developing, updating, and delivering to the project organization *experience packages* (e.g., guide books, models, and training courses).[2] The project organization offers to the experience factory their products, the plans used in their development, and the data gathered

during development and operation. Examples of experience packages include:

- resource models and baselines[3] (e.g., local cost models, resource allocation models)
- change and defect baselines and models (e.g., defect prediction models, types of defects expected for the application)
- project models and baselines (e.g., actual vs. expected product size)
- process definitions and models (e.g., process models for Cleanroom, Ada waterfall model)
- method and technique evaluations (e.g., best method for finding interface faults)
- products and product parts (e.g., Ada generics for simulation of satellite orbits)
- quality models (e.g., reliability models, defect slippage models, ease of change models), and
- lessons learned (e.g., risks associated with an Ada development).

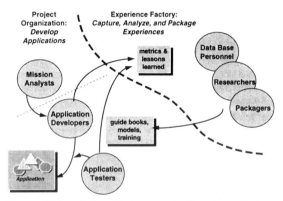

Figure 2 The relationship between the Experience Factory and the project organization as implemented at the Software Engineering Laboratory at NASA/GSFC. This diagram is reused here from [10] with permission of the authors.

3.3 Process Measurement

Process measurement, as used here, means that quantitative information about the process is collected, analyzed, and interpreted. Measurement is used to identify the strengths and weaknesses of processes, and to evaluate processes after they have been implemented and/or changed (e.g., evaluate the ROI from implementing a new process).[4]

---

[2] Also refered to as *process assets*.

[3] Baselines can be interpreted as descriptive reports presenting the current status.

[4] Process measurement may serve other purposes as well. For example, process measurement is useful for managing a software project. Some of these are covered in the Software Engineering Management and

An important assumption made in most process engineering work is illustrated by the path diagram in **Figure 3**. Here, we assume that the process has an impact on process outcomes. Process outcomes could be, for example, product quality (faults per KLOC or per FP), maintainability (effort to make a certain type of change), productivity (LOC or FP per person month), time-to-market, the extent of process variation, or customer satisfaction (as measured through a customer survey). This relationship depends on the particular context (e.g., size of the organization, or size of the project).

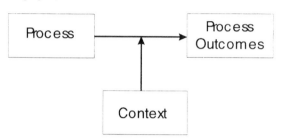

Figure 3 Path diagram showing the relationship between process and outcomes (results). The context affects the **relationship** between the process and process outcomes. This means that this process to process outcome relationship depends on the context value.

Not every process will have a positive impact on all outcomes. For example, the introduction of software inspections may reduce testing effort and cost, but may increase interval time if each inspection introduces large delays due to the scheduling of large inspection meetings [131]. Therefore, it is preferred to use multiple process outcome measures that are important for the organization's business.

In general, we are most concerned about the process outcomes. However, in order to achieve the process outcomes that we desire (e.g., better quality, better maintainability, greater customer satisfaction) we have to implement the appropriate process.

Of course, it is not only process that has an impact on outcomes. Other factors such as the capability of the staff and the tools that are used play an important role.[5] Furthermore, the extent to which the process is institutionalized or implemented (i.e., process fidelity) is important as it may explain why "good" processes do not give the desired outcomes.

One can measure the quality of the software process itself, or the process outcomes. The methodology in Section 3.3.1 is applicable to both. We will focus in Section 3.3.2 on process measurement since the measurement of process

outcomes is more general and applicable in other Knowledge Areas.

3.3.1 Methodology in Process Measurement

A number of guides for measurement are available [108][109][126]. All of these describe a goal-oriented process for defining measures. This means that one should start from specific information needs and then identify the measures that will satisfy these needs, rather than start from specific measures and try to use them. A good practical text on establishing and operating a measurement program has been produced by the Software Engineering Laboratory [123]. This also discusses the cost of measurement. Texts that present experiences in implementing measurement in software organizations include [86][105][115]. An emerging international standard that defines a generic measurement process is also available (ISO/IEC CD 15939: *Information Technology – Software Measurement Process*) [82].

Two important issues in the measurement of software engineering processes are the reliability and validity of measurement. Reliability is concerned with random measurement error. Validity is concerned with the ability of the measure to really measure what we think it is measuring.

Reliability becomes important when there is subjective measurement, for example, when assessors assign scores to a particular process. There are different types of validity that ought to be demonstrated for a software process measure, but the most critical one is predictive validity. This is concerned with the relationship between the process measure and the process outcome. A discussion of both of these and different methods for achieving them can be found in [40][59]. An IEEE Standard describes a methodology for validating metrics (*IEEE Standard for a Software Quality Metrics Methodology*. IEEE Std 1061-1998) [76].

An overview of existing evidence on reliability of software process assessments can be found in [43][49], and for predictive validity in [44][49][59][88].

3.3.2 Process Measurement Paradigms

Two general paradigms that are useful for characterizing the type of process measurement that can be performed have been described by Card [21]. The distinction made by Card is a useful conceptual one. Although, there may be overlaps in practice.

The first is the analytic paradigm. This is characterized as relying on *"quantitative evidence to determine where improvements are needed and whether an improvement initiative has been successful"*.[6] The second, the benchmarking paradigm, *"depends on identifying an 'excellent' organization in a field and documenting its*

---

other KA's. Here we focus on process measurement for the purpose of process implementation and change.

[5] And when evaluating the impact of a process change, for example, it is important to factor out these other influeneces.

---

6   Although qualitative evidence also can play an important role. In such a case, see Section 3.5 on qualitative process analysis.

© IEEE – Trial Version 1.00 – May 2001

practices and tools". Benchmarking assumes that if a less-proficient organization adopts the practices of the excellent organization, it will also become excellent. Of course, both paradigms can be followed at the same time, since they are based on different types of information.

We use these paradigms as general titles to distinguish between different types of measurement.

3.3.2.1 Analytic Paradigm[7]

The analytic paradigm is exemplified by the Quality Improvement Paradigm (QIP) consisting of a cycle of understanding, assessing, and packaging [124].

Experimental and Observational Studies

*   Experimentation involves setting up controlled or quasi experiments in the organization to evaluate processes [101]. Usually, one would compare a new process with the current process to determine whether the former has better process outcomes. Correlational (nonexperimental) studies can also provide useful feedback for identifying process improvements (e.g., for example, see the study described by Agresti [2]).

Process Simulation

*   The process simulation approach can be used to *predict* process outcomes if the current process is changed in a certain way [117]. Initial data about the performance of the current process needs to be collected, however, as a basis for the simulation.

Orthogonal Defect Classification

*   Orthogonal Defect Classification is a technique that can be used to link faults found with potential causes. It relies on a mapping between fault types and fault triggers [22][23]. There exists an IEEE Standard on the classification of faults (or anomalies) that may also be useful in this context (*IEEE Standard for the Classification of Software Anomalies*. IEEE Std 1044-1993) [74].

Statistical Process Control

*   Placing the software process under statistical process control, through the use of control charts and their interpretations, is an effective way to identify stability, or otherwise, in the process. One recent book provides a good introduction to SPC in the context of software engineering [53].

The Personal Software Process

*   This defines a series of improvements to an individual's development practices in a specified order [70]. It is 'bottom-up' in the sense that it stipulates personal data collection and improvements based on the data interpretations.

3.3.2.2 Benchmarking Paradigm

This paradigm involves measuring the maturity of an organization or the capability of its processes. The benchmarking paradigm is exemplified by the software process assessment[8] work. A general introductory overview of process assessments and their application is provided in [135].

*   Process assessment models

    An assessment model captures what are believed to be good practices. The good practices may pertain to technical software engineering activities only, or may also encompass, for example, management, systems engineering, and human resources management activities as well.

Architectures of assessment models

There are two general architectures for an assessment model that make different assumptions about the order in which processes must be measured: the continuous and the staged architectures [110]. At this point it is not possible to make a recommendation as to which approach is better than another. They have considerable differences. An organization should evaluate them to see which are most pertinent to their needs and objectives when selecting a model.

Assessment models

The most commonly used assessment model in the software community is the SW-CMM [122]. It is also important to recognize that ISO/IEC 15504 is an emerging international standard on software process assessments [42][81]. It defines an exemplar assessment model and conformance requirements on other assessment models. ISO 9001 is also a common model that has been applied by software organizations (usually in conjunction with ISO 9000-1) [132]. Other notable examples of assessment models are Trillium [25], Bootstrap [129], and the requirements engineering capability model [128]. There are also maturity models for other software processes available, such as for testing [18][19][20], a measurement maturity model [17], and a maintenance maturity model [36] (although, there have been many more capability and maturity models that have been defined, for example, for design, documentation, and formal methods, to name a few). A maturity model for systems engineering has also been developed, which would be useful where a project or organization is involved in the development and maintenance of systems including software [39]. The applicability of assessment models to small organizations is addressed in [85][120], where assessments models tailored to small organizations are presented.

---

7   These are intended as examples of the analytic paradigm, and reflect what is currently done in practice. Whether a specific organization uses all of these techniaues will depend, at least partially, on its maturity.

8   In some instances the term "appraisal" is used instead of assessment, and the term "capabillity evaluation" is used when the appraisal is for the purpose of contract award.

- Process assessment methods

  In order to perform an assessment, a specific assessment method needs to be followed. In addition to producing a quantitative score that characterizes the capability of the process (or maturity of the organization), an important purpose of an assessment is to create a climate for change within the organization [37]. In fact, it has been argued that the latter is the most important purpose of doing an assessment [38].

  The most well known method that has a reasonable amount of publicly available documentation is the CBA IPI [37]. This method focuses on assessments for the purpose of process improvement using the SW-CMM. Many other methods are refinements of this for particular contexts. Another well known method using the SW-CMM, but for supplier selection, is the SCE [6]. The activities performed during an assessment, the distribution of effort on these activities, as well as the atmosphere during an assessment is different if it is for the purpose of improvement versus contract award. Requirements on both types of methods that reflect what are believed to be good assessment practices are provided in [81][99].

There have been criticisms of various models and methods following the benchmarking paradigm, for example [12][50][62][87]. Most of these criticisms were concerned with the empirical evidence supporting the use of assessments models and methods. However, since the publication of these articles, there has been an accumulation of systematic evidence supporting the efficacy of process assessments [24][47][48][60][64][65][66][94].

3.4 Process Definition

Software engineering processes are defined for a number of reasons, including: facilitating human understanding and communication, supporting process improvement, supporting process management, providing automated process guidance, and providing automated execution support [29][52][68]. The types of process definitions required will depend, at least partially, on the reason.

It should be noted also that the context of the project and organization will determine the type of process definition that is most important. Important variables to consider include the nature of the work (e.g., maintenance or development), the application domain, the structure of the delivery process (e.g., waterfall, incremental, evolutionary), and the maturity of the organization.

There are different approaches that can be used to define and document the process. Under this topic the approaches that have been presented in the literature are covered, although at this time there is no data on the extent to which these are used in practice.

3.4.1 Types of Process Definitions

Processes can be defined at different levels of abstraction (e.g., generic definitions vs. tailored definitions, descriptive vs. prescriptive vs. proscriptive). The differentiation amongst these has been described in [69][97][111].

Orthogonal to the levels above, there are also types of process definitions. For example, a process definition can be a procedure, a policy, or a standard.

3.4.2 Life Cycle Framework Models

These framework models serve as a high level definition of the phases that occur during development. They are not detailed definitions, but only the high level activities and their interrelationships. The common ones are: the waterfall model, throwaway prototyping model, evolutionary prototyping model, incremental/iterative development, spiral model, reusable software model, and automated software synthesis. (see [11][28][84][111][113]). Comparisons of these models are provided in [28][32], and a method for selection amongst many of them in [3].

3.4.3 Software Life Cycle Process Models

Definitions of life cycle process models tend to be more detailed than framework models. Another difference being that life cycle process models do not attempt to order their processes in time. Therefore, in principle, the life cycle processes can be arranged to fit any of the life cycle frameworks. The two main references in this area are ISO/IEC 12207: *Information Technology – Software Life Cycle Processes* [80] and ISO/IEC TR 15504: *Information Technology – Software Process Assessment* [42][81]. Extensive guidance material for the application of the former has been produced by the IEEE (*Guide for Information Technology - Software Life Cycle Processes - Life cycle data*, IEEE Std 12207.1-1998, and *Guide for Information Technology - Software Life Cycle Processes – Implementation. Considerations.* IEEE Std 12207.2-1998) [77][78]. The latter defines a two dimensional model with one dimension being processes, and the second a measurement scale to evaluate the capability of the processes. In principle, ISO/IEC 12207 would serve as the process dimension of ISO/IEC 15504.

The IEEE standard on developing life cycle processes also provides a list of processes and activities for development and maintenance (*IEEE Standard for Developing Software Life Cycle Processes*, IEEE Std 1074-1991) [73], and provides examples of mapping them to life cycle framework models. A standard that focuses on maintenance processes is also available from the IEEE (*IEEE Standard for Software Maintenance*, IEEE Std 1219-1992) [75].

3.4.4 Notations for Process Definitions

Different elements of a process can be defined, for example, activities, products (artifacts), and resources [68]. Detailed frameworks that structure the types of information required to define processes are described in [4][98].

There are a large number of notations that have been used to define processes. They differ in the types of information defined in the above frameworks that they capture. A text that describes different notations is [125].

Because there is no data on which of these was found to be most useful or easiest to use under which conditions, this Guide covers what seemingly are popular approaches in practice: data flow diagrams [55], in terms of process purpose and outcomes [81], as a list of processes decomposed in constituent activities and tasks defined in natural language [80], Statecharts [89][117] (also see [63] for a comprehensive description of Statecharts), ETVX [116], Actor-Dependency modeling [14][134], SADT notation [102], Petri nets [5], IDEF0 [125], rule-based [7], and System Dynamics [1]. Other process programming languages have been devised, and these are described in [29][52][68].

3.4.5 Process Definition Methods

These methods specify the activities that must be performed in order to develop and maintain a process definition. These may include eliciting information from developers to build a descriptive process definition from scratch, and to tailoring an existing standard or commercial process. Examples of methods that have been applied in practice are [13][14][90][98][102]. In general, there is a strong similarity amongst them in that they tend to follow a traditional software development life cycle.

3.4.6 Automation

Automated tools either support the execution of the process definitions, or they provide guidance to humans performing the defined processes. In cases where process analysis is performed, some tools allow different types of simulations (e.g., discrete event simulation).

There exist tools that support each of the above process definition notations. Furthermore, these tools can execute the process definitions to provide automated support to the actual processes, or to fully automate them in some instances. An overview of process modeling tools can be found in [52], and of process-centered environments in [57][58].

Recent work on the application of the Internet to the provision of real-time process guidance is described in [91].

3.5 Qualitative Process Analysis

The objective of qualitative process analysis is to identify the strengths and weaknesses of the software process. It can be performed as a diagnosis before implementing or changing a process. It could also be performed after a process is implemented or changed to determine whether the change has had the desired effect.

Below we present two techniques for qualitative analysis that have been used in practice. Although it is plausible that new techniques would emerge in the future.

3.5.1 Process Definition Review

Qualitative evaluation means reviewing a process definition (either a descriptive or a prescriptive one, or both), and identifying deficiencies and potential process improvements. Typical examples of this are presented in [5][89]. An easily operational way to analyze a process is to compare it to an existing standard (national, international, or professional body), such as ISO/IEC 12207 [80].

With this approach, one does not collect quantitative data on the process. Or if quantitative data is collected, it plays a supportive role. The individuals performing the analysis of the process definition use their knowledge and capabilities to decide what process changes would potentially lead to desirable process outcomes.

3.5.2 Root Cause Analysis

Another common qualitative technique that is used in practice is a "Root Cause Analysis". This involves tracing back from detected problems (e.g., faults) to identify the process causes, with the aim of changing the process to avoid the problems in the future. Examples of this for different types of processes are described in [13][27][41][107].

With this approach, one starts from the process outcomes, and traces back along the path in **Figure 3** to identify the process causes of the undesirable outcomes. The Orthogonal Defect Classification technique described in Section 3.3.2.1 can be considered a more formalized approach to root cause analysis using quantitative information.

3.6 Process Implementation and Change

This topic describes the situation when processes are deployed for the first time (e.g., introducing an inspection process within a project or a complete methodology, such as Fusion [26] or the Unified Process [83]), and when current processes are changed (e.g., introducing a tool, or optimizing a procedure).[9] In both instances, existing practices have to be modified. If the modifications are extensive, then changes in the organizational culture may be necessary.

3.6.1 Paradigms for Process Implementation and Change

Two general paradigms that have emerged for driving process implementation and change are the Quality Improvement Paradigm (QIP) [124] and the IDEAL model

---

[9]   This can also be termed "process evolution".

[100]. The two paradigms are compared in [124]. A concrete instantiation of the QIP is described in [16].

3.6.2 Guidelines for Process Implementation and Change

Process implementation and change is an instance of organizational change. Most successful organizational change efforts treat the change as a project in its own right, with appropriate plans, monitoring, and review.

Guidelines about process implementation and change within software engineering organizations, including action planning, training, management sponsorship and commitment, and the selection of pilot projects, and that cover both the transition of processes and tools, are given in [33][92][95][104][114][120][127][130][133]. An empirical study evaluating success factors for process change is reported in [46]. Grady describes the process improvement experiences at Hewlett-Packard, with some general guidance on implementing organizational change [61].

The role of change agents in this activity should not be underestimated. Without the enthusiasm, influence, credibility, and persistence of a change agent, organizational change has little chance of succeeding. This is further discussed in [72].

Process implementation and change can also be seen as an instance of consulting (either internal or external). A suggested text, and classic, on consulting is that of Schein [121].

One can also view organizational change from the perspective of technology transfer. The classic text on the stages of technology transfer is that by Rogers [119]. Software engineering articles that discuss technology transfer, and the characteristics of recipients of new technology (which could include process related technologies) are [112][118].

3.6.3 Evaluating the Outcome of Process Implementation and Change

Evaluation of process implementation and change outcomes can be qualitative or quantitative. The topics above on qualitative analysis and measurement are relevant when evaluating implementation and change since they describe the techniques. Below we present some conceptual issues that become important when evaluating the outcome of implementation and change.

There are two ways that one can approach evaluation of process implementation and change. One can evaluate it in terms of changes to the process itself, or in terms of changes to the process outcomes (for example, measuring the Return on Investment from making the change). This issue is concerned with the distinction between cause and effect (as depicted in the path diagram in **Figure 3**), and is discussed in [16].

Sometimes people have very high expectations about what can be achieved in studies that evaluate the costs and benefits of process implementation and change. A pragmatic look at what can be achieved from such evaluation studies is given in [67].

Overviews of how to evaluate process change, and examples of studies that do so can be found in [44][59][88][92][93][101].

4   KEY REFERENCES VS. TOPICS MAPPING

Below are the matrices linking the topics to key references. In an attempt to limit the number of references and the total number of pages, as requested, some relevant articles are not included in this matrix. The reference list below provides a more comprehensive coverage.

In the cells, where there is a check mark it indicates that the whole reference (or most of it) is relevant. Otherwise, specific chapter numbers are provided in the cell.

	Elements [45]	SPICE [42]	Pfleeger [111]	Fuggetta [56]	Messnarz [103]	Moore [106]	Madhavji [97]	Dowson [35]
Software Engineering Process Concepts								
Themes								√
Terminology								
Process Infrastructure								
The Software Engineering Process Group								
The Experience Factory								
Process Measurement								
Methodology in Process Measurement								
Process Measurement Paradigms	Ch. 1, 7	Ch. 3						
Process Definition								
Types of Process							√	

	Elements [45]	SPICE [42]	Pfleeger [111]	Fuggetta [56]	Messnarz [103]	Moore [106]	Madhavji [97]	Dowson [35]
Definitions								
Life Cycle Framework Models			Ch. 2					
Software Life Cycle Process Models						Ch. 13		
Notations for Process Definitions				Ch. 1				
Process Definition Methods	Ch. 7							
Automation			Ch. 2	Ch. 2				
Qualitative Process Analysis								
Process Definition Review	Ch. 7							
Root Cause Analysis	Ch. 7							
Process Implementation and Change								
Paradigms for Process Implementation and Change	Ch. 1, 7							
Guidelines for Process Implementation and Change	Ch. 11			Ch. 4	Ch. 16			
Evaluating the Outcome of Process Implementation and Change					Ch. 7			

	Feiler & Humphrey [51]	Briand et al. [15]	SEL [124]	SEPG [54]	Dorfmann & Thayer [34]	El Emam & Goldenson [49]
Software Engineering Process Concepts						
Themes						
Terminology	√					
Process Infrastructure						
The Software Engineering Process Group			√			
The Experience Factory				√		
Process Measurement						
Methodology in Process Measurement		√				√
Process Measurement Paradigms		√				
Process Definition						
Types of Process Definitions						
Life Cycle Framework Models					Ch. 11	
Software Life Cycle Process Models						
Notations for Process Definitions						
Process Definition Methods						

	Feiler & Humphrey [51]	Briand et al. [15]	SEL [124]	SEPG [54]	Dorfmann & Thayer [34]	El Emam & Goldenson [49]
Automation						
Qualitative Process Analysis						
Process Definition Review		√				
Root Cause Analysis		√				
Process Implementation and Change						
Paradigms for Process Implementation and Change			√	√		
Guidelines for Process Implementation and Change			√	√		√
Evaluating the Outcome of Process Implementation and Change			√			√

5 RECOMMENDED REFERENCES FOR SOFTWARE PROCESS

The following are the key references that are recommended for this knowledge area. The mapping to the topics is given in Section 4.

K. El Emam and N. Madhavji (eds.): *Elements of Software Process Assessment and Improvement*, IEEE CS Press, 1999.

This IEEE edited book provides detailed chapters on the software process assessment and improvement area. It could serve as a general reference for this knowledge area, however, specifically chapters 1, 7, and 11 cover quite a bit of ground in a succinct manner.

K. El Emam, J-N Drouin, W. Melo (eds.): *SPICE: The Theory and Practice of Software Process Improvement and Capability Determination*. IEEE CS Press, 1998.

This IEEE edited book describes the emerging ISO/IEC 15504 international standard and its rationale. Chapter 3 provides a description of the overall architecture of the standard, which has since then been adopted in other assessment models.

S-L. Pfleeger: *Software Engineering: Theory and Practice*. Prentice-Hall, 1998.

This general software engineering reference has a good chapter, chapter 2, that discusses many issues related to the process modeling area.

Fuggetta and A. Wolf: *Software Process*, John Wiley & Sons, 1996.

This edited book provides a good overview of the process area, and covers modeling as well as assessment and improvement. Chapters 1 and 2 are reviews of modeling techniques and tools, and chapter 4 gives a good overview of the human and organizational issues that arise during process implementation and change.

R. Messnarz and C. Tully (eds.): *Better Software Practice for Business Benefit: Principles and Experiences*, IEEE CS Press, 1999.

This IEEE edited book provides a comprehensive perspective on process assessment and improvement efforts in Europe. Chapter 7 is a review of the costs and benefits of process improvement, with many references to prior work. Chapter 16 describes factors that affect the success of process improvement.

J. Moore: *Software Engineering Standards: A User's Road Map*. IEEE CS Press, 1998.

This IEEE book provides a comprehensive framework and guidance on software engineering standards. Chapter 13 is the process standards chapter.

N. H. Madhavji: "The Process Cycle". In *Software Engineering Journal*, 6(5):234-242, 1991.

This article provides an overview of different types of process definitions and relates them within an organizational context.

M. Dowson: "Software Process Themes and Issues". In *Proceedings of the 2nd International Conference on the Software Process*, pages 54-62, 1993.

This article provides an overview of the main themes in the software process area. Although not recent, most of the issues raised are still valid today.

P. Feiler and W. Humphrey: "Software Process Development and Enactment: Concepts and Definitions". In *Proceedings of the Second International Conference on the Software Process*, pages 28-40, 1993.

This article was one of the first attempts to define terminology in the software process area. Most of its terms are commonly used nowadays.

L. Briand, C. Differding, and H. D. Rombach: "Practical Guidelines for Measurement-Based Process Improvement".

In *Software Process Improvement and Practice*, 2:253-280, 1996.

This article provides a pragmatic look at using measurement in the context of process improvement, and discusses most of the issues related to setting up a measurement program.

Software Engineering Laboratory: *Software Process Improvement Guidebook*. NASA/GSFC, Technical Report SEL-95-102, April 1996. (available from http://sel.gsfc.nasa.gov/website/documents/online-doc/95-102.pdf)

This is a standard reference on the concepts of the QIP and EF.

P. Fowler and S. Rifkin: *Software Engineering Process Group Guide*. Software Engineering Institute, Technical Report CMU/SEI-90-TR-24, 1990. (available from http://www.sei.cmu.edu/pub/documents/90.reports/pdf/tr24.90.pdf)

This is the standard reference on setting up and running an SEPG.

M. Dorfmann and R. Thayer (eds.): *Software Engineering*, IEEE CS Press, 1997.

Chapter 11 of this IEEE volume gives a good overview of contemporary life cycle models.

K. El Emam and D. Goldenson: "An Empirical Review of Software Process Assessments". In *Advances in Computers*, vol. 53, pp. 319-423, 2000.

This chapter provides the most up-to-date review of evidence supporting process assessment and improvement, as well as a historical perspective on some of the early MIS work.

APPENDIX A – LIST OF FURTHER READINGS

[1]   T. Abdel-Hamid and S. Madnick, *Software Project Dynamics: An Integrated Approach*, Prentice-Hall, 1991.

[2]   W. Agresti, "The Role of Design and Analysis in Process Improvement," in *Elements of Software Process Assessment and Improvement*, K. El-Emam and N. Madhavji (eds.), IEEE CS Press, 1999.

[3]   L. Alexander and A. Davis, "Criteria for Selecting Software Process Models," in *Proceedings of COMPSAC'91*, pp. 521-528, 1991.

[4]   J. Armitage and M. Kellner, "A Conceptual Schema for Process Definitions and Models," in *Proceedings of the Third International Conference on the Software Process*, pp. 153-165, 1994.

[5]   S. Bandinelli, A. Fuggetta, L. Lavazza, M. Loi, and G. Picco, "Modeling and Improving an Industrial Software Process," *IEEE Transactions on Software Engineering*, vol. 21, no. 5, pp. 440-454, 1995.

[6]   R. Barbour, "Software Capability Evaluation - Version 3.0 : Implementation Guide for Supplier Selection," Software Engineering Institute, CMU/SEI-95-TR012, 1996. (available at http://www.sei.cmu.edu/publications/documents/95.reports/95.tr.012.html)

[7]   N. Barghouti, D. Rosenblum, D. Belanger, and C. Alliegro, "Two Case Studies in Modeling Real, Corporate Processes," *Software Process - Improvement and Practice*, vol. Pilot Issue, pp. 17-32, 1995.

[8]   V. Basili, G. Caldiera, and G. Cantone, "A Reference Architecture for the Component Factory," *ACM Transactions on Software Engineering and Methodology*, vol. 1, no. 1, pp. 53-80, 1992.

[9]   V. Basili, G. Caldiera, F. McGarry, R. Pajerski, G. Page, and S. Waligora, "The Software Engineering Laboratory - An Operational Software Experience Factory," in *Proceedings of the International Conference on Software Engineering*, pp. 370-381, 1992.

[10] V. Basili, S. Condon, K. El-Emam, R. Hendrick, and W. Melo, "Characterizing and Modeling the Cost of Rework in a Library of Reusable Software Components," in *Proceedings of the 19th International Conference on Software Engineering*, pp. 282-291, 1997.

[11] B. Boehm, "A Spiral Model of Software Development and Enhancement," *Computer*, vol. 21, no. 5, pp. 61-72, 1988.

[12] T. Bollinger and C. McGowan, "A Critical Look at Software Capability Evaluations," *IEEE Software*, pp. 25-41, July, 1991.

[13] L. Briand, V. Basili, Y. Kim, and D. Squire, "A Change Analysis Process to Characterize Software Maintenance Projects," in *Proceedings of the International Conference on Software Maintenance*, 1994.

[14] L. Briand, W. Melo, C. Seaman, and V. Basili, "Characterizing and Assessing a Large-Scale Software Maintenance Organization," in *Proceedings of the 17th International Conference on Software Engineering*, pp. 133-143, 1995.

[15] L. Briand, C. Differding, and H.D. Rombach, "Practical Guidelines for Measurement-Based Process Improvement," *Software Process Improvement and Practice*, vol. 2, pp. 253-280, 1996.

[16] L. Briand, K. El Emam, and W. Melo, "An Inductive Method for Software Process Improvement: Concrete Steps and Guidelines," in *Elements of Software Process Assessment and Improvement*, K. El-Emam and N. Madhavji (eds.), IEEE CS Press, 1999.

[17] F. Budlong and J. Peterson, "Software Metrics Capability Evaluation Guide," The Software Technology Support Center, Ogden Air Logistics Center, Hill Air Force Base, 1995.

[18] I. Burnstein, T. Suwannasart, and C. Carlson, "Developing a Testing Maturity Model: Part II," *Crosstalk*, pp. 19-26, September, 1996. (available at http://www.stsc.hill.af.mil/crosstalk/)

[19] I. Burnstein, T. Suwannasart, and C. Carlson, "Developing a Testing Maturity Model: Part I," *Crosstalk*, pp. 21-24, August, 1996. (available at http://www.stsc.hill.af.mil/crosstalk/)

[20] I. Burnstein, A. Homyen, T. Suwanassart, G. Saxena, and R. Grom, "A Testing Maturity Model for Software Test Process Assessment and Improvement," *Software Quality Professional*, vol. 1, no. 4, pp. 8-21, 1999.

[21] D. Card, "Understanding Process Improvement," *IEEE Software*, pp. 102-103, July, 1991.

[22] R. Chillarege, I. Bhandhari, J. Chaar, M. Halliday, D. Moebus, B. Ray, and M. Wong, "Orthogonal Defect Classification - A Concept for In-Process Measurement," *IEEE Transactions on Software Engineering*, vol. 18, no. 11, pp. 943-956, 1992.

[23] R. Chillarege, "Orthogonal Defect Classification," in *Handbook of Software Reliability Engineering*, M. Lyu (eds.), IEEE CS Press, 1996.

[24] B. Clark, "The Effects of Software Process Maturity on Software Development Effort," University of Southern California, PhD Thesis, 1997.

[25] F. Coallier, J. Mayrand, and B. Lague, "Risk Management in Software Product Procurement," in *Elements of Software Process Assessment and Improvement*, K. El-Emam and N. H. Madhavji (eds.), IEEE CS Press, 1999.

[26] D. Coleman, P. Arnold, S. Godoff, C. Dollin, H. Gilchrist, F. Hayes, and P. Jeremaes, *Object-Oriented Development: The Fusion Method.*, Englewood Cliffs, NJ:Prentice Hall., 1994.

[27] J. Collofello and B. Gosalia, "An Application of Causal Analysis to the Software Production Process," *Software Practice and Experience*, vol. 23, no. 10, pp. 1095-1105, 1993.

[28] E. Comer, "Alternative Software Life Cycle Models," in *Software Engineering*, M. Dorfmann and R. Thayer (eds.), IEEE CS Press, 1997.

[29] B. Curtis, M. Kellner, and J. Over, "Process Modeling," *Communications of the ACM*, vol. 35, no. 9, pp. 75-90, 1992.

[30] B. Curtis, W. Hefley, and S. Miller, "People Capability Maturity Model," Software Engineering Institute, CMU/SEI-95-MM-02, 1995. (available at http://www.sei.cmu.edu/pub/documents/95.reports/pdf/mm002.95.pdf)

[31] B. Curtis, W. Hefley, S. Miller, and M. Konrad, "The People Capability Maturity Model for Improving the Software Workforce," in *Elements of Software Process Assessment and Improvement*, K. El-Emam and N. Madhavji (eds.), IEEE CS Press, 1999.

[32] A. Davis, E. Bersoff, and E. Comer, "A Strategy for Comparing Alternative Software Development Life Cycle Models," *IEEE Transactions on Software Engineering*, vol. 14, no. 10, pp. 1453-1461, 1988.

[33] R. Dion, "Starting the Climb Towards the CMM Level 2 Plateau," in *Elements of Software Process Assessment and Improvement*, K. El-Emam and N. H. Madhavji (eds.), IEEE CS Press, 1999.

[34] M. Dorfmann and R. Thayer (eds.), "Software Engineering," IEEE CS Press, 1997.

[35] M. Dowson, "Software Process Themes and Issues," in *Proceedings of the 2nd International Conference on the Software Process*, pp. 54-62, 1993.

[36] D. Drew, "Tailoring the Software Engineering Institute's (SEI) Capability Maturity Model (CMM) to a Software Sustaining Engineering Organization," in *Proceedings of the International Conference on Software Maintenance*, pp. 137-144, 1992.

[37] D. Dunnaway and S. Masters, "CMM-Based Appraisal for Internal Process Improvement (CBA IPI): Method Description," Software Engineering Institute, CMU/SEI-96-TR-007, 1996. (available at http://www.sei.cmu.edu/pub/documents/96.reports/pdf/tr007.96.pdf)

[38] K. Dymond, "Essence and Accidents in SEI-Style Assessments or 'Maybe this Time the Voice of the Engineer Will be Heard'," in *Elements of Software Process Assessment and Improvement*, K. El-Emam and N. Madhavji (eds.), IEEE CS Press, 1999.

[39] EIA, "EIA/IS 731 Systems Engineering Capability Model,". (available at http://www.geia.org/eoc/G47/index.html)

[40] K. El-Emam and D. R. Goldenson, "SPICE: An Empiricist's Perspective," in *Proceedings of the Second IEEE International Software Engineering Standards Symposium*, pp. 84-97, 1995.

[41] K. El-Emam, D. Holtje, and N. Madhavji, "Causal Analysis of the Requirements Change Process for a Large System," in *Proceedings of the International Conference on Software Maintenance*, pp. 214-221, 1997.

[42] K. El-Emam, J-N Drouin, and W. Melo, *SPICE: The Theory and Practice of Software Process Improvement and Capability Determination*, IEEE CS Press, 1998.

[43] K. El-Emam, "Benchmarking Kappa: Interrater Agreement in Software Process Assessments," *Empirical Software Engineering: An International Journal*, vol. 4, no. 2, pp. 113-133, 1999.

[44] K. El-Emam and L. Briand, "Costs and Benefits of Software Process Improvement," in *Better Software Practice for Business Benefit: Principles and Experiences*, R. Messnarz and C. Tully (eds.), IEEE CS Press, 1999.

[45] K. El-Emam and N. Madhavji, *Elements of Software Process Assessment and Improvement*, IEEE CS Press, 1999.

[46] K. El-Emam, B. Smith, and P. Fusaro, "Success Factors and Barriers in Software Process Improvement: An Empirical Study," in *Better Software Practice for Business Benefit: Principles and Experiences*, R. Messnarz and C. Tully (eds.), IEEE CS Press, 1999.

[47] K. El-Emam and A. Birk, "Validating the ISO/IEC 15504 Measures of Software Development Process Capability," *Journal of Systems and Software*, vol. 51, no. 2, pp. 119-149, 2000. (available at E:\Articles\ElEmam_Birk_JSS.pdf)

[48] K. El-Emam and A. Birk, "Validating the ISO/IEC 15504 Measures of Software Requirements Analysis Process Capability," *IEEE Transactions on Software Engineering*, vol. 26, no. 6, pp. 541-566, June, 2000.

[49] K. El-Emam and D. Goldenson, "An Empirical Review of Software Process Assessments," *Advances in Computers*, vol. 53, pp. 319-423, 2000.

[50] M. Fayad and M. Laitinen, "Process Assessment: Considered Wasteful," *Communications of the ACM*, vol. 40, no. 11, November, 1997.

[51] P. Feiler and W. Humphrey, "Software Process Development and Enactment: Concepts and Definitions," in *Proceedings of the Second International Conference on the Software Process*, pp. 28-40, 1993.

[52] A. Finkelstein, J. Kramer, and B. Nuseibeh (eds.), "Software Process Modeling and Technology," Research Studies Press Ltd., 1994.

[53] W. Florac and A. Carleton, *Measuring the Software Process: Statistical Process Control for Software Process Improvement*, Addison Wesley, 1999.

[54] P. Fowler and S. Rifkin, "Software Engineering Process Group Guide," Software Engineering Institute, CMU/SEI-90-TR-24, 1990. (available at http://www.sei.cmu.edu/pub/documents/90.reports/pdf/tr24.90.pdf)

[55] D. Frailey, "Defining a Corporate-Wide Software Process," in *Proceedings of the 1st International Conference on the Software Process*, pp. 113-121, 1991.

[56] A. Fuggetta and A. Wolf, *Software Process*, John Wiley & Sons, 1996.

[57] P. Garg and M. Jazayeri, *Process-Centered Software Engineering Environments*, IEEE CS Press, 1995.

[58] P. Garg and M. Jazayeri, "Process-Centered Software Engineering Environments: A Grand Tour," in *Software Process*, A. Fuggetta and A. Wolf (eds.), John Wiley & Sons, 1996.

[59] D. Goldenson, K. El-Emam, J. Herbsleb, and C. Deephouse, "Empirical Studies of Software Process Assessment Methods," in *Elements of Software Process Assessment and Improvement*, K. El-Emam and N. H. Madhavji (eds.), IEEE CS Press, 1999.

[60] D.R. Goldenson and J. Herbsleb, "After the Appraisal: A Systematic Survey of Process Improvement, its Benefits, and Factors that Influence Success," Software Engineering Institute, CMU/SEI-95-TR-009, 1995.

[61] R. Grady, *Successful Software Process Improvement*, Prentice Hall, 1997.

[62] E. Gray and W. Smith, "On the Limitations of Software Process Assessment and the Recognition of a Required Re-Orientation for Global Process Improvement," *Software Quality Journal*, vol. 7, pp. 21-34, 1998.

[63] D. Harel and M. Politi, *Modeling Reactive Systems with Statecharts: The Statemate Approach*, McGraw-Hill, 1998.

[64] J. Herbsleb, A. Carleton, J. Rozum, J. Siegel, and D.Zubrow, "Benefits of CMM-based Software Process Improvement: Initial Results," Software Engineering Institute, CMU/SEI-94-TR-13, 1994.

[65] J. Herbsleb and D. Goldenson, "A Systematic Survey of CMM Experience and Results," in *Proceedings of the International Conference on Software Engineering*, pp. 25-30, 1996.

[66] J. Herbsleb, D. Zubrow, D. Goldenson, W. Hayes, and M. Paulk, "Software Quality and the Capability Maturity Model," *Communications of the ACM*, vol. 40, no. 6, pp. 30-40, 1997.

[67] J. Herbsleb, "Hard Problems and Hard Science: On the Practical Limits of Experimentation," *IEEE TCSE Software Process Newsletter*, vol. 11, pp. 18-21, 1998. (available at http://www.seg.iit.nrc.ca/SPN)

[68] K. Huff, "Software Process Modeling," in *Software Process*, A. Fuggetta and A. Wolf (eds.), John Wiley & Sons, 1996.

[69] W. Humphrey, *Managing the Software Process*, Addison Wesley, 1989.

[70] W. Humphrey, *A Discipline for Software Engineering*, Addison Wesley, 1995.

[71] W. Humphrey, *An Introduction to the Team Software Process*, Addison-Wesley, 1999.

[72] D. Hutton, *The Change Agent's Handbook: A Survival Guide for Quality Improvement Champions*, Irwin, 1994.

[73] IEEE, "IEEE Standard for Developing Software Life Cycle Processes," IEEE Computer Society, IEEE Std 1074-1991, 1991.

[74] IEEE, "IEEE Standard for the Classification of Software Anomalies," IEEE Computer Society, IEEE Std 1044-1993, 1993.

[75] IEEE, "IEEE Standard for Software Maintenance," IEEE Computer Society, IEEE Std 1219-1998, 1998.

[76] IEEE, "IEEE Standard for a Software Quality Metrics Methodology," IEEE Computer Society, IEEE Std 1061-1998, 1998.

[77] IEEE, "Guide for Information Technology - Software Life Cycle Processes - Life cycle data," IEEE Computer Society, IEEE Std 12207.1-1998, 1998.

[78] IEEE, "Guide for Information Technology - Software Life Cycle Processes - Implementation. Considerations," IEEE Computer Society, IEEE Std 12207.2-1998, 1998.

[79] K. Ishikawa, *What Is Total Quality Control ? The Japanese Way*, Prentice Hall, 1985.

[80] ISO/IEC, "ISO/IEC 12207: Information Technology - Software Life Cycle Processes," International Organization for Standardization and the International Electrotechnical Commission, 1995.

[81] ISO/IEC, "ISO/IEC TR 15504: Information Technology - Software Process Assessment (parts 1-9)," International Organization for Standardization and the International Electrotechnical Commission, 1998 (part 5 was published in 1999). (available at http://www.seg.iit.nrc.ca/spice)

[82] ISO/IEC, "ISO/IEC CD 15939: Information Technology - Software Measurement Process," International Organization for Standardization and the International Electrotechnical Commission, 2000. (available at

http://www.info.uqam.ca/Labo_Recherche/Lrgl/sc7/private_files/07n2274.pdf)

[83] I. Jacobson, G. Booch, and J. Rumbaugh, *The Unified Software Development Process*, Addison-Wesley, 1998.

[84] P. Jalote, *An Integrated Approach to Software Engineering*, Springer, 1997.

[85] D. Johnson and J. Brodman, "Tailoring the CMM for Small Businesses, Small Organizations, and Small Projects," in *Elements of Software Process Assessment and Improvement*, K. El-Emam and N. Madhavji (eds.), IEEE CS Press, 1999.

[86] C. Jones, *Applied Software Measurement*, McGraw-Hill, 1994.

[87] C. Jones, "Gaps in SEI Programs," *Software Development*, vol. 3, no. 3, pp. 41-48, March, 1995.

[88] C. Jones, "The Economics of Software Process Improvements," in *Elements of Software Process Assessment and Improvement*, K. El-Emam and N. H. Madhavji (eds.), IEEE CS Press, 1999.

[89] M. Kellner and G. Hansen, "Software Process Modeling: A Case Study," in *Proceedings of the 22nd International Conference on the System Sciences*, 1989.

[90] M. Kellner, L. Briand, and J. Over, "A Method for Designing, Defining, and Evolving Software Processes," in *Proceedings of the 4th International Conference on the Software Process*, pp. 37-48, 1996.

[91] M. Kellner, U. Becker-Kornstaedt, W. Riddle, J. Tomal, and M. Verlage, "Process Guides: Effective Guidance for Process Participants," in *Proceedings of the 5th International Conference on the Software Process*, pp. 11-25, 1998.

[92] B. Kitchenham, "Selecting Projects for Technology Evaluation," *IEEE TCSE Software Process Newsletter*, no. 11, pp. 3-6, 1998. (available at http://www.seg.iit.nrc.ca/SPN)

[93] H. Krasner, "The Payoff for Software Process Improvement: What it is and How to Get it," in *Elements of Software Process Assessment and Improvement*, K. El-Emam and N. H. Madhavji (eds.), IEEE CS Press, 1999.

[94] M. S. Krishnan and M. Kellner, "Measuring Process Consistency: Implications for Reducing Software Defects," *IEEE Transactions on Software Engineering*, vol. 25, no. 6, pp. 800-815, November/December, 1999.

[95] C. Laporte and S. Trudel, "Addressing the People Issues of Process Improvement Activities at Oerlikon Aerospace," *Software Process - Improvement and Practice*, vol. 4, no. 4, pp. 187-198, 1998.

[96] J. Lonchamp, "A Structured Conceptual and Terminological Framework for Software Process Engineering," in *Proceedings of the Second International Conference on the Software Process*, pp. 41-53, 1993.

[97] N. Madhavji, "The Process Cycle," *Software Engineering Journal*, vol. 6, no. 5, pp. 234-242, 1991.

[98] N. Madhavji, D. Hoeltje, W. Hong, and T. Bruckhaus, "Elicit: A Method for Eliciting Process Models," in *Proceedings of the Third International Conference on the Software Process*, pp. 111-122, 1994.

[99] S. Masters and C. Bothwell, "CMM Appraisal Framework - Version 1.0," Software Engineering Institute, CMU/SEI-TR-95-001, 1995. (available at http://www.sei.cmu.edu/pub/documents/95.reports/pdf/tr001.95.pdf)

[100] B. McFeeley, "IDEAL: A User's Guide for Software Process Improvement," Software Engineering Institute, CMU/SEI-96-HB-001, 1996. (available at http://www.sei.cmu.edu/pub/documents/96.reports/pdf/hb001.96.pdf)

[101] F. McGarry, R. Pajerski, G. Page, S. Waligora, V. Basili, and M. Zelkowitz, "Software Process Improvement in the NASA Software Engineering Laboratory," Software Engineering Institute, CMU/SEI-94-TR-22, 1994. (available at http://www.sei.cmu.edu/pub/documents/94.reports/pdf/tr22.94.pdf)

[102] C. McGowan and S. Bohner, "Model Based Process Assessments," in *Proceedings of the International Conference on Software Engineering*, pp. 202-211, 1993.

[103] R. Messnarz and C. Tully (eds.), "Better Software Practice for Business Benefit: Principles and Experiences," IEEE CS Press, 1999.

[104] D. Moitra, "Managing Change for Software Process Improvement Initiatives: A Practical Experience-Based Approach," *Software Process - Improvement and Practice*, vol. 4, no. 4, pp. 199-207, 1998.

[105] K. Moller and D. Paulish, *Software Metrics*, Chapman & Hall, 1993.

[106] J. Moore, *Software Engineering Standards: A User's Road Map*, IEEE CS Press, 1998.

[107] T. Nakajo and H. Kume, "A Case History Analysis of Software Error Cause-Effect Relationship," *IEEE Transactions on Software Engineering*, vol. 17, no. 8, 1991.

[108] Office of the Under Secretary of Defense for Acquisitions and Technology, "Practical Software Measurement: A Foundation for Objective Project Management," 1998. (available at http://www.psmsc.com)

[109] R. Park, W. Goethert, and W. Florac, "Goal-Driven Software Measurement - A Guidebook," Software Engineering Institute, CMU/SEI-96-HB-002, 1996.

(available at http://www.sei.cmu.edu/pub/documents/96.reports/pdf/hb002.96.pdf)

[110] M. Paulk and M. Konrad, "Measuring Process Capability Versus Organizational Process Maturity," in *Proceedings of the 4th International Conference on Software Quality*, 1994.

[111] S-L. Pfleeger, *Software Engineering: Theory and Practice*, Prentice-Hall, 1998.

[112] S-L. Pfleeger, "Understanding and Improving Technology Transfer in Software Engineering," *Journal of Systems and Software*, vol. 47, pp. 111-124, 1999.

[113] R. Pressman, *Software Engineering: A Practitioner's Approach*, McGraw-Hill, 1997.

[114] J. Puffer, "Action Planning," in *Elements of Software Process Assessment and Improvement*, K. El-Emam and N. H. Madhavji (eds.), IEEE C S Press, 1999.

[115] L. Putnam and W. Myers, *Measures for Excellence: Reliable Software on Time, Within Budget*, Yourdon Press, 1992.

[116] R. Radice, N. Roth, A. O'Hara Jr., and W. Ciarfella, "A Programming Process Architecture," *In IBM Systems Journal*, vol. 24, no. 2, pp. 79-90, 1985.

[117] D. Raffo and M. Kellner, "Modeling Software Processes Quantitatively and Evaluating the Performance of Process Alternatives," in *Elements of Software Process Assessment and Improvement*, K. El-Emam and N. Madhavji (eds.), IEEE CS Press, 1999.

[118] S. Raghavan and D. Chand, "Diffusing Software-Engineering Methods," *IEEE Software*, pp. 81-90, July, 1989.

[119] E. Rogers, *Diffusion of Innovations*, Free Press, 1983.

[120] M. Sanders (eds.), "The SPIRE Handbook: Better, Faster, Cheaper Software Development in Small Organisations," European Comission, 1998.

[121] E. Schein, *Process Consultation Revisited: Building the Helping Relationship*, Addison-Wesley, 1999.

[122] Software Engineering Institute, *The Capability Maturity Model: Guidelines for Improving the Software Process*, Addison Wesley, 1995.

[123] Software Engineering Laboratory, "Software Measurement Guidebook (Revision 1),", SEL-94-102, 1995. (available at http://sel.gsfc.nasa.gov/website/documents/online-doc/94-102.pdf)

[124] Software Engineering Laboratory, "Software Process Improvement Guidebook. NASA/GSFC,", SEL-95-102, 1996. (available at http://sel.gsfc.nasa.gov/website/documents/online-doc/95-102.pdf)

[125] Software Productivity Consortium, "Process Definition and Modeling Guidebook,", SPC-92041-CMC, 1992.

[126] R. van Solingen and E. Berghout, *The Goal/Question/Metric Method: A Practical Guide for Quality Improvement of Software Development*, McGraw Hill, 1999.

[127] I. Sommerville and T. Rodden, "Human, Social and Organisational Influences on the Software Process," in *Software Process*, A. Fuggetta and A. Wolf (eds.), John Wiley & Sons, 1996.

[128] I. Sommerville and P. Sawyer, *Requirements Engineering: A Good Practice Guide*, John Wiley & Sons, 1997.

[129] H. Steinen, "Software Process Assessment and Improvement: 5 Years of Experiences with Bootstrap," in *Elements of Software Process Assessment and Improvement*, K. El-Emam and N. Madhavji (eds.), IEEE CS Press, 1999.

[130] D. Stelzer and W. Mellis, "Success Factors of Organizational Change in Software Process Improvement," *Software Process: Improvement and Practice*, vol. 4, no. 4, pp. 227-250, 1998.

[131] L. Votta, "Does Every Inspection Need a Meeting ?," *ACM Software Engineering Notes*, vol. 18, no. 5, pp. 107-114, 1993.

[132] S. Weissfelner, "ISO 9001 for Software Organizations," in *Elements of Software Process Assessment and Improvement*, K. El-Emam and N. Madhavji (eds.), IEEE CS Press, 1999.

[133] K. Wiegers, *Creating a Software Engineering Culture*, Dorset house, 1996.

[134] E. Yu and J. Mylopolous, "Understanding 'Why' in Software Process Modeling, Analysis, and Design," in *Proceedings of the 16th International Conference on Software Engineering*, 1994.

[135] S. Zahran, *Software Process Improvement: Practical Guidelines for Business Success*, Addison Wesley, 1998.

CHAPTER 10

SOFTWARE ENGINEERING TOOLS AND METHODS

David Carrington
Department of Computer Science and Electrical Engineering
The University of Queensland
Brisbane, Qld 4072 Australia
+61 7 3365 3310
davec@csee.uq.edu.au

Table of Contents

1   INTRODUCTION

This chapter provides an initial breakdown of topics within the Software Engineering Infrastructure Knowledge Area as defined by the document "Approved Baseline for a List of Knowledge Areas for the Stone Man Version of the Guide to the Software Engineering Body of Knowledge". Earlier versions of this Knowledge Area included material on integration and reuse, but this has been removed. Consequently the Knowledge Area has been renamed from "Software Engineering Infrastructure" to "Software Engineering Tools and Methods".

The five general software engineering texts [DT97, Moo98, Pfl98, Pre97, and Som96] have been supplemented as primary sources by "The Computer Science and Engineering Handbook" [Tuc96], which provides nine chapters on software engineering topics. Chapter 112, "Software Tools and Environments" by Steven Reiss [Rei96] is particularly helpful for this Knowledge Area. Additional specialized references are identified for particular topics.

One observation from assembling the guide to this knowledge area is that there is a scarcity of recent technical writing on practical software engineering tools. Obviously, there are detailed manuals on specific tools and numerous research papers on innovative software tools, but there is a gap between the two. One difficulty is the high rate of change in software tools. Specific details alter regularly, making it difficult to provide up-to-date concrete examples. There also seems to be an attitude that software engineering tools are prosaic and not worthy of study beyond the level required for use.

2   DEFINITION OF THE SOFTWARE ENGINEERING TOOLS AND METHODS KNOWLEDGE AREA

The Software Engineering Tools and Methods Knowledge Area includes both the software development environments and the development methods knowledge areas identified in the Straw Man version of the guide.

Software development environments are the computer-based tools that are intended to assist the software development process. Tools allow repetitive, well-defined actions to be automated, thus reducing the cognitive load on the software engineer. The engineer is then free to concentrate on the creative aspects of the process. Tools are often designed to support particular methods, reducing any administrative load associated with applying the method manually. Like methods, they are intended to make development more systematic, and they vary in scope from supporting individual tasks to encompassing the complete life cycle.

Development methods impose structure on the software development activity with the goal of making the activity systematic and ultimately more likely to be successful. Methods usually provide a notation and vocabulary, procedures for performing identifiable tasks and guidelines for checking both the process and the product. Development methods vary widely in scope, from a single life cycle phase to the complete life cycle. The emphasis in this Knowledge Area is on methods that encompass multiple lifecycle phases since phase-specific methods are likely to be covered in other Knowledge Areas.

3 BREAKDOWN OF TOPICS FOR SOFTWARE ENGINEERING TOOLS AND METHODS

This section contains a breakdown of topics in the Software Engineering Tools and Methods Knowledge Area, with brief descriptions and references. The Knowledge Area is partitioned at the top level into Software Tools and Software Methods. Two levels of references are provided with topics: the recommended references within brackets and additional references within parentheses. References to a particular chapter are denoted as *Ref*:c*N* where *N* is the chapter number. A similar denotation is used for references to a particular section *Ref*:s*N*. Figure 1 provides a diagrammatic representation of the breakdown of topics.

I. Software Tools

The partitioning of the Software Tools section uses the same structure as the Stone Man Version of the Guide to the Software Engineering Body of Knowledge. The first five subsections correspond to the five Knowledge Areas (Requirements, Design, Construction, Testing, and Maintenance) that correspond to a phase of a software lifecycle, so these sections provide a location for phase-specific tools. The next four subsections correspond to the remaining Knowledge Areas (Process, Quality, Configuration Management and Management), and provide locations for phase-independent tools that are associated with activities described in these Knowledge Areas. Two additional subsections are provided: one for infrastructure support tools that do not fit in any of the earlier sections, and a Miscellaneous subsection for topics, such as tool integration techniques, that are potentially applicable to all classes of tools. Because software engineering tools evolve rapidly and continuously, the hierarchy and description avoids discussing particular tools as far as possible.

A. Software Requirements Tools

Tools for dealing with software requirements have been partitioned into two topics: modeling and traceability. More fine-grained partitioned would certainly be possible but this partition was considered adequate based on the coverage of tools in the literature.

Requirements modeling tools

Tools used for eliciting, recording, analyzing and validating software requirements belong in this section.

Traceability tools

[Pre97:s29.3, DT97:s4.1, DT97:s12.3]

Requirements traceability tools are becoming increasingly important as the complexity of software systems grow, and since traceability tools are relevant also in other lifecycle phases, they have been separated from the other tools for requirements.

B. Software Design Tools

[ ]

This section covers tools for creating and checking software designs. There is a variety of such tools, with much of this variety being a consequence of the diversity of design notations and methods. While this variety of tools exists, no compelling partitions for this topic were found.

C. Software Construction Tools

Software construction tools are concerned with the production and translation of the program representation (commonly known as source code) that is sufficiently detailed and explicit to enable machine execution.

Program editors

Program editors are tools used for creation and modification of programs (and possibly associated documents). These tools can be general-purpose text or document editors, or they can be specialized for a target language. Editing refers to human-controlled development tools.

Compilers and code generators

Traditionally, compilers have been non-interactive translators of source code but there has been a trend to integrate compilers and program editors to provide integrated programming environments. This topic also covers pre-processors, linker/loaders, and code generators.

Interpreters

Interpreters provide software execution through emulation. They can support software construction activities by providing a more controllable and observable environment for program execution.

Debuggers

Debugging tools have been made a separate topic since they support the construction process but are different from program editors or compilers.

D. Software Testing Tools

Testing tools are categorized according to where in the testing process they are used.

Test generators

Test generators assist the development of test cases.

Test execution frameworks

Test execution frameworks enable the execution of test cases in a controlled environment where the behavior of the object under test is observed.

Test evaluation tools

Test evaluation tools support the assessment of the results of test execution, helping to determine whether the observed behavior conforms to the expected behavior.

Test management tools

Test management tools provide support for managing all aspects of the testing process.

Performance analysis tools [ ]

This topic covers tools for measuring and analyzing software performance. It is a specialized form of testing where the goal is to assess the performance behavior rather than the functional behavior (correctness).

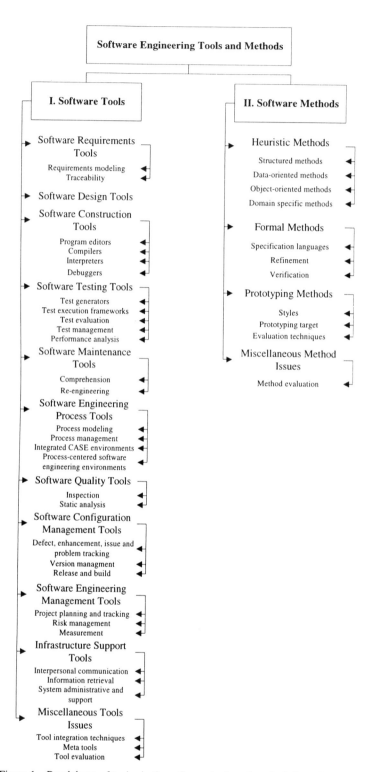

Figure 1 – Breakdown of topics in the software tools and methods knowledge area

E. Software Maintenance Tools

Software maintenance is often presented as additional iterations of the development lifecycle and consequently makes use of tools for all other phases. This category encompasses tools that have particular importance in software maintenance where an existing system is being modified. Two categories are identified: comprehension tools and re-engineering tools.

Comprehension tools

This topic concerns tools to assist human comprehension of programs. Examples include visualization tools such as animators and program slicers.

Re-engineering tools

Re-engineering tools allow translation of a program to a new programming language, or a database to a new format. Reverse engineering tools assist the process by working backwards from an existing product to create abstract artifacts such as design and specification descriptions, which then can be transformed to generate a new product from an old one.

F. Software Engineering Process Tools

Process modeling tools

This topic covers tools to model and investigate software processes.

Process management tools

Integrated CASE environments

(ECMA93, ECMA94, IEEE-1209, IEEE-1348, MNS96)

Computer-aided software engineering tools or environments that cover multiple phases of the software development lifecycle belong in this section. Such tools perform multiple functions and hence potentially interact with the software process that is being enacted.

Process-centered software engineering environments

(GJ96)

This topic covers those environments that explicitly incorporate software process information and that guide and monitor the user according to a defined process.

G. Software Quality Tools

Inspection tools

This topic covers tools to support reviews and inspections.

Static analysis tools

This topic deals with tools that analyze software artifacts, such as syntactic and semantic analyzers, and data, control flow and dependency analyzers. Such tools are intended for checking software artifacts for conformance or for verifying desired properties.

H. Software Configuration Management Tools

Tools for configuration management have been categorized as related to tracking issues associated with a particular software product, management of multiple versions of a product or to managing the task of software release and build.

Defect, enhancement, issue and problem tracking tools

Version management tools

Release and build tools

This category includes installation tools that have become widely used for configuring the installation of software products.

I. Software Engineering Management Tools

Management tools are subdivided into three categories: project planning and tracking, risk management, and measurement.

Project planning and tracking tools

Risk management tools

Measurement tools

J. Infrastructure support tools

This section covers tools that provide interpersonal communication, information retrieval, and system administration and support. These tools, such as e-mail, databases, web browsers and file backup tools, are generally not specific to a particular lifecycle stage, nor to a particular development method.

Interpersonal communication tools

Information retrieval tools

System administration and support tools

K. Miscellaneous tool issues

This section covers issues that are applicable to all classes of tools. Three categories are identified: tool integration techniques, meta-tools and tool evaluation.

Tool integration techniques

[Som96:s25.2]

(Bro94)

Tool integration is important for making individual tools cooperate. This category potentially overlaps with integrated software engineering environments where integration techniques are applied, but it was felt that this topic is sufficiently distinct to merit its own category. The typical kinds of tool integration are platform, presentation, process, data, and control.

Meta tools

Meta-tools generate other tools; compiler-compilers are the classic example.

Tool evaluation

(IEEE-1209, IEEE-1348, Mos92, VB97)

Because of the continuous evolution of software engineering tools, tool evaluation is an essential topic.

II. Software Development Methods

The software development section is divided into four subsections: *heuristic methods* dealing with informal approaches, *formal methods* dealing with mathematically based approaches, *prototyping methods* dealing with software development approaches based on various forms of prototyping, and *miscellaneous method issues*. The first three subsections are not disjoint; rather they represent distinct concerns. For example, an object-oriented method may incorporate formal techniques and rely on prototyping for verification and validation. Like software engineering tools, methodologies evolve continuously. Consequently, the Knowledge Area description avoids naming particular methodologies as far as possible.

A. Heuristic methods

This subsection contains four categories: *structured, data-oriented, object-oriented and domain-specific*. The domain-specific category includes specialized methods for developing systems that involve real-time, safety or security aspects.

Structured methods

Data-oriented methods

Object-oriented methods

Domain-specific methods

B. Formal methods

This subsection deals with mathematically based development methods and is subdivided by different aspects of formal methods. The first topic is the specification notation or language used. Specification languages are commonly classified as model-oriented, property-oriented or behavior-oriented. The second topic deals with how the method refines (or transforms) the specification into a form that is closer to the desired final form of an executable program. The third topic covers the verification properties that are specific to the formal approach and covers both theorem proving and model checking.

Specification languages & notations

Refinement

Verification/proving properties

C. Prototyping methods

This subsection covers methods involving software prototyping and is subdivided into prototyping styles, targets and evaluation techniques.

Styles

(PB92:c1)

The topic of prototyping styles identifies the different approaches: throwaway, evolutionary and the executable specification.

Prototyping target

(PB92:c2)

Example targets of a prototyping method may be requirements, architectural design or the user interface.

Evaluation techniques

This topic covers how the results of a prototype exercise are used.

D. Miscellaneous method issues

The final subsection is intended to cover topics not covered elsewhere in the software method area. The only topic identified so far is method evaluation.

1. Method evaluation

4 BREAKDOWN RATIONALE

The Stone Man Version of the Guide to the Software Engineering Body of Knowledge conforms at least partially with the partitioning of the software life cycle in the ISO/IEC 12207 Standard [ISO95]. Some Knowledge Areas, such as this one, are intended to cover knowledge that applies to multiple phases of the life cycle. One approach to partitioning topics in this Knowledge Area would be to use the software life cycle phases. For example, software methods and tools could be classified according to the phase with which they are associated. This approach was not seen as effective. If software engineering tools and methods could be cleanly partitioned by lifecycle phase, it would suggest that this Knowledge Area could be eliminated by allocating each part to the corresponding life cycle Knowledge Area, e.g., tools and methods for software design to the Software Design Knowledge Area. Such an approach would fail to identify the commonality of, and interrelationships between, both methods and tools in different life cycle phases. However since tools are a common theme to most Knowledge Areas, several reviewers of Version 0.5 of this Knowledge Area suggested that a breakdown based on Knowledge Area for tools would be helpful. The Industry Advisory Board endorsed this suggestion.

There are many links between methods and tools, and one possible structure would seek to exploit these links. However because the relationship is not a simple "one-to-one" mapping, this structure has not been used to organize topics in this Knowledge Area. This means that these links are not always explicitly identified.

Some topics in this Knowledge Area do not have corresponding reference materials identified in the matrices in Appendix 2. There are two possible conclusions: either the topic area is not relevant to this Knowledge Area, or additional reference material needs to be identified. Feedback from the experimentation phase will be helpful to resolve this issue.

5   MATRIX OF TOPICS VS. REFERENCE MATERIAL

I. Software Tools		CW96	DT97	Pfl98	Pre97	Rei96	Som96	Was96
A.	**Software Requirements Tools**		4.1 12.3		11.4.2, 29.3		26.2	
	Requirements modeling tools							
	Traceability tools		7.4					
B.	**Software Design Tools**		12.3		29.3		26.2	
C.	**Software Construction Tools**		12.3		29.3	112.2	26.1	
	Program editors							
	Compilers and code generators							
	Interpreters							
	Debuggers							
D.	**Software Testing Tools**		12.3	7.7, 8.7	29.3	112.3	26.3	
	Test generators							
	Test execution frameworks							
	Test evaluation tools							
	Test management tools							
	Performance analysis tools					112.5		
E.	**Software Maintenance Tools**		12.3	10.5	29.3			
	Comprehension tools					112.5		
	Re-engineering tools							
F.	**Software Engineering Process Tools**		12.3				25, 26, 27	
	Process modeling tools			2.3, 2.4				
	Process management tools							
	Integrated CASE environments				29	112.3, 112.4		
	Process-centered software engineering environments				29.6	112.5		
G.	**Software Quality Tools**		12.3					
	Inspection tools							
	Static analysis tools	X		7.7	29.3	112.5	24.3	
H.	**Software Configuration Management Tools**		12.3	10.5		112.3		
	Defect, enhancement, issue and problem tracking tools				29.3			
	Version management tools				29			
I.	**Software Engineering Management Tools**		12.3					
	Project planning and tracking tools				29.3			
	Risk management tools							
J.	**Infrastructure Support Tools**		12.3					
	Interpersonal communication tools				29.3			
	Information retrieval tools				29.3			
	System administration and support tools				29.3			
K.	**Miscellaneous Tool Issues**		12.3					
	Tool integration techniques			1.8		112.4		X
	Meta tools							
	Tool evaluation			8.10				

II. Development Methods		CW96	DT97	Pfl98	Pre98	Som96	Was96	CW96
A.	**Heuristic Methods**						X	
1.	Structured methods		4.2, 5.2	4.5	10-18	15		
2	Data-oriented methods		4.2, 5.2		12.8			
3	Object-oriented methods		5.1, 5.2	4.4, 7.5	19-23	6.3, 14		
4	Domain-specific methods				15	16		
B.	**Formal Methods**		5.4		24, 25	9-11, 24.4		
1.	Specification languages	X		4.5	24.4			
2.	Refinement				25.3			
3.	Verification/proving properties	X		5.7, 7.3		24.2		
C.	**Prototyping Methods**				2.5	8	X	
1.	Styles		12.2	4.6, 5.6	11.4			
2.	Prototyping targets		12.2					
3.	Evaluation techniques							
D.	**Miscellaneous Method Issues**							
1.	Method evaluation							

6 RECOMMENDED REFERENCES FOR SOFTWARE ENGINEERING TOOLS AND METHODS

This section briefly describes each of the recommended references.

[CW96] Edmund M. Clarke et al. Formal Methods: State of the Art and Future Directions. ACM Computing Surveys, vol. 28, no. 4, dec. 1996, p. 626-643.

This tutorial on formal methods explains techniques for formal specification, model checking and theorem proving, and describes some successful case studies and tools.

[DT97] Merlin Dorfman and Richard H. Thayer (eds.). Software Engineering, IEEE Computer Society Press.

This tutorial volume contains a collection of papers organized into chapters. The following papers are referenced (section numbers have been added to reference individual papers more conveniently in the matrices in the Appendix):

Chapter 4: Software Requirements Engineering and Software Design

4.1 Software Requirements: A Tutorial, Stuart Faulk

4.2 Software Design: An Introduction, David Budgen

Chapter 5: Software Development Methodologies

5.1 Object-oriented Development, Linda M. Northrup

5.2 Object-oriented Systems Development: Survey of Structured Methods, A.G. Sutcliffe

5.4 A Review of Formal Methods, Robert Vienneau

Chapter 7: Software Validation, Verification and Testing

7.4 Traceability, James D. Palmer

Chapter 12 Software Technology

12.2 Prototyping: Alternate Systems Development Methodology, J.M. Carey

12.3 A Classification of CASE Technology, Alfonso Fuggetta

[Pfl98] S.L. Pfleeger. Software Engineering — Theory and Practice, Prentice-Hall.

This text is structured according to the phases of a life cycle so that discussion of methods and tools is distributed throughout the book.

[Pre97] R.S. Pressman. Software Engineering — A Practitioner's Approach (4th Ed.), McGraw-Hill

Chapter 29 covers "Computer-Aided Software Engineering" including a taxonomy of case tools (29.3). There is not much detail about any particular class of tool but it does illustrate the wide range of software engineering tools. The strength of this book is its description of methods with chapters 10-23 covering heuristic methods, chapters 24 and 25 covering formal methods. Section 11.4 describes prototyping methods and tools.

[Rei96] Steven P. Reiss. Software Tools and Environments in The Computer Science and Engineering Handbook. CRC Press, 1996 .

This chapter from [Tuc96] provides an overview of software tools. The emphasis is on programming tools rather than tools for analysis and design although CASE tools are mentioned briefly.

[Som96] Ian Sommerville. Software Engineering (5th Ed.), Addison-Wesley.

Chapters 25, 26 and 27 introduce computer-aided software engineering with the emphasis being on tool integration and large-scale environments. Static analysis tools are covered in Section 24.3. Chapter 9, 10 and 11 introduce formal methods with formal verification being described in Section 24.2 and the Cleanroom method in Section 24.4. Prototyping is discussed in Chapter 8.

[Was96] Anthony I. Wasserman. Toward a Discipline of Software Engineering, IEEE Software, vol. 13, no. 6 Nov. 1996, pp. 23-31.

This general article discusses the role of both methods and tools in software engineering. Although brief, the paper integrates the major themes of the discipline.

APPENDIX A – REFERENCES USED TO WRITE AND JUSTIFY THE KNOWLEDGE AREA DESCRIPTION

[Ber92] Edward V. Berard. Essays on Object-Oriented Software Engineering. Prentice-Hall, 1993.

[BP92] W. Bischofberger and G Pomberger. Prototyping-oriented Software Development: Concepts and Tools. Springer-Verlag, 1992.

[Bro94] Alan W. Brown et al. Principles of CASE Tool Integration. Oxford University Press, 1994.

[CB95] D.J. Carney and A.W. Brown. On the Necessary Conditions for the Composition of Integrated Software Engineering Environments. In Advances in Computers, Volume 41, pages 157-189. Academic Press, 1995.

[CW96] Edmund M. Clarke, Jeanette M. Wing et al. Formal Methods: State of the Art and Future Directions. ACM Computer Surveys, 28(4):626-643, 1996.

[Col94] Derek Coleman et al. Object-Oriented Development: The Fusion Method. Prentice Hall, 1994.

[CGR95] Dan Craigen, Susan Gerhart and Ted Ralston. Formal Methods Reality Check: Industrial Usage, IEEE Transactions on Software Engineering, 21(2):90-98, February 1995.

[DT97] Merlin Dorfman and Richard H. Thayer, Editors. Software Engineering. IEEE Computer Society, 1997.

[ECMA93] ECMA. TR/55 Reference Model for Frameworks of Software Engineering Environments, 3rd edition, June 1993.

[ECMA94] ECMA TR/69 Reference Model for Project Support Environments, December 1994.

[Fin00] Anthony Finkelstein, Editor. The Future of Software Engineering. ACM, 2000.

[GJ96] Pankaj K. Garg and Mehdi Jazayeri. Process-Centered Software Engineering Environments, IEEE Computer Society, 1996.

[HOT00] William Harrison, Harold Ossher and Peri Tarr. Software Engineering Tools and Environments: A Roadmap. In [Fin00], pp. 263-277, 2000.

[IEEE-1175] IEEE. Trial-Use Standard Reference Model for Computing System Tool Interconnections, IEEE Std 1175-1992.

[IEEE-1209] IEEE. Recommended Practice for the Evaluation and Selection of CASE Tools, IEEE Std 1209-1992 (ISO/IEC 14102, 1995).

[IEEE-1348] IEEE Recommended Practice for the Adoption of CASE Tools, IEEE Std 1348-1995 (ISO/IEC 14471).

[ISO-12207] ISO/IEC Standard for Information Technology —Software Life Cycle Processes, ISO/IEC 12207 (IEEE/EIA 12207.0-1996), 1995.

[JH98] Stan Jarzabek and Riri Huang. The Case for User-Centered CASE Tools, Communications of the ACM, 41(8):93-99, August 1998.

[KPP95] B. Kitchenham, L. Pickard, and S.L. Pfleeger. Case Studies for Method and Tool Evaluation, IEEE Software, 12(4):52-62, July 1995.

[Lam00] Axel van Lamsweerde. Formal Specification: A Roadmap. In [fin00], pp. 149-159, 2000.

[Mey97] Bertrand Meyer. Object-oriented Software Construction (2nd Ed.). Prentice Hall, 1997.

[Mul00] Hausi Müller et al. Reverse Engineering: A Roadmap. In [Fin00], pp. 49-60, 2000.

[Moo98] James W. Moore. Software Engineering Standards: A User's Road Map. IEEE Computer Society, 1998.

[Mos92] Vicky Mosley. How to Assess Tools Efficiently and Quantitatively, IEEE Software, 9(3):29-32, May 1992.

(MNS96] H.A. Muller, R.J. Norman and J. Slonim (eds.). Computer Aided Software Engineering, Kluwer, 1996. (A special issue of Automated Software Engineering, 3(3/4), 1996).

[PB96] Gustav Pomberger and Günther Blaschek. Object-orientation and Prototyping in Software Engineering. Prentice Hall, 1996.

[Pfl98] Shari Lawrence Pfleeger. Software Engineering: Theory and Practice. Prentice Hall, 1998.

[Pos96] R.M. Poston. Automating specification-based Software Testing. IEEE, 1996.

[Pre97] Roger S. Pressman. Software Engineering: A Practitioner's Approach. 4th edition, McGraw-Hill, 1997.

[Rei96] Steven P. Reiss. Software Tools and Environments, Ch. 112, pages 2419-2439. In Tucker [Tuc96], 1996.

[RW92] C. Rich and R.C. Waters. Knowledge Intensive Software Engineering Tools, IEEE Transactions on Knowledge and Data Engineering, 4(5):424-430, October 1992.

[Som96] Ian Sommerville. Software Engineering. 5th edition, Addison-Wesley, 1996.

[SO92] Xiping Song and Leon J. Osterweil. Towards Objective, Systematic Design-Method Comparisons, IEEE Software, 9(3):43-53, May 1992.

[Tuc96] Allen B. Tucker, Jr., Editor-in-chief. The Computer Science and Engineering Handbook. CRC Press, 1996.

[VB97] Laura A. Valaer and Robert C. Babb II. Choosing a User Interface Development Tool. IEEE Software, 14(4):29-39, 1997

[Vin90] Walter G. Vincenti. What Engineers Know and How They Know It: Analytical Studies from Aeronautical History. John Hopkins University Press, 1990.

[Was96] Anthony I. Wasserman. Toward a Discipline of Software Engineering, IEEE Software, 13(6): 23-31, November 1996.

[Wie98] Roel Wieringa. A Survey of Structured and Object-Oriented Software Specification Methods and Techniques. ACM Computing Surveys, 30(4):459-527, 1998.

CHAPTER 11

SOFTWARE QUALITY

Dolores Wallace* and Larry Reeker
National Institute of Standards and Technology
Gaithersburg, Maryland 20899 USA
{Dolores.Wallace, Larry.Reeker}@NIST.gov
*Dolores Wallace has retired from NIST (but is still available via her NIST e-mail address at the time of publication.)

Table of Contents

1. INTRODUCTION AND DEFINITION OF THE SOFTWARE QUALITY KNOWLEDGE AREA

This chapter deals with software quality considerations that transcend the life cycle processes. Of course, software quality is a ubiquitous concern in software engineering, so it is considered in many of the other KAs (and the reader will notice pointers those KAs through this KA. There will also be some inevitable duplication with those other KAs as a consequence.

Software Quality Assurance (SQA) and Verification and Validation (V&V) are the major processes discussed in this KA, as they bear directly on the quality of the software product. The term "product" will, however, be extended to mean any artifact that is the output of any process used to build the final software product. Examples of a product include, but are not limited to, an entire system specification, a software requirements specification for a software component of a system, a design module, code, test documentation, or reports from quality analysis tasks. While most treatments of quality are described in terms of the final system's performance, sound engineering practice requires that intermediate products relevant to quality be checked throughout the development and maintenance process. The reason for this extension of "product" is that SQA and V&V can be used to evaluate the intermediate products and the final product. In addition to intermediate products and code, it can be applied to user documentation, which is best developed together with code and can often force issues regarding requirements and code.

Another major topic of this KA is just trying to answer the question "What is software quality?" this is not a simple question, as was concluded by David Garvin [Gar84, Hya96]. Though we will not go into the complexities that he studied, we will present a view for the working software engineer.

The discussion of the purpose and planning of SQA and V&V is a bridge between the discussion of quality and the activities and techniques discussion for SQA and V&V, but it is also an important activity in itself. In the planning process, the activities are designed to be fitted to the product and its purposes, including the quality attributes in the requirements.

Because determining quality of both the final product and intermediate products requires measurement, the topic of measurement is relevant to the other parts of this KA. A separate section is therefore included on the subject of measurement. Measurement of product quality at all levels of the project will in the future become more important than it has been in the past or is today. With increasing sophistication of systems (moving, for example, into areas like intelligent web agents), the questions of quality go beyond whether the system works or not, to how well it achieves measurable quality goals. In addition, the availability of more data about software and its production, along with data mining techniques for analysis of the data, will help to advance measurement definitions and procedures. A more relevant, widely-accepted, robust set of measures will be a sign of maturation in software engineering.

It has been suggested that this chapter should also deal with models and criteria that evaluate the capabilities of software organizations, but those are primarily project organization and management considerations. Of course it is not possible to disentangle the quality of the process from the quality of the product, but the quality of the software engineering process is not a topic specific to this KA, whereas the quality of the software product the assigned topic. So an ability to perform Software Quality Assurance, for instance, is a major component of a quality software engineering program, but SQA is itself relevant to software quality.

2. BREAKDOWN OF TOPICS FOR SOFTWARE QUALITY

The quality of a given product is sometimes defined as "the totality of characteristics [of the product or services] that bear on its ability to satisfy stated or implied needs"[1]. Quality software is sometimes also defined as "the efficient, effective, and comfortable use by a given set of users for a set of purposes under specified conditions". These two definitions can be related to requirements conformance - provided the requirements are well engineered. Both agreement on quality requirements and communication to the engineer information on what will constitute quality requires that the aspects of quality be defined and discussed. For that reason, the first topic is description of product quality and some of the product characteristics that relate to it. The importance of requirements engineering is clearly an issue here.

Sections on the processes — SQA and V&V — that focus on software quality follow the discussion on software quality concepts. These quality-focused processes help to ensure better software in a given project. They also provide, as a by-product, general information to management that can improve the quality of the entire software and maintenance processes. The knowledge areas **Software Engineering Process** and **Software Engineering Management**, discuss quality programs for the organization developing software systems. SQA and V&V can provide relevant feedback for these areas.

Engineering for quality requires the measurement of quality in a concrete way, so this knowledge area contains a section on measurement as applied to SQA and V&V. Other processes for assuring software product quality are discussed in other parts of the SWEBOK. One of these, singled out as a separate KA within the software life cycle, **Software Testing**, is also used in both SQA and V&V.

2.1. Software quality concepts

What is software quality, and why is it so important that it is pervasive in the Software Engineering Body of Knowledge? Within a system, software is a tool, and tools have to be selected for quality and for appropriateness. That is the role of requirements. But software is more than a tool. The software dictates the performance of the system, and is therefore important to the system quality. Much thought must therefore go into the value to place on each quality attribute desired and on the overall quality of the system. This section discusses the value and the attributes of quality.

The notion of "quality" is not as simple as it may seem. For any engineered product, there are many desired qualities relevant to a particular project, to be discussed and

determined at the time that the product requirements are determined. Quality attributes may be present or absent, or may be present in greater or lesser degree, with tradeoffs among them, with practicality and cost as major considerations. The software engineer needs first of all to determine the real purpose for the software, which is a prime point to keep in mind: The customer's needs come first, and they include particular levels of quality, not just functionality. Thus the software engineer has a responsibility to elicit quality requirements that may not even be explicit at the outset and to discuss their importance and the difficulty of attaining them. All processes associated with software quality (e.g. building, checking, improving quality) will be designed with these in mind and carry costs based on the design. Therefore, it is important to have in mind some of the possible attributes of quality.

- Various researchers have produced models (usually taxonomic) of software quality characteristics or attributes that can be useful for discussing, planning, and rating the quality of software products. The models often include measures to "measure" the degree of each quality attribute the product attains. They are not always direct measures of the quality characteristics discussed in the texts of Pressman [Pr], Pfleeger [Pf] and Kan [Kan94]. Each model may have a different set of attributes at the highest level of the taxonomy, and selection of and definitions for the - attributes at all levels may differ. The important point is that requirements define the required quality of the respective software, the definitions of the attributes for quality, and the measurement methods and acceptance criteria for the attributes. Some of the classical thinking in this area is found in McCall [McC77] and Boehm [Boe78].

2.1.1. Measuring the Value of Quality

A motivation behind a software project is a determination that it has a value, and this value may or not be quantified as a cost, but the customer will have some maximum cost in mind. Within that cost, the customer expects to attain the basic purpose of the software and may have some expectation of the necessary quality, or may not have thought through the quality issues or their related costs. The software engineer, in discussing software quality attributes and the processes necessary to assure them, should keep in mind the value of each attribute and the sensitivity of the value of the product to changes in it. Is it merely an adornment or is it essential to the system? If it is somewhere in between, as almost everything is, it is a matter of making the **customer** a part of the decision process and fully aware of both costs and benefits. Ideally, most of this decision process goes on in the Requirements phase (see that KA), but these issues may arise throughout the software life cycle. There is no definite rule for how the decisions are made, but the software engineer should be able to present quality alternatives and their costs. A

---

[1]   From *Quality—Vocabulary*, (ISO 8402: 1986, note 1).

discussion of measuring cost and value of quality requirements can be found in [Wei93], Chapter 8, pp118-134] and [Jon96], Chapter 5.

2.1.2. ISO 9126 Quality Description

Terminology for quality attributes differs from one taxonomy or model of software quality to another; each model may have different numbers of hierarchical levels and a different total number of attributes. A software engineer should understand the underlying meanings of quality characteristics regardless of their names, as well as their value to the system under development or maintenance. An attempt to standardize terminology in an inclusive model resulted in ISO 9126 (*Information Technology-Software Product Quality*, Part 1: Quality Model, 1998), of which a synopsis is included in this KA as Table 1. ISO 9126 is concerned primarily with the definition of quality characteristics in the final product. ISO 9126 sets out six quality characteristics, each very broad in nature. They are divided into 21 sub-characteristics. In the 1998 revision, "compliance" to application-specific requirements is included as a sub-characteristic of each characteristic The approach taken in the 1998 version is discussed in [Bev97].

2.1.3. Dependability

For systems whose failure may have extremely severe consequences, dependability of the overall system (hardware, software, and humans) is the main goal in addition to the realization of basic functionality. Software dependability is the subject of IEC 50-191 and the IEC 300 series of standards. Some types of systems (e.g., radar control, defense communications, medical devices) have particular needs for high dependability, including such attributes as fault tolerance, safety, security, usability. Reliability is a criterion under dependability and also is found among the ISO/IEC 9126 (Table 1). In Moore's treatment [M], Kiang's factors [Kia95] are used as shown in the following list, with the exception of the term Trustability from Laprie [Lap91].

- Availability: The product's readiness for use on demand
- Reliability: The longevity of product performance
- Maintainability: The ease of maintenance and upgrade
- Maintenance support: Continuing support to achieve availability performance objectives
- Trustability: System's ability to provide users with information about service correctness.

There is a large body of literature for systems that must be highly dependable ("high confidence" or "high integrity systems"). Terminology from traditional mechanical and electrical systems that may not include software have been imported for discussing threats or hazards, risks, system integrity, and related concepts, and may be found in the references cited for this section.

2.1.4. Special Types of Systems and Quality Needs

As implied above, there are many particular qualities of software that may or may not fit under ISO 9126. Particular classes of application systems may have other quality attributes to be judged. This is clearly an open-ended set, but the following are examples:

- Intelligent and Knowledge Based Systems – "Anytime" property (guarantees best answer that can be obtained within a given time if called upon for an answer in that amount of time), Explanation Capability (explains reasoning process in getting an answer).
- Human Interface and Interaction Systems – Adaptivity (to user's traits, interests), Intelligent Help, Display Salience.
- Information Systems – Ease of query, High recall (obtaining most relevant information), High Precision (not returning irrelevant information), tradeoffs. 3.5 Quality Attributes of Programming Products

Other considerations of software systems are known to affect the software engineering process while the system is being built and during its future evolution or modification, and these can be considered elements of product quality. These software qualities include, but are not limited to:

- "Stylishness" of Code
- Code and object reusability
- Traceability: From requirements to code/test documentation, and from code/test documentation to requirements
- Modularity of code and independence of modules.

These quality attributes can be viewed as satisfying organizational or project requirements for the software in the effort to improve the overall performance of the organization or project. See the Software Engineering Management and Software Engineering Process KAs for related material.

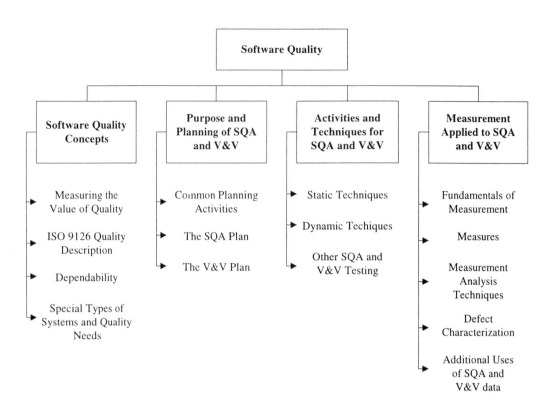

Table 1. Software Quality Characteristics and Attributes – ISO 9126-1998 View	
Characteristics & Subcharacteristics	Short Description of the Characteristics and Subcharacteristics
Functionality	**Characteristics relating to achievement of the basic purpose for which the software is being engineered**
. Suitability	The presence and appropriateness of a set of functions for specified tasks
. **Accuracy**	The provision of right or agreed results or effects
. **Interoperability**	Software's ability to interact with specified systems
. **Security**	Ability to prevent unauthorized access, whether accidental or deliberate, to programs and data.
. **Compliance**	Adherence to application-related standards, conventions, regulations in laws and protocols
Reliability	**Characteristics relating to capability of software to maintain its level of performance under stated conditions for a stated period of time**
. Maturity	Attributes of software that bear on the frequency of failure by faults in the software
. **Fault tolerance**	Ability to maintain a specified level of performance in cases of software faults or unexpected inputs
. **Recoverability**	Capability and effort needed to reestablish level of performance and recover affected data after possible failure
. **Compliance**	Adherence to application-related standards, conventions, regulations in laws and protocols
Usability	**Characteristics relating to the effort needed for use, and on the individual assessment of such use, by a stated or implied set of users**
. Understandability	The effort required for a user to recognize the logical concept and its applicability
. **Learnability**	The effort required for a user to learn its application, operation, input, and output
. **Operability**	The ease of operation and control by users
. **Attractiveness**	The capability of the software to be attractive to the user
. **Compliance**	Adherence to application-related standards, conventions, regulations in laws and protocols
Efficiency	**Characteristic related to the relationship between the level of performance of the software and the amount of resources used, under stated conditions**
. **Time behavior**	The speed of response and processing times and throughput rates in performing its function
. **Resource utilization**	The amount of resources used and the duration of such use in performing its function
. **Compliance**	Adherence to application-related standards, conventions, regulations in laws and protocols
Maintainability	**Characteristics related effort needed to make modifications, including corrections, improvements or adaptation of software to changes in environment, requirements and functional specifications**

 © IEEE – Trial Version 1.00 – May 2001

Table 1. Software Quality Characteristics and Attributes – ISO 9126-1998 View	
Characteristics & Subcharacteristics	**Short Description of the Characteristics and Subcharacteristics**
. Analyzability	The effort needed for diagnosis of deficiencies or causes of failures, or for identification parts to be modified
. Changeability	The effort needed for modification fault removal or for environmental change
. Stability	The risk of unexpected effect of modifications
. Testability	The effort needed for validating the modified software
. Compliance	Adherence to application-related standards, conventions, regulations in laws and protocols
Portability	**Characteristics related to the ability to transfer the software from one organization or hardware or software environment to another**
. Adaptability	The opportunity for its adaptation to different specified environments
. Installability	The effort needed to install the software in a specified environment
. Co-existence	The capability of a software product to co-exist with other independent software in common environment
. Replaceability	The opportunity and effort of using it in the place of other software in a particular environment
. Compliance	Adherence to application-related standards, conventions, regulations in laws and protocols

2.2. Purpose and Planning of SQA and V&V

The KA **Software Requirements** describes how the requirements and their individual features are defined, prioritized and documented and how the quality of that documentation can be measured. The set of requirements has a direct effect on both the intermediate software engineering products, and the delivered software. Building in quality as the process takes place and making careful reference to well-engineered requirements that define the needed measures and attributes of quality are the most important determiners of overall software quality.

The **Software Engineering Process** (discussed overall in that KA) employs multiple *supporting processes* to examine and assure software products for quality. These supporting processes conduct activities to ensure that the software engineering process required by the project is followed. Two related (and sometimes combined) supporting processes most closely related to product quality, SQA and V&V, are discussed in this section. These processes both encourage quality and find possible problems. But they differ somewhat in their emphasis.

SQA and V&V also provide management with visibility into the quality of products at each stage in their development or maintenance. The visibility comes from the data and measurements produced through the performance of tasks to assess and measure quality of the outputs of any software life cycle processes as they are developed. Where strict quality standards are an overriding factor, the tasks used to assess quality and capture data and measurements may be performed by an organization independent of the project organization, in order to provide a higher degree of objectivity to the quality assessment.

The SQA process provides assurance that the software products and processes in the project life cycle conform to their specified requirements by planning a set of activities to help build quality into the software. This means ensuring that the problem is clearly and adequately stated and that the solution's requirements are properly defined and expressed. SQA seeks to retain the quality throughout the

development and maintenance of the product by execution of a variety of activities at each stage that can result in early identification of problems, which are almost inevitable in any complex activity. The SQA role with respect to process is to ensure that planned processes are appropriate and are later implemented according to plan and that relevant measurement processes are provided to the appropriate organization.

The Verification and Validation process determines whether products of a given development or maintenance activity conform to the needs of that activity and those imposed by previous activities, and whether the final software product satisfies its intended use and user needs. Verification attempts to ensure that the product is built correctly, in the sense that the, output products of an activity fulfill requirements imposed on them in previous activities. Validation attempts to ensure that the right product is built, that is, the product fulfills its specific intended use. Both verification and validation processes begin early in the development or maintenance process. They provide an examination of every product relative both to its immediate predecessor and to the system requirements it must satisfy.

In summary, the SWEBOK describes a number of pro ways of achieving software quality. As described in this KA, the SQA and V&V processes are closely related processes that can overlap and are sometimes even combined. They seem largely reactive in nature because they address the processes as practiced and the products as produced; but they have a major role at the planning stage in being proactive as to the procedures needed to attain the quality attributes and degree needed by the stakeholders in the software. They should also produce feedback that can improve the software engineering process. In summary:

- SQA governs the procedures meant to build the desired quality into the products by assuring that the process is well-planned and then applied as prescribed and defined. It helps keep the organization from sliding back into less effective processes and habits, and may provide direct assistance or guidance in applying the current practices.

- V&V is aimed more directly at product quality, in that it is based on testing that can locate deviations and fix them. But it also validates the intermediate products and therefore the intermediate steps of the software engineering process. So it too can affect the software engineering process through that evaluation.

It should be noted that sometimes the terms SQA and V&V are associated with organizations rather than processes. SQA often is the name of a unit within an organization. Sometimes an independent organization is contracted to conduct V&V. Testing may occur in Both SQA and V&V and is discussed in this KA in relation to those processes. Details on testing within the software life cycle are found in the KA on **Software Testing**. The Software Quality KA is not intended to define organizations but rather the purposes and procedures of SQA and V&V, insofar as they relate to software quality. The organizational aspect is mentioned here, however, to tie together different KAs and to help avoid confusion. Some discussion on organizational issues appears in [Hum98], and the IEEE Std. 1012.

2.2.1. Common Planning Activities

Planning for software quality involves (1) defining, the required product in terms of its quality attributes and (2) planning the processes to achieve the required product. Planning of these processes is discussed in other KAs: **Software Engineering Management**, **Software Engineering Design**, and **Software Engineering Methods and Tools**. These topics are different from planning the SQA and V&V processes. The SQA and V&V processes assess predicted adequacy and actual implementation of those plans, that is, how well software products will or do satisfy customer and stakeholder requirements, provide value to the customers and other stakeholders, and meet the software quality needed to meet the system requirements.

System requirements vary among systems, as do the activities selected from the disciplines of SQA and V&V. Various factors influence planning, management and selection of activities and techniques, including:

1. the environment of the system in which the software will reside;
2. system and software requirements;
3. the commercial or standard components to be used in the system;
4. the specific software standards used in developing the software;
5. the software standards used for quality;
6. the methods and software tools to be used for development and maintenance and for quality evaluation and improvement;
7. the budget, staff, project organization, plans and schedule (size is inherently included) of all the processes;
8. the intended users and use of the system, and

9. the integrity level of the system.

Information from these factors influences how the SQA and V&V processes are organized, and documented, how specific SQA and V&V activities are selected, and what resources are needed or will impose bounds on the efforts. The integrity level of a system can be used as an example. The integrity level is determined based on the possible consequences of failure of the system and the probability of failure. For software systems where safety or security is important, techniques such as hazard analysis for safety or threat analysis for security may be used to develop a planning process that would identify where potential trouble spots lie. Failure history of similar systems may also help in identifying which activities will be most useful in detecting faults and assessing quality.

If the SQA and V&V organizations are the same, their plans may be combined, but we will treat them as separate plans below, as they are often distinguished from one another.

2.2.2. The SQA Plan

The SQA plan defines the processes and procedures that will be used to ensure that software developed for a specific product meets its requirements and is of the highest quality possible within project constraints. To do so, it must first ensure that the quality target is clearly defined and understood. The plan may be governed by software quality assurance standards, life cycle standards, quality management standards and models, company policies and procedures for quality and quality improvement. It must consider management, development and maintenance plans for the software. Standards and models such as ISO9000, CMM, Baldrige, SPICE, TickIT are related to the **Software Engineering Process** and may influence the SQA plan.

The specific activities and tasks are laid our, with their costs and resource requirements, their overall management, and their schedule in relation to those in the software management, development or maintenance plans. The SQA plan should be cognizant of the software configuration plan also (see the KA for **Software Configuration Management**) The SQA plan identifies documents, standards, practices, and conventions that govern the project and how they will be checked and monitored to ensure adequacy or compliance. The SQA plan identifies measures, statistical techniques, procedures for problem reporting and corrective action, resources such as tools, techniques and methodologies, security for physical media, training, and SQA reporting and documentation to be retained. The SQA plan addresses assurance of any other type of function addressed in the software plans, such as supplier software to the project or commercial off-the-shelf software (COTS), installation, and service after delivery of the system. It can also contain some items less directly related to quality: acceptance criteria, activity deadlines, reporting, and management activities that feed experiences into the development process.

2.2.3. The V&V Plan

The V&V plan is the instrument to explain the requirements and management of V&V and the role of each technique in satisfying the objectives of V&V. An understanding of the different purposes of each verification and validation activity will help in planning carefully the techniques and resources needed to achieve their purposes. IEEE standard 1012, section 7, specifies what ordinarily goes into a V&V plan.

Verification activities examine a specific product, that is, output of a process, and provide objective evidence that specified requirements have been fulfilled. The "specified requirements" refer to the requirements of the examined product, relative to the product from which it is derived. For example, code is examined relative to requirements of a design description, or the software requirements are examined relative to system requirements.

Validation examines a specific product to provide objective evidence that the requirements for a specific intended use are fulfilled. The validation confirms that the product traces back to the software system requirements and satisfies them. This includes planning for system testing more or less in parallel with the system and software requirements process. This aspect of validation often serves as part of a requirements verification activity. While some communities separate completely verification from validation, the activities of each actually service the other.

V&V activities can be exercised at every step of the life cycle, often on the same product, possibly using the same techniques in some instances. The difference is in the technique's objectives for that product, and the supporting inputs to that technique. Sequentially, verification and validation will provide evidence from requirements to the final system, a step at a time. This process holds true for any life cycle model, gradually iterating or incrementing through the development. The process holds in maintenance also.

The plan for V&V addresses the management, communication, policies and procedures of the V&V activities and their iteration, evaluation of methods, measures, and tools for the V&V activities, defect reports, and documentation requirements. The plan describes V&V activities, techniques and tools used to achieve the goals of those activities.

The V&V process may be conducted in various organizational arrangements. First, to re-emphasize, many V&V techniques may be employed by the software engineers who are building the product. Second, the V&V process may be conducted in varying degrees of independence from the development organization. Finally, the integrity level of the product may drive the degree of independence.

2.3. Activities and techniques for SQA and V&V

The SQA and V&V processes consist of activities to indicate how software plans (e.g., management, development, configuration management) are being implemented and how well the evolving and final products are meeting their specified requirements. Results from these activities are collected into reports for management before corrective actions are taken. The management of SQA and V&V are tasked with ensuring the quality of these reports, that is, that the results are accurate.

Specific techniques to support the activities software engineers perform to assure quality may depend upon their personal role (e.g., programmer, quality assurance staff) and project organization (e.g., test group, independent V&V). To build or analyze for quality, the software engineer understands development standards and methods and the genesis of other resources on the project (e.g., components, automated tool support) and how they will be used. The software engineer performing quality analysis activities is aware of and understands considerations affecting quality assurance: standards for software quality assurance, V&V, testing, the various resources that influence the product, techniques, and measurement (e.g., what to measure and how to evaluate the product from the measurements).

The SQA and V&V activities consist of many techniques; some may directly find defects and others may indicate where further examination may be valuable. These may be referred to as direct-defect finding and supporting techniques. Some often serve as both, such as people-intensive techniques like reviews, audits, and inspection (as used here, not to be confused with the term "inspection" used for static analysis of work products) and some static techniques like complexity analysis and control flow analysis. The SQA and V&V techniques can be categorized as two types: static and dynamic. Static techniques do not involve the execution of code, whereas dynamic techniques do. Static techniques involve examination of the documentation (e.g., requirements specification, design, plans, code, test documentation) by individuals or groups of individuals and sometimes with the aid of automated tools. Often, people tend to think of testing as the only dynamic technique, but simulation is an example of another one. Sometimes static techniques are used to support dynamic techniques, and vice-versa. An individual, perhaps with the use of a software tool, may perform some techniques; in others, several people are required to conduct the technique. Such techniques, requiring two or more people, are "people-intensive". Depending on project size, other techniques, such as testing, may involve many people, but are not people-intensive in the sense described here.

Static and dynamic techniques are used in either SQA or V&V. Their selection, specific objectives and organization depend on project and product requirements. Discussion in the following sections and the tables in the appendices provide only highlights about the various techniques; they are not inclusive. There are too many techniques to define in this document but the lists and references provide a flavor of SQA and V&V techniques and will yield insights for selecting techniques and for pursuing additional reading about techniques.

2.3.1. Static Techniques

Static techniques involve examination of the project's documentation, software and other information about the software products without executing them. The techniques may include people intensive activities, as defined above, or analytic activities conducted by individuals, with or without the assistance of automated tools. These support both SQA and V&V processes and their specific implementation can serve the purpose of SQA, verification, or validation, at every stage of development or maintenance.

2.3.1.1. People-Intensive Techniques

The setting for people-intensive techniques, including audits, reviews, and inspections, may vary. The setting may be a formal meeting, an informal gathering, or a desk-check situation, but (usually, at least) two or more people are involved. Preparation ahead of time may be necessary. Resources in addition to the items under examination may include checklists and results from analytic techniques and testing. Another technique that may be included in this group is the walkthrough. They may also be done on-line. These activities are discussed in IEEE Std. 1028 on reviews and audits, [Fre82], [Hor96], and [Jon96], [Rak97].

Reviews that specifically fall under the SQA process are technical reviews, that is, on technical products. However, the SQA organization may be asked to conduct management reviews as well. Persons involved in the reviews are usually a leader, a recorder, technical staff, and -in the management review - management staff.

Management reviews determine adequacy of and monitor progress or inconsistencies against plans and schedules and requirements. These reviews may be exercised on products such as audit reports. progress reports, V&V reports and plans of many types including risk management, project management, software configuration management, software safety, and risk assessment, among others. See the **Software Engineering Management** KA for related material.

Technical reviews examine products (again, anything produced a stage of the software engineering project, such as software requirement specifications, software design documents, test documentation, user documentation, installation procedures), but the coverage of the material may vary with purpose of the review. The subject of the review is not necessarily the completed product, but may be a portion of it. For example, a subset of the software requirements may be reviewed for a particular set of functionality, or several design modules may be reviewed, or separate reviews may be conducted for each category of test for each of its associated documents (plans, designs, cases and procedures, reports).

An audit is an independent evaluation of conformance of software products and processes to applicable regulations, standards, plans, and procedures. Audits may examine plans like recovery, SQA, and maintenance, design documentation. The audit is a formally organized activity, with participants having specific roles, such as lead auditor, other auditors, a recorder, an initiator, and a representative of the audited organization. While for reviews and audits there may be many formal names such as those identified in the IEEE Std. 1028, the important point is that they can occur on almost any product at any stage of the development or maintenance process.

Software inspections generally involve the author of a product, while reviews likely do not. Other persons include a reader and some inspectors. The inspector team may consist of different expertise, such as domain expertise, or design method expertise, or language expertise, etc. Inspections are usually conducted on a relatively small section of the product. Often the inspection team may have had a few hours to prepare, perhaps by applying an analytic technique to a small section of the product, or to the entire product with a focus only on one aspect, e.g., interfaces. A checklist, with questions germane to the issues of interest, is a common tool used in inspections. Inspection sessions can last a couple of hours or less, whereas reviews and audits are usually broader in scope and take longer.

The walkthrough is similar to an inspection, but is conducted by only members of the development group, who examine a specific part of a product. With the exception of the walkthrough – primarily an assurance technique used only by the developer, these people-intensive techniques are traditionally considered to be SQA techniques, but may be performed by others. The technical objectives may also change, depending on who performs them and whether they are conducted as verification or as validation activities. Often, when V&V is an organization, it may be asked to support these techniques, either by previous examination of the products or by attending the sessions to conduct the activities.

2.3.1.2 Analytic Techniques

An individual generally applies analytic techniques. Sometimes several people may be assigned the technique, but each applies it to different parts of the product. Some are tool-driven; others are primarily manual. With the References (Section 7.1) there are tables of techniques according to their primary purpose. However, many techniques listed as support may find some defects directly but are typically used as support to other techniques. Some however are listed in both categories because they are used either way. The support group of techniques also includes various assessments as part of overall quality analysis. Examples of this group of techniques includes complexity analysis, control flow analysis, algorithm analysis, and use of formal methods.

Each type of analysis has a specific purpose and not all are going to be applied to every project. An example of a support technique is complexity analysis, useful for determining that the design or code may be too complex to develop correctly, to test or maintain; the results of a complexity analysis may be used in developing test cases. Some listed under direct defect finding, such as control flow analysis, may also be used as support to another activity. For a software system with many algorithms, algorithm analysis is important, especially when an incorrect algorithm could cause a catastrophic result. There are too many analytic techniques to define in this document but the lists and references provide a flavor of software analysis and will yield to the software engineer insights for selecting techniques and for pursuing additional reading about techniques.

A class of analytic techniques that is gaining greater acceptance is the use of formal methods to verify software requirements and designs. Proof of correctness may also be applied to different parts of programs. Their acceptance to date has mostly been in verification of crucial parts of critical systems, such as specific security and safety requirements [NAS97].

2.3.2. Dynamic Techniques

Different kinds of dynamic techniques are performed throughout the development and maintenance of software systems. Generally these are testing techniques, but techniques such as simulation, model checking, and symbolic execution may be considered dynamic. Code reading is considered a static technique but experienced software engineers may execute the code as they read through it. In this sense, code reading may also fit under dynamic. This discrepancy in categorizing indicates that people with different roles in the organization may consider and apply these techniques differently.

Some testing may fall under the development process, the SQA process, or V&V, again depending on project organization. The discipline of V&V encompasses testing and requires activities for testing at the very beginning of the project. Because both the SQA and V&V plans address testing, this section includes some commentary about testing. The knowledge area on **Software Testing** provides discussion and technical references to theory, techniques for testing, and automation. Supporting techniques for testing fall under test management, planning and documentation. V&V testing generally includes component or module, integration, system, and acceptance testing. V&V testing may include test of commercial off-the-shelf software (COTS) and evaluation of tools to be used in the project (see section 5.3).

The assurance processes of SQA and V&V examine every output relative to the software requirement specification to ensure the output's traceability, consistency, completeness, correctness, and performance. This confirmation also includes exercising the outputs of the development and maintenance processes, that is, the analysis consists of validating the code by testing to many objectives and strategies, and collecting, analyzing and measuring the results. SQA ensures that appropriate types of tests are planned, developed, and implemented, and V&V develops test plans, strategies, cases and procedures.

2.4. Other SQA and V&V Testing

Two types of testing fall under SQA and V&V because of their responsibility for quality of materials used in the project:

Evaluation and test of tools to be used on the project (See ISO/IEC 12119 Information Technology – Guidance for the Evaluation and Selection of CASE Tools)

Conformance test (or review of conformance test) of components and COTS products to be used in the product. There now exists a standard for software packages (see section 7.2.4.)

The SWEBOK knowledge area on **Software Testing** addresses special purpose testing. Many of these types are also considered and performed during planning for SQA or V&V testing. Occasionally the V&V process may be asked to perform these other testing activities according to the project's organization. Sometimes an independent V&V organization may be asked to monitor the test process and sometimes to witness the actual execution, to ensure that it is conducted in accordance with specified procedures. And, sometimes, V&V may be called on to evaluate the testing itself: adequacy of plans and procedures, and adequacy and accuracy of results.

Another type of testing that may fall under a V&V organization is third party testing. The third party is not the developer or in any way associated with the development of the product. Instead, the third party is an independent facility, usually accredited by some body of authority. Their purpose is to test a product for conformance to a specific set of requirements. Discussion on third party testing appears in the July/August 1999 *IEEE Software* special issue on software certification.

2.5. Measurement applied to SQA and V&V

SQA and V&V discover information at all stages of the development and maintenance process that provides visibility into the software development and maintenance processes. Some of this information involves counting and classifying defects, where "defect" refers to errors, faults, and failures. Typically, if the word "defect" is used, it refers to "fault" as defined below, but different cultures and standards may differ somewhat in their meaning for these same terms, so there have been attempts to define them. Partial definitions taken from the IEEE Std 610.12-1990

("IEEE Standard Glossary of Software Engineering Terminology") are these:

- Error: "A difference...between a computed result and the correct result"
- Fault: "An incorrect step, process, or data definition in a computer program"
- Failure: "The [incorrect] result of a fault"
- Mistake: "A human action that produces an incorrect result".

Mistakes (as defined above) are the subject of the quality improvement process, which is covered in the Knowledge Area **Software Engineering Process**. Failures found in testing as the result of software faults are included as defects in the discussion of this section. Reliability models are built from failure data collected during system testing or from systems in service, and thus can be used to predict failure and to assist decisions on when to stop testing.

Information on inadequacies and defects found during SQA and V&V techniques may be lost unless it is recorded. For some techniques (e.g., reviews, audits, inspections), recorders are usually present to record such information, along with issues, and decisions. When automated tools are used, the tool output may provide the defect information. Sometimes data about defects are collected and recorded on a "trouble report" form and may further be entered into some type of database, either manually or automatically from an analysis tool. Reports about the defects are provided to the software management and development organizations.

One probable action resulting from SQA and V&V reports is to remove the defects from the product under examination. Other actions enable achieving full value from the findings of the SQA and V&V activities. These actions include analyzing and summarizing the findings with use of measurement techniques to improve the product and the process ands to track the defects and their removal. Process improvement is primarily discussed in **Software Engineering Process** with SQA and V&V process being a source of information..

2.5.1. Fundamentals of Measurement

The theory of measurement establishes the foundation on which meaningful measurements can be made. It tells us, for instance, that the statement that it is twice as warm today as yesterday if it is 40 degrees Fahrenheit today but only 20 degrees yesterday is not meaningful because degrees Fahrenheit is not a "ratio scale" but a similar statement concerning degrees Kelvin would have a physical meaning. Measurement is defined in the theory as "the assignment of numbers to objects in a systematic way to represent properties of the object." If the property is just a constant assigned by counting some aspect it is an "absolute" measure, but usually not very meaningful. More meaningful scales are relative to a classification or scale, and for those, measurement theory provides a succession of

more and more constrained ways of assigning the measures. If the numbers assigned are merely to provide labels to classify the objects, they are called "nominal". If they are assigned in a way that ranks the objects (e.g. good, better, best), they are called "ordinal". If they deal with magnitudes of the property relative to a defined measurement unit, they are "interval" (and the intervals are uniform between the numbers unless otherwise specified, and are therefore additive). Measurements are at the "ratio" level if they have an absolute zero point, so ratios of distances to the zero point are meaningful (as in the example of temperatures given earlier).

Key terms on software measures and measurement methods have been defined in ISO/IEC FCD 15939 on the basis of the ISO international vocabulary of metrology [ISO93]. Nevertheless, readers will encounter terminology differences in the literature; for example, the term "metric" is sometimes used in place of "measure".

Software measures of all of these types have been defined. A simple example of a ratio scale in software, for instance, is the number of defects discovered per module. In module 1, there may be 10 defects per function point (where a function point is a measure of size based on functionality) in module 2, 15 and in module 3, 20. The difference between module 1 and 2 is 5 and module 3 has twice as many defects as module 1. Theories of measurement and scales are discussed in [Kan94], pp. 54-82. The standard for functional size measurement is ISO/IEC 14143-1 and additional, supporting standards are under development. A number of specific methods, suitable for different purposes, are available.

Measurement for measurement's sake does not help define quality. Instead, the software engineer needs to define specific questions about the product, and hence the objectives to be met to answer those questions. Only then can specific measures be selected. ISO/IEC FCD 15939 defines the activities and tasks necessary to implement a software measurement process as well a measurement information model. Another approach is "Plan-Do-Check-Act" discussed in [Rak97] . Others are discussed in the references on software measurement. The point is that there has to be a reason for collecting data, that is, there is a question to be answered.

Measurement programs are considered useful if they help project stakeholders (1) understand what is happening during their processes, and (2) control what is happening on their projects [Fen95,97, Pf]. For measurement to work well, it is critical to establish measurement planning, collection, interpretation and reporting activities as part of a larger organizational process, for example requirements engineering, design, or software construction. The measurement process and its implementation should be documented in the form of a measurement plan. It defines the measurement process with exact information on stakeholders involved, measurement frequency, sources of measurement data, measurement rules, measurement data interpretation rules, tools support, reports to be produced, and action items that can be taken based on the measurement data. In this way, the plan represents a communication vehicle to ensure that all team members agree with the measurement approach, while also serving as the ongoing reference model to manage the implementation of reuse measures.

Other important measurement practices deal with experimentation and data collection. Experimentation is useful in determining the value of a development, maintenance, or assurance technique and results may be used to predict where faults may occur. Data collection is non-trivial and often too many types of data are collected. Instead, it is important to decide what is the purpose, that is, what question is to be answered from the data, then decide what data is needed to answer the question and then to collect only that data. While a measurement program has costs in time and money, it may result in savings. Methods exist to help estimate the costs of a measurement program. Discussion on the following key topics for measurement planning are found in ([Bas84], [Kan94], [Pr], [Pf], [Rak97], [Zel98]):

- Experimentation
- Selection of approach for measurement
- Methods
- Costing
- Data Collection process.

2.5.2. Measures

Measurement models and frameworks for software quality enable the software engineer to establish specific product measures as part of the product concept. Models and frameworks for software quality are discussed in [Kan94], [Pf], and [Pr].

If they are designed properly measures can support software quality (among other aspects of the software engineering process) in multiple ways. They can help management decision-making. They can find problematic areas and bottlenecks in the software product; and they can help the developers in assessing the quality of their work for SQA purposes and for longer term process quality assessment.

Data can be collected on various characteristics of software products. Many of the measures are related to the quality characteristics defined in **Section 2** of this Knowledge Area. Much of the data can be collected as results of the **static techniques** previously discussed and from various testing activities (see **Software Testing** Knowledge Area). The types of measures for which data are collected generally fall into one or more of these categories and are discussed in [Jon96], [Lyu96], [Pf], [Pr], [Lyu96], and [Wei93]:

- Quality characteristics measures
- Reliability models & measures

- Defect features (e.g., counts, density)
- Customer satisfaction
- Product features (e.g., size, which includes source lines of code)and/or function points [Abr96], number of requirements)
- Structure measures (e.g., modularity, complexity, control flow)
- Object-oriented measures.

2.5.3. Measurement Analysis Techniques

While the measures for quality characteristics and product features may be useful in themselves (for example, the number of defective requirements or the proportion of requirements that are defective), mathematical and graphical techniques can be applied to aid in interpretation of the measures. These fit into the following categories and are discussed in [Fen97], [Jon96], [Kan94], [Lyu96] and [Mus98].

- Statistically based (e.g., Pareto analysis, run charts, scatter plots, normal distribution)
- Statistical tests (e.g., binomial test; chi-squared test)
- Trend analysis
- Prediction, e.g., reliability models.

The statistically based techniques and tests often provide a snapshot of the more troublesome areas of the software product under examination. The resulting charts and graphs are visualization aids that the decision-makers can use to focus resources where they appear most needed. Results from trend analysis may indicate whether a schedule may be slipped, such as in testing, or may indicate that certain classes of faults will gain in intensity unless some corrective action is taken in development. And the predictive techniques assist in planning test time and predicting failure. More discussion on these appears in **Software Engineering Process** and **Software Engineering Management**.

2.5.4. Defect Characterization

SQA and V&V processes discover defects. Characterizing those defects enables understanding of the product, facilitates corrections to the process or the product, and informs the project management or customer of the status of the process or product. Many defect (fault) taxonomies exist and while attempts have been made to get consensus on a fault and failure taxonomy, the literature indicates that quite a few are in use (IEEE Std. 1044, [Bei90], [Chi92], [Gra92]). Defect (anomaly) characterization is used in audits and reviews, too, with the review leader often presenting a list of anomalies provided by team members for consideration at a review meeting.

As new design methodologies and languages evolve, along with advances in overall application technologies, new classes of defects appear, or, the connection to previously defined classes requires much effort to realize. When tracking defects, the software engineer is interested not only in the count of defects, but the types. Without some classification, information will not really be useful in identifying the underlying causes of the defects because no one will be able to group specific types of problems and make determinations about them. The point, again, as in selecting a measurement approach with quality characteristics, measures and measurement techniques, is to establish a defect taxonomy that is meaningful to the organization and software system.

The above references as well as [Kan94], [Fen95] and [Pf], and [Jon89] all provide discussions on analyzing defects. This is done by measuring defect occurrences and then applying statistical methods to understand the types of defects that occur most frequently, that is, answering questions about where mistakes occur most frequently (their density). They also aid in understanding the trends and how well detection techniques are working, and, how well the development and maintenance processes are doing.[2] Measuring test coverage helps to estimate how much test effort remains and to predict possible remaining defects. From these measurement methods, one can develop defect profiles for a specific application domain. Then, for the next software system within that organization, the profiles can be used to guide the SQA and V&V processes, that is, to expend the effort where the problems are likeliest to occur. Similarly, benchmarks, or defect counts typical of that domain, may serve as one aid in determining when the product is ready for delivery.

The following topics are useful for establishing measurement approaches for the software products:

• Defect classification and descriptions

• Defect analysis

• Measuring adequacy of the SQA and V&V activities

• Test coverage

• Benchmarks, profiles, baselines, defect densities.

2.5.5. Additional Uses of SQA and V&V data

The measurement section of this KA on SQA and V&V touches only minimally on measurement, for measurement is a major topic itself. The purpose here is only to provide some insight on how the SQA and V&V processes use measurement directly to support achieving their goals. There are a few more topics which measurement of results from SQA and V&V may support. These include some assistance in deciding when to stop testing. Reliability models and benchmarks, both using fault and failure data, are useful for this objective. Again, finding a defect, or perhaps trends among the defects, may help to locate the source of the problem.

The cost of SQA and V&V processes is almost always an issue raised in deciding how to organize a project. Often generic models of cost, based on when the defect is found and how much effort it takes to fix the defect relative to finding the defect earlier, are used. Data within an organization from that organization's projects may give a better picture of cost for that organization. Discussion on this topic may be found in [Rak97], pp. 39-50. Related information can be found in the **Software Engineering Process** and **Software Engineering Management** KAs.

Finally, the SQA and V&V reports themselves provide valuable information not only to these processes but to all the other software engineering processes for use in determining how to improve them. Discussions on these topics are found in [McC93] and IEEE Std. 1012.

3. BREAKDOWN RATIONALE

One breakdown of topics is provided for this area. The rationale for that breakdown is largely stated in the KA introduction. This has been developed through an evolutionary process as the various rewrites and review cycles took place.

The original name of the topic, as it came out of the first meeting of the Industrial Review Board, was "Software Quality Analysis, and it had resulted from a fusion of

• Software Quality Assurance

• Verification and Validation

• Dependability and Quality

• The jump-start document (produced by the same authors as this current KA version) suggested three breakdowns . They were based on

• Criteria for Quality of Software (Basic General Criteria, Examples of Implicit Requirements, Special Situations with Additional Quality Criteria)

• Maintaining and Improving Quality in Software (Process or Project Quality, Product Quality, Techniques for Effective V&V)

• Verification and Validation Across the Software Life Cycle (Initial Project V&V Management, Software Requirements V&V, Software Design V&V, Coding V&V, Testing Phase)

It soon became clear that the topic was intended to transcend life cycle divisions, and that the third suggested breakdown could be covered by references to the KAs covering stages of the life cycle. The first two breakdowns did not really have major overlaps, but each dealt with topics that related to quality, so they were merged into a single breakdown.

An attempt to define the title "Software Quality Analysis" was included in early versions, and it distinguished Quality Process and Quality Product. The Product portion dwelt in

---

[2] Discussion on using data from SQA and V&V to improve development and maintenance processes appears in **Software Engineering Management** and **Software Engineering Process**.

some detail on views of quality characteristics. The Process section included SQA and V&V and some management-oriented considerations.

Later it was determined that the management portions were covered well elsewhere in the SWEBOK, and that the purpose of this KA was really Quality Product. Other KAs were describing the process, including quality concerns, in their descriptions. Nevertheless, there was a place for the processes (SQA and V&V) whose major concern was quality, as this would pull together fragmented discussions in the life cycle KAs and emphasize that these processes were in principle the same over all stages.

Since the ISO 9126 characteristics are well set out in the standard, and there are other views of quality characteristics as well, the detailed examination of them that appeared in earlier versions has also been reduced and dealt with

through references. This was suggested by reviewers and by space considerations.

In summary, the breakdown is a product of the original concept of the editorial team; the suggestions of the Industrial Advisory Board; the material developed by other KA authors; and the opinions voiced by dozens of individuals, representing different points of view, who have reviewed this KA. During the process, the word "Analysis" was dropped from the KA title, since it was causing confusion as to the purpose of the KA by implying to some readers a scholarly area, rather than an area of concern to the practitioner.

It is intended that the KA as a whole and its breakdown of the topic will now evolve based on experience by users, reflecting its usefulness in fulfilling the multiple objectives of the SWEBOK.

4. MATRIX OF TOPICS VS. REFERENCE MATERIAL

Software Quality Concepts	[Boe78]	[D]	[Fen97]	[Kia95]	[Lap91]	[Lew92]	[Lyu96]	[M]	[Mus98]	[Pf]	[Pr]	[Rak97]	[S]	[Wal96]	[Wei93]
Value of Quality	X									X					X
Functionality												X			
Reliability							X	X	X	X	X	X	X	X	
Efficiency							X	X				X			
Usability			X			X		X		X	X	X	X		
Maintainability			X	X		X		X		X	X		X		
Portability								X		X	X	X	X		
Dependability			X		X		X	X	X	X	X		X	X	
Other Qualities		X				X		X		X	X		X	X	

Definition & Planning for Quality	[Gra92]	[Hor96]	[Kaz99]	[Lew92]	[Lyu96]	[McC93]	[M]	[Mus98]	[Pf]	[Pr]	[Rak97]	[Sch98]	[S]	[Wal89]	[Wal96]
Overall							X		X	X			X		
SQA		X	X			X	X		X	X	X	X	X		
VV			X				X		X	X	X	X	X	X	X
Independent V&V			X						X	X	X		X	X	X
Hazard, threat anal.							X		X	X			X		X
Risk assessment	X	X		X	X		X	X					X		
Performance analysis			X						X	X					

Techniques Requiring Two or More People	[Ack97]	[Ebe94]	[Fre82]	[Gra92]	[Hor96]	[Lew92]	[McC93]	[Pf]	[Pr]	[Rak97]	[Sch98]	[S]	[Wal89]	[Wal96]
Audit			X		X	X				X			X	
Inspection	X	X	X	X	X		X	X	X	X	X	X	X	X
Review			X		X	X	X	X	X			X	X	X
Walkthrough			X		X		X	X	X			X	X	X

Support to Other Techniques	[Bei90]	[Con86]	[Fri95]	[Het84]	[Lev95]	[Lew92]	[Lyu96]	[Mus98]	[Pf]	[Pr]	[Rak97]	[Rub94]	[S]	[Fri95]	[Wal89]	[Wal96]
Change Impact Anal.							X		X	X			X			
Checklists				X		X					X	X				
Complexity Analysis	X	X					X	X			X					
Coverage Analysis	X						X	X								
Consistency Analysis									X	X		X				
Criticality Analysis					X	X					X					X
Hazard Analysis			X		X						X	X	X			
Sensitivity Analysis			X												X	
Slicing	X														X	X
Test documents	X	X					X	X							X	X
Tool evaluation						X	X								X	
Traceability Analysis						X	X		X				X		X	X
Threat Analysis			X				X		X	X			X			

Testing Special to SQA or V&V	[Fri95]	[Lev95]	[Lyu96]	[Mus98]	[Pf]	[Pr]	[Rak97]	[Rub94]	[Sch98]	[S]	[Voa99]	[Wak99]	[Wal89]
Conformance Test.	X											X	
Configuration Test.						X							
Certification Testing			X	X			X	X		X		X	X
Reliability Testing	X	X	X	X					X				
Safety Testing	X		X	X					X				
Security Testing						X							
Statistical Testing			X	X	X	X			X	X			
Usability Testing					X			X					
Test Monitoring													X
Test Witnessing													X

Defect Finding Techniques	[Bei90]	[Fen95]	[Fri95]	Hetzel	[Hor96]	[Ipp95]	[Lev95]	[Lew92]	[Lyu96]	[M]	[Mus98]	[Pf]	[Pr]	[Rak97]	[Rub94]	[Sch98]	[S]	[Wak99]	[Wal89]
Algorithm Analysis		X		X				X										X	X
Boundary Value Anal.			X									X	X					X	X
Change Impact Anal.									X			X	X	X		X	X		
Checklists					X		X							X					
Consistency Analysis												X			X				
Control Flow Analysis	X	X						X	X			X	X					X	X
Database Analysis	X	X	X					X							X			X	X
Data Flow Analysis	X	X	X					X	X	X					X			X	X
Distrib. Arch. Assess.																X			
Evaluation of Docts.: Concept, Reqmts.			X					X	X						X			X	X

Defect Finding Techniques	[Bei90]	[Fen95]	[Fri95]	[Hetzel]	[Hor96]	[Ipp95]	[Lev95]	[Lew92]	[Lyu96]	[M]	[Mus98]	[Pf]	[Pr]	[Rak97]	[Rub94]	[Sch98]	[S]	[Wak99]	[Wal89]
Evaluation of Docts.: Design, Code, Test			X					X	X						X			X	
Evaluation of Doc.: User, Installation			X					X	X						X			X	
Event Tree Analysis			X																X
Fault Tree Analysis			X			X			X	X					X				
Graphical Analysis	X	X									X							X	
Hazard Analysis		X	X			X	X		X						X				
Interface Analysis	X		X		X			X	X						X				X
Formal Proofs			X						X	X					X				X
Mutation Analysis			X						X									X	X
Perform. Monitoring									X										X
Prototyping			X						X	X					X				X
Reading			X																X
Regression Analysis			X		X			X	X									X	X
Simulation			X																X
Sizing & Timing Anal.			X					X	X	X								X	X
Threat Analysis									X	X					X				

Measurement in Software Quality Analysis	[Bas84]	[Bei90]	[Con86]	[Chi96]	[Fen95]	[Fen97]	[Fri95]	[Gra92]	[Het84]	[Hor96]	[Jon96]	[Kan94]	[Lew92]	[Lyu96]	[Mus89]	[Mus98]	[Pen92]	[Pf]	[Pr]	[McC93]	[Rak97]	[Sch98]	[S]	[Wak99]	[Wei93]	[Zel98]
Benchmarks, profiles, etc.		X			X													X		X		X				
Company Measures Progs.				X	X			X				X						X	X							
Costing		X	X					X	X			X				X		X		X	X	X	X		X	
Customer satisfaction											X	X										X				
Data Collection process	X	X		X	X			X			X															
Debugging		X	X		X									X						X				X		
Defect Analysis		X	X	X				X	X	X		X		X		X	X	X	X	X	X					
Defect Classif. and Descr.		X		X	X	X		X			X	X	X	X		X		X	X							
Defect Features		X	X		X			X			X	X		X							X					
Example of applied GQM						X		X																		
Experimentation:		X	X	X	X											X										X
Framework				X	X																					
GQM	X			X	X			X				X												X		
Methods		X		X				X				X		X		X					X					
Measures			X		X			X	X			X		X				X	X	X			X	X	X	
Models				X	X									X		X										
Prediction						X								X		X	X				X					
Prod. features: O/O Metr.																								X		
Prod. Features: Structure		X		X	X			X				X									X					
Product features: Size			X		X			X			X	X														

Measurement in Software Quality Analysis	[Bas84]	[Bei90]	[Con86]	[Chi96]	[Fen95]	[Fen97]	[Fri95]	[Gra92]	[Het84]	[Hor96]	[Jon96]	[Kan94]	[Lew92]	[Lyu96]	[Mus89]	[Mus98]	[Pen92]	[Pf]	[Pr]	[McC93]	[Rak97]	[Sch98]	[S]	[Wak99]	[Wei93]	[Zel98]
Quality Attributes													X					X	X				X			
Quality Character. Meas.					X								X			X					X					
Reliab. Models & Meas.			X		X	X						X		X		X				X	X					
Scales			X	X	X							X														
SQA & V&V reports *							X									X					X			X		
Statistical tests			X		X									X			X	X					X			
Statistical Analysis & measurement			X	X	X			X				X		X			X	X			X					
Test coverage																X					X					
Theory			X	X	X							X														
Trend analysis														X												
When to stop testing*						X							X	X												

Standards	Quality Requirements & planning	Reviews/ Audits	SQA/V&V planning	Safety/security analysis, tests	Documentation of quality analysis	Measurement
ISO 9000	X	X			X	X
ISO 9126	X					
IEC 61508	X			X		X
ISO/IEC 14598				X	X	X
ISO/IEC 15026	X					
ISO FDIS 15408	X			X		
FIPS 140-1	X			X		
IEEE 730		X	X		X	
IEEE 1008			X			
IEEE 1012		X	X	X	X	
IEEE 1028		X				
IEEE 1228				X		
IEEE 829					X	
IEEE 982.1,.2						X
IEEE 1044						X
IEEE 1061						X

5. RECOMMENDED REFERENCES FOR SOFTWARE QUALITY

5.1. Basic SWEBOK References

Dorfman, M., and R.H. Thayer, *Software Engineering*. IEEE Computer Society Press, 1997. [D]

Moore, J.W., *Software Engineering Standards: A User's Road Map*. IEEE Computer Society Press, 1998. [M]

Pfleeger, S.L., *Software Engineering – Theory and Practice*. Prentice Hall, 1998. [Pf]

Pressman, R.S., *Software Engineering: A Practitioner's Approach* (4th edition). McGraw-Hill, 1997. [Pr]

Sommerville, I., *Software Engineering* (5th edition). Addison-Wesley, 1996. [S]

5.2. Software Quality KA References

Ackerman, Frank A., "Software Inspections and the Cost Effective Production of Reliable Software," in [D] pp. 235-255. [Ack97]

Basili, Victor R. and David M. Weiss, A Methodology for Collecting Valid Software Engineering Data, IEEE

Transactions on Software Engineering, pp. 728-738, Vol. SE-10, no. 6, November 1984. [Bas84]

Beizer, Boris, *Software Testing Techniques,* International Thomson Press, 1990. [Bei90]

Boehm, B.W. et al., *Characteristics of Software Quality",* TRW series on Software Technologies, Vol. 1, North Holland, 1978. [Boe78]

Chilllarege, Ram, Chap. 9, pp359-400, in [Lyu96]. [Chi96]

Conte, S.D., et al, *Software Engineering Metrics and Models,* The Benjamin / Cummings Publishing Company, Inc., 1986. [Con86]

Ebenau, Robert G., and Susan Strauss, *Software Inspection Process,* McGraw-Hill, 1994. [Ebe94]

Fenton, Norman E., *Software Metrics: A rigorous and practical approach (2nd edition),* International Thomson Computer Press, 1995. [Fen95]

Fenton, Norman E., and Shari Lawrence Pfleeger, Software Metrics, International Thomson Computer Press, 1997. [Fen97]

Freedman, Daniel P., and Gerald M. Weinberg, Handbook of Walkthroughs, Inspections, and Technical Reviews, Little, Brown and Company, 1982. [Fre82]

Friedman, Michael A., and Jeffrey M. Voas, *Software Assessment: reliability, safety testability,* John Wiley & Sons, Inc., 1995. [Fri95]

Grady, Robert B, *Practical Software Metrics for project Management and Process Management,* Prentice Hall, Englewood Cliffs, NJ 07632, 1992. [Gra92]

Hetzel, William, *The Complete Guide to Software Testing,* QED Information Sciences, Inc., 1984, pp177-197. [Het84]

Horch, John W., *Practical Guide to Software Quality Management,* Artech-House Publishers, 1996. [Hor96]

Ippolito, Laura M. and Dolores R. Wallace, NISTIR 5589, A Study on Hazard Analysis in High Integrity Software Standards and Guidelines,@ U.S. Department. of Commerce, Technology Administration, National Institute of Standards and Tech., Jan 1995. http://hissa.nist.gov/HAZARD/ [Ipp95]

Jones, Capers, Applied Software Measurement: Assuring Productivity and Quality, McGraw-Hill, Inc., 2nd edition, 1996.; (Chapters on Mechanics of Measurement and User Satisfaction). [Jon96]

Kan, Stephen, H., *Metrics and Models in Software Quality Engineering,* Addison-Wesley Publishing Co., 1995. [Kan94]

Kazman, R., M. Barbacci, M. Klein, S. J. Carriere, S. G. Woods, Experience with Performing Architecture Tradeoff Analysis, *Proceedings of ICSE 21,* (Los Angeles, CA), IEEE Computer Society, May 1999, 54-63. [Kaz99]

Kiang, David, Harmonization of International Software Standards on Integrity and Dependability, *Proc. IEEE International Software Engineering Standards Symposium,*

IEEE Computer Society Press, Los Alamitos, CA, 1995, pp. 98-104. [Kia95]

Laprie, J.C., *Dependability: Basic Concepts and Terminology in English, French, German, Italian and Japanese, IFIP WG 10.4,* Springer-Verlag, New York 1991. [Lap91]

Leveson, Nancy, *SAFEWARE: System Safety and Computers,* Addison-Wesley, 1995. [Lev95]

Lewis, Robert O., *Independent Verification and Validation: A Life Cycle Engineering Process for Quality Software ,* John Wiley & Sons, Inc., 1992. [Lew92]

Lyu , Michael R., *Handbook of Software Reliability Engineering,* McGraw Hill, 1996. [Lyu96]

McCall, J.A. - Factors in Software Quality - General Electric, n77C1502, June 1977 [McC77]

McConnell, Steve C., *Code Complete: a practical handbook of software construction,* Microsoft Press, 1993. [McC93]

Musa, John D., and A. Frank Ackerman, "Quantifying Software Validation: When to stop testing?" *IEEE Software,* vol. 6, no. 3, May 1989, 19-27. [Mus89]

Musa, John, *Software Reliability Engineering: More Reliable Software, Faster Development and Testing,* McGraw Hill, 1999. [Mus98]

Peng, Wendy W. and Dolores R. Wallace, "Software Error Analysis," NIST SP 500-209, National Institute of Standards and Technology, Gaithersburg, MD 20899, December 1993.] http://hissa.nist.gov/SWERROR/. [Pen92]

Rakitin, Steven R., *Software Verification and Validation, A Practitioner's Guide,* Artech House, Inc., 1997. [Rak97]

Rubin, Jeffrey, *Handbook of Usability Testing: How to Plan, Design, and Conduct Effective Tests,* John Wiley & Sons, 1994. [Rub94]

Schulmeyer, Gordon C., and James I. McManus, *Handbook of Software Quality Assurance,* Third Edition, Prentice Hall, NJ, 1999. [Sch98]

Voas, Jeffrey, "Certifying Software For High Assurance Environments, " *IEEE Software,* Vol. 16, no. 4, July-August, 1999, pp. 48-54. [Voa99]

Wakid, Shukri, D. Richard Kuhn, and Dolores R. Wallace, "Toward Credible IT Testing and Certification," *IEEE Software,* July-August 1999, 39-47. [Wak99]

Wallace, Dolores R., and Roger U. Fujii, "Software Verification and Validation: An Overview," *IEEE Software,* Vol. 6, no. 3, May 1989, 10-17. [Wal89]

Wallace, Dolores R., Laura Ippolito, and Barbara Cuthill, Reference Information for the Software Verification and Validation Process,@ NIST SP 500-234, NIST, Gaithersburg, MD 20899, April, 1996. http://hissa.nist.gov/VV234/. [Wal96]

Weinberg, Gerald M., Quality Software Management, Vol 2: First-Order Measurement, Dorset House, 1993. (Ch. 8, Measuring Cost and Value). [Wei93]

Zelkowitz, Marvin V. and Dolores R. Wallace, Experimental Models for Validating Technology, *Computer*, Vol. 31 No.5, 1998 pp.23-31. [Zel98]

Appendix A – List of Further Readings

A.1 Books and Articles

Abran, A.; Robillard, P.N. , Function Points Analysis: An Empirical Study of its Measurement Processes, in IEEE Transactions on Software Engineering, vol. 22, 1996, pp. 895-909. [Abr96]

Bevan, N., "Quality and usability: a new framework", in Achieving Software Product Quality, ed. E. van Veenendaal & J. McMullan, Uitgeverij Tutein Nolthenius, Holland, 1997.[Bev97]

Department of Defense and US Army, Practical Software and Systems Measurement : A Foundation for Objective Project Management, Version 4.0b, October 2000. Available at : www.psmsc.com [DOD00]

Garvin, D., "What Does 'Product Quality' Really Mean?" Sloan Management Review, Fall 1984, pp 25-45. [Gar84]

Humphrey, Watts S., Managing the Software Process, Addison Wesley, 1989 Chapters 8, 10, 16. [Hum89]

Hyatt, L.E. and L. Rosenberg, A Software Quality Model and Metrics for Identifying Project Risks and Assessing Software Quality, 8th Annual Software Technology Conference, Utah, April 1996. [Hya96]

Ince, Darrel, *ISO 9001 and Software Quality Assurance*, McGraw-Hill, 1994. [Inc94]

NASA, *Formal Methods Specification and Analysis Guidebook for the Verification of Software and Computer Systems, Volume II: A Practitioner's Companion*, [NASA-GB-001-97], 1997, http://eis.jpl.nasa.gov/quality/Formal_Methods/. [NAS97]

Palmer, James D., "Traceability," In: [Dorf], pp. 266-276. [Pal97]

Rosenberg, Linda, Applying and Interpreting Object-Oriented Metrics, Software Tech. Conf. 1998, http://satc.gsfc.nasa.gov/support/index.html. [Ros98]

Vincenti, W.G., What Engineers Know and How They Know It – Analytical Studies form Aeronautical History. Baltimore and London: John Hopkins, 1990. [Vin90]

A.2 Relevant Standards

FIPS 140-1, 1994, Security Requirements for Cryptographic Modules

IEC 61508 Functional Safety - Safety -related Systems Parts 1,2,3

IEEE 610.12-1990, Standard Glossary of Software Engineering Terminology

IEEE 730-1998 Software Quality Assurance Plans

IEEE 829 -1998 Software Test Documentation

IEEE Std 982.1 and 982.2 Standard Dictionary of Measures to Produce Reliable Software

IEEE 1008-1987 Software Unit Test

IEEE 1012-1998 Software Verification and Validation

IEEE 1028 -1997 Software Reviews

IEEE 1044 -1993 Standard Classification for Software Anomalies

IEEE Std 1061-1992 Standard for A Software Quality Metrics Methodology

IEEE Std 1228-1994 Software Safety Plans

ISO 8402-1986 Quality - Vocabulary

ISO 9000-1994 Quality Management and Quality Assurance Standards

ISO 9001-1994 Quality Systems

ISO/IEC 9126-1999: Software Product Quality

ISO 12207 Software Life Cycle Processes 1995

ISO/IEC 12119 Information technology - Software package - Quality requirements and test

ISO/IEC 14598-1998: Software Product Evaluation

ISO/IEC 15026:1998, Information technology -- System and software integrity levels.

ISO/IEC 25939: Information Technology – Software Measurement Process, International Organization for Standardization and the International Electrotechnical Commission, 2000. Available at www.info.uqam.ca/ Labo_Recherche/Lrgl/sc7/private_files/07n2410.pdf

The Common Criteria for Information Technology Security Evaluation (CC) VERSION 2.0 / ISO FDIS 15408.

APPENDIX A

KNOWLEDGE AREA DESCRIPTION SPECIFICATIONS FOR THE TRIAL VERSION OF THE GUIDE TO THE SOFTWARE ENGINEERING BODY OF KNOWLEDGE

Pierre Bourque and Alain Abran
École de technologie supérieure

Robert Dupuis
Université du Québec à Montréal

James W. Moore
The MITRE Corporation

Leonard Tripp
1999 President IEEE Computer Society

1 INTRODUCTION

This document presents a final version (version 0.9) of the specifications provided by the Editorial Team to the Knowledge Area Specialist regarding the Knowledge Area Descriptions of the Guide to the Software Engineering Body of Knowledge (Trial Version). The Editorial Team definitely views the development of these specifications as an iterative process and strongly encourages comments, suggested improvements and feedback on these specifications from all involved.

This set of specifications may of course be improved through feedback obtained from the next phase – Ironman – of the project.

This document begins by presenting specifications on the contents of the Knowledge Area Description. Criteria and requirements are defined for proposed breakdowns of topics, for the rationale underlying these breakdowns and the succinct description of topics, for the rating of these topics according to Bloom's taxonomy, for selecting reference materials, and for identifying relevant Knowledge Areas of Related Disciplines. Important input documents are also identified and their role within the project is explained. Non-content issues such as submission format and style guidelines are also discussed in the document.

2 CONTENT GUIDELINES

The following guidelines are presented in a schematic form in the figure found below. While all components are part of the Knowledge Area Description, it must be made very clear that some components are essential, while other are not. The breakdown(s) of topics, the selected reference material and the matrix of reference material versus topics are essential. Without them there is no Knowledge Area Description. The other components could be produced by other means if, for whatever reason, the Specialist cannot provide them within the given timeframe and should not be viewed as major stumbling blocks.

2.1 Criteria and requirements for proposing the breakdown(s) of topics within a Knowledge Area

The following requirements and criteria should be used when proposing a breakdown of topics within a given Knowledge Area:

a) Knowledge Area Specialists are expected to propose one or possibly two complementary breakdowns that are specific to their Knowledge Area. The topics found in all breakdowns within a given Knowledge Area must be identical.

b) These breakdowns of topics are expected to be "reasonable", not "perfect". The Guide to the Software Engineering Body of Knowledge is definitely viewed as a multi-phase effort and many iterations within each phase as well as multiple phases will be necessary to continuously improve these breakdowns. At least for the Stone Man version, "soundness and reasonableness" are being sought after, not "perfection".

c) The proposed breakdown of topics within a Knowledge Area must decompose the subset of the Software Engineering Body of Knowledge that is "generally accepted". See section found below for a more detailed discussion on this.

d) The proposed breakdown of topics within a Knowledge Area must not presume specific application domains, business needs, sizes of organizations, organizational structures, management philosophies, software life cycle models, software technologies or software development methods.

e) The proposed breakdown of topics must, as much as possible, be compatible with the various schools of thought within software engineering.

f) The proposed breakdown of topics within Knowledge Areas must be compatible with the breakdown of software engineering generally found in industry and in the software engineering literature and standards.

g) The proposed breakdown of topics is expected to be as inclusive as possible. It is deemed better to suggest too many topics and have them be abandoned later than the reverse.

h) The Knowledge Area Specialist are expected to adopt the position that even though the following "themes" are common across all Knowledge Areas, they are also an integral part of all Knowledge Areas and therefore must be incorporated into the proposed breakdown of topics of each Knowledge Area. These common themes are quality (in general) and measurement.

Please note that the issue of how to properly handle these "cross-running" or "orthogonal topics" and whether or not they should be handled in a different manner has not been completely resolved yet.

i) The proposed breakdowns should be at most two or three levels deep. Even though no upper or lower limit is imposed on the number of topics within each Knowledge Area, Knowledge Area Specialists are expected to propose a reasonable and manageable number of topics per Knowledge Area. Emphasis should also be put on the selection of the topics themselves rather than on their organization in an appropriate hierarchy.

j) Proposed topic names must be significant enough to be meaningful even when cited outside the Guide to the Software Engineering Body of Knowledge.

k) The description of a Knowledge Area will include a chart (in tree form) describing the knowledge breakdown.

l) Knowledge Area Specialists are also expected to propose a breakdown of topics based on the categories of engineering design knowledge defined in Chapter 7 of Vincenti's book. This exercise should be regarded by the Knowledge Area specialists as a tool for viewing the proposed topics in an alternate manner and for linking software engineering itself to engineering in general. Please note that effort should not be spent on this classification at the expense of the three essential components of the Knowledge Area Description. (Please note that a classification of the topics as per the categories of engineering design knowledge has been produced but will be published on the web site at a latter date in a separate working document. Please contact the editorial team for more information).

2.2 Criteria and requirements for describing topics and for describing the rationale underlying the proposed breakdown(s) within the Knowledge Area

a) Topics need only to be sufficiently described so the reader can select the appropriate reference material according to his/her needs.

b) Knowledge Area Specialists are expected to provide a text describing the rationale underlying the proposed breakdown(s).

2.3 Criteria and requirements for rating topics according to Bloom's taxonomy

a) Knowledge Area Specialists are expected to provide an Appendix that states for each topic at which level of Bloom's taxonomy a "graduate plus four years experience" should "master" this topic. This is seen by the Editorial Team as a tool for the Knowledge Area Specialists to ensure that the proposed material meets the criteria of being "generally accepted". Additionally, the Editorial Team views this as a means of ensuring that the Guide to the Software Engineering Body of Knowledge is properly suited for the educators that will design curricula and/or teaching material based on the Guide and licensing/certification officials defining exam contents and criteria.

Please note that these appendices will all be combined together and published as an Appendix to the Guide to the Software Engineering Body of Knowledge.

2.4 Criteria and Requirements for selecting Reference Material

a) Specific reference material must be identified for each topic. Each reference material can of course cover multiple topics.

b) Proposed Reference Material can be book chapters, refereed journal papers, refereed conference papers or refereed technical or industrial reports or any other type of recognized artifact such as web documents. They must be generally available and must not be confidential in nature. Please be as precise as possible by identifying what specific chapter or section is relevant.

c) Proposed Reference Material must be in English.

d) A reasonable amount of reference material must be selected for each Knowledge Area. The following guidelines should be used in determining how much is reasonable:

♦ If the reference material were written in a coherent manner that followed the proposed breakdown of topics and in a uniform style (for example in a new book based on the proposed Knowledge Area description), an average target for the number of pages would be 500. However, this target may not be attainable when selecting existing reference material due to differences in style, and overlap and redundancy between the selected reference material.

- The amount of reference material would be reasonable if it consisted of the study material on this Knowledge Area of a software engineering licensing exam that a graduate would pass after completing four years of work experience.

- The Guide to the Software Engineering Body of Knowledge is intended by definition to be selective in its choice of topics and associated reference material The list of reference material for each Knowledge Area should be viewed and will be presented as an "informed and reasonable selection" rather than as a definitive list.

- The classification of topics according to Bloom's taxonomy should be used to allot the appropriate amount and level of depth of the reference material selected for each topic.

- Additional reference material can be included in a "Further Readings" list. These further readings still must be related to the topics in the breakdown. They must also discuss generally accepted knowledge. However, the further readings material will not be made available on the web nor should there be a matrix between the reference material listed in Further Readings and the individual topics.

e) If deemed feasible and cost-effective by the IEEE Computer Society, selected reference material will be published on the Guide to the Software Engineering Body of Knowledge web site. To facilitate this task, preference should be given to reference material for which the copyrights already belong to the IEEE Computer Society or the ACM. This should however not be seen as a constraint or an obligation.

f) A matrix of reference material versus topics must be provided.

2.5 Criteria and Requirements for identifying Knowledge Areas of the Related Disciplines

a) Knowledge Area Specialists are expected to identify in a separate section which Knowledge Areas of the Related Disciplines that are sufficiently relevant to the Software Engineering Knowledge Area that has been assigned to them be expected knowledge by a graduate plus four years of experience.

This information will be particularly useful to and will engage much dialogue between the Guide to the Software Engineering Body of Knowledge initiative and our sister initiatives responsible for defining a common software engineering curricula and standard performance norms for software engineers.

The list of Knowledge Areas of Related Disciplines can be found in the Proposed Baseline List of Related Disciplines. If deemed necessary and if accompanied by a justification, Knowledge Area Specialists can also propose additional Related Disciplines not already included or identified in the Proposed Baseline List of Related Disciplines. (Please note that a classification of the topics from the Related Disciplines has been produced but will be published on the web site at a latter date in a separate working document. Please contact the editorial team for more information).

2.6 Common Table of Contents

a) Knowledge Area descriptions should use the following table of contents:

- Table of contents

- Introduction

- Definition of the Knowledge Area

- Breakdown of topics of the Knowledge Area (for clarity purposes, we believe this section should be placed in front and not in an appendix at the end of the document. Also, it should be accompanied by a figure describing the breakdown)

- Breakdown rationale

- Matrix of topics vs. Reference material

- Recommended references for the Knowledge Area being described (please do not mix them with references used to write the Knowledge Area description)

- List of Further Readings

- References used to write and justify the Knowledge Area description.

2.7 What do we mean by "generally accepted knowledge"?

The software engineering body of knowledge is an all-inclusive term that describes the sum of knowledge within the profession of software engineering. However, the Guide to the Software Engineering Body of Knowledge seeks to identify and describe that subset of the body of knowledge that is generally accepted or, in other words, the core body of knowledge. To better illustrate what "generally accepted knowledge" is relative to other types of knowledge, Figure 1 proposes a draft three-category schema for classifying knowledge.

The Project Management Institute in its Guide to the Project Management Body of Knowledge[1] defines "generally accepted" knowledge for project management in the following manner:

"'Generally accepted' means that the knowledge and practices described are applicable to most projects most of the time, and that there is widespread consensus about their value and usefulness. "Generally accepted" does not mean that the knowledge and practices described are or should be applied uniformly on all projects; the project management team is always responsible for determining what is appropriate for any given project.'

The Guide to the Project Management Body of Knowledge is now an IEEE Standard.

At the Mont-Tremblant kick off meeting, the Industrial Advisory Board better defined "generally accepted" as knowledge to be included in the study material of a software engineering licensing exam that a graduate would pass after completing four years of work experience. These two definitions should be seen as complementary.

Knowledge Area Specialists are also expected to be somewhat forward looking in their interpretation by taking into consideration not only what is "generally accepted" today and but what they expect will be "generally accepted" in a 3 to 5 years timeframe.

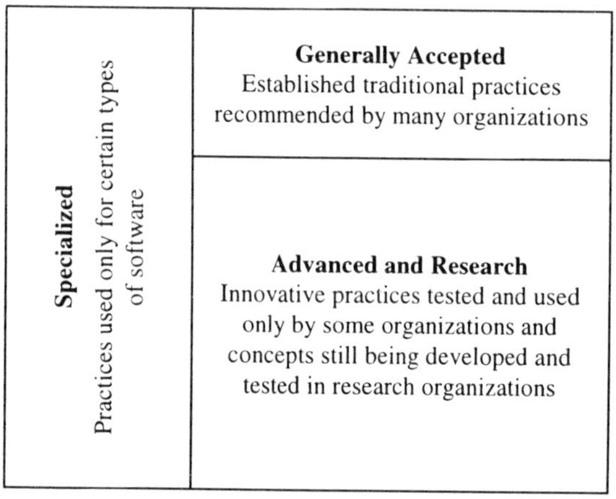

Figure 1 Categories of knowledge

2.8 Length of Knowledge Area Description

Knowledge Area Descriptions are currently expected to be roughly in the 10 pages range using the format of the International Conference on Software Engineering format as defined below. This includes text, references, appendices and tables etc. This, of course, does not include the reference materials themselves. This limit should, however, not be seen as a constraint or an obligation.

2.9 Role of Editorial Team

Alain Abran and James W. Moore are the Executive Editors and are responsible for maintaining good relations with the IEEE CS, the ACM, the Industrial Advisory Board and the Panel of Experts as well as for the overall strategy, approach, organization and funding of the project.

Pierre Bourque and Robert Dupuis are the Editors and are responsible for the coordination, operation and logistics of this project. More specifically, the Editors are responsible for developing the project plan, the Knowledge Area description specification and for coordinating Knowledge Area Specialists and their contribution, for recruiting the reviewers and the review captains as well as coordinating the various review cycles.

The Editors are therefore responsible for the coherence of the entire Guide and for identifying and establishing links between the Knowledge Areas. The resolution of gaps and overlaps between Knowledge Areas will be negotiated by the Editors and the Knowledge Area Specialists themselves.

2.10 Summary

The following figure presents in a schematic form the Knowledge Area Description Specifications

---

[1] See [1] W. R. Duncan, "A Guide to the Project Management Body of Knowledge," Project Management Institute, Upper Darby, PA 1996. Can be downloaded from www.pmi.org

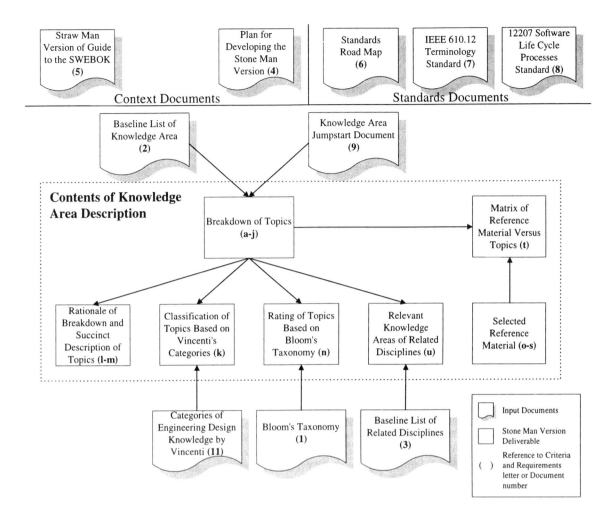

IMPORTANT RELATED DOCUMENTS (in alphabetical order of first author)

1. Bloom *et al.*, Bloom's Taxonomy of the Cognitive Domain

Please refer to chiron.valdosta.edu/whuitt/col/cogsys/bloom.html for a short description of Bloom's taxonomy. The original source is Bloom, B.S. (Ed.) (1956) Taxonomy of educational objectives: The classification of educational goals: Handbook I, cognitive domain. New York ; Toronto: Longmans, Green.

2. P. Bourque, R. Dupuis, A. Abran, J. W. Moore, L. Tripp, D. Frailey, A Baseline List of Knowledge Areas for the Stone Man Version of the Guide to the Software Engineering Body of Knowledge, Université du Québec à Montréal, Montréal, February 1999.

Based on the Straw Man version, on the discussions held and the expectations stated at the kick off meeting of the Industrial Advisory Board, on other body of knowledge proposals, and on criteria defined in this document, this document proposes a baseline list of ten Knowledge Areas for the Trial Version of the Guide to the Software Engineering Body of Knowledge. This baseline may of course evolve as work progresses and issues are identified during the course of the project.

This document is available at www.swebok.org.

3. P. Bourque, R. Dupuis, A. Abran, J. W. Moore, L. Tripp. A Proposed Baseline List of Related Disciplines for the Stone Man Version of the Guide to the Software Engineering Body of Knowledge, Université du Québec à Montréal, Montréal, February 1999.

Based on the Straw Man version, on the discussions held and the expectations stated at the kick off meeting of the Industrial Advisory Board and on subsequent work, this document proposes a baseline list of Related Disciplines and Knowledge Areas within these Related Disciplines. This document has been submitted to and discussed with the Industrial Advisory Board and a recognized list of Knowledge Areas still has to be identified for certain Related Disciplines. Knowledge Area Specialists will be informed of the evolution of this document.

The current version is available at www.swebok.org

4. P. Bourque, R. Dupuis, A. Abran, J. W. Moore, L. Tripp, D. Frailey, Approved Plan, Stone Man Version of the Guide to the Software Engineering Body of Knowledge, Université du Québec à Montréal, Montréal, February 1999.

This report describes the project objectives, deliverables and underlying principles. The intended audience of the Guide is identified. The responsibilities of the various contributors are defined and an outline of the schedule is traced. This documents defines notably the review process that will be used to develop the Stone Man version. This plan has been approved by the Industrial Advisory Board.

This document is available at www.swebok.org

5. P. Bourque, R. Dupuis, A. Abran, J. W. Moore, L. Tripp, K. Shyne, B. Pflug, M. Maya, and G. Tremblay, Guide to the Software Engineering Body of Knowledge - A Straw Man Version, Université du Québec à Montréal, Montréal, Technical Report, September 1998.

This report is the basis for the entire project. It defines general project strategy, rationale and underlying principles and proposes an initial list of Knowledge Areas and Related Disciplines.

This report is available at www.swebok.org.

6. J. W. Moore, Software Engineering Standards, A User's Road Map. Los Alamitos: IEEE Computer Society Press, 1998.

This book describes the scope, roles, uses, and development trends of the most widely used software engineering standards. It concentrates on important software engineering activities — quality and project management, system engineering, dependability, and safety. The analysis and regrouping of the standard collections exposes you to key relationships between standards.

Even though the Guide to the Software Engineering Body of Knowledge is not a software engineering standards development project per se, special care will be taken throughout the project regarding the compatibility of the Guide with the current IEEE and ISO Software Engineering Standards Collection.

7. IEEE Standard Glossary of Software Engineering Terminology, IEEE, Piscataway, NJ std 610.12-1990, 1990.

The hierarchy of references for terminology is Merriam Webster's Collegiate Dictionary (10th Edition), IEEE Standard 610.12 and new proposed definitions if required.

8. Information Technology – Software Life Cycle Processes, International Standard, Technical ISO/IEC 12207:1995(E), 1995.

This standard is considered the key standard regarding the definition of life cycle process and has been adopted by the two main standardization bodies in software engineering: ISO/IEC JTC1 SC7 and the IEEE Computer Society Software Engineering Standards Committee. It also has been designated as the pivotal standard around which the Software Engineering Standards Committee (SESC) is currently harmonizing its entire collection of standards. This standard was a key input to the Straw Man version.

Even though we do not intend that the Guide to the Software Engineering Body of Knowledge be fully 12207-compliant, this standard remains a key input to the Stone Man version and special care will be taken throughout the project regarding the compatibility of the Guide with the 12207 standard.

9. Knowledge Area Jumpstart Documents

A "jumpstart document" has already been provided to all Knowledge Area Specialists. These "jumpstart documents" propose a breakdown of topics for each Knowledge Area based on the analysis of the four most widely sold generic software engineering textbooks. As implied by their title, they have been prepared as an enabler for the Knowledge Area Specialist and the Knowledge Area Specialist are not of course constrained to the proposed list of topics nor to the proposed breakdown in these "jumpstart documents".

10. Merriam Webster's Collegiate Dictionary (10th Edition).

See note for IEEE 610.12 Standard.

11. W. G. Vincenti, What Engineers Know and How They Know It - Analytical Studies from Aeronautical History. Baltimore and London: Johns Hopkins, 1990.

The categories of engineering design knowledge defined in Chapter 7 (The Anatomy of Engineering Design Knowledge) of this book were used as a framework for organizing topics in the various Knowledge Area "jumpstart documents " and are imposed as decomposition framework in the Knowledge Area Descriptions because:

•   they are based on a detailed historical analysis of an established branch of engineering: aeronautical engineering. A breakdown of software engineering topics based on these categories is therefore seen as an important mechanism for linking software engineering with engineering at large and the more established engineering disciplines;

- they are viewed by Vincenti as applicable to all branches of engineering;

- gaps in the software engineering body of knowledge within certain categories as well as efforts to reduce these gaps over time will be made apparent;

- due to generic nature of the categories, knowledge within each knowledge area could evolve and progress significantly while the framework itself would remain stable;

3 AUTHORSHIP OF KNOWLEDGE AREA DESCRIPTION

The Editorial Team will submit a proposal to the project's Industrial Advisory Board to have Knowledge Area Specialists recognized as authors of the Knowledge Area description.

4 STYLE AND TECHNICAL GUIDELINES

Knowledge Area Descriptions should conform to the International Conference on Software Engineering Proceedings format (templates are available at http://sunset.usc.edu/icse99/cfp /technical_papers.html).

Knowledge Area Descriptions are expected to follow the IEEE Computer Society Style Guide. See http://computer.org/author/style/cs-style.htm

Microsoft Word 97 is the preferred submission format. Please contact the Editorial Team if this is not feasible for you.

4.1 Other Detailed Guidelines:

When referencing the guide, we recommend that you use the full title "Guide to the SWEBOK" instead of only "SWEBOK."

For the purpose of simplicity, we recommend that Knowledge Area Specialists avoid footnotes. Instead, they should try to include their content in the main text.

We recommend to use in the text explicit references to standards, as opposed to simply inserting numbers referencing items in the bibliography. We believe it would allow to better expose the reader to the source and scope of a standard.

The text accompanying figures and tables should be self-explanatory or have enough related text. This would ensure that the reader knows what the figures and tables mean.

Make sure you use current information about references (versions, titles, etc.)

To make sure that some information contained in the Guide to the SWEBOK does not become rapidly obsolete, please avoid directly naming tools and products. Instead, try to name their functions. The list of tools and products can always be put in an appendix.

You are expected to spell out all acronyms used and to use all appropriate copyrights, service marks, etc.

The Knowledge Area Descriptions should always be written in third person.

5 EDITING

Knowledge Area Descriptions will be edited by IEEE Computer Society staff editors. Editing includes copy editing (grammar, punctuation, and capitalization), style editing (conformance to the Computer Society magazines' house style), and content editing (flow, meaning, clarity, directness, and organization). The final editing will be a collaborative process in which IEEE Computer Society staff editors and the authors work together to achieve a concise, well-worded, and useful a Knowledge Area Description.

6 RELEASE OF COPYRIGHT

All intellectual properties associated with the Guide to the Software Engineering Body of Knowledge will remain with the IEEE Computer Society. Knowledge Area Specialists were asked to sign a copyright release form.

It is also understood that the Guide to the Software Engineering Body of Knowledge will be put in the public domain by the IEEE Computer Society, free of charge through web technology, or other means.

For more information, See http://computer.org/copyright.htm

APPENDIX B

A LIST OF RELATED DISCIPLINES FOR
THE STONE MAN VERSION OF THE GUIDE TO THE SWEBOK

In order to circumscribe software engineering, it is necessary to identify the other disciplines with which SE shares a common boundary. These disciplines are called Related Disciplines. In this regard, the mandate of the Guide to the SWEBOK project is to Identify other disciplines that contain knowledge areas that are important to a software engineer. The list of such Knowledge areas would be useful to attain the fifth objective of the project: Provide a foundation for curriculum development and individual certification and licensing material.

Therefore, this appendix identifies:

◆ a list of Related Disciplines, based on the Strawman Guide, on the discussions of the Industrial Advisory Board at the Industrial Advisory Board kick-off meeting in Mont-Tremblant (Canada) and on subsequent work and discussions;

◆ a list of knowledge areas for these Related Disciplines, based on as authoritative a source as found.

These lists were to be as large as possible because we considered it easier to eliminate topics than adding them further on in the process.

The SWEBOK KA Specialists were asked to identify from these lists the Knowledge Areas of the Related Disciplines that are sufficiently relevant to the Software Engineering KA that has been assigned to them to be expected knowledge from a graduate with four years of experience. If deemed necessary and if accompanied by a justification, Knowledge Area Specialists could also propose additional Related Disciplines not already. These choices are presented in Appendix D. The level and extent of knowledge that a software engineer should posses within these knowledge areas is not specified at this point. This will be done by other projects according to their needs.

LIST OF RELATED DISCIPLINES AND SOURCES OF KNOWLEDGE AREAS.

Computer Science

◆ It was agreed in Mont-Tremblant that the reference for this Related Discipline would be obtained through an initiative called the IEEE Computer Society and ACM Joint Task Force on "Year 2001 Model Curricula for Computing: CC-2001". To ensure proper coordination

with this initiative, Carl Chang, Joint Task Force Co-Chair is a member of the Industrial Advisory Board and was present in Mont-Tremblant. Appendix B.1 lists the preliminary Knowledge Areas of Computer Science as determined by the CC-2001 group.

Mathematics

◆ It was agreed in Mont-Tremblant that the Computing Curricula 2001 initiative would be the "conduit" to mathematics. So far, we have not received such a list of Knowledge Areas (Knowledge Units in the CC-2001 vocabulary), for Mathematics but it is expected that CC-2001 will provide it. In the mean time, the project refers to the list defined by the Computing Curriculum 1991[1] initiative and found in Appendix B.2.

Project Management

◆ The reference for this Related Discipline is "A Guide to the Project Management Body of Knowledge"[2] published by the Project Management Institute. This document is currently being adopted as an IEEE software engineering standard. The list of Knowledge Areas for project management can be found in Appendix B.3.

Computer Engineering

A list of Knowledge Areas for Computer Engineering and found in Appendix B.4 was compiled from the integration of:

◆ The syllabus for the British licensing exam for the field of Computer Systems Engineering[3].

◆ The Principles and Practice of Engineering Examination - Guide for Writers and Reviewers in Electrical Engineering of the National Council of Examiners for Engineering and Surveying (USA). An appendix listed Computer Engineering Knowledge Areas for which questions should be put to the candidates.

◆ The Computer Engineering undergraduate program at the Milwaukee School of Engineering[4]. This program

---

[1] See http://computer.org/educate/cc1991/
[2] See www.pmi.org to download this report.
[3] See http://www.engc.org.uk

is considered to be a typical example of an American accredited program by the director of the Computer Engineering and Computer Science Department at MSOE.

Systems Engineering

Appendix B.5 contains a proposed list of Knowledge Areas for Systems Engineering. The list was compiled from:

- The EIA 632 and IEEE 1220 (Trial-Use) standards;
- the Andriole and Freeman paper[5];
- the material available on the INCOSE (International Council on Systems Engineering) website[6];
- a curriculum for a graduate degree in Systems Engineering at the University of Maryland[7];

Three experts in the field were also consulted, John Harauz, from Ontario Hydro, John Kellogg from Lockheed Martin, and Claude Laporte consultant, previously with the Armed Forces of Canada and Oerlikon Aerospace.

Management and Management Science

No definitive source has been identified so far for a list of Management and Management Science Knowledge Areas relevant to software engineering. A list was therefore compiled from

- the Technology Management Handbook[8] which contains many relevant chapters;
- the Engineering Handbook[9] which contains a section on Engineering Economics and Management covering many of the relevant topics;
- an article by Henri Barki and Suzanne "Rivard titled A Keyword Classification Scheme for IS Research Literature: An Update"[10].

The proposed list of knowledge areas for Management and Management Science can be found in Appendix B.6.

Cognitive Sciences and Human Factors

Appendix B.7 contains a list of proposed Knowledge Areas for Cognitive Sciences and Human Factors. The was compiled from the list of courses offered at the John Hopkins University Department of Cognitive Sciences[11] and from the ACM SIGCHI Curricula for Human-Computer Interaction[12].

---

4   See http://www.msoe.edu/eecs/ce/index.htm
5   Stephen J. Andriole and Peter A. Freeman, *Software systems engineering: the case for a new discipline*, System Engineering Journal, Vol. 8, no 3, May 1993, pp. 165-179.
6   See www.incose.org
7   See http://www.isr.umd.edu/ISR/education/msse/
8   See CRC Press
9   See Crc Press
10 See MIS Quaterly, June 1993, pp. 209-226
11 See http://www.cogsci.jhu.edu/
12 See TABLE 1. Content of HCI at http://www.acm.org/sigchi/cdg/cdg2.html

The list was then refined by three experts in the field: two from UQAM and W. W. McMillan, from Eastern Michigan University. They were asked to indicate which of these topics should be known by a software engineer. The topics that were rejected by two of the three respondents were removed from the original list.

APPENDIX B.1 – KNOWLEDGE AREAS OF COMPUTER SCIENCE.

0. [MP] Mathematics and Physical Sciences

1. [FO] Foundations

   Complexity analysis

   Complexity classes

   Computability and undecidability

   Discrete mathematics (logic, combinatorics, probability)

   Proof techniques

   Automata (regular expressions, context-free grammars, FSMs/PDAs/TMs)

   Formal specifications

   Program semantics

2. [AL] Algorithms and Data Structures

   Basic data structures

   Abstract data types

   Sorting and searching

   parallel and distributed algorithms

3. [AR] Computer Architecture

   Digital logic

   Digital systems

   Machine level representation of data

   Number representations

   Assembly level machine organization

   Memory system organization and architecture

   Interfacing and communication

   Alternative architectures

   Digital signal processing

   Performance

4. [IS] Intelligence Systems (IS)

   Artificial intelligence

   Robotics

   Agents

   Pattern Recognition

   Soft computing (neural networks, genetic algorithms, fuzzy logic)

5. [IM] Information Management

   Database models

Search Engines

Data mining/warehousing

Digital libraries

Transaction processing

Data compression

6. [CI] Computing at the Interface

Human-computer interaction (usability design, human factors)

Graphics

Vision

Visualization

Multimedia

PDAs and other new hardware

User-level application generators

7. [OS] Operating Systems

Tasks, processes and threads

Process coordination and synchronization

Scheduling and dispatching

Physical and virtual memory organizations

File systems

Networking fundamentals (protocols, RPC, sockets)

Security

Protection

Distributed systems

Real-time computing

Embedded systems

Mobile computing infrastructure

8. [PF] Programming Fundamentals and Skills

Introduction to programming languages

Recursive algorithms/programming

Programming paradigms

Program-solving strategies

Compilers/translation

Code Generation

9. [SE] Software Engineering

Software Engineering will not be a related discipline to Software Engineering

This focus group will be coordinated with the SWEBOK project in order to avoid double definitions of the field.

10. [NC] Net-centric Computing

Computer-supported cooperative work

Collaboration Technology

Distributed objects computing (DOC/CORBA/DCOM/ JVM)

E-Commerce

Enterprise computing

Network-level security

11. [CN] Computational Science

Numerical analysis

Scientific computing

Parallel algorithms

Supercomputing

Modeling and simulation

12. [SP] Social, Ethical, Legal and Professional Issues

Historical and social context of computing

Philosophical ethics

Intellectual property

Copyrights, patents, and trade secrets

Risks and liabilities

Responsibilities of computing professionals

Computer crime

APPENDIX B.2 – KNOWLEDGE AREAS OF MATHEMATICS

Discrete Mathematics: sets, functions, elementary propositional and predicate logic, Boolean algebra, elementary graph theory, matrices, proof techniques (including induction and contradiction), combinatorics, probability, and random numbers.

Calculus: differential and integral calculus, including sequences and series and an introduction to differential equations.

Probability: discrete and continuous, including combinatorics and elementary statistics.

Linear Algebra: elementary, including matrices, vectors, and linear transformations.

Mathematical Logic: propositional and functional calculi, completeness, validity, proof, and decision

APPENDIX B.3 – KNOWLEDGE AREAS OF PROJECT MANAGEMENT

The list of Knowledge Areas defined by the Project Management Institute for project management is:

- Project Integration Management
- Project Scope Management
- Project Time Management
- Project Cost Management
- Project Quality Management
- Project Human Resource Management

- Project Communications Management
- Project Risk Management
- Project Procurement Management

APPENDIX B.4 – KNOWLEDGE AREAS OF COMPUTER ENGINEERING.

Digital Data Manipulation
Processor Design
Digital Systems Design
Computer Organization
Storage Devices and Systems
Peripherals and Communication
High Performance Systems
System Design
Measurement and Instrumentation
Codes and Standards
Circuit Theory
Electronics
Controls
Combinational and Sequential Logic
Embedded Systems Software
Engineering Systems Analysis with Numerical Methods
Computer Modeling and Simulation

APPENDIX B.5 – KNOWLEDGE AREAS OF SYSTEMS ENGINEERING

PROCESS
    Need Analysis
    Behavioral Analysis
    Enterprise Analysis
    Prototyping
    Project Planning
    Acquisition
    Requirements Definition
    System definition
    Specification trees
    System breakdown structure
    Design
    Effectiveness Analysis
    Component specification
    Integration

    Maintenance & Operations
    Configuration Management
    Documentation
    Systems Quality Analysis and Management
    Systems V & V
    System Evaluation
    Systems Lifecycle Cost Estimation
    Design of Human-Machine Systems
    Fractals and self-similarities
ESSENTIAL FUNCTIONAL PROCESSES: (IEEE 1220)
    Development
    Manufacturing
    Test
    Distribution
    Operations
    Support
    Training
    Disposal
TECHNIQUES & TOOLS (IEEE 1220)
    Metrics
    Privacy
    Process Improvement
    Reliability
    Safety
    Security
    Vocabulary
    Effectiveness Assessment

APPENDIX B.6 – KNOWLEDGE AREAS OF MANAGEMENT AND MANAGEMENT SCIENCE

BUSINESS STRATEGY
FINANCE
EXTERNAL ENVIRONMENT
    Economic Environment
    Legal Environment
    Regulation processes
ORGANIZATIONAL ENVIRONMENT
    Organizational Characteristics
    Organizational Functions
    Organizational Dynamics
INFORMATION SYSTEMS MANAGEMENT
    Data Resource Management

Information Resource Management
Personnel Resource Management
IS Staffing
INNOVATION AND CHANGE
ACCOUNTING
TRAINING
MANAGEMENT SCIENCE
    Models
        Financial Models
        Planning Models
    Optimization
        Optimization methods
        Heuristics
        Linear Programming
        Goal Programming
        Mathematical Programming
    Statistics
    Simulation

Ergonomics
Computer System and Interface Architecture
    Input and Output Devices
    Dialogue Techniques
    Dialogue Genre
    Computer Graphics
Dialogue Architecture
Development Process
    Design Approaches
    Implementation Techniques
    Evaluation Techniques
    Example Systems and Case Studies

APPENDIX B.7 – KNOWLEDGE AREAS OF COGNITIVE SCIENCES AND HUMAN FACTORS

Cognition
Cognitive AI I: Reasoning
Machine Learning and Grammar Induction
Formal Methods in Cognitive Science: Language
Formal Methods in Cognitive Science: Reasoning
Formal Methods in Cognitive Science:
    Cognitive Architecture
Cognitive AI II: Learning
Foundations of Cognitive Science
Information Extraction from Speech and Text
Lexical Processing
Computational Language Acquisition
The Nature of HCI
    (Meta-)Models of HCI
Use and Context of Computers
    Human Social Organization and Work
    Application Areas
    Human-Machine Fit and Adaptation
Human Characteristics
    Human Information Processing
    Language, Communication, Interaction

APPENDIX C

CLASSIFICATION OF TOPICS ACCORDING TO BLOOM'S TAXONOMY

INTRODUCTION

Bloom's taxonomy is the best known and most widely used classification of cognitive educational goals. In order to help all audiences in that field who wish to use the Guide as a tool in designing course material, programs or accreditation criteria, the project was mandated to provide a first draft evaluation of the topics included in the Knowledge Areas breakdowns according Bloom's Taxonomy. This should only be seen as a jump-start document to be further developed by other steps in other, related projects.

Knowledge Area Specialists were asked to provide an Appendix that states for each topic at which level of Bloom's taxonomy a "graduate plus four years experience" should "master" this topic. The resulting table could also be used by the specialists themselves as a guide to choose the amount and level of reference material appropriate for each topic.

This appendix contains, for each Knowledge Area[1], a table identifying the topics and the associated Bloom's taxonomy level of understanding on each topic for a graduate with four years experience. The levels of understanding from lower to higher are: knowledge, comprehension, application, analysis, synthesis, and evaluation. The version used can be found at http://www.valdosta.peachnet.edu/~whuitt/psy702/cogsys/bloom.html

SOFTWARE REQUIREMENTS

TOPIC	Bloom Level
Requirements engineering process	
Process models	Knowledge
Process actors	Knowledge
Process support	Knowledge
Process quality and improvement	Knowledge
Requirements elicitation	
Requirements sources	Comprehension
Elicitation techniques	Application
Requirements analysis	
Requirements classification	Comprehension
Conceptual modeling	Comprehension
Architectural design and requirements allocation	Analysis
Requirements negotiation	Analysis
Requirement specification	
The requirements definition document	Application
The software requirements specification (SRS)	Application
Document structure	Application
Document quality	Analysis
Requirements validation	
The conduct of requirements reviews	Analysis
Prototyping	Application
Model validation	Analysis
Acceptance tests	Application
Requirements management	
Change management	Analysis
Requirement attributes	Comprehension
Requirements tracing	Comprehension

---

[1] Ratings for the Software Construction Area and the Software Maintenance Knowledge Area have been omitted for this edition.

SOFTWARE DESIGN

Software Design Topic	Knowledge	Comprehension	Application	Analysis	Synthesis	Evaluation
I. SOFTWARE DESIGN BASIC CONCEPTS						
General design concepts		X				
The context of software design		X				
The software design process				X		X
Enabling techniques for software design				X		
II. Key issues in Software Design						
Concurrency			X			
Control and handling of events			X			
Distribution			X			
Exception handling			X			
Interactive systems			X			
Persistence			X			
III. SOFTWARE STRUCTURE AND ARCHITECTURE						
Architectural structures and viewpoints			X			
Architectural styles (macro-architecture)				X		X
Design patterns (micro-architecture)				X		X
Families of programs and frameworks			X			
IV. SOFTWARE DESIGN QUALITY ANALYSIS AND EVALUATION						
Quality attributes				X		
Quality analysis and evaluation tools			X	X		
Measures			X	X		
V. SOFTWARE DESIGN NOTATIONS						
Structural descriptions (static view)			X	X		
Behavioral descriptions (dynamic view)			X	X		

Software Design Topic	Knowledge	Comprehension	Application	Analysis	Synthesis	Evaluation
VI. SOFTWARE DESIGN STRATEGIES AND METHODS						
General strategies			X			
Function-oriented design			X			
Object-oriented design				X		X
Data-structure centered design		X				
Other methods		X	X			

Note: As mentioned in the URL used as reference for "Bloom's et al.'s Taxonomy of the Cognitive Domain", Evaluation has been considered to be at the same level as Synthesis, but using different cognitive processes.

SOFTWARE CONSTRUCTION

Rating has been omitted for this edition.

SOFTWARE TESTING

Topic	Bloom's level
A. Testing Basic Concepts and definitions	
Definitions of testing and related terminology	Analysis
Faults vs. failures	Analysis
Test selection criteria/Test adequacy criteria (or stopping rules)	Application
Testing effectiveness/Objectives for testing	Comprehension
Testing for defect identification	Comprehension
The oracle problem	Comprehension
Theoretical and practical limitations of testing	Application
The problem of infeasible paths	Comprehension
Testability	Comprehension
Testing vs. Static Analysis Techniques	Application
Testing vs. Correctness Proofs and Formal Verification	Knowledge
Testing vs. Debugging	Comprehension
Testing vs. Programming	Application
Testing within SQA	Application
Testing within CMM	Knowledge
Testing within Cleanroom	Knowledge
Testing and Certification	Comprehension
B. Test Levels	
Unit testing	Application
Integration testing	Application
System testing	Application
Acceptance/qualification testing	Application
Installation testing	Application
Alpha and Beta testing	Application
Conformance testing/Functional testing/Correctness testing	Application
Reliability achievement and evaluation by testing	Comprehension
Regression testing	Application
Performance testing	Comprehension
Stress testing	Comprehension
Back-to-back testing	Knowledge
Recovery testing	Comprehension
Configuration testing	Comprehension
Usability testing	Comprehension
C. Test Techniques	
Ad hoc	Synthesis
Equivalence partitioning	Application
Boundary-value analysis	Application
Decision table	Knowledge
Finite-state machine-based	Knowledge
Testing from formal specifications	Knowledge
Random testing	Application
Reference models for code-based	Application

Topic	Bloom's level
testing (flow graph, call graph)	
Control flow-based criteria	Application
Data flow-based criteria	Comprehension
Error guessing	Application
Mutation testing	Knowledge
Operational profile	Comprehension
SRET	Knowledge
Object-oriented testing	Application
Component-based testing	Comprehension
GUI testing	Knowledge
Testing of concurrent programs	Knowledge
Protocol conformance testing	Knowledge
Testing of distributed systems	Knowledge
Testing of real-time systems	Knowledge
Testing of scientific software	Knowledge
Functional and structural	Synthesis
Coverage and operational/Saturation effect	Knowledge
D. Test related measures	
Program measurements to aid in planning and designing testing.	Synthesis
Types, classification and statistics of faults	Application
Remaining number of defects/Fault density	Application
Life test, reliability evaluation	Comprehension
Reliability growth models	Knowledge
Coverage/thoroughness measures	Application
Fault seeding	Knowledge
Mutation score	Knowledge
Comparison and relative effectiveness of different techniques	Comprehension
E. Managing the Test Process	
Attitudes/Egoless programming	Application
Test process	Synthesis
Test documentation and workproducts	Synthesis
Internal vs. independent test team	Comprehension
Cost/effort estimation and other process metrics	Application
Termination	Application
Test reuse and test patterns	Application
Planning	Application
Test case generation	Application
Test environment development	Application
Execution	Application
Test results evaluation	Application
Problem reporting/Test log	Application
Defect tracking	Application

SOFTWARE MAINTENANCE

Rating has been omitted for this edition.

SOFTWARE CONFIGURATION MANAGEMENT

SCM TOPIC	Bloom Level
I. Management of the SCM Process	Knowledge
A. Organizational Context for SCM	Knowledge
B. Constraints and Guidance for SCM	Knowledge
C. Planning for SCM	Knowledge
1. SCM Organization and Responsibilities	Knowledge
2. SCM Resources and Schedules	Comprehension
3. Tool Selection and Implementation	Knowledge
4. Vendor/Subcontractor Control	Knowledge
5. Interface Control	Comprehension
D. Software Configuration Management Plan	Knowledge
E. Surveillance of SCM	Comprehension
1. SCM Metrics and Measurement	Comprehension
2. In-Process Audits of SCM	Knowledge
II. Software Configuration Identification	Comprehension
A. Identifying Items to be controlled	Comprehension
1. Software Configuration	Comprehension
2. Software Configuration Items	Comprehension
3. Software configuration item relationships	Comprehension
4. Software Versions	Comprehension
5. Baselines	Comprehension
6. Acquiring Software Configuration Items	Knowledge
B. Software Library	Comprehension
III. Software Configuration Control	Application
A. Requesting, Evaluating, and Approving Software Changes	Application
1. Software Configuration Control Board	Application
2. Software Change Request Process	Application
B. Implementing Software Changes	Application
C. Deviations & Waivers	Comprehension
IV. Software Configuration Status Accounting	Comprehension
A. Software Configuration Status Information	Comprehension
B. Software Configuration Status Reporting	Comprehension
V. Software Configuration Auditing	Knowledge
A. Software Functional Configuration Audit	Knowledge
B. Software Physical Configuration Audit	Knowledge
C. In-process Audits of a Software Baseline	Knowledge
VI. Software Release Management & Delivery	Comprehension
A. Software Building	Comprehension
B. Software Release Management	Comprehension

SOFTWARE ENGINEERING MANAGEMENT

Topic	Level
A. Organizational Management	
Policy management	Comprehension
Personnel management	Analysis
Communication management	Analysis
Portfolio management	Comprehension
Procurement management	Knowledge
B. Process/project Management	
Determination and negotiation of requirements	Comprehension
Feasibility analysis	Application
Review/revision of requirements	Comprehension
Process planning	Analysis
Project planning	Application
Determine deliverables	Comprehension
Effort, schedule and cost estimation	Analysis
Resource allocation	Application
Risk management	Synthesis
Quality management	Synthesis
Plan management	Application
Implementation of plans	Application
Implementation of measurement process	Application
Monitor process	Application
Control process	Application
Reporting	Application
Determining satisfaction of requirements	Comprehension
Reviewing and evaluating performance	Application
Determining closure	Application
Closure activities	Comprehension
C. Software Engineering Measurement	
Organizational objectives	Synthesis
Software process improvement goals	Synthesis
Goal-driven measurement selection	Application
Measurement validity	Comprehension
Size measurement	Analysis
Structure measurement	Analysis
Resource measurement	Analysis
Quality measurement	Analysis
Survey techniques and form design	Knowledge
Automated and manual data collection	Knowledge
Model building, calibration and evaluation	Application
Implementation, interpretation and refinement of models	Analysis

SOFTWARE ENGINEERING PROCESS

Topic	Level
Software Engineering Process Concepts	
Themes	Comprehension
Terminology	Knowledge
Process Infrastructure	
The Software Engineering Process Group	Comprehension
The Experience Factory	Comprehension
Process Measurement	
Methodology in Process Measurement	Comprehension
Process Measurement Paradigms	Comprehension
Analytic Paradigm	Comprehension
Benchmarking Paradigm	Comprehension
Process Definition	
Types of Process Definitions	Application
Life Cycle Framework Models	Application
Software Life Cycle Process Models	Application
Notations for Process Definitions	Application
Process Definition Methods	Application
Automation	Knowledge
Qualitative Process Analysis	
Process Definition Review	Comprehension
Root Cause Analysis	Comprehension
Process Implementation and Change	
Paradigms for Process Implementation and Change	Comprehension
Guidelines for Process Implementation and Change	Comprehension
Evaluating the Outcome of Process Implementation and Change	Comprehension

SOFTWARE ENGINEERING TOOLS AND METHODS

Topic	Bloom Level
Software Tools	
Software Requirements Tools	Application
Requirements Modeling Tools	Application
Traceability Tools	Comprehension
Software Design Tools	Application
Software Construction Tools	
Program Editors	Application
Compilers and Code Generators	Application
Interpreters	Application
Debuggers	Application
Software Testing Tools	
Test Generators	Comprehension
Test Execution Frameworks	Application
Test Evaluation Tools	Application
Test Management Tools	Comprehension
Performance Analysis Tools	Comprehension
Software Maintenance Tools	
Comprehension Tools	Application
Re-engineering Tools	Knowledge
Software Engineering Process Tools	
Process Modeling Tools	Knowledge
Process Management Tools	Knowledge
Integrated CASE Environments	Application
Process-centered Software Engineering Environments	Comprehension
Software Quality Tools	
Inspection Tools	Comprehension
Static Analysis Tools	Application
Software Configuration Management Tools	
Defect, Enhancement, Issue and Problem Tracking Tools	Application
Version Management Tools	Application
Release and Build Tools	Application
Software Engineering Management Tools	
Project Planning and Tracking Tools	Application
Risk Management Tools	Comprehension
Measurement Tools	Application
Infrastructure Support Tools	
Interpersonal Communication Tools	Application
Information Retrieval Tools	Application
System Administration and Support Tools	Comprehension

Topic	Bloom Level
Miscellaneous Tools Issues	
Tool Integration Techniques	Knowledge
Meta Tools	Comprehension
Tool Evaluation	Application
Software Methods	
Heuristic Methods	Application
Structured Methods	Application
Data-oriented Methods	Application
Object-oriented Methods	Application
Domain-specific Methods	Comprehension
Formal Methods	
Specification Languages	Comprehension
Refinement	Knowledge
Validation/Proving Properties	Comprehension
Prototyping Methods	
Styles	Comprehension
Prototyping Targets	Application
Evaluation	Comprehension
Miscellaneous Method Issues	
Method Evaluation	Application

SOFTWARE QUALITY

All software engineers are responsible for the quality of the products they build. We consider that the knowledge requirements for topics in Software Quality vary depending on the role of the software engineer. We use the roles of programmer, SQA/VV specialist, and project manager. The programmer will design and build the system, possibly be involved in inspections and reviews, analyze his work products statically, and possibly perform unit test. This person may turn over the products to others who will conduct integration and higher levels of testing, and may be asked to submit data on development tasks, but will not conduct analyses on faults or on measurements. The SQA/VV specialist will plan and implement the processes for software quality analysis, verification, and validation. The project manager of the development project will use the information from the software quality analysis processes to make decisions. Of course, in a small project, the software engineer may have to assume all of these roles, in which case, the highest of the three is appropriate.

Software Quality Topic (Numbered as to Section in this KA)	Bloom Level*, By Job Responsibility		
	Programmer	*SQA/VV Spec.*	*Project Manager*
Software Quality Concepts			
Measuring the Value of Quality	Comprehension	Comprehension	Analysis
ISO 9126 Quality Description	Comprehension	Comprehension	Comprehension
Dependability	Comprehension	Comprehension	Comprehension
Special Types of Systems and Quality Needs	Comprehension	Comprehension	Comprehension
Purpose and Planning of SQA and V&V			
Common Planning Activities			
The SQA Plan	Application	Synthesis	Evaluation
The V&V Plan	Application	Synthesis	Evaluation
Activities and Techniques for SQA and V&V			
Static Techniques			
Audits, Reviews, and Inspections	Application	Evaluation	Analysis
Analytic Techniques	Application	Evaluation	Analysis
Dynamic Techniques	Application	Evaluation	Analysis
Measurement Applied to SQA and V&V			
Fundamentals of Measurement	Application	Evaluation	Analysis
Metrics	Application	Evaluation	Analysis
Measurement Techniques	Application	Evaluation	Analysis
Defect Characterization	Application	Evaluation	Analysis
Additional uses of SQA and V&V data	Application	Evaluation	Analysis

*The levels, in ascending order: Knowledge, Comprehension, Application, Analysis, Synthesis, Evaluation

© *IEEE – Trial Version 1.00 – May 2001*

APPENDIX D

A PROPOSED BREAKDOWN FOR A COMPONENT INTEGRATION KNOWLEDGE AREA

Submitted by
Michel Boivin, CGI, Canada

One of the topics whose inclusion in the Guide was hotly debated is Component Integration. While it certainly is an important part of software practice today, there were disagreements about the existence of a generally accepted body of knowledge on that topic. One of the reviewers proposed the breakdown presented here. It was decided to included it as an appendix to make sure that discussions about the topic and about this view would start as soon as possible. It is therefore a jumpstart breakdown, intended to be discussed in the following phase of the project. That is the procedure that was used for the other ten Knowledge Areas. Future efforts concerning this topic will be announced on the project web site.

1. Component Integration

A. Component definition

1. Interface specification

2. Protocol specification

3. Off-the-shelf components

B. Reference model

1. Patterns

2. Frameworks

3. Standard architectures

4. Semantic interoperability

C. Reuse

1. Type of reuse

2. Re-engineering

3. Reuse repositories

4. Cost/Benefit Analysis

2. Application Integration

A. Planning

1. Environments definition

2. Software integration strategies

3. Data integration strategies

B. Selection

1. Applications selection

2. Services selection

3. Components selection

4. Communication protocols selection

5. Integration standards selection

C. Implementation

1. Software assembly

2. Data conversion

3. Integration Testing

4. Deployment